ARCHAEOLOGICAL APPROACHES TO CULTURAL IDENTITY

ONE WORLD ARCHAEOLOGY
Series Editor: P. J. Ucko

Animals into Art
H. Morphy (ed.), vol. 7

Archaeological Heritage Management in the Modern World
H. F. Cleere (ed.), vol. 9

Archaeology and the Information Age: a global perspective
P. Reilly & S. Rahtz (eds), vol. 21

The Archaeology of Africa: food, metals and towns
T. Shaw, P. Sinclair, B. Andah & A. Okpoko (eds), vol. 20

Centre and Periphery: comparative studies in archaeology
T. C. Champion (ed.), vol. 11

Conflict in the Archaeology of Living Traditions
R. Layton (ed.), vol. 8

Domination and Resistance
D. Miller, M. J. Rowlands & C. Tilley (eds), vol. 3

The Excluded Past: archaeology in education
P. Stone & R. MacKenzie (eds), vol. 17

Foraging and Farming: the evolution of plant exploitation
D. R. Harris & G. C. Hillman (eds), vol. 13

From the Baltic to the Black Sea: studies in medieval archaeology
D. Austin & L. Alcock (eds), vol. 18

Hunters of the Recent Past
L. B. Davis & B. O. K. Reeves (eds), vol. 15

The Meanings of Things: material culture and symbolic expression
I. Hodder (ed.), vol. 6

The Origins of Human Behaviour
R. A. Foley (ed.), vol. 19

The Politics of the Past
P. Gathercole & D. Lowenthal (eds), vol. 12

Sacred Sites, Sacred Places
D. L. Carmichael, J. Hubert, B. Reeves & A. Schanche (eds), vol. 23

The Presented Past: heritage, museums and education
P. G. Stone & B. L. Molyneaux (eds), vol. 25

Signifying Animals: human meaning in the natural world
R. G. Willis (ed.), vol. 16

Social Construction of the Past: representation as power
G. C. Bond & A. Gilliam (eds), vol. 24

State and Society: the emergence and development of social hierarchy and political centralization
J. Gledhill, B. Bender & M.T. Larsen (eds), vol. 4

Tropical Archaeobotany: applications and developments
J.G. Hather (ed.), vol. 22

The Walking Larder: patterns of domestication, pastoralism, and predation
J. Clutton-Brock (ed.), vol. 2

What is an Animal?
T. Ingold (ed.), vol. 1

What's New? A closer look at the process of innovation
S. E. Van der Leeuw & R. Torrence (eds), vol. 14

Who Needs the Past? Indigenous values and archaeology
R. Layton (ed.), vol. 5

ARCHAEOLOGICAL APPROACHES TO CULTURAL IDENTITY

Edited by Stephen Shennan

Department of Archaeology, University of Southampton

London and New York

First published by Unwin Hyman Ltd in 1989

First published in paperback 1994
by Routledge
11 New Fetter Lane, London EC4P 4EE

Simultaneously published in the USA and Canada
by Routledge
29 West 35th Street, New York, NY 10001

Typeset in 10 on 11 point Bembo by
Computape (Pickering) Ltd, Pickering, North Yorkshire
Printed and bound in Great Britain at the University Press, Cambridge

British Library Cataloguing in Publication Data
   Archaeological approaches to cultural identity. –
   (One world archaeology: 10).
   1. Cultural processes. Archaeological sources
   I. Shennan, Stephen   II. Series
   306

Library of Congress Cataloging in Publication Data
   Archaeological approaches to cultural identity/edited by S. J. Shennan.
       p. cm. (One world archaeology: 10)
   Chiefly papers presented at the World Archaeological Congress,
   held Sept. 1986, at Southampton, England.
   Includes bibliographies and index.
   1. Ethnoarchaeology – Congresses.
   2. Ethnicity – Congresses.
   3. Ethnic barriers – Congresses.
   I,. Shennan, Stephen. II. World Archaeological Congress
   (1986: Southampton, England). III. Series.
   CC79.E85A73 1989 930.1 – dc19 88–25145

ISBN 0–415–09557–3

List of contributors

Dean E. Arnold, Department of Anthropology, Wheaton College, Wheaton, Illinois, USA.

Csanád Bálint, Archaeological Institute of the Hungarian Academy of Sciences, Budapest, Hungary.

Luis Alberto Borrero, Programa de Estudios Prehistóricos, Conicet, Buenos Aires, Argentina.

Christopher R. DeCorse, Department of Archaeology, University of Ghana, Legon, Ghana.

Paul M. Dolukhanov, Leningrad Branch of the Institute of Archaeology, Academy of Sciences of the USSR, Leningrad, USSR.

Brian Durrans, Museum of Mankind, British Museum, London, UK.

Omotoso Eluyemi, Department of Archaeology, Obafemi Awolowo University, Ile-Ife, Nigeria.

Natalie R. Franklin, Department of Archaeology, La Trobe University, Bundoora, Victoria, Australia.

Jean-Claude Gardin, Ecole des Hautes Etudes en Sciences Sociales, Paris, France.

Carol W. Hill, Independent Researcher, New York, USA.

Zbigniew Kobyliński, Institute for the History of Material Culture, Polish Academy of Sciences, Warsaw, Poland.

Lars Larsson, Institute of Archaeology, Lund University, Lund, Sweden.

Jes Martens, Institute of Prehistoric Archaeology, University of Aarhus, Moesgaard, Denmark.

Marcela Mendoza, Centro de Estudios en Antropologias Especiales, University of Buenos Aires, Argentina.

Michael S. Nassaney, Department of Anthropology, University of Massachusetts, Amherst, USA.

Ann Osborn, Fundación de Investigaciones Arqueológicas Nacionales del Banco de la República, Bogotá, Colombia.

Andras Pálóczi-Horváth, Hungarian Agricultural Museum, Budapest, Hungary.

Ralph M. Rowlett, Department of Anthropology, University of Missouri–Columbia, Columbia, Missouri, USA.

Stephen Shennan, Department of Archaeology, University of Southampton, UK.

Ulrich Veit, Institut für Ur- und Frühgeschichte, University of Münster, West Germany.

Wang Ningsheng, Yunnan Nationalities Research Institute, Kunming, Yunnan, China.

Dorothy K. Washburn, Department of Anthropology, University of Rochester, New York, USA.

Pablo G. Wright, Centro Argentino de Etnologia, Buenos Aires, Argentina.
Alison Wylie, Department of Philosophy, University of Western Ontario,
    London, Canada.

Foreword

This book is one of a major series of more than 20 volumes resulting from the World Archaeological Congress held in Southampton, England, in September 1986. The series reflects the enormous academic impact of the Congress, which was attended by 850 people from more than 70 countries, and attracted many additional contributions from others who were unable to attend in person.

The *One World Archaeology* series is the result of a determined and highly successful attempt to bring together for the first time not only archaeologists and anthropologists from many different parts of the world, as well as academics from a host of contingent disciplines, but also non-academics from a wide range of cultural backgrounds, who could lend their own expertise to the discussions at the Congress. Many of the latter, accustomed to being treated as the 'subjects' of archaeological and anthropological observation, had never before been admitted as equal participants in the discussion of their own (cultural) past or present, with their own particularly vital contribution to make towards global, cross-cultural understanding.

The Congress therefore really addressed world archaeology in its widest sense. Central to a world archaeological approach is the investigation not only of how people lived in the past but also of how, and why, changes took place resulting in the forms of society and culture which exist today. Contrary to popular belief, and the archaeology of some 20 years ago, world archaeology is much more than the mere recording of specific historical events, embracing as it does the study of social and cultural change in its entirety. All the books in the *One World Archaeology* series are the result of meetings and discussions which took place within a context that encouraged a feeling of self-criticism and humility in the participants about their own interpretations and concepts of the past. Many participants experienced a new self-awareness, as well as a degree of awe about past and present human endeavours, all of which is reflected in this unique series.

The Congress was organized around major themes. Several of these themes were based on the discussion of full-length papers which had been circulated some months previously to all who had indicated a special interest in them. Other sessions, including some dealing with areas of specialization defined by period or geographical region, were based on oral addresses, or a combination of precirculated papers and lectures. In all cases, the entire sessions were recorded on cassette, and all contributors were presented with the recordings of the discussion of their papers. A major part of the thinking behind the Congress was that a meeting of many hundreds of participants that did not leave behind a published record of its academic discussions would be little more than an exercise in tourism.

Thus, from the very beginning of the detailed planning for the World Archaeological Congress, in 1982, the intention was to produce post-Congress books containing a selection only of the contributions, revised in the light of discussions during the sessions themselves as well as during subsequent consultations with the academic editors appointed for each book. From the outset, contributors to the Congress knew that if their papers were selected for publication, they would have only a few months to revise them according to editorial specifications, and that they would become authors in an important academic volume scheduled to appear within a reasonable period following the Southampton meeting.

The publication of the series reflects the intense planning which took place before the Congress. Not only were all contributors aware of the subsequent production schedules, but also session organizers were already planning their books before and during the Congress. The editors were entitled to commission additional chapters for their books when they felt that there were significant gaps in the coverage of a topic during the Congress, or where discussion at the Congress indicated a need for additional contributions.

One of the main themes of the Congress was devoted to 'Archaeological "Objectivity" in Interpretation', where consideration of the precirculated full-length papers on this theme extended over four and a half days of academic discussion. The particular sessions on 'Archaeological "Objectivity" in Interpretation' were under my overall control, the main aim being to focus attention on the way that evidence of the past – including archaeological evidence – has been used and viewed by particular groups (whether local, regional or national) at different times. Essential to this aim was the exploration of the reasons why particular interpretations might have been chosen, or favoured, by individual societies and traditions at specific points in their development, or at certain stages in their activities. The whole theme attempted, therefore, a unique mix of critical assessment of the basis of archaeological methodology with critical awareness of the social contexts of the use (and possible manipulation) of the evidence of the past.

Central to this re-evaluation of the strengths and weaknesses of archaeological approaches to the interpretation, and indeed 'display', of the past – whether through academic articles or by means of formal or informal curricula, or through museums or site presentation – is an assessment of the methodologies and approaches to the significance of material culture. This has long been a core issue in archaeological discussion, but it badly needed re-examination. Throughout the history of archaeology as a discipline material culture, or at least the repetitive association of distinctive material culture objects, has been taken to reflect activities of specific social groups or 'societies' whose physical movements across a geographic stage have often been postulated on the basis of the distribution patterns of such objects, and whose supposed physical or ethnic identity (see also *State and society*, edited by J. Gledhill, B. Bender & M. T. Larsen) have often been assumed to correlate with such artefactual groupings. More recently archaeologists have been forced to recognize, often through lessons gained from ethnography, that a distinctive material culture complex may represent the activities of a vast variety of social groupings and subgroups, and that archaeological classification may often serve to camouflage the subtle message of style and technique (see also *Animals into art*, edited by H. Morphy, and *Domination and resistance*, edited by D. Miller, M. J. Rowlands & C. Tilley) which probably symbolize complex patterns of behaviour, as well as individual aspirations, within any society.

If the very basis of the equation between a material culture complex and a social grouping is ambiguous, then much of archaeological interpretation must remain subjective, even at this fundamental level of its operations. Whenever the archaeological data of material culture are presented in museums, on sites, in literature, in schools or in textbooks, as the evidence for the activities of 'races', 'peoples', 'tribes', 'linguistic groups' or other socially derived ethnic amalgamations, there should be at least scepticism if not downright suspicion. In a large number of such cases, what we are witnessing is the none-too-subtle ascription of racial/cultural stereotypes to static material culture items.

The overall theme therefore took as its starting point the proposition that archaeological interpretation is a subjective matter. It also assumed that to regard archaeology as somehow constituting the only legitimate 'scientific' approach to the past needed re-examination and possibly even rejection. A narrow parochial approach to the past which simply assumes that a linear chronology based on a 'verifiable' set of 'meaningful' 'absolute' dates is the only way to tackle the recording of, and the only way to comprehend, the past completely ignores the complexity of many literate and of many non-literate 'civilizations' and cultures. However, a world archaeological approach to a concept such as 'the past' focuses attention on precisely those features of archaeological enquiry and method which archaeologists all too often take for granted, without questioning the related assumptions.

Discussions on this theme during the Congress were grouped around seven headings, and have led to the publication of five books. The first subtheme, organized by Stephen Shennan, Department of Archaeology, University of Southampton, which lasted for almost a day, was concerned with 'Multiculturalism and Ethnicity in Archaeological Interpretation' and the second, under the control of Ian Hodder, Department of Archaeology, University of Cambridge, which occupied more than a day, was on 'Material Culture and Symbolic Expression'. The fourth subtheme, 'The Politics of the Past: Museums, Media, and other Presentations of Archaeology' was organized by Peter Gathercole of Darwin College, Cambridge, and also lasted for more than a day. Each of these subthemes has led to a separate book: this volume, *The meanings of things*, edited by I. Hodder, and *The politics of the past*, edited by P. Gathercole & D. Lowenthal (until recently of the Department of Geography, University College London). The fifth subtheme on 'The Past in Education' was organized by Robert MacKenzie, Central Training Department, National Association of Citizens' Advice Bureaux, and discussion of this topic (which lasted formally for half a day at the Congress and informally throughout the week by means of displays and educational events) has been expanded into the book *The excluded past*, under the editorship of Peter Stone (of English Heritage) and R. MacKenzie. David Bellos of the Department of French, University of Manchester, was responsible for a short discussion session on the sixth subtheme 'Mediations of the Past in Modern Europe', and contributions from this subtheme have been combined either with those from the third on 'Contemporary Claims about Stonehenge' (a short discussion session organized by Christopher Chippindale, of the Department of Archaeology, University of Cambridge), or with those from the seventh subtheme on 'Indigenous Perceptions of the Past' which lasted for almost a day. Robert Layton of the Department of Anthropology, University of Durham, was in charge of this seventh topic and has also edited the two resulting books, *Who needs the past?* and *Conflict in the archaeology of living traditions*. The latter also incorporates several contributions from a one-day discussion on 'Material Culture and the Making of the Modern United States: Views from Native America', which had been organized by Russell Handsman of the American Indian Archaeological Institute, Washington, and Randall McGuire of the Department of Anthropology of the State University of New York at Binghamton.

The whole of the 'Archaeological "Objectivity" in Interpretation' theme had been planned as the progressive development of an idea and the division of it into subthemes was undertaken in the full knowledge that there would be considerable overlap between them. It was accepted that it would, in many ways, be impossible, and even counter-productive, to split, for example, education from site presentation, or literary presentations of the past from indigenous history. In the event, while each of the books resulting from this overall theme has its own coherence, they also share a concern to make explicit the responsibility of recognizing the various ways of interpreting humanly created artefacts. In addition they recognize the social responsibility of archaeological interpretation, and the way that this may be used, consciously or unconsciously, by others for their own ends. The contributions in these books, directly or indirectly, explicitly or implicitly, epitomize the view that modern archaeology must recognize and confront its new role, which is to address the wider community. It must do this with a sophisticated awareness of the strengths and the weaknesses of its own methodologies and practices.

A world archaeological approach to archaeology as a 'discipline' reveals how subjective archaeological interpretation has always been. It also demonstrates the importance that all rulers and leaders (politicians) have placed on the legitimization of their positions through the 'evidence' of the past. Objectivity is strikingly absent from most archaeological exercises in interpretation. In some cases there has been conscious manipulation of the past for national political ends (as in the case of Ian Smith's Rhodesian regime over Great Zimbabwe, or that of the Nazis with their racist use of archaeology). But, apart from this, archaeologists themselves have been influenced in their interpretations by the received wisdom of their times, both in the sort of classificatory schemes which they consider appropriate to their subject, and in the way that their dating of materials is affected by their assumptions about the capabilities of the humans concerned. Nowhere is archaeological explanation immune to changes in interpretative fashion. This is as true of Britain as of anywhere else – Stonehenge, in particular, has been subjected to the most bizarre collection of interpretations over the years, including all sorts of references to its having been constructed by Mycenaeans and Phoenicians. Although, at first sight, it is tempting to assume that such contentions are different from attempts by politicians to claim that the extraordinary site of Great Zimbabwe was constructed by Phoenicians using black slaves, the difference is not very easy to sustain.

Realization of the flexibility and variety of past human endeavour all over the world directs attention back to those questions that are at the very basis of archaeological interpretation. How can static material culture objects be equated with dynamic human cultures? How can we define and recognize the 'styles' of human activity, as well as their possible implications? In some contexts these questions assume immense political importance. For example, the archaeological 'evidence' of cultural continuity, as opposed to discontinuity, may make all the difference to an indigenous land claim, the right of access to a site/region, or the disposal of a human skeleton to a museum, as against its reburial.

All these factors lead in turn to a new consideration of how different societies choose to display their museum collections and conserve their sites. As the debates about who should be allowed to use Stonehenge, and how it should be displayed, make clear, objects or places may be considered important at one time and 'not worth bothering about' at others. Who makes these decisions and in what contexts? Who is responsible, and why, for what is taught about the past in schools or in adult education? Is such education based on a narrow local/regional/national framework of archaeology and history, or is it oriented towards multiculturalism and the variety of human cultural experiences in a world–wide context? What should the implications be for the future of archaeology?

The main themes in *Archaeological approaches to cultural identity* have been discussed in detail in its editorial Introduction. My aim in what follows is to examine a few of the points which have struck me personally as being of particular interest and fascination.

In this book Stephen Shennan and his contributors return to one of the most – possibly *the* most – fundamentally important questions of archaeological enquiry and interpretation. What can be legitimately inferred about the social groups which produced the material culture objects which are the primary evidence of archaeology? More particularly, when can such presumed groups of people legitimately be assumed to have thought themselves to be distinct from other contemporaneous social groups of human beings?

Traditionally, archaeology of the Western European tradition has concen-

trated, using various criteria and techniques, on the classification of archaeological discoveries such as pottery and flint tools into groups, or types. Such
types have then often been grouped into larger classes or families sharing
supposedly distinctive features. Traditionally, it is these 'types', 'classes',
and 'families' of similar objects which have been taken as indicators of
chronological and cultural relationships between different human cultures of
the past. Already in the works of Gordon Childe such a simple correlation
between apparently distinctive items of material culture and a human
'society' was considered to be too facile. Instead, he posited the equation of
societies with the archaeological evidence of material culture only when
more than one regularly associated 'type' of object occurred with another.
The existence of a specific past human society was, therefore, assumed only
when there was a demonstrable association between certain kinds of material
culture evidence.

Since the time of Gordon Childe, archaeology has striven to become much
more rigorous, and much more sophisticated, in its methods of drawing
social inferences from material evidence. Nevertheless, an equation between
tool types and 'peoples', as well as reliance on physical migrations as
explanation, are often still in evidence. Thus, for example, Kozłowski and
Bandi (1981) are strongly critical of early efforts to explain the first peopling
of the Americas, including 16th-century attempts to class the Amerindians as
a Semitic group which had arrived from the West. They are also critical of
later attempts to derive them from Ancient Egypt on the basis of the claimed
similarity between their respective pyramids. They also dismiss those who,
then and later, postulated that the vanished Atlantis had once joined Spain to
the New World, and others who either claimed that the Indians were direct
descendants of a local fossil ape or that they had been forced out from the
Arctic with their reindeer in Pleistocene times, had crossed the Bering Strait,
and having arrived via Siberia in Europe, had then reversed their route (at the
end of the Upper Palaeolithic) to become what we now recognize as the
Eskimo culture(s). In the 1920s different theories continued unabated,
including the view that the earliest discoverers of the Americas had been of
Malayo/Polynesian/Melanesian/Australian stock who had crossed the Antarctic. In 1963 it was even claimed that the Atlantic had been crossed in skin
boats.

After a detailed review of all the artefactual material and the available
dates, Kozłowski and Bandi concluded (1981, pp. 24–5) that there had been
no less than three separate and distinct migrations of East Asian peoples into
America via Alaska between c.20 000 BC and c.8 000 BC when Beringia
disappeared – all these mass movements of people being inferred from the
supposed similarities of stone tool manufacturing techniques and flint tool
morphologies.

Part of the increase in methodological rigour has consisted of attempts to
define and understand the nature of what constitutes 'style(s)', and has also
led to specially oriented fieldwork with living peoples. Several chapters in
this book continue discussion of this central concern (and see also *The*

meanings of things, edited by I. Hodder, *Animals into art*, edited by H. Morphy and *Domination and resistance*, edited by D. Miller *et al.*). There is no doubt that an anthropological or archaeological definition of style remains an analytical tool which may or may not be coterminous with any classification recognized by the society concerned. Even when 'different' styles can be expressed in scientific terms, they may reflect a whole range of different social concerns, some of current political import to the social groups themselves, and others derived from the particular histories of the individuals and groups who make use of them. It would, therefore, be incorrect to simply assume that where the archaeologist can recognize stylistic differences in the material culture of the past, it is legitimate to infer the existence of social groups who considered themselves to be distinct from others.

At various times in the history of archaeology, the apparently distinctive nature of tool, artistic, or weapon types have been assumed to reflect not only human societies but actual races of people with distinctive languages. As this book demonstrates (see also *The politics of the past*, edited by P. Gathercole and D. Lowenthal), such an equation between material culture and racial groups is not only unwarranted but has been subject to changing interpretation and weighting of one side or the other of the supposed balance according to often complex political and ideological considerations (and see *Conflict in the archaeology of living traditions*, edited by R. Layton). Some of these have led to abuse and extremism. The history of archaeological interpretation was, until relatively recently, a mosaic of assumed migrations, invasions and annihilations of peoples and cultures. Several of the contributors to *Archaeological approaches to cultural identity* provide much more satisfactory explanations for the archaeological record without having to assume extensive migrations or equations with later 'groups' in historic literature.

Many chapters in this book demonstrate the now long-accepted fact that all societies are continually changing, and can be assumed to have always been far from static. It is even possible to recognize the effects of assimilation in some archaeological records. Peoples' practices and beliefs have always adapted to changing events and circumstances even in those areas, such as burial practices, where the outside observer as well as the people of the culture itself would both be (wrongly) inclined to expect and claim continuity of belief and practice.

Given such well-documented changes in style, practices and attitudes, *Archaeological approaches to cultural identity* brings into the open the question whether there are, or are not, social or biological entities which can be assumed to be unchanging, and to have existed and be recognizable in the record of the past. If the answer is in the affirmative then the question turns to the problems of demonstrating continuity of such groups into the present. The former question raises all the problems of what it is that is 'congealed' in the material culture record (Trigger 1986), and the latter question is also central to the political role of archaeology in the aspirations of 'indigenous minorities' and others in the modern world (and see *Archaeological heritage management in the modern world*, edited by H. F. Cleere, for the way that 'World' and 'National' legislation makes no, or little, allowance for any prior rights accruing to such indigenous groups).

The literature on what constitutes 'culture', 'race' and 'tribe' is a vast one. Chapters in this book stress that there is no necessary one-to-one correlation between material culture and language or art style, nor between either of the former and what a living group may consider the extent of its own culture. In attempting to rid itself of the various connotations which have become attached to terms such as 'race' and 'tribe', anthropologists and archaeologists have, over the past few years, adopted the term 'ethnic group(s)', and a considerable body of literature has concentrated on this supposed category of human beings, often, but not exclusively, in the context of the Fourth World and the relations between the (now) minority 'ethnic' indigenes and the groups in political power in such areas. However, by simply shifting nomenclature and by trying to isolate social groupings on the basis of emic attitudes towards others, the problems for the archaeologists have not necessarily decreased. Much as debate rages about whether or not there is an 'objective' past to be discovered somewhere 'out there' (see also *Who needs the past?* and *Conflict in the archaeology of living traditions*, both edited by R. Layton, and *The politics of the past*, edited by P. Gathercole and D. Lowenthal), so the question shifts to attempts to determine whether the feelings of identity of ethnic groupings derive from original distinct biological and/or linguistic groups. Alternatively, are ethnic identities merely social constructs whose compositions have adapted through time to changing conditions and political allegiances? The matter is one of intense debate at the current time. The evidence of this book demonstrates, in various different contexts, many of the extreme problems of matching the archaeological and ethnographic record, a lack of congruence which does little to support the view of continuity in ethnic identities. Even where stylistically distinctive traditions can be identified in the material culture record it may be that what is being attested to is no more than the effects of training skills and logistics of production rather than the shared distinctive experiences and preconceptions of an ethnic group.

Archaeological approaches to cultural identity explores some of the kinds of archaeological data which may adduce evidence of ethnicity in the past. In no case is it an easy matter of evidence and proof. To most of us it would seem, as a starting point, that disposal of the dead in distinctive fashions, coupled to the skeletal evidence itself, should be a major source of data. However, as already indicated, methods of disposal of the dead are subject to changes of fashion and practice. Nor, as suggested in this book, is it entirely clear how the practice of grave robbing (in any period) should be interpreted – whether it can be taken to be evidence of effective political marginality from, or within, a group or as the actions of people from ethnic groups other than those whose human remains are being disturbed or desecrated. Furthermore, as is well known (Ucko 1969), there is no simple correlation between the boundaries of an ethnic (or cultural) group and the adoption of only one standardized and consistent disposal practice (Hubert 1989). In addition, archaeologist. have the added disadvantage that it is only very rarely that exact temporal contemporaneity can be demonstrated between the modes of disposal of two or more supposed distinct ethnic groups. Nor is the analysis of skeletal morphology capable of fine discriminations of a kind that might adduce evidence of ethnicity, if it can indeed be assumed that such ethnic groupings had a biological basis. As this book reveals, the *same* archaeological and osteological material has been taken to represent evidence of the Avars *and* of the Hungarians.

If it is not the traditional analyses by typology and classification of tools and dwellings that can securely reveal the existence of ethnicity, then it is tempting to assume that the occasional evidence of artistic depiction may be more rewarding. Indeed the study of prehistoric rock art (and see *Animals into art*, edited by H. Morphy) has been characterized by attempts to assign animals to species and subspecies, and humans to different racial types. By and large these attempts have not been very successful for the Palaeolithic period (Ucko & Rosenfeld 1972, Ucko in press), and the analysis of Chinese bronzes in this book can do no more than show that in the Iron Age there, stylistic conventions for hair and beard appear to divide human beings into groupings which are not only meaningful to our own 20th-century perceptions but resemble those distinctive characteristics which can still be seen in the area today. The difficulty comes in arguing backwards from our own categories to the seemingly similar evidence of the past, whether it be of those with whom the Iron Age Chinese might have been in contact, or from the so-called tribal European groups mentioned in the first Classical literature to the archaeological evidence of the earlier Iron Age. There is a further problem regarding the interpretation of art works in the context of ethnic identifications, for the visual image is often a vehicle for stereotyping. As is well documented for European images of Australian Aborigines (Maynard n.d.), visual assumptions and racial attitudes in such art works change and linger according to philosophical ideas and social theories. In such situations there can be no *a priori* assumption either that the 'groups' depicted as such were indeed exclusive groups or, alternatively, were compound creations from a heterogeneous set of individuals by the 'dominant' observers. In an archaeological context, in particular, these questions are both very complex and very important. At one level of analysis, the archaeologist's interest in material culture is focused on the determination of what kind of social group, or subgroup (sexual, technological or whatever), has been responsible for the particular patterning in the material culture record which has been observed. At another level, however, the archaeologist is also bound to be concerned with any larger groupings of identity or practice, whether or not they be the results of 'imposed' categorizations from outside, once such groups become visible in the archaeological record – and whether or not they were accompanied by feelings of 'identity' and 'belonging'.

A recent conference of the Association of Social Anthropologists (1987) was devoted to 'History and Ethnicity', the term ethnicity having been often discussed in the social anthropological literature. It appears that, by now, the term has acquired two very distinct meanings, the first being simply an alternative to 'culture' and the second assuming a genetic basis to the ethnic group. The weight of evidence produced at the conference left no doubt that despite the emotions of ethnic identification, and the claims of members of groups recognized as ethnic today, membership of such groups is in fact often fluid and dependent upon agreement between the individual claiming to be a member and acceptance by the group of the claimant. If this is indeed the case in living cultures, the critical question remains as to whether the nature of a distinctive ethnic identity is based on fiction or is derived from the past. The most likely explanation is that ethnicity does derive from the past but that the relationship is not a direct one. Instead it appears that the borders and nature of an ethnic group will change according to the later needs and social circumstances of the groups concerned (Ucko 1983a); the need to be, and feel, distinctive is not an unchanging circumstance, neither are the needs and wishes of dominant societies which may manipulate by changing the bases of peoples' allegiances (see also *State and society*, edited by J. Gledhill *et al.*). What remains completely obscure, however, is the detailed nature of the relationship between what did in fact happen in the past to the particular group concerned and the later details of claimed ethnic separateness and distinctiveness.

Several chapters in this book demonstrate how ethnic (or cultural) groupings have in fact changed in composition, and adapted their modes of production, in response to political change and political influence. Other books in this *One World Archaeology* series have contained eloquent evidence of the need for individuals and groups to be able to have access to their 'own' pasts. In this book the added point is made by Hill in a poignant discussion of her own self-identity that material culture by itself does not seem to be a good indicator for differentiating between particular American Indian cultural groupings with their own distinctive oral traditions. It appears that archaeology is not in a position to pinpoint what are ethno-specific artefacts in most, or any, situations. As contributors point out, there are numerous examples of the same archaeological data being interpreted quite differently in terms of their ethnic implications by different researchers. As I have stressed elsewhere (1983a, 1983b, 1987) it is this very characteristic of subjectivity in the equation of groups (quite apart from the nature of the groups concerned) with past material culture complexes which has made archaeological evidence so amenable to political interpretation and even manipulation. It is a striking feature of this book, therefore, that despite the fact that its subject matter is traditionally at the very heart of archaeological interpretation and has received much discussion over the past 100 years, it is also at the very centre of debate about current political power. As other books in this series have shown, the ability to be able to demonstrate primacy is often a political matter, not just in specific contexts such as land rights claims, but also in wider issues. Indigenous ethnicity has, at least in a Fourth World context, often acquired a political momentum of its own, as rival political powers claim to care most about the demands of indigenous peoples for distinctive and special treatment. In all these cases, part of the distinctiveness of the situation involves the special relationship which such groups have traditionally shared with the land and the sacred sites and areas within their estates. Archaeologists have already been forced to enter into debates about the nature of the archaeological evidence for ethnic continuity and discontinuity in specific localized situations (Ucko 1983a, 1983b). Now, however, the context for deciding how far archaeological evidence is capable of interpretation is probably changing. No longer is it merely a question of determining chronological primacy and deducing matters of continuity and discontinuity within a particular archaeological context, for the argument is growing (e.g. Diaz-Polanco 1987) that archaeological and anthropological claims for indigenous distinctive ethnicity are being used by national governments and international agencies to separate out such groups (and those who sympathize with them), from other migrant non-indigenous (ethnic and cultural) groups with whom they in fact share many of the common features of the disadvantaged. Such claims demand that the chronology of distinctive ethnicity be seen to be of less importance than the current economic and social positions of such groups. In the context of all these changing and complex interests in the nature of the pasts of different social groups of apparently distinctive peoples, archaeology has to be very sure of its own basic interpretative methods and assumptions. The discussions in *Archaeological approaches to cultural identity*, which attempt to elucidate many of these key concepts, are therefore bound to have a profound effect upon future developments and attitudes to the role and nature of archaeology on the world's political stage.

P. J. Ucko
Southampton

References

Diaz-Polanco, H. 1987. *Neoindigenismo* and the ethnic question in Central America. *Latin American Perspectives* **14**, 87–100.

Hubert, J. 1988. The disposition of the dead. *World Archaeological Bulletin* **2**, 12–39.

Hubert, J. 1989. A proper place for the dead: a critical review of the 'reburial' issue. In *Conflict in the archaeology of living traditions*, R. Layton (ed.), ch. 10. London: Unwin Hyman.

Kozłowski, J. K. & H.–G. Bandi 1981. Le problème des racines asiatiques du premier peuplement de l'Amérique. *Bull. Société Suisse des Américanistes* **45**, 7–42.

Maynard, N. n.d. *European images of Aborigines.* (24 slides with notes and sound cassette.) Melbourne: Educational Media International.

Trigger, B. G. 1986. Prospects for a world archaeology. *World Archaeology* **18**, 1–20.

Ucko, P. J. 1969. Ethnography and archaeological interpretation of funerary remains. *World Archaeology* **1**, 262–80.

Ucko, P. J. 1983a. The politics of the indigenous minority. *Journal Biosocial Science*, suppl. **8**, 25–40.

Ucko, P. J. 1983b. Australian academic archaeology: Aboriginal transformation of its aims and practices. *Australian Archaeology* **16**, 11–26.

Ucko, P. J. 1987. *Academic freedom and apartheid: the story of the World Archaeological Congress*. London: Duckworth.

Ucko, P. J. in press. Subjectivity and the recording of palaeolithic cave art. *Altamira Celebration Volume*. Santander.

Ucko, P. J. & A. Rosenfeld 1972. Anthropomorphic representation in palaeolithic art. *Actas del Simposium Internacional de Arte Rupestre*. Santander.

Contents

List of contributors   *page* vii

Foreword   P. J. Ucko   ix

Preface   Stephen Shennan   xxvii

Introduction: archaeological approaches to cultural identity
   Stephen Shennan   1

   Rationality and relativism   1
   Archaeological 'cultures'   5
   Ethnicity and archaeology   14
   Spatial variation, style and identity   17
   Archaeological approaches to cultural identity   22
   Conclusion   29
   References   30

OBJECTIVITY, INTERESTS AND CULTURAL
DIFFERENCE IN ARCHAEOLOGICAL INTERPRETATION   33

1 *Ethnic concepts in German prehistory: a case study on the*
   relationship between cultural identity and archaeological
   objectivity   Ulrich Veit   35

   The case of Kossinna and its consequences   36
   'Settlement archaeology'. Kossinna's method and
   contemporary criticisms   39
   'Archaeological culture' and ethnicity since 1945:
   some examples   42
   Cultural identity and archaeological objectivity   47
   Acknowledgements   51
   References   51

2 *The Vandals: myths and facts about a Germanic tribe of the first half*
   of the 1st millennium AD   Jes Martens   57

   The history of the Vandals   58
   The theories of the Vandals   58
   The history of the Vandal theories   60
   The future of the Vandals   63
   References   64

3 *Theory, profession, and the political rôle of archaeology*
   Brian Durrans   67

   Acknowledgements   74
   Note   74
   References   74

4 *An epistemological enquiry into some archaeological and historical*
   interpretations of 17th century Native American–European
   relations   Michael S. Nassaney   76

   Introduction   76
   Rethinking objectivity: the case of culture contact   77
   Historical context   79
   Narragansett cosmology and mortuary ritual   81
   Legitimating the quotidian: the RI 1000 cemetery   82
   Another way of telling   85
   Summary and conclusions   89
   Acknowledgements   90
   References   91

5 *Matters of fact and matters of interest*   Alison Wylie   94

   The problem of epistemic limits   94
   Theoretical and methodological foundations   95
   The objectivist response   98
   Paradigm relativity   103
   In defence of qualified objectivism   105
   Conclusions   107
   References   108

6 *The rôle of 'local knowledge' in archaeological interpretation*
   Jean-Claude Gardin   110

   'Universal' semantics and 'local' semantics   110
   Setting up schemas and rules for inferences   111
   The local character of the rules of inference   113
   'Locality', objectivity and subjectivity   115
   The prospection of 'possible worlds'   116
   Local knowledge and ethnography   118
   Conclusion   120
   References   121

CULTURAL IDENTITY AND ITS MATERIAL EXPRESSION IN THE PAST AND THE PRESENT   123

7 *Material aspects of Limba, Yalunka and Kuranko ethnicity:
   archaeological research in northeastern Sierra Leone*
   Christopher R. DeCorse   125

   The geographical and culture setting   125
   Material aspects of Limba, Yalunka and Kuranko ethnicity 128
   Discussion and conclusions   137
   References   139

8 *Multiculturalism in the eastern Andes*   Ann Osborn   141

   Language   144
   The agricultural-cum-ceremonial system   146
   Material culture   148
   Food, fertility and race   151
   Concluding remarks   153
   Acknowledgements   154
   References   155

9 *The property of symmetry and the concept of ethnic style*
   Dorothy K. Washburn   157

   Introducton   157
   The perception of symmetry   159
   The individuals who participated in the case study   160
   The preference tests   161
   Results   165
   Discussion   171
   Acknowledgements   172
   References   172

10 *Patterns of learning, residence and descent among potters in Ticul,
   Yucatan, Mexico*   Dean E. Arnold   174

   The population of potters in Ticul   175
   Discussion   180
   Implications for archaeology   181
   Acknowledgements   182
   Notes   182
   References   183

11 *Some ethnospecific features in central and eastern European
   archaeology during the early Middle Ages: the case of Avars and
   Hungarians*   Csanád Bálint   185

   Introduction   185

The area of interest   186
On the ethnospecific rôle of objects   186
On the ethnospecific rôle of archaeological culture   189
References   193

12   *Ancient ethnic groups as represented on bronzes from Yunnan,*
     China   Wang Ningsheng   195

     Introduction   195
     A brief outline of the economic and social life of the Dian
     kingdom   197
     The ethnic classification of human figures on the bronzes   199
     The identification of ethnic groups on the bronzes   204
     Conclusion   205
     References   205

13   *The archaeology of the Yoruba: problems and possibilities*
     Omotoso Eluyemi   207

     Introduction   207
     Archaeological data   207
     Shrines and the African gods   209
     References   209

14   *Ethnicity and traditions in Mesolithic mortuary practices of southern*
     Scandinavia   Lars Larsson   210

     References   217

15   *Detecting political units in archaeology – an Iron Age example*
     Ralph M. Rowlett   219
     Political units   225
     References   230

THE GENESIS, MAINTENANCE AND DISAPPEARANCE
OF ETHNICITY AND CULTURAL VARIATION   231

16   *Who is what? A preliminary enquiry into cultural and physical*
     identity   Carol W. Hill   233

     Introduction   233
     The prehistoric and early historic period in Virginia   233
     Microraces in the eastern USA   234
     Racial categorization and social behaviour   236
     The personal dimension   238
     Material culture   238
     Conclusions   239
     Acknowledgements   240
     References   240

17   *Sociocultural and economic elements of the adaptation systems of the
     Argentine Toba: the Nacilamolek and Taksek cases of Formosa
     Province*   Marcela Mendoza and Pablo G. Wright   242

     Introduction   242
     Ethnohistory   244
     Environment   246
     Demography   247
     Subsistence technology   248
     Domestic economy   249
     Political economy   251
     Discussion   253
     Acknowledgements   256
     Note   256
     References   256

18   *Spatial heterogeneity in Fuego-Patagonia*   Luis Alberto Borrero   258

     Introduction   258
     Cultural differentiation   259
     Conclusion   264
     References   265

19   *Cultural and ethnic processes in prehistory as seen through the
     evidence of archaeology and related disciplines*
     P. M. Dolukhanov   267

     Approaches to prehistoric ethnic processes   267
     Palaeolithic Europe   269
     The origins of agriculture   272
     Conclusion   275
     References   276

20   *Research with style: a case study from Australian rock art*
     Natalie R. Franklin   278
     Style as a measure of social interaction and social boundaries 278
     Stochastic versus Emblemic: a case study   282
     References   288

21   *Steppe traditions and cultural assimilation of a nomadic people: the
     Cumanians in Hungary in the 13th–14th century*
     Andras Pálóczi-Horváth   291

     Grave goods   293
     Settlements   296
     References   300

22   *An ethnic change or a socio-economic one? The 5th and 6th centuries
     AD in the Polish lands*   Zbigniew Kobylínski   303
     References   310

Index   313

Preface

This book originated in the session on 'Multiculturalism and Ethnicity in Archaeological Interpretation', the first part of the 'Archaeological Objectivity' theme, at the World Archaeological Congress. However, the differences between the book and the session with its precirculated papers are quite considerable. In particular, after some considerable thought, the structure of the project was changed. This led to the exclusion from the book of a number of the papers presented in the session, the inclusion of three presented in other sessions, and the commissioning of three others to fill in obvious gaps. Thus, the chapters by Durrans, by Dolukhanov and by Veit are new, whereas those of Arnold, Franklin and Washburn were originally placed elsewhere in the Congress proceedings.

It was decidedly nerve-racking on the first day of the Congress being the organizer of the session which started off the key theme of 'Archaeological Objectivity'. I would like to express my thanks to the contributors to the session and to the chairmen – Per Mathiesen, Bozidar Slapsak and Polly Wiessner – for helping things to run as smoothly as they did.

Much of the success of the meeting was due to Professor M.G. Smith's 'summing up' of the day's session – a staggering feat of concentration and erudition. Subsequently, Mike Smith wrote up his comments in chapter form, and I am most grateful to him for having allowed me to make use of them in my Introduction.

Finally, I would like to thank Peter Ucko for making the whole enterprise work and for taking his critical rôle as general editor of this series very seriously. If the book reflects even a fraction of the excitement which was felt by those present at the Congress, then it will have been more than worthwhile.

Stephen Shennan
Southampton

Introduction: archaeological approaches to cultural identity

STEPHEN SHENNAN

The essence of the argument in this book is that the phenomenon of cultural difference raises profound problems for archaeology at all levels of both theory and practice. This introduction outlines some of these problem areas, and the individual chapters examine various aspects of them from a variety of different viewpoints.

Rationality and relativism

Climates of thought and the interests of particular groups strongly affect the questions which archaeologists bring to their material. They go on to affect the interpretations which are produced: the arrows of cultural influence on the archaeological map go one way or the other, depending on whether the archaeologist is Polish or German (Martens, Ch. 2); the interpretation of the 17th century New England cemetery is played one way or the other, in relation to the current interests of the Native American group who see it as part of their heritage (Nassaney, Ch. 4). In short, one's position affects how one sees the world:

> What then is truth? A mobile army of metaphors, metonyms and anthropomorphisms – in short a sum of human relations, which have been enhanced, transposed and embellished poetically and rhetorically, and which after long use seem firm, canonical and obligatory to a people: truths are illusions about which one has forgotten that this is what they are . . . .
>
> (Nietzsche 1873, quoted in Hollis & Lukes 1982)

The idea that the different traditions within an academic discipline may be seen as so many cultures, with different criteria of relevance, significance and meaning has long been commonplace. Hollis & Lukes (1982, p. 1) spell out the point clearly:

> Recent upheavals in the philosophy of science have turned the historian or sociologist of science into something of an anthropologist, an explorer of alien cultures. It is as if scientific paradigms and theoretical

frameworks were strung out in time like islands across an archipelago. Other minds, other cultures, other languages and other theoretical schemes call for understanding from within. . . . Is not the world, as interpreted in our scheme of things, but one of many? Are not our forms of reasoning and tests of truth as parochial as any other?

Questions about why people prefer one tradition to another, or one explanation to another, then become a matter not of reference to external standards of objectivity or evidence, but of their interests – economic or otherwise – and the milieu in which they were enculturated, whether as students into a particular academic discipline or as people growing up within a particular social group and acquiring its traditions. Of course, on this view there is no reason to restrict the range of choices of explanation to those available within the academic discipline itself. As far as reconstructing and explaining the past is concerned, traditional origin myths are as good as archaeology, which is, in fact, simply a way of producing origin myths which are congenial to the way of thinking of a particular kind of society. It is all a question of upbringing.

Taken to its radical conclusion, this view calls into question the deeply entrenched belief that there was a real past in which people produced the material which has come down to us as the 'archaeological record', that if we study this material we can reconstruct what they did, and possibly why they did it, and furthermore, that it is only by using 'evidence' – whether archaeological or documentary – that we can gain access to that past.

The starting point of these radical arguments is now very well known. It is a rejection of the idea that deciding between different hypotheses is simply a matter of collecting 'objective facts' and seeing which view they support. This rejection is based on two arguments: first, theories are *always* under-determined by data; that is to say, a given set of data will always support more than one interpretation, so the choice of one rather than another will also be based on other factors. This is not just a problem for archaeology (cf. Mellor 1973). Secondly, data only become data in the context of specific theories: observations are 'theory-laden'. In other words, we do not see the world as if we were indiscriminate sensing devices; on the contrary, the ideas that we have and the problems in which we are interested direct our attention to particular 'facts' or data which some chain of argument (implicit or explicit) leads us to believe are relevant to our problem.

In their discussion of these questions Hollis & Lukes (1982) draw a series of useful distinctions which tend to be overlooked by those who leap from the view that archaeological hypotheses are not totally determined by the facts to the conclusion that anything beyond description of the material is specu-lative guesswork, in which one person's guess is as good as anyone else's. In fact, what is striking is the great variety of distinctions that it is possible to make, and the existence of tenable positions between the two extremes.

This is clearly demonstrated by the chapters in the first part of this book, whose response to the problems just outlined is generally to argue for a qualified or limited objectivism, in the sense that at some point external criteria involving the concept of 'evidence' are relevant to deciding between hypotheses. This approach is explicit in Wylie's chapter (Ch. 5), but implicit, and in some ways against the run of his argument, in Nassaney's chapter (Ch. 4). The position is clearly distinct from the outright relativism of authors such as Barnes & Bloor (for example, 1982) in the philosophy of science, or the recent work of Shanks & Tilley (1987) in archaeology, who take the view that preferences within the discipline for one hypothesis over another depend entirely on factors arising from the sociology of the practitioners, rather than from constraints given by the objects that they study.

However, even strong forms of relativism do not necessarily imply outright subjectivity, as some of the more superficial discussions of these issues in archaeology seem to suggest. Subjectivity implies 'that some proposition, with a content independent of reasoning, could be held to be true or false according to the mode of reasoning we adopt' (Hacking 1982, p. 65); a strong relativism, 'that their very sense and their being true or false depends on how we reason about them, that alternative styles of reasoning yield other categories of truth-or-falsehood than ours' (Hollis & Lukes 1982, p. 14). However, to accept this does not produce an indeterminacy of translation, or incompatibility of meaning:

> The indeterminacy of translation . . . is empirically empty, because we know that unequivocal translation evolves between any two communities in contact. It is the wrong theoretical notion because it starts from an idea of truth-preserving matching of sentences. In fact, the possibilities available in one language are not there in the other. To get them into the second language one has to learn a way of reasoning and when that has been done there is no problem of translation at all, let alone indeterminacy.
>
> There is perfect commensurability, and no indeterminacy of translation in those boring domains of observations that we share with all people as people. Where we as people have branched off from others as people, we find new interests, and a looseness of fit between their and our commonplaces. Translation of truths is irrelevant. Communication of ways to think is what matters.
>
> (Hacking 1982, pp.60–1)

Horton (1982) also takes note of the non-problematical aspect of communication with regard to Hacking's 'boring domains', but goes on to develop it as the basis for arguing that at a certain level there exist human universals which undermine strong relativist conclusions derived from anthropological studies of different systems of thought. By this Horton means 'a strong core of human cognitive rationality common to the cultures of all places on earth and all times since the dawn of properly human social life' (Horton 1982, p. 256). This core of rationality is based on the common evolutionary heritage of the human species, and it revolves around what Horton calls 'primary theory', developed to cope with a world of middle-sized objects, 'interrelated . . . in terms of a push–pull conception of causality, in which spatial and temporal contiguity are seen as crucial to the transmission of change' (*ibid*. 1982, p. 228). It is this primary theory which 'provides the cross-cultural voyager with his intellectual bridgehead' (*ibid*. 1982, p. 228).

However, such 'primary theory' is insufficient to account for everything that goes on in the world, and all cultures have developed what Horton calls 'secondary theory' in an attempt to transcend it. Such 'secondary theory' varies greatly from culture to culture, although it often involves postulating the action of hidden entities and processes, whether these be particles and currents or gods and spirits. On Horton's view the reason why some societies postulate particles and others spirits is nothing to do with differences in rationality between the cultures concerned, but rather with the fact that 'in different technological, economic and social settings, the "logic of the situation" dictates the use of different intellectual means to achieve the same ends' (*ibid*. 1982, p. 257).

Horton's arguments provide one way, although certainly not the only one, for archaeologists to maintain a universalist position, rather than a relativist one which denies the possibility of the growth of archaeological knowledge. His approach is attractive for two reasons: it does not seek to deny the importance of context in formulating explanations, and it accords explanatory primacy to 'the technological, economic and social setting' rather than to differences in rationality, which are not nearly so accessible to the prehistoric archaeologist.

It is perhaps worth making clear that to talk of a 'universal rationality', as Horton does, is not to postulate the operation of universal laws governing human history; it is to designate a species-wide capacity to relate to the phenomena with which 'primary theory' is concerned in a similar fashion, arising from a common evolutionary heritage. The psychologist James Gibson has made a similar point concerning the nature of human perception, which he sees as deriving from a functional relation to the environment based on human needs in the course of evolutionary history (see Costall 1982).

However, the problem of reconstructing and explaining specific situations on the basis of archaeological evidence remains, and even if we allow that the process of doing this is not totally subjective or arbitrary, that does not mean it is easy. In the face of our lack of direct access to the nature and basis of the cultural schemes which lie behind the situations that we wish to reconstruct, how do we know that we are making valid inferences concerning the significance of the patterning in material culture which we observe? Binford has tried to solve this problem by arguing that the cultural schemes are irrelevant (see, for example, Binford 1983), because we can explain what seem at first sight to be arbitrarily chosen cultural practices as adaptive solutions to problems posed by the environment. However, as Wylie (Ch. 5) points out, this does not work, because it is only too easy to find particular examples of material culture in today's world whose features are not explicable in terms of adaptive rationality.

Conversely, Gardin (Ch. 6) is concerned with developing a framework which will cope not only with the specificity of the situations that the archaeologist investigates, but also with that of the archaeologist operating in a current context. This involves the formulation of locally relevant rules which have empirical implications; for example, that in certain contexts but not in others representations of a bird sitting on a man's gloved hand can be interpreted in terms of the practice of falconry (cf. also Eluyemi, Ch. 13). In doing this Gardin is prepared to concede that there are clear limits to the possibilities of inference in particular situations, as indeed does Wylie.

However, it is insufficient for archaeologists to take a particular pattern of cultural variation at some point in the past as a static given situation which poses problems for interpretation. Archaeology has shown that these patterns come into existence and disappear again, and documenting and understanding the nature of these changes is one of its prime tasks, both as an end in itself and because changing cultural patterns imply changing rules of archaeological interpretation. Local knowledge (in Gardin's terms) is bounded in time as well as space.

Archaeological 'cultures'

It is very easy indeed to demonstrate that the way in which people conduct their lives varies from time to time and from place to place, and, as we have seen, this variation is important to archaeological interpretation. However, from this simple truism archaeologists have elaborated a complex and unsatisfactory explanatory edifice, based on the idea of the archaeological 'culture', which has in general served to confuse rather than enlighten (for example, Rouse 1972). In order to avoid this confusion it is essential at this point to anatomize the archaeological 'culture' and the ideas associated with it:

(a)   as a result of the fact that people living in different places conduct their lives differently to a greater or lesser extent, the material residues (and therefore the archaeological record) of those ways of life will also differ;

(b)   archaeologists have classified these patterns of spatial variation into entities called archaeological 'cultures': 'a culture must be distinguished by a plurality of well-defined diagnostic types that are repeatedly and exclusively associated with one another and, when plotted on a map, exhibit a recognizable distribution pattern . . .' (Childe 1956, p. 123);

(c)   these entities which have been constructed have been regarded as actors on the historical stage, playing the rôle for prehistory that known individuals and groups have in documentary history;

(d)   in playing this rôle these 'cultures' have been regarded as indicators of ethnicity – self-conscious identification with a particular social group; and

(e)   in their rôle as indicators of ethnicity, archaeological 'cultures' have had, and continue to have, a political rôle as legitimators of the claims of modern groups to territory and influence.

These are controversial, but essential, tenets of much archaeological methodology today and the remainder of this introduction is devoted to discussing them. However, first some short comments on each of them may be useful.

(a)   Spatial variation in human ways of life: there is no problem in accepting this, and it will be suggested below that it has some interesting evolutionary implications.

(b)   'Cultures' as a way of classifying spatial variation in the archaeological record: it can be useful to summarize spatial variation in this way for shorthand descriptive purposes, but it has been disastrous to use the results of this classification procedure for many analytical goals. Furthermore, the adoption of this particular kind of summary is not simply the result of some kind of neutral inductive reasoning from the data but also of preconceptions arising out of points (c)–(e), above.

(c)   Cultures as historical actors: 'cultures' cannot be considered as historical actors since they are not real entities. They have been regarded as such for reasons arising out of (d) and (e), above. In a parallel fashion some sociologists (for example, Mann 1986) have recently suggested that 'societies' are not real entities.

(d)   'Cultures' and ethnic identity: the question of the origin of ethnic groups in the sense of self-conscious identity groups is an interesting and important one, but it is analytically distinct from that of the nature of archaeological 'cultures'.

(e)   The political significance of archaeological 'cultures': it is precisely because of their political rôle through their identification with ethnic groups that 'cultures' have played such an important part in archaeological interpretation. This was the reason for their introduction to the discipline in the 19th century, and it is why they have again become important in recent years after a period during which their significance declined. In other words, it is only rarely, and then usually only on a local scale, a question of objective groupings of material being discovered by the archaeologist which are then available for use in political arguments (for example, Ucko 1983a, b). More frequently political interests have conditioned archaeologists' ideas about the type of grouping that they ought to be constructing.

These arguments should come as no surprise after the discussion of rationality and relativism above. It is now necessary to document them, so that they become more than mere assertions. It is appropriate to begin with the political significance of 'cultures', since this takes us back to the origin of their introduction to the discipline of archaeology, and shows how political and other considerations arising from the intellectual milieu of the time affected the development and use of the 'culture' concept.

The political and intellectual context of the concept of the archaeological 'culture' and its link with ethnic identity

The early interest in archaeological cultures and their ethnic identification arose from 19th century romantic nationalism in Europe and its attempt to show the long history of the peoples and nation–states which were then emerging as important political entities (Veit 1984, Ch. 1, this volume, A. D. Smith 1986, Gellner 1987a, Muehlmann 1985). The newly emergent late-19th century German *Reich* had particular problems from the point of view of establishing its historical legitimacy as a unified national state within its newly acquired German-speaking territories, as A. D. Smith (1986, p. 141) points out:

'Germany' was not aided by its ragged geography, nor really by its Holy Roman imperial polity, since here, too, the boundaries fluctuated and political memories were vague. Hence the increasing recourse to ethnic, especially linguistic, criteria, crossed, however, with historical memories of former statehoods in the area.

However, the idea of the importance of such criteria for German identity goes back earlier than this. Hegelian concepts of history no doubt played a rôle (cf. Gellner 1987b), while Muehlmann (1985, p. 11) has indicated other factors, including an extensive misuse of Tacitus' *Germania* as evidence for the German past:

Tacitus' 'Germania', discovered in 1455, played an important role in the ethnocentric self-definition of the Germans. Fichte's 'Talks to the German People' of 1807–8 had a similar influence on a concern with ancestry and origins, especially the idea of a primaeval German people and of a primaeval language. Also important in the case of Friedrich Ludwig Jahn was the idea of an opposed French and Jewish type with which it was not permissible to mix.

Girtler (1982) identifies a different, but not unrelated, set of factors when he suggests that ideas of *Volk* and *Nation* are to be linked with the French Revolution and the setting up of new social categories in contrast to the class strata of feudalism. The *Volk* or *Nation* was considered to be a totality, a closed whole which was culturally uniform.

It was in this context that Kossinna developed his approach to prehistory (see Veit 1984, Ch. 1, this volume), with the aim of documenting the antiquity of the Germans in the new state of Germany. In the course of this

he created a set of methods and interpretative principles for the new
discipline of prehistoric archaeology: the method involved the definition of
archaeological 'culture provinces', and the interpretative principles postulated a link between such culture provinces and the territories of prehistoric
peoples. In addition, for Kossinna the peoples of prehistory were not all
equal – the Germans, or the Nordic race of which they were representatives,
were held to be superior, as Veit (Ch. 1) points out.

Ideas of racial superiority were by no means restricted to Germany, but
were part of a widespread racist ideology current in the later 19th and early
20th century (Gould 1981). It was based on an evolutionary view which saw
races as hierarchically arranged in terms of their capacities, and which
produced the nascent discipline of physical anthropology, together with IQ
testing, with the aim of 'scientifically documenting' these varying capacities,
as Gould shows. Again, it was not just in Germany that this view had
repercussions:

> Americans of European origin were thought to belong to one of three
> entirely distinct physical types, Nordic (which included Anglo-Saxon
> and Teutonic, or Aryan), Alpine, or Mediterranean. Nordics were
> viewed as superior, but their dominance was believed threatened by the
> mass immigration of 'inferior' types from eastern and southern Europe.
> This theory, later entirely discredited, was the basis of the discrimina-
> tory immigration quotas [into the USA] enacted in the 1920s and not
> repealed until 1965.
> (Thernstrom *et al.* 1980, p. 749, quoted in M. G. Smith 1982)

The significance of this climate of thought is difficult to overemphasize,
since it coloured so much of the thinking about socio-economic processes
current during the later 19th and earlier 20th centuries.

Thus, Kossinna had a powerful set of ingredients with which to produce
his picture of the European prehistoric past and the method on which it was
based: a belief, derived from the present, of nation–states as historical actors,
whose predecessors were the 'peoples' whose character and movements
were described by classical authors at the dawn of recorded history; and an
explanation of variations in social and economic patterns in terms of the
innate capacities of the 'peoples' producing them, ranked on a widely agreed
scale of evolutionary superiority.

As Veit (1984, pp. 349–50) makes clear, it was Kossinna's achievement to
project these assumptions into prehistory by linking 'peoples' with material
culture distributions and then explaining the changes in these distributions in
terms of the activities of these 'peoples'. Childe too, of course, initially held
similar views to Kossinna, as is seen in his discussion of the Aryans (Childe
1925), but then largely gave them up in favour of a concern with socio-
economic evolutionary processes (for example, Childe 1936, see Veit 1984
for an extensive discussion of the relationship between Childe and
Kossinna).

Nevertheless, it is a measure of the power of Kossinna's 'settlement archaeology' method that it has continued to be widely used, particularly in continental European circles, albeit now without its racist overtones (see Veit, Ch. 1, this volume, Gebuehr 1987). Traditional European archaeologists take a concern with cultures as self-evidently of importance, and use them as the basis of much routine archaeological activity. In doing so they have largely lost sight of the origins of the 'culture' concept in the romantic nationalism of the 19th century, and have taken their definition as a simple matter of inductive pattern recognition in the way discussed above. Indeed, as Veit (Ch. 1) points out (see also Shennan 1978) some of them have regarded the definition of such entities as one of the few legitimate goals which prehistoric archaeology can pursue, given the data at its disposal.

However, this unreflecting continuation of Kossinna's legacy in European archaeology must be distinguished from a new concern with the history of cultural entities which has appeared in recent years as a result of what has been called an 'ethnic revival' (A. D. Smith 1981, cf. Gellner 1983), a development which has occasioned some surprise (cf. Friedman 1988). Regional groups have emerged in the nation–states of Europe questioning the legitimacy of the states to which they belong and asserting their own special identity; as in the 19th century, the past has become an arena for the establishment of that authentic identity. In the developing world too, similar issues have arisen, often in a starker form, because there the process of nation-building within the boundaries left by the European colonists is still actively continuing. The old white-dominated colonies, such as Australia, Canada and the USA, have also been faced with similar issues, often related to claims on the mineral or other resources of particular areas, which have depended on evidence concerning the identity of the occupiers of the area in the past. Even within Europe, with its long tradition of written history, archaeological evidence has played an important rôle in the arguments. Outside Europe, where in many cases written history begins with the colonial era, archaeology is of even greater significance.

There are several elements in this re-awakened interest in cultural identity, to which A. D. Smith (1986) has drawn attention:

> . . . nostalgia for one's ethnic past has become more acute and widespread and persistent in the modern era, with the decline of tradition and salvation religions. In this sense, ethnic nationalism becomes a 'surrogate' religion which aims to overcome the sense of futility engendered by the removal of any vision of an existence after death, by linking individuals to persisting communities whose generations form indissoluble links in a chain of memories and identities.

The issue is also discussed by Friedman (1988), who links the phenomenon to other general cultural trends and suggests that many of the causes of its most recent massive resurgence are to be sought in global scale economic patterns:

The tendency to cultural fragmentation is, in our view, not part of a process of development, of the emergence of a post-industrial order, an information society on a global scale. It is, rather, a question of real economic fragmentation, a decentralization of capital accumulation, an accompanying increase in competition, a tendency for new centres of accumulation to concentrate both economic and political power in their own hands, i.e. the beginning of a major shift in hegemony in the world system.

In looking at the development of these cultural identities and their historical justification, the question arises of whether the past is merely an invention designed to meet current needs (Rowlands 1984, A. D. Smith 1986); this point takes us back to the issues already discussed in our examination of rationality and relativism. Smith clearly believes in the importance of evidence: some societies, he suggests (A. D. Smith 1986, pp. 177–8), have very 'full' pasts, in the sense that a great deal is known about them; in presenting this past it is possible to be decidedly selective, but there are limits to the possibilities of manipulation. In other cases the past is relatively 'empty' – that is to say, little is actually known about it – so that production of the past amounts to a conjectural reconstruction in which there is considerably more latitude. The possibilities of archaeology in producing life-like reconstructions of 'the atmosphere and drama of past epochs in the life of the community' (*ibid.*, p. 180–1) are considerable:

How can one truly re-enter the past? This is where modern, scientific disciplines like . . . archaeology . . . can help. They are able to translate the idealised images of the ethnic past into tactile realities, according to modern canons of knowledge. Archaeology has been, perhaps, the most useful of these disciplines in recovering communal pasts. . . . Through our archaeological discoveries and interpretations we locate 'ourselves' and dignify 'our communities' by reference to an ancient pedigree and time-honoured environment. The material remains uncovered bring home to us, as only tactile objects can, the physical immediacy of former eras and archaic peoples, lending vivid substance to the records of chronicle and epics.
For a 'returning intelligentsia' bent on rediscovering its 'roots', this physical presence confirms on the ground its re-entry into a living past; for a secular intelligentsia, committed to rationalism and empiricism, archaeology and philology provide the surest basis for their reconstructions.

However, in this sense archaeology is a double-edged weapon: if it can be used to legitimate new national states by giving them a past, then it can also be employed to undermine them by its use to demonstrate that different groups within the state have different cultural histories (Ucko 1983b). Many arguments can be made for and against the use of the past to define identity in this way. A. D. Smith tends to take a positive view of the enterprise as a valid one. From a Marxist point of view Diaz-Polanco (in press) is sceptical, arguing that the whole approach is a romantic and unproductive one, associated with an ethnic separatism based around the idea of preserving indigenous groups in some sort of primeval condition. Such a viewpoint, argues Diaz-Polanco, encouraged by philosophers of Western capitalism, ensures that working-class interests and ethnic-minority interests in Third World countries are seen as being opposed to one another when in fact they are largely identical, a divide-and-rule policy which is to the benefit of multinational capitalist interests.

Given that archaeology is being used in this way, however, and that such a use implies an acceptance of the idea (or at least lip-service to it) that archaeology provides *evidence* relevant to such debates, we are entitled to ask whether such a use is valid in archaeological terms. This brings us back to the questions about the nature of archaeological 'cultures' as entities, and their ethnic equivalence, which have already been raised.

'Cultures' as entities

It has been suggested above that archaeological 'cultures' have traditionally been treated as entities acting on the historical stage, and that such a treatment is mistaken: they are summary descriptions of patterns of spatial variation, not merely useless for analytical purposes, but positively misleading if taken as the basis of an approach to prehistory. The arguments for taking this view are many and varied.

(a) Part of the reason why they have been regarded as entities is because they have been regarded as equivalent to other entities, such as 'tribes', 'societies' and 'ethnic groups'. However, we can question not only the equivalence (see, for example, Clarke 1968, Ucko 1969, Hodder 1978a, b, Renfrew 1987) but even the existence of these other supposed entities.

Mann (1986) has argued that individual 'societies' do not exist; instead we should think in terms of overlapping social networks of varying scales relating to different types of social power, whether ideological, economic, military or political. Fried (1967, 1968) has argued that 'tribes' as we usually conceive them are an artefact of the political situations which arose in many parts of the world with the expansion of Western influence.

Similarly, Geary (1983) has cast doubt on what has always been one of the pillars of an ethnic interpretation of prehistory, in Europe at least – the protohistorical migrations of 'peoples' of the Roman and post-Roman period. One important problem is that of understanding the meanings and uses of ethnic terminology by contemporary authors (Geary 1983, p. 16):

Early medieval authors stress origin, customs, languages and law, as the most significant characteristics by which ethnicity is determined. In contemporary terms each of these characteristics was subjective and together [they] do not provide a means by which one can determine the ethnic identity of individuals or groups.

When one examines the actual uses of ethnic labels, one finds that these articulated criteria in fact had a very limited role in determining the vocabulary of ethnicity. Apparently ethnic identity became conscious to writers largely within the context of politics, and ethnicity was perceived and molded as a function of the circumstances which related most specifically to the interests of lordship.

Geary's conclusion is that medieval historians have started from the mistaken assumption that ethnicity, or ethnic group identity or membership, was an objective fact about the past which they could go out and find – a category 'amenable to precise determination'. On the contrary (Geary 1983, p. 16):

Early medieval ethnicity should be viewed as a subjective process by which individuals and groups identified themselves or others within specific situations and for specific purposes.

One concludes that ethnicity did not exist as an objective category but rather as a subjective and malleable category by which various pre-existing likenesses could be manipulated symbolically to mold an identity and a community.

Hill's chapter (Ch. 16), in the third part of this book, dealing with the very different case of changing ethnic identities among Native Americans in the eastern USA over the past 200 years, leads to similar conclusions, as, of course, do a number of the contributions to Barth's (1969a) well-known book on ethnic groups and boundaries.

(b) The second reason to reject the idea that archaeological 'cultures' are entities arises from the fact that spatial variation in archaeological material is the product of a variety of different factors, not merely of the fact that different people in different places have different ideas about how to do things. The most powerful critic of this latter view has been Binford, who characterizes it as follows (Binford 1972b, pp. 197–8):

Culture is viewed as a vast flowing stream with minor variations in ideational norms concerning appropriate ways of making pots, getting married, treating one's mother-in-law, building houses or temples (or not building them, as the case may be) and even dying.

On this view changes observed in the archaeological record are the result of changing ideas about how to do things. Ideas change either because the people who hold them are replaced by different people with different ideas, or because their ideas are influenced from outside, by diffusion.

Binford's argument is that cultural variation results from all sorts of different factors, operating in various ways and in varying combinations.

Thus, different aspects of variation in pottery, for example, may relate to vessel function, cooking techniques, the size of the domestic group, the rank of the individuals using the pottery, whether the pottery is made by specialists, as well as the milieu in which the potters learned their craft (on this latter subject, see Arnold, Ch. 10).

The lesson from this is not that migration and diffusion never occur and are never reflected in the archaeological record, but that archaeological data must be subjected to a process of analysis, and that we can no longer continue with implicit interpretative principles which assume precisely what should be open to question and investigation. In treating cultures as entities this is exactly the mistake we make.

(c) The third reason for rejecting the idea that archaeological 'cultures' are entities is an empirical one, but it arises because archaeological distributions are the product of a variety of different processes in the way just described. If we examine the distributions of individual types of archaeological material, especially if we use quantitative rather than mere presence–absence information, we find not neatly bounded entities but an enormous variety of cross-cutting patterns. Childe, in fact, was not unaware of this, but his answer was to throw away the information that did not fit (Childe 1956, p. 124, emphasis added):

> We may have to be content . . . with saying that only in culture A are types a, b, c and d repeatedly associated though type b, in association with types e, f and g may distinguish culture B, types c, h, j and k culture C and so on. *Our aim should be demoting b and c from the rank of diagnostic types by finding other types l, m, n. . . . that, being exclusively associated together and with a, should better define A.*

In *Analytical archaeology* Clarke (1968) rejected Childe's approach and argued for a polythetic definition of cultures (see Osborn, Ch. 8). However, although Clarke differed from Childe in the way that cultures should be defined, both regarded the results of their process of definition as entities representing the cultural traditions of human groups (in other words as 'organic totalities' in the terms of Girtler 1982). Both adopted classificatory expedients to remove the untidiness in the cross-cutting distributions, rather than taking the more radical step of recognizing that this untidiness is, in fact, the essence of the situation, arising from the fact that there are no such entities as 'cultures', simply the contingent interrelations of different distributions produced by different factors.

(d) Finally, the examination of the origins of the concept of the archaeological 'culture' presented above (see also Veit 1984, Ch. 1, this volume) has already provided further reasons for being profoundly sceptical of it as a real entity, as Girtler (1982) has also argued.

What are we left with at this point? Cultures have been dismissed as imaginary entities which simply confuse an analysis of social and historical processes. Ethnic identity appears to be an evanescent situational construct, not a solid enduring fact through which we can trace the destinies of peoples. Furthermore, as we have seen, the notion of individual 'societies' has also come under attack.

Is the answer, then, to dismiss all questions relating to such topics as meaningless and irrelevant? This is tempting but unsatisfactory, since the concerns from which they arise are valid even if approaches to them have been misconceived. As already stated, human practices (and therefore local interpretative principles) *do* vary from place to place and the patterns change over time. Furthermore, the phenomenon of ethnicity plays an important rôle in the modern world, and the question of the circumstances of its origin is an important one.

Ethnicity and archaeology

Ethnicity must be distinguished from mere spatial variation and should refer to self-conscious identification with a particular social group at least partly based on a specific locality or origin. If we accept this definition, then it appears that prehistoric archaeology is in a difficult position as far as investigating it is concerned, since it does not have access to people's self-conscious identifications (cf. Arutiunov & Khazanov 1981). The position of documentary history is no better. As we have seen already, Geary (1983) has shown that the ethnic labels applied by early writers do not necessarily correspond to our definition of self-conscious identity groups. All too frequently the mere existence of documentary sources is taken to be conclusive in any argument, whereas such sources should simply be viewed as one more piece of evidence.

However, it is a question of general importance for the history of human societies to establish when the phenomenon of ethnicity in the sense defined above first appeared, and what factors brought it into existence. Gellner (1983) takes the view that entities of the ethnic group type are essentially characteristic of the onset of industrialism and its impact – before that they did not exist. In the preceding agrarian civilizations it was class identity that mattered, with a clear distinction between an élite stratum and a peasantry, the former typified by widespread élite styles and the latter by the prevalence of village communities which were largely insulated from one another and which were differentiated only in the sense of the existence of a certain amount of spatial variation between them.

On the other hand, A. D. Smith (1986, p. 45) traces ethnic entities back much further:

> But it was with the emergence of the first city-states and patrimonial kingdoms in the early 3rd millennium BC . . . that we find a growing sense of a more than local ethnic consciousness and sentiment, notably among the Egyptians and Sumerians.

Given that these statements are ultimately based on contemporary documentary sources, we are faced with the problem raised by Geary (1983) which has already been discussed: that ethnic identity is better considered as a subjective and changing phenomenon rather than as an objective and enduring one, and we cannot assume that the 'peoples' described in the sources correspond to the self-conscious identity groups which are essential to the definition of ethnicity. At present this problem remains unresolved.

However, if for the moment we take the view that the 'peoples' described were indeed 'ethnic groups', then obviously Gellner is wrong, Smith is right and further questions about the origins of such entities arise, most importantly whether ethnic identity arose as a product of the development of the earliest states, whose documents provide us with our references to 'peoples', or is a more general phenomenon which also arises in other economic, social and political contexts not characterized by the presence of states. Several arguments can be advanced in favour of the view that it is indeed a product of the appearance of states.

As we have seen already, Fried (1967, 1968) suggested that 'tribes' as real entities arose as a result of external pressure from more-complex societies; they coalesced on the basis of a segmentary principle in the face of an outside threat, and when they were incorporated into expanding empires they were treated and administered as a fixed unit. Without such pressure, Fried argues, there are merely temporary and fluctuating patterns of groupings and alliances. In a similar fashion Bentley (1987) sees ethnicity as very much associated with complex societies and the impact they have on people in terms of social and economic upheavals.

Bentley's model is an interesting one because it offers an explanation of the form that ethnicity takes, links it to the larger-scale society in terms of the conditions in which it appears, and has some implications for attempts to infer the presence of ethnicity in the past. He rejects what he calls the *instrumentalist* and *primordialist* views of ethnicity. The former sees ethnic groups appearing as the result of the pursuit of common interests, the latter as the result of a desire for 'rootedness' which gives rise to communal sentiments. Bentley (1987, p. 27) argues that neither model stands up to empirical testing or specifies how collectivities of interest and sentiment come into existence:

> At base ethnicity makes a claim to be a particular kind of person . . ., ethnic identity claims involve symbolic construal of sensations of likeness and difference, and these sensations must somehow be accounted for.

Instead he suggests that the conscious sensations of affinity involved in membership of an ethnic group arise from a 'subliminal awareness of objective commonalities in practice' (*ibid.*, p. 27), that is to say, in the terms of Bourdieu (1977), whom Bentley takes as the basis of his theoretical position, from similarities in the *habitus*.

Ethnic identity is therefore not something which is completely arbitrary, whether guided by interests or emotion, but rather 'ethnic identities are anchored internally in experience as well as externally in the cognitive distinctions in terms of which that experience is ordered' (Bentley 1987, p. 36). In other words, the *habitus* is the link between subjective identity and objective context. However, having provided a basis for the generation of ethnic sentiment, Bentley still has to deal with the question of why and how an ethnic sentiment comes into existence. This is usually taken to arise from contexts of competition (cf. Hodder 1979), although other possibilities also exist (Barth 1969b, p. 19). For Bentley, examining ethnicity in the modern world, ethnic mobilization is related to 'a shift in conceptions of personal identity as new modes of domination are instituted in response to changed environmental circumstances' (Bentley 1987, p. 45), that is, in the light of the pervasive political, social and economic changes of recent times.

Bentley (1987, p. 48) concludes that Bourdieu's theory accounts for the power that is available to the ethnic dimension once it has been mobilized:

> Rooted in preconscious patterns of practice that are not susceptible to conscious apprehension or alteration, ethnic identities implicate . . . who people are. It is this authenticity that advocates of instrumentalist models deny. At the same time, the idea of *habitus* accounts for ethnic group formation and coordinated ethnic action without having to assume that ethnic identities represent either artifice or the product of some psychologically improbable process of unconscious interest aggregation.

To understand ethnicity it is necessary to have a historical perspective, because only then can we see how it comes into existence, what resources it uses, what rôle it plays in the process of social reproduction, and why it might have been mobilized. Archaeologically, the suggestions of Bentley are interesting, as they emphasize the cultural nature of the process of ethnic identity creation, which provides a key reason for the emotional power associated with it. On this basis the creation of ethnic identities should have repercussions in terms of the self-conscious use of specific cultural features as diacritical markers, a process which might well be reflected in the archaeological record. However, the process of ethnic identity creation only comes to have its power in a situation in which pre-existing forms of identity creation and maintenance – kinship, for example – are being destroyed; this is often seen as a key feature of the processes at the root of the origins of states (for example, Crone 1986).

Outside of such societies and their spheres of influence the formulation of collective interests is very much a situational phenomenon; a kind of segmentary principle operates, producing the coalescence and disintegration of groups depending on what people's current interests are (cf. Gellner 1987c). Personal identity is not so strongly implicated. In other words, if one follows through the implications of this line of argument, ethnicity as defined above, and discussed by Bentley, Smith and others, does not exist outside the orbit of early states.

Spatial variation, style and identity

This still leaves the question of the nature and significance of the spatial variation which is apparent almost universally in the archaeological record. We have already seen that the concept of the 'archaeological culture' is a hopelessly unsatisfactory way of dealing with it, so some alternative must be offered. That suggested here has three elements:

(a) an emphasis derived from Binford on the importance of dissecting cultural phenomena;
(b) an analytical approach to the concept of style; and
(c) a suggested theoretical basis to account for the prevalence of spatial variation.

The analytical approach to variation in the archaeological record

This has already been discussed in the course of arguing for the unsatisfactory nature of archaeological 'cultures' as entities. Variation in artefacts across space and time arises as a result of an enormous range of different processes, from the problems of coping with a specific environment to the distribution of social power, the organization of material production or changing patterns of religion and iconography. Despite all the subsequent attacks on the 'New Archaeology' of the 1960s, the need for the analysis of processes has remained a fundamental premise of modern archaeology even if the explanations for those different processes have since changed considerably from the initial emphasis on functional adaptation.

The nature of style

There is one key aspect of spatial variation which has not yet been considered – style:

> Clearly, the meanings of style have become many. However, all the more central usages of the word refer first to form as against substance, manner as against content. Secondly, they imply some consistency of forms. And third, they may suggest that the forms used in the style cohere sufficiently to integrate into a series of related patterns.
>
> (Kroeber 1957, p. 4)

Many Anglo-American archaeologists have accepted all of the points about archaeological cultures outlined above, and the importance of dissecting cultural processes, but they have argued that the phenomenon of stylistic variation in artefacts remains unaccounted for. In fact, many of the discussions which in the past concerned the nature of archaeological 'cultures' and the kinds of entity that they represented have not disappeared, but have become refocused around the concept of style.

The most influential view of style in Anglo-American archaeology in recent years has seen it in terms of information exchange (Wobst 1977). Stylistic variation in artefacts functions to transmit messages of one kind or another which facilitate social interaction, especially at intermediate social distances. Thus, Wobst cited a modern example of different styles of hat conveying an instantly visible message concerning the ethnic identity of the hat wearers.

Wiessner has developed these ideas in a series of important papers (1983, 1984, 1985) which have involved her in a debate with Sackett (1982, 1985) about the nature and significance of stylistic variation. Wiessner has argued for an essentially active view of style, suggesting that it has two aspects: *emblemic* and *assertive*. Emblemic style is (Wiessner 1983, p. 257):

> formal variation in material culture that has a distinct referent and transmits a clear message to a defined target population about conscious affiliation or identity. . . . Most frequently its referent will be a social group . . ., and thus it will be used to express objective social attributes of identity. Because it has a distinct referent, emblemic style carries information about the existence of groups and boundaries and not about degree of interaction across or between them.

Assertive style, on the other hand, is (*ibid.*, p. 258):

> formal variation in material culture which is personally based and which carries information supporting individual identity. . . . It has no distinct referent as it supports, but does not directly symbolise, individual identity and may be employed either consciously or unconsciously.
>
> . . . consequently [it] has the potential to diffuse with acculturation and enculturation, providing a measure of interpersonal contact for archaeologists. . . . Whether it carries such information, however, is a complex matter that depends on a number of decisions of the maker and on the natural, functional and social properties of the object . . . .

In her particular case study Wiessner demonstrated that San projectile points were characterized by emblemic style, in the sense of being a good indicator of linguistic group boundaries. She also sketched out certain features which might be expected to characterize vehicles of emblemic style.

Sackett (1982, 1985) does not actually exclude such a rôle altogether, but regards the vast majority of stylistic variation in artefacts – or, as he prefers to call it, 'isochrestic variation' – as passive. In his view material culture inevitably carries a heavy load of ethnic symbolism because it is produced in ethnically bounded contexts.

In another book in this *One World Archaeology* series, however, Wiessner (1989) has outlined a view which integrates her 'emblemic' and 'assertive' categories, as well as Sackett's isochrestic variation, in a single framework, based on the idea of 'identification by comparison' operating in different conditions (Wiessner 1989, ch. 2):

> The specificity of the referent for a given style [i.e. the extent to which it is emblemic or assertive] is . . . dependent on context and conditions, i.e. whether distinctive social units are recognized in a society, whether factors such as competition make it advantageous to send a clear stylistic message to a defined target population, and so on.

Isochrestic variation simply arises where particular artefacts, or aspects of them, are not of great importance, so that choices about how to make and use them are largely automatic or subconscious, arising from the local pattern of enculturation, rather than being used in the process of identification by comparison. It is important to note that (*ibid.*)

> since it is the context and conditions affecting social and stylistic comparison that create different aspects of style, no distinct line can be drawn to separate isochrestic variation from style. If during times of change an item takes on new social and symbolic value, its profile of variation may change radically.

These distinctions made by Wiessner are extremely useful ones and fit in very well with the ideas of Bentley (1987) discussed above. They also make clear the confusion in the original concept of isochrestic variation. It is mistaken and unhelpful to think of isochrestic variation expressing 'ethnicity', or carrying a load of 'ethnic symbolism'; this is precisely what, as isochrestic variation, it does not do. We have argued already that ethnicity must be distinguished from mere spatial variation and should refer to self-conscious identification with a particular social group. Once some aspect of style has an ethnic reference, it is by definition 'emblemic', since it has acquired a different and specific value. As we have noted several times already, spatial variation always exists (or certainly has done since the origins of modern man), but ethnicity is a specific and contingent phenomenon, the product of particular situations, involving the mobilization of an ethnic identity, which may well involve new uses for old styles. 'Ethnicity' may, as we have suggested, be a rather special kind of group identity associated with the appearance of states, in contrast with other kinds of more-flexible group definition involving the use of emblemic style (see below).

The concept of isochrestic variation may also be criticized for other reasons: it may lead us to think that we have explained something when all we have done is give it a label. It refers to the largely automatic choices about how to do things which arise from local patterns of enculturation, but it does not take us very far in analysing or explaining those patterns. In fact, it is vulnerable to precisely the same criticisms as Binford made of the ideas behind traditional culture history – it views spatial variation and change purely in terms of variation in people's 'mental templates' of how to do things. Understanding why such variation takes the form that it does involves the detailed dissection of a series of adaptive and other processes.

Bentley's use of Bourdieu's concept of the *habitus* discussed can be seen to correspond in many respects to Sackett's isochrestic variation, except of course that it refers not just to material culture, but to social life in general: what people are enculturated to do and think from birth onwards without conscious reflection, simply by virtue of having been brought up in one place rather than another. This provides the resources for ethnic identity, and indeed for 'emblemic' and 'assertive' uses of style in general. As a result such uses of style perhaps have a stronger and more genuine basis than Wiessner, with her emphasis on conscious identity creation related to context, is prepared to allow. On the other hand, the *habitus* is not in itself ethnic identity, any more than is isochrestic variation, nor can it be regarded as representing the bedrock explanatory level – it must itself be subjected to a process of further analysis.

Emblemic style and identity

In the above discussion of ethnicity it was speculated that it was a phenomenon deriving from the social and economic dislocation associated with the existence of states and that outside of such situations the formation of collective interests and supralocal groups is a more situational phenomenon. Nevertheless, it may still involve the use of 'emblemic style', as Wiessner (1989) illustrates in her description of the way in which members of a swidden horticultural group use material means to create an impression of strength, unity and wealth on the occasion of major ceremonials involving the participation of groups from several different valleys.

However, 'emblemic style' has a wider relevance than to the creation and definition of supralocal or ethnic groups. As Schortman's (in press) discussion of 'salient identity' emphasizes, individuals have a variety of aspects to their identity, which they can use to construct aspects of differentiation which are important in different situations; for example, age, sex and social class (where present), as well as group membership. In a particular context 'emblemic style' may relate to any of these. Precisely why particular aspects emerge as salient in a particular context is a matter of considerable importance, and it is quite likely that there will be interactions between them. This point is well illustrated by two interesting recent ethno-archaeological studies from East Africa (Hodder 1985, Larick 1986). In both cases the form and material expression of inter-'tribe' relations are connected with patterns of intra-group social differentiation. From a different perspective such links between local and larger-scale socio-economic processes are also emphasized in some of the archaeological work using 'neo-Marxist' and 'world systems' perspectives (for example, Kristiansen 1982, 1984, Rowlands 1980).

It follows from this that archaeology has the task of recognizing any emblemic uses of style in the definition of groups arising from particular interests in particular social networks of differing scales (cf. Mann 1986). Emblemic uses must be distinguished from other aspects of stylistic variation, and the nature of the reference group to which the emblemic style refers must be determined. This is not necessarily a hopeless task by any means. There may well be at least partly independent lines of evidence to establish whether age, gender or social class are relevant, whereas changes over time in the structure of spatial distributions can give an indication that a particular material attribute has acquired an emblemic rôle. Nevertheless, obvious problems exist. If, for example, patterns of group definition are short-term and fluctuating, as we have suggested they often will be, then any material aspect of them may not be detectable at the relatively low levels of chronological resolution normally available to prehistorians.

To sum up, Wiessner's view of style, which has been adopted here, is of considerable importance, with its emphasis on the process of identification by comparison, in which 'emblemic' and 'assertive' style and 'isochrestic variation' are distinct but not totally unrelated. Indeed, in principle a given attribute – for example, a particular type of decoration on pottery – could over a period, and without changing its form, play an 'assertive' rôle, an 'emblemic' one and represent mere 'isochrestic variation'. Precisely which is relevant at a given time depends on the context and conditions, as Wiessner points out. This further emphasizes the argument presented above that it is impossible to regard what goes on within social groups as independent of what happens in the relations between them, and again brings home the importance of detailed analysis of archaeological data and their social and economic implications.

Darwinian models for style and isochrestic variation

Archaeology has usually taken as the limit of its brief the description of the patterns of variation, most often in terms of 'cultures', and the explanation of the specific patterns observed in particular cases, traditionally on the basis of a 'culture = people' hypothesis. However, it is reasonable to ask the more general and more basic question, why is the world like this at all? Why do such patterns of variation as those discussed in this introduction exist? It is possible to suggest some answers to this question by looking at it from a Darwinian viewpoint.

Wiessner (1983, 1989) does this in her discussion of 'assertive style'. She suggests (following Crook 1981) that there would be an advantage in natural selection terms in the creation of a positive self-image, since it would encourage others to engage in desirable social relations, and that the use of assertive style is one way of achieving this (Wiessner 1983, p. 258):

Desire to present a positive image to partners in reciprocity and to members of the opposite sex was the most frequent motive for stylistic effort given by San informants. . . . If Crook's hypothesis is correct, one would expect assertive style to appear first in the archaeological record with the origins of regular, delayed and unbalanced reciprocal relations.

However, Darwinian explanations may also be adduced for the general phenomenon that differing areas of uniform 'practice' – patterns of isochrestic variation – are a general occurrence. This is because in a context where culture is much more important than genes from the selection point of view, it will usually be advantageous to take decisions based not on individual learning, but on imitation of existing culturally transmitted practices, especially those which are most frequent. Thus, the transmission of cultural, as opposed to genetic, variation from generation to generation is not a process of random intermixing of the available material. Common variants of cultural practices will tend to be transmitted preferentially within an area, rather than the random intermixing of the genes which occurs in genetic inheritance. Of course, the result of this is the generation of areas of cultural uniformity with respect to the various phenomena in question, where people tend to do things in the same way. It follows from this that specific populations will tend to be far more homogeneous culturally than genetically.

This kind of imitation may operate at various levels of consciousness, and at the conscious level may be accompanied by another phenomenon, which Boyd & Richerson (1985) called 'indirect bias': this is a tendency to imitate those who appear particularly successful in their society, not just in the specific aspects that are relevant to their success, but also in other aspects of their behaviour and appearance. This would lead to the appearance of areas of similarity in the expression of 'assertive style'. Wiessner's account explains why people should want to use 'assertive style'; 'indirect bias' explains why the content of 'assertive style' is not unique to each individual, but shows widespread patterns of similarity in particular places at particular times.

In short, there is every reason to believe that the human species, or rather the culture which characterizes it, will inevitably exhibit spatially varying patterns of isochrestic variation and assertive style. These need to be analysed essentially in the ways already discussed. As we have seen, these patterns provide the material from which emblemic uses of style, including the construction of ethnicity, can develop.

Archaeological approaches to cultural identity

This book is divided into three sections, each relating to a different aspect of the problems discussed above.

The first part of the book deals with general theoretical and philosophical questions revolving around the question of objectivity in archaeological interpretation, and the possibility of acquiring knowledge about the past, and in particular prehistory, by archaeological means.

Veit's chapter discusses the development of the concept of the archaeological 'culture' by Kossinna, a very appropriate place to begin, given that Kossinna's work has set the agenda for a century of subsequent discussion. However, in exploring the subsequent development of Kossinna's ideas, a key part of Veit's argument is the ambivalence of German archaeologists since World War II with regard to the 'culture' concept, because of its origins in the attempt to demonstrate the antiquity and superiority of the Germans and its consequent use by the Nazis. Clearly, they still accept the importance of archaeological 'cultures' as entities, and do not subscribe to the arguments against them outlined above, but they have attempted to strip them of any significance other than the purely archaeological. In various ways this has tended to lead to sterility at the theoretical level, as Veit describes.

Martens (Ch. 2) presents a case study which very effectively illustrates many of Veit's arguments. He shows how a concern with the antecedents of the historical Vandals led to an extremely dubious linkage between this historically known group and an archaeological 'culture' located in Poland. Since the Vandals were 'Germanic', this became a further excuse for Nazi plans of expansion to the East, and it was argued that the 'culture' itself had appeared in Poland as a result of a Germanic migration from Jutland. Once the Nazis were defeated, Polish archaeologists argued that the arrows of migration should be reversed, but subsequently archaeologists with evolutionist preconceptions, who placed more emphasis on internal social developments, ignored similarities in the archaeological record of Poland and Jutland, and suggested that Iron Age developments in the two areas were independent of one another. Nothing could illustrate better the tenuous nature of 'evidence' in archaeological arguments.

Durrans, in Chapter 3, continues the emphasis on the rôle of interests and ideology, as opposed to 'evidence', in archaeological interpretation. However, the sources of ideology that he discusses come less from preconceptions about ethnicity and more from the problems faced by archaeologists working within the context of capitalism, although to the extent that this includes imperialism it also has a racist component. Durrans argues for a critical rôle for archaeology in exposing the false consciousness characteristic of capitalist societies. If it is to achieve this rôle, then the knowledge of the past that it provides is necessary but not sufficient; archaeologists must also involve themselves in political action, since it is only by this means that they will come to a realization of the ideological preconceptions governing their work. This is why, he suggests, 'some of the sharpest criticism of orthodox archaeology is now coming from the Third (and Fourth) World and from blacks and women in the West' (Ch. 3, p. 73).

In the same way that Martens provides a case study illustrating some of Veit's general points, Nassaney's study (Ch. 4) of interpretations of a cemetery of the Narragansett, a Native American group, complements Durrans. He refers to it as an enterprise in the 'ethnography of archaeology',

and supports his own interpretation of the cemetery with reference to two
very different sets of criteria. First, it is an improvement in its fit to the data,
since it is consistent with a wider range of evidence than previous interpretations were. Secondly, it is potentially acceptable to the current Narragansett
and to archaeologists, and assigns a creative rôle to the Narragansett of the
17th century in their dealings with European encroachment. That the
interpretation is satisfactory in relation to both of these sets of criteria is very
convenient. One wonders what the outcome would have been if it had
satisfied the first, but not the second. In any event, he suggests, the
Narragansett concern with such questions is itself a response to demands by
the modern state in which they belong to demonstrate continuity and
persistence if they wish to claim legitimacy, demands which inevitably lead,
to some extent, to the invention of tradition. These questions of how
groups emerge and define themselves are also discussed by Hill (Ch. 16).

Wylie (Ch. 5) treats the same questions of objectivity and interests, but
from a general philosophical and epistemological point of view; her focus is
the epistemological debates which have taken place within archaeology
concerning the possibility of acquiring knowledge about the past by using
the methods of archaeology. Binford (1972a) argues for a strongly objectivist point of view, stating that we can find out anything we want to about the
past, so long as we use the right methods in the context of a generalizing
approach based on the central importance of the ecosystem. Wylie argues
against this view, and against its opposite, which presupposes that 'if
knowledge claims about the past are not established with certainty, then they
are nothing but arbitrary speculation' (Ch. 5, p. 108). On the contrary,
appeals to evidence can constrain the free play of archaeological interpretation, but the extent of that constraint is variable and changing: 'what can be
known of the past and the security of this knowledge will change as the
relevant background (or "middle-range") knowledge and associated technologies develop' (Ch. 5, p. 108).

A similar position is taken by Gardin (Ch. 6), who also shares Wylie's
emphasis on the importance of ethno-archaeology and related research. He,
too, takes the view that there are contingent limits on what we can say about
the past, while emphasizing the constraining rôle of data, on the one hand,
and the lack of universal interpretative principles, on the other. According to
Gardin, what we must do is establish rigorous rules of archaeological
interpretation which take into account the essential specificity and local
nature of cultural situations: they must be local rules rather than universal
laws, they must be internally consistent and fit the data, and they should
contain a statement of the limits of their own application. Although he can
accept the relevance of interests to choosing a question to investigate or a
model to test, there should be no room for them, when it comes to model
validation, even if that means drawing very tight limits round the possibilities of archaeological interpretation.

The need emphasized by Gardin and Wylie for ethno-archaeological and
other work which enables us to see processes at work and their outcomes has

been widely felt in recent years, especially in Anglo-American archaeology. In addition, as we have already seen, examination of more-general ethnographic information collected without archaeologists in mind demonstrates (see, for example, Clarke 1968, Ucko 1969, Hodder 1978a, b, Renfrew 1987) an enormous range of different possibilities with regard to the relationship between material culture distributions, language distributions and the boundaries (if indeed there are any) of social groups.

The second section of the book deals with these questions of the relationship between cultural identity and variation in material culture. It includes several ethno-archaeological studies in which information has been collected on people's cultural identity, on variation in material culture, and the relationships between them, thus enabling an examination of the factors behind spatial variation in material culture. Other chapters in this section are more purely archaeological or are based on archaeological and documentary evidence, but they are careful to avoid assuming an equation, of the kind criticized above, between archaeological 'culture' and ethnic group. They use their information analytically to discuss questions of cultural identity, ethnicity and even, in the case of Rowlett (Ch. 15), political boundaries.

DeCorse (Ch. 7) presents an ethno-archaeological study from Sierra Leone, in which he examined variation in a number of aspects of the material culture of three adjacent distinct ethnic groups and found that it showed relatively little relation to the ethnic divisions, although he sketches out some possibilities for future research which might be more successful at defining them.

Osborn's contribution (Ch. 8) is also based on ethnography. Its special interest lies in its demonstration of a situation in which there are no clear boundaries except at the very edge of the system. The U'wa of the Colombian Andes are made up of several different groups which are culturally distinct from one another in a wide variety of different and complex respects but in a polythetic fashion. There are no characteristics which are specific to one group and not to any of the others, merely an overall dissimilarity which increases with distance. Here Clarke's (1968) emphasis on the polythetic nature of archaeological 'cultures' would be relevant, although how successful the archaeologist would be at identifying the correct real groups, or even the correct spatial scale of group, is another matter. At the boundary between the U'wa, on the one hand, and whites and lowland Indians, on the other, there is a very clear boundary but, in keeping with what has been said above about contexts for the creation of clear and enduring boundaries, Osborn suggests it is a result of colonial disruption (Ch. 8, p. 154):

> I do not believe that in pre-Conquest times radical differences were drawn between people living in different areas of the northeastern Andes. It seems much more probable that the Spanish conquest, with its disruption of native beliefs, was a prime factor in the development of sharper boundaries. . . . As time passed this situation was exacerbated

by the dispersal and disappearance of many of those groups that had once formed links in a more-or-less continuous chain.

Washburn's ethno-archaeological study (Ch. 9) is much more specific. Following on the criticisms of the archaeological 'culture' concept outlined above, she is concerned to identify aspects of the archaeological record which can confidently be used to specify group boundaries, and argues that most of those used in recent attempts to solve this problem are too superficial and object-specific. Washburn's answer is to suggest that the analysis of patterns of symmetry may be a better method of distinguishing ethnic groups, and she carries out a survey which demonstrates that members of a particular ethnic group do, indeed, have consistent preferences with regard to symmetry patterns. As Washburn points out, however, this is very much a preliminary study which establishes that members of two groups from different parts of the world have different preferences. An important next step would be to investigate the way in which symmetry preferences vary between groups within a given region.

Arnold (Ch. 10) tackles the important question of the microprocesses of cultural transmission within a single community with respect to pottery, and demonstrates that it does, indeed, relate to kinship in this case, despite suggestions to the contrary from elsewhere, which he reviews. Children learn pottery making within the household, and recruitment to households is based on kinship. The aspects of the pottery in which this situation is reflected are those related to the 'basic motor habits of vessel fabrication' (Ch. 10, p. 181) rather than decorative patterns, which are much more prone to variation relating to other influences. Like Washburn's chapter (Ch. 9), this chapter provides some interesting suggestions for further work.

As we have already seen, when the information available to us is no longer ethnographic but historical and archaeological, we have to be more clear-minded than ever. Such clear-mindedness is well illustrated by Balint's chapter (Ch. 11) on what he calls 'ethnospecific' features of the archaeological record in eastern Europe during the early Medieval period. He shows the complex relations between distributions of material culture items and historically known groups, and the way in which ideas about the definition of these groups and the material culture associated with them have varied with changing patterns of nationalism in the area in the recent past. As Smith (1986) pointed out, Balint also suggests that the 'so-called Bijelo Brdo culture' in the 10th and 11th centuries AD represents 'the archaeological culture of the Hungarian state', created by Hungarian commoners 'blending their own culture with those found on the spot'; if it is correct, this represents an interesting comparison with situations like the USA, where a state culture has developed, produced by several ethnic groups.

Wang (Ch. 12) has a remarkable data set with which to explore the definition of ethnic groups in the Yunnan area of China c. 500–100 BC – a series of bronzes depicting scenes from people's daily lives and other activities, including battle scenes and ceremonies. He uses this information, linked with ancient documentary sources and modern ethnography, to suggest that four ethnic groups can be defined which have survived relatively unchanged for more than 2000 years, up to the present. The quality of the data sources is very high indeed, and this makes this suggestion far more convincing than such arguments usually are – it confirms Wylie's and Gardin's proposal that the limits of inference in specific cases are contingent rather than absolute. The study is also interesting for other reasons: first, because it achieves, apparently convincingly (to someone who is not a specialist on the Chinese data), precisely what Kossinna was trying to achieve when he developed his 'culture' concept – the projection of current ethnic groups into the past. Secondly, it demonstrates that ethnic identity can in certain circumstances be an extraordinarily enduring phenomenon.

Eluyemi, in Chapter 13, who does not have access to data sources of the same quality as Wang, discusses the problems of trying to trace the ethnohistory of the Yoruba by archaeological means, and notes the problems that archaeologists have if they do not have access to what Gardin would call the 'local knowledge' to understand what they find.

Larsson (Ch. 14) provides a case study relevant to the classic archaeological problem of making inferences about cultural identity in prehistory. After discussing the various problems which can arise in this enterprise, such as poor preservation conditions and general lack of data, as well as the non-contemporaneity of different sites, he eventually does suggest that there may have been ethnic differences in late Mesolithic southern Scandinavia, on the basis of consistent differences in burial ritual between the two regions he discusses. In my view he makes the case that there are differences in burial practice, but not necessarily that they should be considered ethnic; there are many reasons for spatial variation, of which ethnicity is only one.

In recent years archaeologists have become at least as interested in trying to establish the boundaries of political units as cultural or ethnic ones: the emphasis on social archaeology has directed attention to the study of political processes, and the demonstration that the link between cultural distributions and political entities is very much a contingent one has made it clear that defining political entities constitutes a separate problem. The problem has led to the use of several expedients to 'guesstimate' them, for example Thiessen polygons. In a study of Iron Age material from France, Rowlett (Ch. 15) suggests that certain cultural distributions did indeed have a political significance by demonstrating that their edges are characterized by very high incidences of grave-robbing, which he attributes to intertribal raiding. As Smith (1986) pointed out, there is more that we need to know before we can accept this interesting and provocative idea. For example, it might be that the heavily looted graves were in a less rich or less well-connected part of the region, so that they had a greater need to recycle grave goods to meet the demands of the population for the often rich ornaments that were buried.

The definition and understanding of spatial variation in material culture beyond the level of the individual site is clearly of central importance to

archaeology, as indeed is the reconstruction of patterns of ethnicity, or
indeed the lack of it. However, such reconstructions cannot be an end in
themselves. Rather, they are a means to an end, since the archaeologist is not
normally content with reconstructing a static picture of cultural variation at a
particular point in time, but in diachronic change in such patterns. Why these
variations occur, and the extent to which ethnic group distinctiveness, or the
loss of it, is characteristic of them, are questions of major importance which
are the object of the chapters in the third section of this book, all of which are
concerned with change, albeit in a wide variety of different contexts.

In contrast with the long duration of ethnic identity identified by Wang,
Hill's chapter (Ch. 16) demonstrates how situations can be disrupted by
rapid and violent social change, in this case the effect of the European
colonization of North America. To what extent identities before this were
ethnic in the sense discussed above (and cf. Osborn, Ch. 8) is an open
question, but the pace and complexity of ethnic group formation which
followed the disruption it caused is remarkable. Hill also demonstrates the
subtlety of the factors which lead people to identify themselves with one
group rather than another, and the fact that the way in which groups have
defined themselves is strongly affected by the power of the dominant group
in the larger society. It is in the face of this that Native American groups have
been trying to define a heritage for themselves in recent years, a process of
which Nassaney's study (Ch. 4) gives us an example.

Mendoza & Wright present a case study (Ch. 17) which is somewhat
similar, in the sense of examining trajectories of change of two groups in the
Argentine Toba as white influence has increased. Their detailed and wide-
ranging analysis shows how initial differences in adaptation and spatial
position have led them in rather different directions as they have interacted
increasingly with the outside world. Its examination of changing subsistence
and consumption patterns deals with areas which are fairly directly accessible
to archaeologists. However, Smith (1986) criticized their use of Marvin
Harris' cultural materialist approach as a framework for their study:

> In that theory the infrastructure, structure and superstructure are
> aligned by relations of linear determinism, though conceptually and in
> practice they are inseparably associated at emic and etic levels so that the
> deterministic relations that link them are systemic and recursive rather
> than unilinear.

Borrero's chapter (Ch. 18) also deals with Argentina, but this time from a
much longer time perspective (from 12 000 years ago to the present)
concerned with the appearance and expansion of human populations in this
area. As a result he focuses on general ecological issues, and gives an
interesting account of the colonization process from this point of view.

Dolukhanov (Ch. 19) also adopts a macroscale approach, both chronologically and spatially, but ventures some speculative and provocative
arguments about the relationship between archaeological evidence and

language with reference to the appearance and spread of proto-Indo-European languages. Renfrew (1987) has recently again made this a topical question, and many of Dolukhanov's arguments follow a similar line to Renfrew's, in particular the suggestion that the spread of these languages is associated with the spread of agriculture.

Franklin (Ch. 20) examines changes in rock art styles and their distributional patterns in Australia, and argues for a view of them in terms of what she calls 'stochastic style', a concept not dissimilar to Sackett's 'isochrestic variation' discussed above. She specifically rejects the concept of 'emblemic style' (see above), on the grounds that its use presupposes that stylistic variation is related to differences between ethnic groups. However, as we have seen above, 'emblematic' and 'isochrestic' are not mutually exclusive concepts: establishing whether a particular style is emblemic is a matter for empirical investigation in a given case. By excluding it *a priori*, Franklin excludes the very possibility that style might be used in this way.

Of course, Franklin is in the difficult position of the prehistorian, not the case for Paloczi-Horvath, whose study (Ch. 21) of cultural assimilation in medieval Hungary is based on both archaeological and historical sources. It has several similarities to Balint's chapter (Ch. 11), in the second section of the book, but belongs here because the main object of concern is not the correlation or otherwise of material variation and historically documented groups, but the process of cultural assimilation itself. In providing this detailed and fascinating account, based on good-quality information, Paloczi-Horvath pursues the approach advocated above of documenting change in a variety of different spheres and demonstrating their inter-relations. The situation he presents makes an interesting comparison with those of Hill and Mendoza & Wright (Chs 16 & 17).

Kobylinski (Ch. 22) similarly presents a study of change, this time concerned with Poland in the 5th and 6th centuries AD. Despite the date, the sources of information available mean that Kobylinski is, in effect, working as a prehistorian, and the bulk of his chapter presents archaeological arguments related to the question of continuity over this period in Poland. This is not a neutral zone. The questions being posed are highly emotive ones, such as the origins of the Slavs, and the answers are seen to hinge on archaeological evidence: we have already noted the case study of the Vandals by Martens (Ch. 2), which raises similar issues, but examined from a rather different viewpoint. In discussing the evidence, Kobylinski shows an acute awareness of the various theoretical issues which his chapter raises and which are, in fact, the main theme of this book.

Conclusion

The importance of ethnic issues and conflicts of interest in the modern world at least partly explains and justifies our interest in them in the past. Unfortunately, in investigating these questions, as with so many others, we have tended to create the past in our own image. The challenge for the future, to which I hope this book is a contribution, is to try to transcend this parochial subjectivism. We can only do this by remaining constantly aware of what is in effect the main lesson of this book: problems of theory, aims, methods and results, especially the link between substantive patterns in the past and the approaches that we use to investigate them, are inextricably bound up with one another and with the problems of the wider world of which archaeologists are members.

References

Arutiunov, S. A. & A. M. Khazanov 1981. Das Problem der archaeologischen Kriterien mit ethnischer Spezifik. *Ethnographisch–Archaeologische Zeitschrift* **22**, 669–85.

Barnes, B. & D. Bloor 1982. Relativism, rationalism and the sociology of knowledge. In *Rationality and relativism*, M. Hollis & S. Lukes (eds), 21–47. Oxford: Basil Blackwell.

Barth, F. (ed.) 1969a. *Ethnic groups and boundaries*. London: Allen & Unwin.

Barth, F. 1969b. Introduction. In *Ethnic groups and boundaries*, F. Barth (ed.), 9–38. London: Allen & Unwin.

Bentley, G. C. 1987. Ethnicity and practice. *Comparative Studies in Society and History* **29**, 24–55.

Binford, L. R. 1962 (1972a). Archaeology as anthropology. *American Antiquity* **28**, 217–25. (Reprinted in Binford, L. R. 1972. *An archaeological perspective*, 20–32. New York: Seminar Press.)

Binford, L. R. 1965 (1972b). Archaeological systematics and the study of culture process. *American Antiquity* **31**, 203–10. (Reprinted in Binford, L. R. 1972. *An archaeological perspective*, 195–207. New York: Seminar Press.)

Binford, L. R. 1983. Forty-seven trips: a case study in the character of archaeological formation processes. In *Working at archaeology*, 243–68. New York: Academic Press.

Bourdieu, P. 1977. *Outline of a theory of practice*. Cambridge: Cambridge University Press.

Boyd, R. & P. J. Richerson 1985. *Culture and the evolutionary process*. Chicago: University of Chicago Press.

Childe, V. G. 1925. *The Aryans*. London: Routledge & Kegan Paul.

Childe, V. G. 1936. *Man makes himself*. London: Collins.

Childe, V. G. 1956. *Piecing together the past*. London: Routledge & Kegan Paul.

Clarke, D. L. 1968. *Analytical archaeology*. London: Methuen.

Costall, A. 1982. On how so much information controls so much behaviour. In *Infancy and epistemology*, G. Butterworth (ed.), 30–51. Brighton: Harvester Press.

Crone, P. 1986. The tribe and the state. In *States in history*, J. A. Hall (ed.), 48–77. Oxford: Basil Blackwell.

Crook, J. H. 1981. The evolutionary ethology of social processes in man. In *Group cohesion*, H. Kellerman (ed.), 86–108. New York: Grune & Stratton.

Diaz-Polanco, H. in press. Ethnic questions and social change in Latin America. *World Archaeological Bulletin* **3**.

Fried, M. H. 1967. *The evolution of political society*. New York: Random House.

Fried, M. H. 1968. On the concepts of 'tribe' and 'tribal society'. In *Essays on the problem of tribe*, J. Helm (ed.), 3–22. Seattle: University of Washington Press.

Friedman, J. 1988. Culture, identity and world process. In *Domination and resistance*, D. Miller, M. Rowlands & C. Tilley (eds), ch. 1. London: Unwin Hyman.

Geary, P. J. 1983. Ethnic identity as a situational construct in the early middle ages. *Mitteilungen der Anthropologischen Gesellschaft in Wien* **113**, 15–26.

Gebuehr, M. 1987. Das Allerletzte: Montelius und Kossinna im Himmel. *Archaeologische Informationen* **10**, 109–15.

Gellner, E. 1983. *Nations and nationalism*. Oxford: Basil Blackwell.

Gellner, E. 1987a. *Culture, identity and politics*. Cambridge: Cambridge University Press.

Gellner, E. 1987b. Zeno of Cracow. In *Culture, identity and politics*, 47–74. Cambridge: Cambridge University Press.

Gellner, E. 1987c. The roots of cohesion. In *Culture, identity and politics*, 29–46. Cambridge: Cambridge University Press.

Girtler, R. 1982. 'Ethnos', 'Volk' und soziale Gruppe. *Mitteilungen der Anthropologischen Gesellschaft in Wien* **112**, 42–57.

Gould, S. J. 1981. *The mismeasure of Man*. New York: W. W. Norton.

Hacking, I. 1982. Language, truth and reason. In *Rationality and relativism*, M. Hollis & S. Lukes (eds), 48–65. Oxford: Basil Blackwell.

Hodder, I. 1978a. Simple correlations between material culture and society: a review. In *The spatial organisation of culture*, I. Hodder (ed.), 3–24. London: Duckworth.

Hodder, I. 1978b. The spatial structure of material 'cultures': a review of some of the evidence. In *The spatial organisation of culture*, I. Hodder (ed.), 93–111. London: Duckworth.

Hodder, I. 1979. Social and economic stress and material culture patterning. *American Antiquity* **44**, 446–54.

Hodder, I. 1985. Boundaries as strategies. In *The archaeology of frontiers and boundaries*, S. W. Green & S. M. Perlman (eds), 141–59. Orlando: Academic Press.

Hollis, M. & S. Lukes 1982. Introduction. In *Rationality and relativism*, M. Hollis & S. Lukes (eds), 1–20. Oxford: Basil Blackwell.

Horton, R. 1982. Tradition and modernity revisited. In *Rationality and relativism*, M. Hollis & S. Lukes (eds), 201–60. Oxford: Basil Blackwell.

Kristiansen, K. 1982. The formation of tribal systems in later European prehistory: northern Europe, 4000–500 BC. In *Theory and explanation in archaeology*, C. Renfrew, M. J. Rowlands & B. Segraves (eds), 241–80. New York: Academic Press.

Kristiansen, K. 1984. Ideology and material culture. In *Marxist perspectives in archaeology*, M. Spriggs (ed.), 72–100. Cambridge: Cambridge University Press.

Kroeber, A. L. 1957. *Style and civilizations*. Cornell University Press.

Larick, R. 1986. Age grading and ethnicity in the style of Loikop (Samburu) spears. *World Archaeology* **18**, 269–83.

Mann, M. 1986. *The sources of social power*, vol. I: *A history of power from the beginning to AD 1760*. Cambridge: Cambridge University Press.

Mellor, D. 1973. On some methodological misconceptions. In *The explanation of culture change*, C. Renfrew (ed.), 493–8. London: Duckworth.

Muehlmann, W. E. 1985. Ethnogonie und Ethnogenese: theoretisch–ethnologische und ideologiekritische Studie. In *Studien zur Ethnogenese* (Abhandlungen der Rheinisch-Westfaelischen Akademie der Wissenschaften 72), 9–26. Opladen: Westdeutscher Verlag.

Nietzsche, F. 1873. On truth and lie in an extra-moral sense. A posthumous fragment included in *The portable Nietzsche*, W. Kaufman (ed.). New York: Viking Press (1954).

Renfrew, C. 1987. *Archaeology and language: the puzzle of Indo-European origins*. London: Jonathan Cape.

Rouse, I. 1972. *Introduction to prehistory: a systematic approach*. New York: McGraw-Hill.

Rowlands, M. J. 1980. Kinship, alliance and exchange in the European Bronze Age. In *Settlement and society in the British later Bronze Age*, J. Barrett & R. Bradley (eds), 15–55. Oxford: British Archaeological Reports.

Rowlands, M. J. 1984. Objectivity and subjectivity in archaeology. In *Marxist perspectives in archaeology*, M. Spriggs (ed.), 108–13. Cambridge: Cambridge University Press.

Sackett, J. R. 1982. Approaches to style in lithic archaeology. *Journal of Anthropological Archaeology* **1**, 59–112.

Sackett, J. R. 1985. Style and ethnicity in the Kalahari: a reply to Wiessner. *American Antiquity* **50**, 151–9.

Schortman, E. M. in press. Interregional interaction in prehistory: the need for a new perspective.

Shanks, M. & C. Tilley 1987. *Re-constructing archaeology*. Cambridge: Cambridge University Press.

Shennan, S. J. 1978. Archaeological 'cultures': an empirical investigation. In *The spatial organisation of culture*, I. Hodder (ed.), 113–39. London: Duckworth.

Smith, A. D. 1981. *The ethnic revival*. Cambridge: Cambridge University Press.

Smith, A. D. 1986. *The ethnic origins of nations*. Oxford: Basil Blackwell.

Smith, M. G. 1982. Ethnicity and ethnic groups in America: the view from Harvard. *Ethnic and Racial Studies* **5**, 1–22.

Smith, M. G. 1986. Some cultural and ethnic problems in archaeology. Concluding remarks on the session 'Multiculturalism and Ethnicity in Archaeological Interpretation'. World Archaeological Congress, September.

Thernstrom, S., A. Orlov & O. Handlin (eds) 1980. *Harvard encyclopedia of American ethnic groups*. Cambridge, Massachusetts: Harvard University Press.

Ucko, P. J. 1969. Ethnography and archaeological interpretation of funerary remains. *World Archaeology* **1**, 262–80.

Ucko, P. J. 1983a. Australian academic archaeology: Aboriginal transformations of its aims and practices. *Australian Archaeology* **16**, 11–26.

Ucko, P. J. 1983b. The politics of the indigenous minority. *Journal of Biosocial Science Supplement* **8**, 25–40.

Veit, U. 1984. Gustaf Kossinna und V. Gordon Childe: Ansaetze zu einer theoretischen Grundlegung der Vorgeschichte. *Saeculum* **35**, 326–64.

Wiessner, P. 1983. Style and social information in Kalahari San projectile points. *American Antiquity* **48**, 253–76.

Wiessner, P. 1984. Reconsidering the behavioural basis of style. *Journal of Anthropological Archaeology* **3**, 190–234.

Wiessner, P. 1985. Style or isochrestic variation? A reply to Sackett. *American Antiquity* **50**, 221–4.

Wiessner, P. 1989. Style and changing relations between the individual and society. In *The meanings of things: material culture and symbolic expression*, I. Hodder (ed.), ch. 2. London: Unwin Hyman.

Wobst, M. 1977. Stylistic behavior and information exchange. In *For the director: research essays in honor of James B. Griffin* (Museum of Anthropology, University of Michigan, Anthropological Papers 61), C. E. Cleland (ed.), 317–42. Ann Arbor: Museum of Anthropology, University of Michigan.

OBJECTIVITY, INTERESTS AND CULTURAL DIFFERENCE IN ARCHAEOLOGICAL INTERPRETATION

1 *Ethnic concepts in German prehistory: a case study on the relationship between cultural identity and archaeological objectivity*

ULRICH VEIT

(translated by Stephen Shennan)

> It is almost fashionable to be derogatory about Kossinna's theories, but his methods were perhaps not as bad as the way he himself misused them.
>
> (McWhite 1956, p. 7)

Historians of the development of anthropology seem to be united in the belief that the past decade has seen a major change in the whole scene. Just as there has been a trend in society as a whole towards a new traditionalism, so the science of man has largely said goodbye to modernism, and consequently to a belief in the progress of civilization and to the idea of a single world society (Friedman 1988). Thus, it is not surprising that in the field of prehistoric archaeology too the self-styled guardians of modernism are on the retreat.

In the 1960s the liberation of archaeology from the fetters of culture history was proclaimed under the banner of a 'New Archaeology'. Today we can perceive an opposite trend. History has a future once more. It is no longer the pursuit of cultural universals that is at stake. It is the variety and specificity of cultural developments on which people's efforts are focused. In the context of systems theoretical approaches the term 'culture' was at times reduced to the level of an extrasomatic means of adaptation to the natural environment. However, now there is a renewed interest in 'cultures' in the plural and not merely 'culture' in general. One result of this development is that 'cultural identity' is increasingly becoming a key term for the self-definition of a 'post-processual' archaeology. Questions about problems such as ethnicity and multiculturalism, which people long thought they could avoid by regarding them as unimportant, or even unscientific (for example, Hagen 1980, p. 8) are again open to archaeological debate.

In the light of these developments, it seems to me to be important to remember that there were areas of prehistoric research where problems of ethnicity and multiculturalism had always remained of interest. However, these lay outside the approaches mentioned above which have determined the direction of theoretical discussion in the subject since the 1960s. This is also true of prehistoric research in the German-speaking countries. Here the topic of cultures and ethnicity has traditionally had considerable significance, although specific academic and historical circumstances to which we will return below have meant that in recent decades this line of enquiry has not always been looked at with as much open-mindedness and soberness as one would wish.

Apart from language difficulties, historical circumstances may also be one of the reasons why, outside Germany, approaches to the question of 'ethnic interpretations' of archaeological data have not taken the corresponding German tradition into account. Remarkably enough, even in a recent work by McGuire (1982) on 'The study of ethnicity in historical archaeology' one finds not a single reference to the old Central European research tradition concerning the 'ethnic interpretation' of archaeological data. On the other hand, German research since World War II has largely ignored such discussions going on outside Germany, and even more so outside Europe, although occasional forays over the language barrier convincingly demonstrate how profitable an argument with the other side can be (McWhite 1956, Cullberg 1977, Trigger 1978, 1984, Narr 1981, 1985). What follows below cannot in itself provide such an argument, but it does aim to make a contribution, mainly from the perspective of the history of research, as an attempt to provide admittedly subjective glimpses into the German tradition of the ethnic interpretation of archaeological finds. Thus, the following presentation is intended more as a discussion of some general theoretical and methodological problems in prehistoric archaeology (on the question of different technical terms in the German- and English-speaking archaeological traditions; see Narr 1966) than as a treatment of the problem of the *Germani*, which is, in fact, inseparable from the question of ethnic interpretation. However, this is not an area in which the author can claim the necessary factual knowledge and technical competence (for recent summaries of this topic, see Hachmann 1975, Mildenberger 1986, cf. Martens, Ch. 2, this volume).

The case of Kossinna and its consequences

As far as German research is concerned, the argument about the problem of 'the ethnic interpretation of archaeological culture areas' remains inseparably linked with the name of Gustaf Kossinna. Although competing with other schools of archaeological thought, such as the 'Marburg school', the fate of his teachings exemplifies the rise and fall of German archaeology in the first half of the 20th century. Indeed, in many respects, even today he casts a shadow over the subject, a phenomenon which Smolla (1979–1980, 1984–1985, 1986) recently characterized by the convenient term, 'the Kossinna syndrome'. Therefore, it is necessary to start by at least spotlighting the causes and symptoms of this syndrome, which can serve us as a case study of the relationship between archaeological objectivity and cultural identity.

First it must be made clear that Gustaf Kossinna (b. 1858), who was originally trained in Germanic philology and entered prehistory via his antiquarian study of the *Germani* (see Stampfuß 1935, Schwerin von Krosigk 1982, Smolla 1978–1980, 1984–1985, 1986), was by no means the first person who attempted to ascribe archaeological finds to specific peoples (on the question of his predecessors see, for example, Wahle 1941, Eggers 1959, Meinander 1981, Hachmann 1987). Certainly today it is his name which is associated with this idea; this is because he, like no other person, brought the question of ethnic interpretation to the centre of prehistoric thought. In doing this he made a lasting contribution to the establishment of prehistory as an academic discipline. Undoubtedly, the rising tide of nationalism at the beginning of this century was remarkably convenient for him in this respect. Indeed, one could go so far as to say that it was this which made possible the rise in the status of prehistory to that of an independent academic subject (Smolla 1979–1980).

Kossinna first stepped on to the archaeological stage with a paper on 'The prehistoric distribution of the Germani in Germany', presented at a meeting of the Anthropological Society in Kassel in 1895 (Kossinna 1896). In this paper he had already sketched out the principles of his so-called 'settlement archaeological method'. He continued to develop these in the following decades, and tried to apply them on a large scale to European prehistory. An extended presentation of his methodological basis combined with a polemical settling of accounts with his academic opponents appeared in 1911 under the title *The origin of the Germani. On the settlement archaeological method* (Kossinna 1911a). It was in this that he made his famous statement 'Sharply defined archaeological culture areas correspond unquestionably with the areas of particular peoples or tribes' (*ibid.*, p. 3). Fifteen years later, after Kossinna had in the meantime succeeded in obtaining a professorship in German archaeology at the University of Berlin, a revised version of his volume on methods of 1911 appeared, under the title *Origin and distribution of the Germani in the prehistoric and early historic periods* (Kossinna 1926). Between these two dates lay a period of extremely intensive work as an author, as a university lecturer and as an organizer. The last of these applies especially to his presidency of the newly founded German Society for Prehistory, and his editorship of the journal *Mannus* and of the monograph series of the same name associated with it.

As well as academic publications in the strict sense, Kossinna produced a whole series of publications intended to influence a wider non-academic audience. The title of his popular book, *German prehistory, a pre-eminently national discipline* (Kossinna 1914) gives an adequate impression of the nationalistic, indeed racist, attitude which was inseparably associated with Kossinna's work. In his concept of an Aryan, Nordic ideal race, superior to all other peoples – his *Germani*, or their supposedly even more upright predecessors the Indo-Europeans – he saw the key to an unwritten history, as it lay hidden in his prehistoric find groups. According to him, in ever-repeated advances towards the south these *Germani* gave the decisive push to the course of history (Schwerin von Krosigk 1982, p. 71) – a slim, tall, light-complexioned, blonde race, calm and firm in character, constantly striving, intellectually brilliant, with an almost ideal attitude towards the world and life in general.

In the light of these ideas, it comes as no surprise that Kossinna finally attempted to derive political demands from the results of his ethnohistoric research. Apart from his explicit war propaganda during World War I, these included as a political footnote his flawed attempt to influence the political decisions made at Versailles. His demands were laid down in his book *The German Ostmark, a homeland of the Germani* (Eggers 1959, pp. 231ff.)

Kossinna died in 1931, and did not live to experience the upsurge of his subject, and especially of his theories, which followed the seizure of power by the Nazis. However, it goes without saying that, had he still been alive, he would have hailed it with considerable satisfaction, even if the new propagandists did not do adequate justice to his work. Posthumously, Kossinna became, albeit less on the basis of his academic achievements and more because of his 'political influence', the conceptual father and the leading figure of a National Socialist popular (*völkischen*) prehistory (Stampfuß 1935). After the Nazi seizure of power its representatives occupied the key positions in the discipline, once the academic world of Germany had been brought into line according to the ideological prescriptions of the 'Rosenberg office' (Bolmus 1970, Kater 1974). Most members of the discipline, however, especially in those circles which had no direct connection with Kossinna and his school, behaved more discreetly and waited to see what would happen. More direct opposition to the ideological takeover of the discipline, which was connected with a vulgarization of the subject, is certainly not to be detected. The courageous methodological criticisms concerning the 'Kossinna method', raised by Wahle (1941), will be discussed below.

If the rise of Kossinna with the National Socialist takeover was logical, then his fall after 1945 was equally inevitable. Apart from a few of his pupils (Wahle 1950–1951, Jahn 1952), hardly any of those still using his methodological principles were prepared to take his side. The name Kossinna became a non-word. Enormous quantities of paper were printed with explanations that were supposed to demonstrate that the working methods of their respective authors had nothing to do with the Kossinna method, now fallen into disrepute.

However, inasmuch as people from now on anathematized Kossinna's work, and thus did not subject it to a proper critique, they were committing the same mistake as in 1933, albeit with the opposite premises. With the verbal damnation of Kossinna's method and his convenient branding as the only guilty party – a view which was also widely taken up outside Germany (for example, Clark 1957, Renfrew 1976, p. 38) – the reasons for the ideological misuse of his ideas, which were, after all, based on the nature of archaeological knowledge, remained largely unexplained.

On the other hand, most scholars continued to work with Kossinna's principles, and not just in Germany (cf. Martens, Ch. 2, this volume). Probably the best-known pupil of Kossinna was no less than Childe, who had introduced Kossinna's principles into Great Britain during the 1920s, but stripped of their ideological baggage (Childe 1927, 1929). In view of the political developments in Germany after 1933, this connection tended to be forgotten (Childe 1933). It was Childe himself who, late in life, pointed it out again (Childe 1958, Trigger 1980, McNairn 1980; also, in greater detail, Veit 1984).

'Settlement archaeology'. Kossinna's method and contemporary criticisms

It is now necessary to ask ourselves what there is really of consequence in the 'Kossinna method', much maligned but actually frequently used by its critics (in addition, see in detail Wahle 1941, Eggers 1959, Hachmann 1970, Klejn 1974a). The core of Kossinna's methodological principles is summed up in his well-known axiom of 1911. In its expanded 1926 version this states: 'Clearly defined, sharply distinctive, bounded archaeological provinces correspond unquestionably to the territories of particular peoples and tribes' (Kossinna 1926, p. 21). This guiding principle is linked with the retrospective method, which involves using the (ethnic) conditions of the present (or the historically documented past) to infer the situation in prehistory. The two together make up the so-called 'settlement archaeological method'. Working backwards from early historical times, Kossinna tried to throw light on the development of peoples in prehistory by tracing continuities within particular settlement areas. The basis for this was provided by the 'typological method', which he had taken over from Montelius. Typology enabled him to establish time horizons for the chronological ordering of the material remains of the past (although for Kossinna the principle of the closed find, which had been so important for Montelius, as well as the stratigraphic principle, were both less important than typology; Schwerin von Krosigk 1982, p. 35). Once these chronological horizons had been defined, Kossinna's next step was to make use of the cartographic method in order to distinguish those specific spatial units – find areas or culture provinces – which were supposed to be characterized by the greatest possible homogeneity of material, but most of all by being sharply bounded from neighbouring culture provinces. Kossinna's interpretation of these units had two aspects, which it is important to differentiate:

(a) on the one hand, they were regarded as an expression of ethnic groups, or peoples; and
(b) on the other hand, they were equated with the peoples or tribes first documented historically in a given area.

It is obvious that the hypothetical character of such identifications of peoples increases as one goes further back in time. Kossinna tried to come to terms with this problem by means of an idea influenced by evolutionary principles and deriving from linguistic concepts. It was the notion of apparently less-complex 'primeval cultures' or 'primeval peoples', which supposedly enabled him to 'reconstruct' the former relationships between 'peoples' over a timespan stretching as far back as the Mesolithic. In reality he simply deluded himself about the limited possibility of archaeological knowledge arising from the fragmentary nature of the sources.

Even during his lifetime Kossinna did not lack critics, a fact due at least in part to the provocative and polemical style of his work. Kossinna's argument with Carl Schuchardt is well known and still has an almost legendary ring to it. Josef Kostrzewski was one of Kossinna's own pupils who turned against him. However, this did not represent a refutation of his method, but only of his results with regard to the ethnic identity of the archaeological groups on what is now Polish soil (Eggers 1959, p. 236, also Martens, Ch. 2, this volume).

Two factors in particular rendered difficult, if not impossible, a proper critique of Kossinna's methodological approaches, thus preventing a sober reassessment of the problem of ethnic interpretation.

The first was his inadmissible equation of people and race (probably a secondary accretion to his method) and the way this notion slipped into an ideology of the Germanic master race due to the nationalistic euphoria of the time.

Secondly, it must be held against Kossinna that, despite his verbal rigour, he quite frequently did not stick to his own methodological principles, with regard both to the definition of sharply defined culture provinces and to the evidence for continuity from purely prehistoric cultures to cultures in early historical times. Given the state of research at the time, he could probably not do this without renouncing altogether the reconstruction of the supposed prehistoric peoples. Thus, it is typical of much of the lively debate about the 'Kossinna method' that, under the guise of examining the method, it mainly criticized its applications.

Luckily, the extreme racist component of Kossinna's ideas was not taken over by many of his pupils. Thus, even at an early date Blume, Jahn and others (Blume 1912, Hahne 1922, Jahn 1941, 1952) concerned themselves with a further development of the factual and theoretical basis of Kossinna's settlement archaeology, while largely excluding racial aspects. For example, Blume speaks more appropriately of the 'ethnographic method' and Jahn later of the 'ethnohistorical method', even if the idea of the 'people' or 'folk' as a unit that is objectively present and above all historically significant remains untouched. This is also true of Menghin (1931, 1936, 1952). He was the main representative of the prehistoric branch of the *Kulturkreislehre*, who made Kossinna's principles his own and tried to apply them universally. However, in Menghin's work we begin to see a replacement of the term 'people' by the more neutral and supposedly less dubious term 'culture', a development which continued after World War II. However, Kossinna's followers continued to ignore the more fundamental doubts that were being expressed with regard to the equation between peoples and cultures, and more generally about the true culture-historical character of the discipline.

Several scholars come to mind in this connection, including Hoernes (1905, p. 238) and Sprockhoff (1930, p. vii), but the most important is K. H. Jacob-Friesen. Already in Kossinna's lifetime he published a wide-ranging theoretical volume entitled *Basic questions of prehistoric research* (K. H. Jacob-Friesen 1928), with the more explicit subtitle: *A critique of the current state of research on races, peoples and cultures in prehistory*. Here he concluded (p. 144):

> Today it is still extraordinarily difficult to identify the areas of cultures with the areas of peoples when we know little more than the names of those peoples from historical sources. To make this kind of equation in periods millennia earlier than the first historical mention of those peoples is a claim which can only be rejected.

Jacob-Friesen was, of course, influenced by the ethnological '*Kulturkreis*' school, as represented by Leo Frobenius; accordingly, he saw the practical task of prehistory first of all as 'defining as many individual distribution areas of given forms as possible, gathering these together into *Kulturkreise* and establishing their chronological succession' (K. H. Jacob-Friesen 1928, p. 145).

It was during World War II, in 1941, against the background of the dominance of Nazi prehistory, that Wahle published a small book that became famous, entitled *On the ethnic interpretation of early historical culture provinces*. It was Wahle who rekindled the debate about the Kossinna method, which under the surface had never quite died out. Because of the particular circumstances of the time, the immediate published reaction was confined to a rejection of the critique of Kossinna by his pupil Jahn (1941, at greater length 1952). On the basis of various examples from the early historical period, Wahle presented cases of ethnic boundaries which did *not* find an expression in clearly defined cultural provinces. However, with this he basically criticized only the reversal of Kossinna's principle (Narr 1985, pp. 58f.). Recognizing the legitimacy of the ethnic interpretation at least of early historical culture provinces, he used this as a basis for criticizing the schematic treatment of prehistory apparent in Kossinna's method. In opposition to this, he demanded that 'rational–ahistorical' thought in prehistory should be overcome. By this he meant especially the typological–

evolutionary approach. This, Wahle held, should be superseded in future by the investigation of the driving forces operating in history, above all in the history of 'prehistoric peoples'. It is apparent from the idealistic concepts with which Wahle approached his subject – for example, the concept of 'vital power' (*Lebenskraft*) – that his demands are difficult to realize in practice. However, even his more concrete hypotheses about the possible factors which could have produced particular distributions of finds often remain very vague. Apart from his demand for a greater emphasis on the question of the association of various find groups with one another (Wahle 1941, p. 133), these did not lead to any new perspectives. His ethnic reconstructions depend largely on written sources, and therefore they are not transferable to periods where such evidence is lacking. Indeed, on the basis of *a priori* assumptions about the nature of sociopolitical evolution, he tried to cast doubt on the existence of peoples or other units for the earlier periods of prehistory, and in certain areas called them into question altogether (*ibid.*, p. 116), a procedure which is just as problematical as Kossinna's completely unhistorical concept of 'peoples'.

'Archaeological culture' and ethnicity since 1945: some examples

Wahle's (1941) book largely determined the direction of discussion in the discipline after 1945. Two lines of enquiry were pursued. In the field of early history, on the basis of an increasingly refined source-critical approach, an increasingly good grip was obtained on both the possibility and the necessity of ethnic interpretation. However, the possibility of doing this on the basis of archaeological sources alone was completely rejected, as being beyond the range of possibility of archaeological knowledge (Kirchner 1950, Werner 1950, Jankuhn 1952, Eggers 1959, von Uslar 1955, 1961, 1965, Kilian 1960; most recently Daim 1982). However, this last principle immediately came into conflict with current research practice, in which – hidden behind the supposedly more neutral term 'archaeological culture' – the old ethnic concepts continued to survive. Although many scholars gave up speaking of Indo-Europeans or even Germani, the notion that 'peoples' must be hiding behind the various archaeological groupings remained something taken for granted, albeit not made explicit (Lüning 1972, Bergmann 1972, 1973–1974, 1974, Angeli 1976). The 'archaeological culture' became – as for Childe (1929) – a quasi-ideology-free substitute for the term 'ethnic unit'. By means of this safeguard the problem of ethnic interpretation was removed from explicit discussion. Incidentally, this observation is equally true of prehistoric research in the eastern part of Germany, newly oriented as it was to the principles of historical materialism. Here we are faced with a vehement polemic directed against both Kossinna and his followers, and against more-recent 'bourgeois' approaches apparently thought to be outdated. Nevertheless, the term 'socio-economic areas' meant essentially the same as the term 'archaeological culture' (Behrens 1984, p. 57; cf., for example, Otto 1953, Hermann 1965, 1977). Lack of space here precludes an extensive treatment of materialist approaches (cf. also Russian and Polish authors: Klejn 1974a, 1974b, 1981, Hensel 1977).

As far as ethnic interpretation in the field of early historical cultures is concerned, a strict division between the various arguments of the individual disciplines involved became the standard demand. With the methodological maxim 'march separately, strike together' – a rather disturbing slogan in the light of recent history (see Wenskus 1979, p. 637) – people thought they could avoid the mistakes of that past. The disciplines involved – history, linguistics and prehistory, i.e. archaeology – should first of all evaluate their respective sources, and only at the final stage should their various results be brought together. A classic example of this approach is provided in a book written jointly by Hachmann, Kossack, and Kuhn. This impressive study by two archaeologists and one philologist appeared in 1962 under the title, *Peoples between Germani and Celts. Written sources, archaeological finds and information from names, for the history of North-West Germany around the time of Christ.* Similarly, Eggers' *Introduction to prehistory* (1959), a trail-blazing textbook in post-World War II Germany, recommends a three-stage dialectical sequence in archaeological source criticism: 'archaeological thesis, literary antithesis, historical synthesis'.

Although at first sight the application of these principles seems advisable, it soon became apparent that they did not do justice to the actual procedures current in the discipline. According to the historian Wenskus, they are both unsubtle and impracticable. Instead he argues for a broad interdisciplinary approach, in a similar fashion to Klejn (1974b, 1981). Wenskus' book on the formation and composition of the gentes of the early middle ages, published in 1961, remains today the starting point for all attempts at an interdisciplinary approach to the problem of ethnic interpretation in the early historical period, and these have been attempted from various sides (for example, Hachmann 1970, 1975, Capelle 1971, F. Fischer 1972; summaries in Daim 1982, Mildenberger 1986).

Here, however, I wish to restrict my reflections to the following question: how significant a rôle have ethnic concepts played since 1945 in that larger segment of the discipline for which no historical data are available as a corrective? The significance which the term 'archaeological culture' came to have in this connection has already been pointed out above (cf. recently Hachmann 1987). It increasingly became an ideologically untainted and therefore useful synonym for the term 'ethnic unit'. Unfortunately, in doing this it encouraged a tendency to obscure the real problem, a point of criticism already made by Hodson (1980) of the English-speaking archaeological scene. Of course, it is important to note here that in this connection the phrase 'ethnic interpretation' no longer referred to the equation of specific groups of finds with historically attested ethnic units, but solely to the interpretation of certain find groups as the expression of once-existing ethnic groups whose names have not come down to us.

Apart from Bronze Age work (for example, Bergmann 1970), a look at research on the Central European Neolithic is worthwhile in this regard. This is a topic which provides the practical prerequisites for a discussion of this type of question, because of the considerable expansion of the available data base which has taken place over the years. In this respect U. Fischer's (1956) book, *The graves of the Stone Age in the Saale area*, was of outstanding importance for German research in the post-World War II period, from both a practical and a theoretical point of view. Starting from the rich corpus of finds of Neolithic burials in the central German area, the question was raised by the author of whether the grave finds would confirm or even refine the existing ordering of 'cultural groups', predominantly based on an appraisal of the pottery. From this investigation it emerged clearly that, on the whole, the pottery groups correspond to the groups based on burial ritual. From this U. Fischer (1956, p. 256) concluded, contrary to his original hope, that

> the burial rite cannot be used to bridge cultural differences diachronically. Our problem field thus appears to have gained a truly historical dimension. The quest for historical continuity lies beyond the range of our sources. The changes in grave and burial form appear completely embedded in the change of cultural forms, in that 'historische Tiefendimension' which must remain inaccessible to a purely ethnographic treatment.

Thus, within this limited area, Fischer provided the empirical evidence for the 'recurrent assemblage of types' (here pottery and burial types) which Childe (1956) had demanded as the characteristic feature of an 'archaeological culture'. He rightly saw the problem area as raised to an 'historical dimension'. This means nothing more nor less than that he saw appearing behind the groupings of finds historically influential units, 'peoples', or if one wishes, more non-committally, 'ethnic groups'. On the other hand, in establishing not only the spatial but also the chronological discontinuity of his material, it was made clear by Fischer that a pursuit of such groups across various periods is impossible, at least on the basis of the material currently available.

It is unfortunate that subsequently people have not always kept to the standards set by Fischer for the analysis of archaeological cultures. Such cultures have been postulated even without the possibility of being able to demonstrate a combination of various cultural elements, functionally independent of one another. This kind of approach has been rightly criticized in recent years. In the field of Neolithic research, fundamental observations go to the credit of Lüning (1972, 1979; cf. Mandera 1965). Taking as his starting point the results of recent empirical investigations which point to a marked degree of continuity within the Neolithic cultural development of western Central Europe, Lüning (1979, p. 101) demanded a rethinking of the term 'culture' in its old ethnically influenced sense:

Under the influence of an ethnically based cultural theory, earlier research worked in the main from the assumption that the neolithic pottery groups represented 'cultures' in an inclusive and organic sense. This produced a 'block-like' cultural model which regarded the pottery as an exact expression of sociocultural, ethnic and economic entities, and in effect as a passive reflection of them. Their duration and their spatial distribution could thus be regarded as a substitute for a 'culture' in the wider sense. This approach made ethno-historic and politico-historic interpretations a great deal easier.

Contrary to this approach, Lüning argued, it is necessary to free the term 'archaeological culture' from its ethnic and other implications and to restrict it to its chronological dimension. In the context of this new 'paradigm' for the early and late Neolithic periods in Central Europe, influenced by the concept of an extensive continuity, 'archaeological cultures' should be regarded solely 'as components of a chronological–terminological system' which should not be overburdened with too much weight of meaning (Lüning 1972, p. 169):

This term culture is thus suitable for quite specific tasks, and only for these. In the context of the present state of knowledge it gives us full information about the chronological position of the material, but implies little about its spatial position and almost nothing about either the combined treatment of these two, possible functional connections between individual cultural elements or areas, or about the relationship to political, social, religious, military, economic and other categories of neolithic people. It is important to be clear about this if one wants to look at the neolithic from other than a chronological point of view and in doing this mistakenly makes use of the cultures as apparently given entities.

What, then, is the value of such a concept of culture with its narrowly bounded explanatory potential? Here I cannot go into all of the practical problems connected with the Lüning paradigm. Nevertheless, it should be pointed out that the assumption of a strong degree of continuity may be supported by the material only under certain conditions. With his concept of a prevailing continuity – debatable because it may only be maintained on the assumption that apparent breaks in the development are to be interpreted exclusively as gaps in the finds record – Lüning explicitly contradicts the results of Fischer and others. It is worth calling to mind that they had to conclude – in some cases contrary to their initial assumptions – that discontinuity rather than continuity characterized the archaeological material. When Lüning starts from the assumption of a general continuity in Neolithic development, in contrast with earlier research, then he is not simply basing his argument on empirical observations, but primarily replacing one set of premises with another. In fact, the implicit postulate of continuity makes one wonder whether his culture concept is unsuitable for detecting continuity or discontinuity not only in the spatial dimension, but also in the chronological dimension. At the more practical level this seems to be borne out by Lüning's habit of frequently using the terms 'chronological succession' and 'genetic succession' interchangeably. In this regard Sangmeister (1973, p. 387, more generally 1967) has pointed out that a chronological succession, 'B comes after A', is not necessarily the same as a genetic derivation, 'B developed from A'. In the last analysis a chronological *a priori* of this kind is as problematical as a comparable chorological or geographical *a priori*, such as the culture-area concept of American archaeology (Wissler 1917, 1923).

As far as the theoretical framework of the discipline is concerned, the new empirical observations which Lüning adduces as a basis for his argument ultimately do not necessitate a change of paradigm. The stress laid on unity and continuity in the Central European early and middle Neolithic appears (but only appears) to be an emphasis emerging from certain empirical investigations. Their results could equally well be explained exclusively in terms of the 'culture-historical' paradigm, and not by recourse to a concept which excludes the existence of such entities at the outset. The overhasty equation made between archaeological cultures and quasi-ethnic entities was less the result of incorrect methods, and much more the consequence of two shortcomings: a lack of methodological purity and an overestimation of the possibilities of acquiring knowledge in the context of a comparatively poor state of research. The quest for groupings which extend beyond the individual settlement unit remains valid, for the Neolithic as well as for other periods, even if today it can no longer claim its earlier monopoly position, and even if the problems involved may never be completely resolved by archaeological means.

The practical conclusion of this discussion must surely be that we shall continue to use the old culture concept as conceived by Kossinna and developed by others, even though we are conscious that in talking of an 'archaeological culture' we are not necessarily dealing with the material expression of a 'people', but primarily with an archaeological heuristic device. In this way, and contrary to Lüning's demand, the term, as the most important unit of archaeological classification, should finally be freed from its burden of chronostratigraphic implications (Müller-Beck 1977, p. 195). An 'archaeological culture' is thus to be understood as a term for an entity which is spatially and chronologically distinguishable within the general cultural development. The degree of spatial (or chronological) uniformity (Kossinna) or the extent to which a coincidence of individual features can be detected (Childe) – that is, the combination of individual, functionally independent elements (Narr 1981) – must be investigated empirically in each particular case (on methodological questions, see Hodder 1978, Shennan 1978).

Furthermore, depending on the degree of uniformity within the distribution of types and the extent to which individual elements coincide, it must be permissible to accept as an heuristic principle the ethnic nature of such entities, if other more-simple explanations, such as ecological or economic factors, can be excluded. Since Wahle's (1941) work, early historical archaeology has provided a variety of important methodological assessments (for example, Werner 1950, Kirchner 1950, Jankuhn 1952, Eggers 1959, Hachmann et al. 1962, Hachmann 1970). As far as the Neolithic is concerned, such reflections have only begun recently. Here special mention should be made of the work of Narr (1985), dealing with the 'Schönfeld Group' of the central German Neolithic and archaeological groups from the southwestern USA.

However, in all these endeavours it is important to be aware that no more than a rough approximation to former conditions is possible. Thus, if one accepts that the decisive feature of an ethnic unit is the consciousness of individuals in it of belonging to it (Wenskus 1961) – a consciousness of belonging together within a definite group extending beyond the local settlement unit – it is apparent that evidence for this can never be observed by archaeological means alone. Nevertheless, we may take as an heuristic starting point that the greater the differences between such a group and other groups are, the greater the probability is that these will be reflected in the field of material culture. Ethnic groups are not primarily objective organic entities detectable by means of language, material culture or race whose ancestry can be traced back through the ages. They are rather to be considered as structures or entities which can only be experienced subjectively, in the sense of belonging or not belonging to them, and whose individual form and content depend on a variety of cultural, social, religious, economic and other factors (Hodder 1977, 1978, especially pp. 248ff., Wernhardt 1979, Girtler 1982, Geary 1983). In this connection it would be mistaken to regard a mutual cultural distinction between such groups as a measure of their isolation. On the contrary, ethnic boundaries have their justification and gain importance through intensive interethnic contact (Barth 1969). To this extent the supposedly more neutral term 'interaction sphere' (Mischung 1986, also critically Shennan 1978), often valued as a substitute, is at least misleading.

To sum up, the problem of the ethnic interpretation of archaeological data which has been the object of controversial discussion for so long does not differ significantly in nature from the problem of their sociological interpretation. In both cases we are faced with the question of inferring the status of a specific group of individuals when that status is not directly detectable by archaeological means. In the final analysis it is a matter of demonstrating a symbolic connection which is not in itself evident. It is therefore not credible for people to engage in the business of sociological interpretation while damning the enterprise of ethnic interpretation; of course, the reverse also applies.

Cultural identity and archaeological objectivity

The relationship between culture and ethnicity has certainly not been the primary goal of German prehistory in the post-World War II years.

However, as I have tried to show, despite Kossinna and his consequences, the time-honoured discussion of the problem of the interpretation of find groups, types and assemblages in terms of ethnic units has never ceased, even though this discussion has frequently made use of a strangely coded form of expression, due to the special historical circumstances prevailing. Nevertheless, as a result of the events which followed 1933, this paradigm, and with it the discipline as a whole, has lost most of its former influence on historical thinking in Germany. At the beginning of the 20th century prehistory was able to establish itself as a discipline within our universities, above all because it succeeded in securing a strong position in the writing of the history of Germany before it became a nation. Inevitably the vulgarization and misuse of the subject by the Nazis shook this initiative. The attempt to establish prehistory as an historical discipline was almost wrecked, thereby confirming the views of those who had always expressed doubts about whether archaeology could produce real historical knowledge. Prehistoric archaeology became what many earlier had wished to make of it, 'a preeminently antiquarian discipline', to use the phrase with which Torbrügge (1959, p. 4) played on Kossinna's (1914) well-known dictum. This change of direction is expressed in the predominantly pragmatic orientation of the discipline as far as prehistory is concerned, and its strong emphasis on descriptive–classificatory and chronological problems (Narr 1966, Eggert 1978a). This restriction of the discipline to a specific area of method and the refusal to set theoretical goals of any consequence can only be understood as a reaction against the inflated knowledge claims of Nazi studies in prehistory. However, it had the opposite effect to that intended, in at least one respect – it did not lead to the rehabilitation of German prehistoric studies outside Germany.

In the 1920s German prehistory pioneered the development of the discipline as a whole, thanks above all to Kossinna and his school. However, this position, which was lost at the latest by 1933, could not be regained after World War II. In the English-speaking world in particular, ecological, economic and sociological questions came increasingly to the forefront of research, notably thanks to the works of Childe and Clark, and consequently theoretical perspectives broadened. In the Federal Republic of Germany pragmatism prevailed (with a few notable exceptions: for example, Jankuhn 1952, 1977, Narr 1954, some of the contributions to the short-lived journal *Archaeologia Geographica*) and the discipline moved increasingly towards the theoretically irrelevant (Eggert 1978a, Härke 1983). This 'common-sense attitude' is documented not least by the fact that people shunned the influences now coming from abroad and from neighbouring disciplines. Thus, a serious debate with the protagonists of the 'New Archaeology' never took place – apart from a few significant exceptions (Eggert 1978b, Wolfram 1986) – despite the availability of good arguments for a culture-historical approach.

The attitude that prevailed in the post-World War II period is still reflected where theoretical abstinence was abandoned in favour of a new theoretical foundation. Thus, the 'Lüning paradigm' discussed above basically represents nothing other than a justification of the archaeological practice of the post-World War II period, and therefore of a position rejecting theory as such. This is borne out by the fact that Lüning believes that he can finally reject such concepts as people, ethnos or culture which transcend the practice of prehistorians, and which have been an indispensable part of anthropological thought since the beginning of this century. In his view prehistory should be satisfied with the goal of demonstrating the 'development, correlation and structure of individual cultural phenomena' (Lüning 1972, pp. 169f.). Eggert (1978a, p. 18) instead was certainly right to remark, 'that archaeology, like all the other human sciences, cannot do without a definition of culture which is primarily theoretical, in other words, explanatory and interpretative'. For this reason he urges prehistorians to take as active a part as possible in theoretical discussions within anthropology, a point of view which has long been taken for granted elsewhere. However, here too the problem arises of the nature of ethnic entities or 'cultures' and their possible material expression, a question which has received a great variety of different answers within cultural anthropology over the past 100 years.

In my view it has been one of the shortcomings of post-World War II German prehistory with major implications that, apart from a few exceptions, it has failed to take up anew the extremely fruitful debate between the anthropological and historical traditions already established at the origin of our discipline. It was the assumption of Kossinna and many of his followers that the so-called Aryan–Germanic culture was superior to other cultures and incomparable, that discredited a co-operation with anthropology (the German *Ethnologie*) which could still be successfully practised in the 1920s (Kossinna 1911b, pp. 128f.). However, after 1945 it is a mistaken claim of methodological absolutism which must be adduced as the basis of the supposed uselessness of such a co-operation. In this respect the shambles of the patriotic–nationalist and the sceptical tendencies formed an unholy alliance which led in most parts of prehistoric archaeology to the general abandonment of the anthropological roots of the discipline (an exception is palaeolithic research). As I see it, this is the major reason for the deep-rooted reluctance still prevalent in the German-speaking world to use ethnographic data in the interpretation of prehistoric facts, particularly from the more recent periods. Inasmuch as people restricted themselves to analogies from the present and historical past of Europe in order to interpret archaeological facts, they were bound to restrict the potential of our knowledge in an inadmissible fashion. Following the implicit premise that 'European prehistory can *only* be explained through European history', ethnocentric prejudice partly took the place of empirical comparison. Thus, in a certain fashion Kossinna, who had only recently been publicly banned, re-entered the discipline through the back door (however, in this context it is worth noting that it was a similar belief in the superiority of European culture, albeit based on different motives, which was unconsciously at least partly responsible for Childe's negative attitude to ethnographic parallels). This unconscious ethnocentric fixation continues to hinder in Germany the breakthrough of ethno-archaeology which has taken place in the English-speaking world in recent decades. Attempts from the ethnological side, especially on the subject of 'ethnicity' (Vossen 1969, Liesegang 1973), were largely ignored. The same is true of similar attempts at an interdisciplinary rapprochement on this subject in the context of a certain renaissance of the 'old anthropology' (Wernhardt 1979, Girtler 1982, Daim 1982, Spindler 1983, Winkler 1983, *Studien zur Ethnogenese* 1985).

Finally, if we look from a more abstract point of view at the relationship of the aspirations of 'ethnic archaeology' and 'ethnoarchaeology', there appear to be certain parallels. An ideological one-sidedness was at the root of both trends: in the one case an excessive nationalism has been noted, in the other case a similarly authoritarian internationalism may be detected. Both were specific products of their time, but hopefully both have now outlived their stage of ideological excess, if the indications are correct. Are they not turning out to be theoretically complementary concepts that may prove to be useful in the long term for the study of archaeological data as the expression of past human thought and action?

However, what does all this signify for the relationship between archaeology and politics? I believe that if we are able to draw one lesson from the German example, it is that archaeology is not an appropriate medium for the contemporary debate and foundation of ethnic or national interests. I emphasize this not least in relation to the variety of archaeologies now being established outside Europe. The current problems arising out of the factor of ethnicity which are increasingly impinging on the general consciousness (for example, Smith 1981) can certainly not be solved by the introduction of archaeological or prehistoric arguments into the debate. The amusing case of Kossinna's unsatisfactory intervention at the Versailles peace conference exemplifies this opinion in an almost surrealistic fashion. A prehistory which makes a claim to be taken seriously as an academic discipline must, like history, defend itself all the more vigorously against every form of takeover by outside interests. This is a demand which Kossinna's contemporaries did not take sufficiently seriously. Like all of the other human sciences, prehistoric archaeology too must insist on a division between archaeological knowledge and the process of life, for the sake of its objectivity and its capacity to make progress. Prehistory does not provide a finished picture of the past which can be applied without further ado to directing social activity.

On the other hand, there can be no prehistoric research outside the interests of society. Archaeological knowledge is not neutral and apolitical by virtue of its very nature (Hodder 1984, 1986, Ucko 1983). However, the acknowledgement that an objective and value-free archaeology is impossible in principle leads directly to the demand for permanent self-reflection within the discipline (Rüsen 1977, from the position of a historian). There will be a great deal of work on this subject in the future – especially in western Germany. This point is equally valid for the discussion of the rôle of archaeology in public education. Here, too, it was the shock of Nazi prehistory in Germany which allowed statements on the subject from the 1920s to lapse into oblivion (Marienfeld 1979).

The qualifications made above do not mean that we can draw no lessons from prehistory. However, in going ahead with drawing lessons we should always bear in mind that 'History "obtained from archaeology" ', as Smolla (1979–1980, p. 8) put it, 'is exposed to greater dangers, because the facts can have more than one meaning, and are thus more prone to manipulation; moreover, because the "beginnings" and "origins" can so easily be turned into myth'.

Acknowledgements

I am grateful to Dr S. J. Shennan for his kind invitation to contribute to this book and also for carrying out the translation. In addition I owe a debt of gratitude to the University of Münster, which contributed to my travel costs and thus made possible my attendance at the World Archaeological Congress. I also wish to thank Professor G. Smolla (Frankfurt) for valuable background information on questions to do with the history of research. I must also thank Dr H. Vierck (Münster) for his critical comments on both this, and an earlier version, of this chapter. Finally, special thanks must go to Professor K. J. Narr (Münster) for his great encouragement of this topic and for taking the trouble to read the manuscript.

References

Angeli, W. 1976. Zum Kulturbegriff in der Urgeschichtswissenschaft. In *Festschrift für R. Pittioni*. *Archaeologia Austriaca*, Beiheft **13**, I, 3–6. Wien: Deuticke.

Barth, F. (ed.) 1969. *Ethnic groups and boundaries. The social organization of culture difference*. Bergen, Oslo: Universitets Forlaget and London: Allen & Unwin.

Behrens, H. 1984. *Die Ur- und Frühgeschichtswissenschaft in der DDR von 1945–1980*. Arbeiten zur Urgeschichte des Menschen. H. Ziegert (ed.). Frankfurt-am-Main: Lang.

Bergmann, J. 1970. *Die ältere Bronzezeit Nordwestdeutschlands. Neue Methoden zur ethnischen und historischen Interpretation urgeschichtlicher Quellen*. Kasseler Beiträge zur Vor- und Frühgeschichte **2**, Teil A/B. Marburg: Elgwert.

Bergmann, J. 1972. Ethnos und Kulturkreis. Zur Methodik der Urgeschichtswissenschaft. *Prähistorische Zeitschrift* **47**, 105–10.

Bergmann, J. 1973–1974. Zum Kulturkreis. Zur Denkweise in der Urgeschichtswissenschaft. *Archäologische Informationen* **2–3**, 189–91.

Bergmann, J. 1974. Zum Begriff des Kulturkreises in der Vorgeschichtswissenschaft. *Prähistorische Zeitschrift* **49**, 129–38.

Blume, E. 1912. *Die germanischen Stämme und die Kulturen zwischen Oder und Passarge zur römischen Kaiserzeit*. Mannus-Bibliothek 8. Würzburg: Kabitzsch.

Bolmus, R. 1970. *Das Amt Rosenberg und seine Gegener. Zum Machtkampf im nationalsozialistischen Herrschaftssystem*. Stuttgart: Deutsche Verlags-Anstalt.

Capelle, T. 1971. *Studien über elbgermanische Gräberfelder in der ausgehenden Latènezeit und der älteren römischen Kaiserzeit.* Münstersche Beiträge zur Vor- und Frühgeschichte 6. Hildesheim: Lax.

Childe, V. G. 1927. Rezension von: Kossinna 1926. *Man* **27**, 54f.

Childe, V. G. 1929. *The Danube in prehistory.* Oxford: Clarendon Press.

Childe, V. G. 1933. Is prehistory practical? *Antiquity* **7**, 410–18.

Childe, V. G. 1956. *Piecing together the past. The interpretation of archaeological data.* London: Routledge & Kegan Paul.

Childe, V. G. 1958. Retrospect. *Antiquity* **32**, 69–74.

Clark, G. 1957. *Archaeology and society. Reconstructing the prehistoric past,* 3rd edn. London: Methuen. (1st edn 1939; 2nd edn 1947.)

Cullberg, C. 1977. Kossinna in Florida. In *Festschrift zum 50jährigen Bestehen des Vorgeschichtlichen Seminars Marburg.* O.-H. Frey (ed.). Marburger Studien zur Vor- und Frühgeschichte 1. Gladenbach: Kempkes.

Daim, F. 1982. Gedanken zum Ethnosbegriff. *Mitteilungen der Anthropologischen Gesellschaft in Wien* **112**, 58–71.

Eggers, H. J. 1959. *Einführung in die Vorgeschichte* (new edn 1974). Munich: Piper.

Eggert, M. K. H. 1978a. Zum Kulturkonzept in der prähistorischen Archäologie. *Bonner Jahrbücher* **178**, 1–20.

Eggert, M. K. H. 1978b. Prähistorische Archäologie und Ethnologie. Studien zur amerikanischen New Archaeology. *Prähistorische Zeitschrift* **53**, 6–164.

Fischer, F. 1972. Die Kelten bei Herodot. *Madrider Mitteilungen* **13**, 109ff.

Fischer, U. 1956. *Die Gräber der Steinzeit im Saalegebiet. Studien über neolithische und frühbronzezeitliche Grab- und Bestattungsformen in Sachsen-Thüringen.* Berlin: de Gruyter.

Friedman, J. 1988. Culture, identity and world process. In *Domination and resistance,* D. Miller, M. Rowlands & C. Tilley (eds), ch. 1. London: Unwin Hyman.

Geary, P. J. 1983. Ethnic identity as a situational construct in the early middle ages. *Mitteilungen der Anthropologischen Gesellschaft in Wien* **113**, 15–26.

Girtler, R. 1982. 'Ethnos', 'Volk' und soziale Gruppe. Zum Problem eines zentralen Themas in den anthropologischen Wissenschaften. *Mitteilungen der Anthropologischen Gesellschaft in Wien* **112**, 42–57.

Hachmann, R. 1970. *Die Goten und Skandinavien.* Berlin: de Gruyter.

Hachmann, R. 1975. Der Begriff des Germanischen. *Jahrbuch für Internationale Germanistik* **7**, 113–44.

Hachmann, R. (ed.) 1987. *Studien zum Kulturbegriff in der Vor- und Frühgeschichtsforschung.* (Saarbrückener Beiträge zur Altertumskunde, Bd. 48.) Bonn: Habelt.

Hachmann, R., G. Kossack & H. Kuhn 1962. *Völker zwischen Germanen und Kelten. Schriftquellen, Bodenfunde und Namengut zur Geschichte des nördlichen Westdeutschlands um Christi Geburt.* Neumünster: Wachholtz.

Hagen, A. 1980. Trends in Scandinavian archaeology at the transition to the 1980s. *Norwegian Archaeological Review* **13**, 1–8.

Hahne, H. (ed.) 1922. *25 Jahre Siedlungsarchäologie. Arbeiten aus dem Kreise der Berliner Schule.* Mannus-Bibliothek Nr 22. Leipzig: Kabitzsch.

Härke, H. (ed.) 1983. *Archäologie und Kulturgeschichte. Symposium zu Zielvorstellungen der deutschen Archäologie.* Unkel.

Hermann, J. 1965. Archäologische Kulturen und sozialökonomische Gebiete. *Ethnographisch–Archäologische Zeitschrift* **6**, 97–128.

Hermann, J. 1977. Archäologie als Geschichtswissenschaft. In *Archäologie als Geschichtswissenschaft. Studien und Untersuchungen,* J. Hermann (ed.), 9–28. Berlin: Akademie-Verlag.

Hensel, W. 1977. A method of ethnic qualification of archaeological sources. *Archaeologia Polona* **18**, 7–35.

Hodder, I. 1977. The distribution of material culture items in the Baringo district, Western Kenya. *Man (New Series)* **12**, 239–69.

Hodder, I. (ed.) 1978. *The spatial organization of culture.* New Approaches in Archaeology. London: Duckworth.

Hodder, I. 1984. Archaeology in 1984. *Antiquity* **58**, 25–32.

Hodder, I. 1986. Politics and ideology in the World Archaeological Congress 1986. *Archaeological Review for Cambridge* **5**(1), 113–19.

Hodson, F. R. 1980. Cultures as types? Some elements of classification theory. *Bulletin of the Institute of Archaeology, University of London* **17**, 1–10.

Hoernes, M. 1905. Die Hallstattperiode. *Archiv für Anthropologie (Neue Folge)* **3**, 233–81.

Jacob-Friesen, K. H. 1928. *Grundfragen der Urgeschichtsforschung. Stand und Kritik der Forschung über Rassen, Völker und Kulturen in urgeschichtlicher Zeit.* Hannover: Helwing.

Jahn, M. 1941. Die deutsche Vorgeschichtsforschung in einer Sackgasse? *Nachrichtenbaltt für deutsche Vorzeit* **17**, 73–82.

Jahn, M. 1952. *Die Abgrenzung von Kulturgruppen und Völkern in der Vorgeschichte.* Berichte über die Verhandlungen der sächsischen Akademie der Wissenschaften zu Leipzig. Philologisch–historische Klasse, Vol. 99, No. 3. Berlin: Akademie Verlag.

Jankuhn, H. 1952. Klima, Besiedlung und Wirtschaft der älteren Eisenzeit im westlichen Ostseebecken. *Archaeological Geographica* **3** (1/3), 23–35.

Jankuhn, H. 1977. *Einführung in die Siedlungsarchäologie.* Berlin and New York: de Gruyter.

Kater, M. H. 1974. *Das 'Ahnenerbe' der SS 1935–1945. Ein Beitrag zur Kulturpolitik des Dritten Reiches.* Stuttgart: Deutsche Verlags-Anstalt.

Kilian, L. 1960. Zum Aussagewert von Fund- und Kulturprovinzen. *Swiatowit* **23**, 41–85.

Kirchner, H. (ed.) 1950. *Ur- und Frühgeschichte als historische Wissenschaft. Festschrift zum 60. Geburtstag von E. Wahle.* Heidelberg: Winter.

Klejn, L. S. 1974a. Kossinna im Abstand von vierzig Jahren. *Jahresschrift für mitteldeutsche Vorgeschichte* **58**, 7–55.

Klejn, L. S. 1974b. Regressive Purifizierung und exemplarische Betrachtung. Polemische Bemerkungen zur Integration der Archäologie mit der schriftlichen Geschichte und Sprachwissenschaft bei der ethnischen Deutung des Fundgutes. *Ethnographisch–Archäologische Zeitschrift* **15**, 223–54.

Klejn, L. S. 1981. Die Ethnogenese als Kulturgeschichte, archäologisch betrachtet, neue Grundlagen. In *Beiträge zur Ur- und Frühgeschichte I. Festschrift für W. Coblenz,* 13–25. Berlin: Akademie Verlag.

Kossinna, G. 1896. Die vorgeschichtliche Ausbreitung der Germanen in Deutschland. *Zeitschrift des Vereins für Volkskunde* **6**, 1–14.

Kossinna, G. 1911a. *Die Herkunft der Germanen. Zur Methode der Siedlungsarchäologie.* Mannus-Bibliothek 6. Würzburg: Kabitzsch.

Kossinna, G. 1911b. Anmerkungen zum heutigen Stand der Vorgeschichtsforschung. *Mannus* **3**, 127–30.

Kossinna, G. 1914. *Die deutsche Vorgeschichte eine hervorragend nationale Wissenschaft,* 2nd edn. Mannus-Bibliothek 9. Würzburg: Kabitzsch.

Kossinna, G. 1926. *Ursprung und Verbreitung der Germanen in vor- und frühgeschichtlicher Zeit.* Mannus-Bibliothek 6. Würzburg: Kabitzsch.

Liesegang, G. 1973. 'Ethnische Gruppen' und rezente keramische Komplexe (oder Formenkreise) im südlichen Mosambik: ein Beitrag zur Frage der 'ethnischen Deutung'. In *Festschrift zum 65. Geburtstag von Helmut Petri*, K. Tauchmann (ed.). Kölner Ethnologische Mitteilungen 5, 289–317. Cologne: Böhlau.

Lüning, J. 1972. Zum Kulturbegriff im Neolithikum. *Prähistorische Zeitschrift* **47**, 145–73.

Lüning, J. 1979. Über den Stand der neolithischen Stilfrage in Südwestdeutschland. *Jahrbuch des Römisch–Germanischen Zentralmuseum Mainz* **26**, 75–113.

McGuire, R. H. 1982. The study of ethnicity in historical archaeology. *Journal of Anthropological Archaeology* **1**, 159–78.

McNairn, B. 1980. *The theory and method of V. G. Childe*. Edinburgh: Edinburgh University Press.

McWhite, E. 1956. On the interpretation of archaeological evidence in historical and sociological terms. *American Anthropologist* **58**, 3–25.

Mandera, H.-E. 1965. Zur Deutung neolithischer Kulturen. Probleme urgeschichtlicher Methodik. *Nassauische Annalen* **76**, 1–14.

Marienfeld, W. 1979. *Ur- und Frühgeschichte im Unterricht. Zugleich ein Beitrag zur Geschichte des Geschichtsunterrichts*. Frankfurt-am-Main: Diesterweg.

Martens, J. 1989. The Vandals: myths and facts about a Germanic tribe of the first half of the first millennium AD. In *Archaeological approaches to cultural identity*, S. J. Shennan (ed.), ch. 2. London: Unwin Hyman.

Meinander, C. F. 1981. The concept of culture in European archaeological literature. In *Towards a history of archaeology. Conference on the history of archaeology in Aarhus 1978*, G. Daniel (ed.), 100–11. London: Thames & Hudson.

Menghin, O. 1931. *Weltgeschichte der Steinzeit*. Wien: Schroll.

Menghin, O. 1936. Grundlinien einer Methodik der urgeschichtlichen Stammeskunde. In *Germanen und Indogermanen. Festschrift für H. Hirt*, 41–67. Heidelberg: Winter.

Menghin, O. 1952. Urgeschichtliche Grundfragen. In *Historia Mundi*, Vol. 1: *Frühe Menschheit*, 229–58. Munich: Lehnen.

Mildenberger, G. 1986. Die Germanen in der archäologischen Forschung nach Kossinna. In *Germanenprobleme in heutiger Sicht*, H. Beck (ed.). Reallexikon der germanischen Altertumskunde, Ergänzungsband 1. Berlin and New York: de Gruyter.

Mischung, R. 1986. Rezension von: Studien zur Ethnogenese. In *Germania* **64**(2), 677–82.

Müller-Beck, H. 1977. Ein Beitrag zur urgeschichtlich–archäologischen Terminologie. *Regio Basiliensis* **18**(I), 187–95.

Narr, K. J. 1954. Formengruppen und Kulturkreise im europäischen Paläolithikum. *Berichte der Römisch–Germanischen Kommission* **34**, (1951–1953), 1–40.

Narr, K. J. 1966. Archäologie und Vorgeschichte. In *Sowjetsystem und demokratische Gesellschaft – eine vergleichende Enzyklopädie*, C. D. Kernig (ed.), Vol. 1, 369–86. Freiburg: Herder. (English edn: Archaeology and prehistory. In *Marxism, communism and Western society. A comparative encyclopedia*, 161–70. New York: Herder & Herder (1972).)

Narr, K. J. 1981. Struktur und Ereignis: einige urgeschichtliche Aspekte. *Grenzfragen* **11**, 35–61.

Narr, K. J. 1985. Kulturelle Vereinheitlichung und sprachliche Zersplitterung: Ein Beispiel aus dem Südwesten der Vereinigten Staaten. In *Studien zur Ethnogenese*, 57–99. Opladen: Westdeutscher Verlag.

Otto, K. H. 1953. Archäologische Kulturen und die Erforschung der konkreten

Geschichte von Stämmen und Völkerschaften. *Ethnographisch–Archäologische Forschungen* **1**, 1–27.

Renfrew, C. 1976. *Before civilisation: the radiocarbon revolution and prehistoric Europe.* Harmondsworth: Penguin.

Rüsen, J. 1977. Historik und Didaktik. Ort und Funktion der Geschichtstheorie im Zusammenhang von Geschichtsforschung und historischer Bildung. In *Geschichtswissenschaft. Didaktik – Forschung – Theorie*, E. Kosthorst (ed.), 48–64. Göttingen: Vandenhoeck & Ruprecht.

Sangmeister, E. 1967. Methoden der Urgeschichtswissenschaft. *Saeculum* **18**, 199–245.

Sangmeister, E. 1973. Zur relativen Chronologie des Neolithikums in Südwestdeutschland und der Schweiz. *Germania* **51**(2), 387–403.

Schwerin von Krosigk, H. 1982. *G. Kossinna. Der Nachlaß – Versuch einer Analyse.* Offa-Ergänzungsreihe Vol. 6. Neumünster: Wachholtz.

Shennan, S. J. 1978. Archaeological cultures: an empirical investigation. In *The spatial organization of culture*, I. Hodder (ed.), 113–39. London: Duckworth.

Smith, A. D. 1981. *The ethnic revival in the modern world.* Cambridge: Cambridge University Press.

Smolla, G. 1979–1980. Das Kossinna-Syndrom. *Fundberichte aus Hessen* **19/20**, 1–9.

Smolla, G. 1984–1985. Gustaf Kossinna nach 50 Jahren. Kein Nachruf. *Acta Praehistorica et Archaeologica* **16/17**, 9–14.

Smolla, G. 1986. Rezension von Schwerin von Krosigk 1982. *Germania* **64**(2), 682–6.

Spindler, P. 1983. Das Ethnos-Problem vom Standpunkt der Humanethologie. *Mitteilungen der Anthropologischen Gesellschaft in Wien* **113**, 1–3.

Sprockhoff, E. 1930. *Zur Handelsgeschichte der germanischen Bronzezeit.* Vorgeschichtliche Forschungen 7. Berlin: de Gruyter.

Stampfuß, R. 1935. *Gustaf Kossinna, ein Leben für die deutsche Vorgeschichte.* Leipzig: Kabitzsch.

Studien zur Ethnogenese 1985. Abhandlungen der Rheinisch–Westfälischen Akademie der Wissenschaften, Vol. 72. Opladen: Westdeutscher Verlag.

Torbrügge, W. 1959. Die Bronzezeit in Bayern. Stand und Forschungen zur relativen Chronologie. *Berichte der Römisch–Germanischen Kommission* **40**, 1–78.

Trigger, B. G. 1978. *Time and traditions. Essays in archaeological interpretation.* Edinburgh: Edinburgh University Press.

Trigger, B. G. 1980. *Gordon Childe. Revolutions in archaeology.* London: Thames & Hudson.

Trigger, B. G. 1984. Alternative archaeologies. Nationalist, colonialist, imperialist. *Man* **19**, 355–70.

Ucko, P. J. 1983. The politics of the indigenous minority. *Journal of Biosocial Science Supplement* **8**, 25–40.

Veit, U. 1984. Gustaf Kossinna und V. G. Childe. Ansätze zu einer theoretischen Grundlegung der Vorgeschichte. *Saeculum* **35**, 326–64.

von Uslar, R. 1955. Über den Nutzen spekulativer Betrachtung vorgeschichtlicher Funde. *Jahrbuch des Römisch–Germanischen Zentralmuseums Mainz* **2**, 1–20.

von Uslar, R. 1961. Germanische Bodenaltertümer um Christi Geburt als Interpretationsbeispiel. *Jahrbuch des Römisch–Germanischen Zentralmuseums Mainz* **8**, 38–65.

von Uslar, R. 1965. Stämme und Fundgruppen. Bermerkungen zu 'Stammesbildung und Verfassung' von R. Wenskus. *Germania* **43**, 138–48.

Vossen, R. 1969. *Archäologische Interpretation und ethnographischer Befund. Eine Analyse anhand rezenter Keramik des westlichen Amazonasbeckens.* Hamburger Reihe zur Kultur und Sprachwissenschaft 1. Munich: Renner.

Wahle, E. 1941. *Zur ethnischen Deutung frühgeschichtlicher Kulturprovinzen. Grenzen der frühgeschichtlichen Erkenntnis I*. Sitzungsberichte der Heidelberger Akademie der Wissenschaften, Philologisch–historische Klasse. Jahrgang 1940–1, 2nd edn. Heidelberg: Winter.

Wahle, E. 1950–1951. Geschichte der prähistorischen Forschung. *Anthropos* **45**, 497–538; **46**, 49–112.

Wenskus, R. 1961. *Stammesbildung und Verfassung. Das Werden der frühmittelalterlichen gentes*. Cologne and Graz: Böhlau.

Wenskus, R. 1979. Randbemerkungen zum Verhältnis von Historie und Archaëologie, insbesondere mittelalterlicher Geschichte und Mittelalterarchäologie. In *Geschichtswissenschaft und Archäologie*, H. Jankuhn & R. Wenskus (eds). Forschungen und Vorträge 22, 637–57. Sigmaringen: Thorbecke.

Werner, J. 1950. Zur Entstehung der Reihengräberzivilisation. Ein Beitrag zur Methode der frühgeschichtlichen Archäologie. *Archaeologica Geographica* **1**(2), 23–32.

Wernhardt, K. 1979. 'Ethnosnotiz' – Bemerkungen zu einem Zentralbegriff der anthropologischen Disziplinen. *Mitteilungen der Anthropologischen Gesellschaft in Wien* **109**, 173–9.

Winkler, E.-M. 1983. Volk, Kultur, Ethnos, Population, Typus. Zur Methodik der 'ethnischen Deutung'. *Mitteilungen der Anthropologischen Gesellschaft in Wien* **113**, 5–14.

Wissler, C. 1917. *The American Indian. An introduction to the anthropology of the New World*. New York.

Wissler, C. 1923. *Man and culture*. New York.

Wolfram, S. 1986. *Zur Theoriediskussion in der prähistorischen Archäologie Großbritanniens. Ein forschungsgeschichtlicher überblick über die Jahre 1968–1982*. BAR International Series 306. Oxford: BAR.

2 The Vandals: myths and facts about a Germanic tribe of the first half of the 1st millennium AD

JES MARTENS

The first association we have, when we hear the word 'vandal' mentioned, is 'vandalism'. Instinctively we imagine the taste of blood on our tongue, the sound of breaking glass on the main street around midnight, or gravestones overturned and covered with graffiti. 'Vandalism' has a similar horrifying connotation with chaos: meaningless violence and a lack of respect for cultural and human values. It instills in us the same feeling of bottomless uncertainty as the word 'anarchy', and similarly the modern meaning pays little or no respect at all to the origins of the word.

As a matter of fact, the first to use the word 'vandal' in its modern sense was a French bishop of the late 18th century. He used it to characterize the revolutionaries who burned down libraries and tore down church monuments during the French Revolution (Jahn 1940, pp. 1022ff.). The people who lent their name to this expression – a Germanic tribe living on Roman territory during the 5th and 6th centuries AD – were not themselves in particular 'vandals' in this sense of the word. Though they appear to us as such through the contemporary Roman sources, we must keep in mind that we hear only one part of the case. Besides, they were just one among many tribes drawn to Rome by the glare of power and incomprehensible luxury.

A possible reason why the Vandals acquired such a bad reputation seems to be that they never had their own chronicler, as many of the other important Germanic tribes had. In addition, unlike the other conquerors of Rome, they accepted neither the superiority of the Byzantine emperor nor that of the Roman Pope. The latter fact is of especial importance, as it was the Church which later became the bearer of the written tradition. Thus, it is surely no coincidence that it was an ecclesiastic who was the first to turn their name into a word of shame.

The history of the Vandals

The first to mention the Vandals was the Greek historian Cassius Dio (AD 150–235). He recorded their appearance on the borderlands of the Roman Empire during the Markomannian wars at the end of the 2nd century AD. The Vandals – or that part of them that called themselves the Hasdings – lived here between Goths and Markomans. It was probably at this time that they converted to Christianity. They chose, however, not Roman Catholicism but Arianism, which was then popular among the Germanic tribes of the Eastern Roman borders.

At the end of the fourth century the pressure from the Huns made the Goths uneasy. The Vandals then broke up and moved north-west along the Limes. In AD 406 the joint forces of the Vandals, the Sueves and the Alans invaded Gaul. Approximately 10 years later they ended up in Spain, which they divided into a Sueve, an Alan and two Vandal territories – a Silingian and a Hasdingian. The West Roman Emperor then engaged the West Goths to force the barbarians out of Spain. This project was quite successful because the Silingians and the Alan kingdoms were wiped out. Under Gothic pressure the remaining Vandal and Alan forces crossed the Strait of Gibraltar and occupied the Roman provinces of North Africa. Here they set up an independent state in AD 429.

At the height of their success the Vandals ruled the waves of the western Mediterranean and rejected as the first Barbarians on Roman territory the superiority of the Eastern Roman Emperor and the Roman Pope. Instead, they erected a national church organization based on Arian beliefs. In this way they opposed the local population, and this enabled them to remain a distinct social unity despite their ethnic diversity and the fact that they formed only a negligible minority in their new 'homeland'.

However, their good fortune was limited. The kingdom fell apart as a result of the attack of the Byzantine Emperor Justinian in AD 533 – and the Vandals would have become extinct from history – if not for the French bishop 1200 years later . . . (Schmidt 1934, pp. 100ff., Jahn 1940 *passim*, Courtois 1955 *passim*, Haüsler 1983, pp. 647ff.).

The theories of the Vandals

It is uncertain who was the first to point out as the original home of the Vandals the southern and central parts of Poland. The classical sources are quite ambiguous on this point. Before they appeared in the proximity of the Limes, we have no record of the Vandals. Pliny the Elder gives us a piece of information that describes the 'Vandils' as a union of several tribes; among these were peoples like the 'Gutones' (Goths?), the 'Burgodiones' (Burgunds?), the 'Charins' and the 'Varins'. Somewhat later, Tacitus mentioned, in the introduction to his survey of the Germanic tribes, that the original names of the Germans probably were the 'Suebes', the 'Vandils', and so on.

However, this union is not presented at all later in the book (Pliny, pp. 99–100, Tacitus, p. 2). It is therefore most likely that the Vandils were a union of tribes that dissolved in the early part of the first century AD, and had little or nothing to do with the Vandals (Jahn 1940, p. 945). Again, to use the words of Pliny, to locate the Vandils is not an easy task. Based on his works we can only say that they lived 'somewhere up northeast in Germania Libra'. A much later source, the Gothic chronicler Jordanes, mentioned that the Goths had to fight with the Vandals when arriving on the continent from 'Scandza'. However, this source is much later, and consequently is of very dubious authority.

Pre-World War II German archaeologists did not hesitate in their interpretation of Pliny. Strongly supported by the first lines of Jordanes' *Romana et Getica*, they claimed that the Vandals lived south-east of the Baltic Sea somewhere between the Odra and the Vistula. This was adopted as a fact by the majority of German scholars after a lecture of Gustaf Kossinna in 1895 (Kossinna 1896, 1929, Nerman 1930, Hülle 1936). They identified the Vandals with those people represented in the archaeological record by the so-called Przeworsk culture, occupying the central and southern parts of Poland at the turn of the millennium. The question of how far back we can trace them is where the disagreements begin.

Kossinna originally pointed to the East Pommeranian culture as the material expression of the Vandils or the Vandals (Kossinna 1912, 1929). According to him, this cultural group was generated by a synthesis of local western Germanic people and newcomers arriving from somewhere in Scandinavia at the end of the Bronze Age (Kossinna 1912, pp. 155f). The Vandils later expanded southwards deeper into the areas of what is today Poland. From where in Scandinavia they came could not be established at the time, but Kossinna supposed that they had the same genetic roots as the inhabitants of the Northern Jutland district of Vendsyssel – in earlier times called Vendila. Thus, opposing a far older assumption that the Vandals originated from Vendsyssel, he maintained that the Eastern Germanic tribes were to be derived from Scandinavian North Germanic tribes (Kossinna 1929, p. 233). Both of these theories were still mainly based on philological assumptions, and were only vaguely supported by early studies of the archaeological record of the areas in question (for example, Jahn 1922, Nerman 1924, Kossinna 1929).

The first to bring in more materials and to give an archaeological basis to the theories was Baron Bolko von Richthofen, who had a knowledge of the Danish material, and called attention to the striking similarities between the late pre-Roman pottery of Vendsyssel, especially that from Kraghede, and that of Silesia. Those similarities that were previously known were of a much later date and were taken by Kossinna as an indication of a minor migration from the south-east to the north-west. The direction was now reversed, as the Vendsyssel material was supposed to have a local chronological and typological background, whereas it was claimed that the Polish had none (Richthofen 1930, Nerman 1930).

From this point onwards the supporters of this theory had the upper hand, as it seemed impossible to prove any continuity between the early pre-Roman and the late pre-Roman Iron Age cultures in Poland, and in the years before World War II they produced one work after another showing that the origin of the Polish Vandal culture must be sought in the Northern Kattegat area (Petersen 1932, Jahn 1937, Peschek 1939, Jahn 1940). They even boldly skipped the philological and historical sources which were the starting points of the whole discussion (Jahn 1940, p. 946) in favour of what they believed they saw in the archaeological material. The location of the Vandals in the 1st century AD was now 'proved' by the expansion of the Przeworsk culture into the areas of Slovakia and Hungary at the end of the 2nd century AD, at the time when Cassius Dio mentions the arrival of the Vandals in the same area. It was further believed that the Lugians of the 1st century AD, whom Tacitus mentions living in Poland, must be identical with the Vandals of the 2nd century (Tacitus, p. 43, Jahn 1940, p. 944). This tribe is even mentioned as early as around the birth of Christ living somewhere in the neighbourhood of the Markomans and possibly the Goths (Butones) (Strabo, 7.1.3).

The Vandal migration theory never really gained support either in Poland or in Denmark (for example, Brøndsted 1941). After World War II the opposition gained force, while German archaeology from now on kept silent on the subject. Meanwhile, Poland produced a strongly autochthonous school of archaeologists under the leadership of Józef Kostrzewski. A great effort was invested in proving the unbroken settlement and population continuity of the Slavs in People's Poland. To this end Kostrzewski wrote a remarkable reversed history of Poland, going backwards from Medieval times to the Neolithic period (Kostrzewski 1965).

Around this time the Swedish and Danish scholars Moberg and Klindt-Jensen visited Poland, preparing their doctorates (Moberg 1941). They became strongly influenced by his ideas, and consequently again the similarities in the ceramics which no-one still denied were explained by the reverse interpretation. This idea has survived until today (Kaszewska 1980, p. 38, Godlowski 1981, p. 59). However, in 1976 Carl Axel Moberg called together modern scientists to renew the discussion on the matter. At the meeting, held in Gothenburg, it appeared that nobody felt any need for explaining the emerging Iron Age cultures in their respective research areas by means of a migration. As everything could be derived from local prototypes, the conclusion inevitably was that there were no connections at all between the areas in question (Kaelas 1976, Kaelas & Wigfors 1980).

The history of the Vandal theories

The history of the Vandal migration theory has a striking similarity with that of the Vandals themselves. For a long time the theory struggled for its own existence, like the Vandals fighting their way through Europe. Finally, it found firm ground, as they did in North Africa, but, similarly, only to vanish shortly thereafter. How can this be? The death of the theory seems to occur at the end of World War II. This coincides with the death of the third Reich and its philosophy.

The works of Gustaf Kossinna and the Kossinna school can be designated as nationalist, or even as national chauvinist, writings, but not as National Socialist propaganda, at least not at the outset. The Kossinna classic of 1912, *German prehistory – an outstanding national science*, was reprinted at least nine times. Five years and three issues after the death of the author in 1931 this book was elevated to be a cornerstone in the National Socialist ideology. In the 7th edition, of 1936, Adolf Hitler is quoted in the foreword, speaking about the need for common national pride and that 'the Germans already 1000 years before the foundation of Rome had experienced a cultural prime' (Hülle 1936).

In the period between the World Wars, a defeated Germany needed dreams like these of a greater past in order to be able to face the present. This was well understood by the Nazis, who integrated history at all levels, to the extent that even minor local periodicals of historical societies were turned into pamphlets of National Socialism (for example, *Altschlesische Blätter* 1936, No. 5). Perhaps many of the archaeologists, even those of the Kossinna school, were not convinced Nazis, but many of them still provided the great Nazi propaganda machine with ammunition, as in the question of their rights to the Polish territories. By their talk about Eastern Germanic tribes like the Goths and the Vandals living in the Polish lands, the archaeologists offered expansionist plans an alibi (for example, Jahn 1940, p. 1030). It is therefore no wonder that the Vandal theory was buried with World War II. It had become synonymous with Nazi expansionism.

Only one pupil of the Kossinna school continued to write in the old way: the Pole Józef Kostrzewski. During the years between the World Wars he was fighting vigorously against German archaeology, listening to the view that Slav culture was an *Unkultur*. During the German occupation of Poland he had to remain underground, watching the occupiers systematically destroy the Slav heritage, while the SS officer and archaeologist Ernst Petersen was looking for him (Jazdzewski 1980). Now, finally, Kostrzewski got the opportunity to take revenge. He took it. He proved that the Slavs originated in the Polish lands, by postulating a continuity in material culture from today back to the Neolithic. Thus, they were much older as a people than the Germans, who first arrived in Germany during the Early Iron Age (Kostrzewski 1965). As these theories were presented as facts to Moberg and Klindt-Jensen, they easily spread to Scandinavia, and since the Early pre-Roman Iron Age was still somewhat little known in Denmark, and the Kraghede cemetery in Vendsyssel was almost the only material published, it was easy to change the direction of the influences once again (Moberg 1941, Brøndsted 1941).

However, it might seem strange that the re-examination of the problem in 1976 in Gothenburg did not rekindle the discussion. After all, almost every scholar of the first half of the 20th century at least agreed about the

similarities between Northern Jutland and the Przeworsk culture. Even this
was now being denied (Becker 1980). The reason must be sought in a general
change of paradigm in Western archaeology, from concentrating on typology and culture historical explanations to a focus on economic and
sociohistorical processes; in short, a change from external to internal
explanatory models. Migration theories were no longer 'in', and no-one
believed in the possibilities of identifying historically known tribes in the
archaeological record. In addition to this, the Poles who attended the
meeting belonged mainly to the Kostrzewski school. Their aim was primarily to prove the ethnohistorical legitimacy of the modern Polish
territories.

Modern Danish research has shown that the so-called 'Kraghede group' of
Vendsyssel is not that strange, but has a comprehensive local background
(Becker 1961, 1980, Bech 1975, 1980, Bech & Lysdahl 1976). At the same
time modern Polish research has demonstrated that the continuity between
the Early and the Late pre-Roman Iron Age in Poland is not that certain at all
(Nieweglowski 1981, Dabrowska 1977). Again, the basic materials have
been altered, and one could easily turn to the old north–south migration
theory. However, that would not bring us any further.

The major difference between the migration theories of the Poles and the
Germans was in the direction of the influence. The methods and the materials
were the same: artefacts were taken as identifiers of different prehistoric
peoples, and similarities in separated archaeological cultures were taken as a
sign of genetic relationships. As the methods were the same but the
conclusions conflicting, it is tempting to seek the reason for this not in the
scientific arguments, but in the sociocultural context: the question of the
rights to the Polish lands.

The third point of view – that there are no connections at all – is just as
scientifically based as the other two. As mentioned above, it is only an
expression of the general change of focus in Western archaeology from
external to internal cultural processes. Here, again, we suggest that the
reason for this shift is not to be found within the discipline of archaeology
but in its environment, where at that time materialism, and especially
historical materialism, was enjoying widespread popularity.

However, it should be obvious that neither exclusively internal nor
purely external factors can adequately account for the course of a sociocultural development. Unfortunately, there is insufficient space here to
develop a model embodying them both (for an attempt, see Martens 1984),
since the major aim of this paper is the reassessment of migration theory,
based on the example of the archaeological Vandal theories.

For this purpose, some points must be made clear.

(a)   Neither migration theories nor ethnic theories should or can be used to
      justify any political or historical claim on territories or ethnic rights.
(b)   The identification of historically known peoples and tribes is a very
      difficult task because the means of expressing ethnic unity and diver-

sity, and the need for it, varies through space and time with the general cultural and political situation of the period in question.

(c)   The migration 'solution' has been more or less popular through the ages due to changes in the general nature of shifting world systems.

(d)   A total replacement of one ethnic group by another, as so often claimed by pre-World War II German archaeology, is a very unusual situation; normally one would find a mixture of indigenous inhabitants and newcomers.

(e)   A migrating and conquering group might be strong in the political and military sense but at the same time weaker in the general cultural sense than those defeated – as was the case with the German conquerors of Rome; thus many migrations might not leave any trace in the archaeo-logical record.

The future of the Vandals

If we want to reopen the case, the first step that must be taken is to make a distinction between the historical and the 'archaeological' Vandals. The historical ones began their lives in the borderlands of the Roman Empire during the years of the Markoman wars. The archaeological 'Vandals' lived in southern and central Poland from the beginning of the Late La Tène period. So far no archaeological investigation has proved any connection between them, and thus we should rather call the latter complex the Przeworsk culture, as modern Polish archaeology does. If we do claim an identity, however, would it then be wrong to expect that we should be able to follow them all the way through Europe to North Africa?

A problem arising here is that we know that the historical Vandals were Christians, whereas the archaeological ones were pagan. Another point is that a considerable change in their social organization must be expected, due to external pressure during their journey through Europe and internal social instability caused by the sudden wealth of war spoils. It seems that they arrived in Spain as a rather loose organization not able to form a lasting superstructure of larger scale, whereas a more centralized kingship emerged as they crossed to Africa. At this point the culture of the conquerors was already completely subjected to Roman civilization, even in the way in which they expressed their opposition to it (i.e. their confession of the Arian faith). For this reason, and because the later Roman writers were interested in the deeds (or misdeeds) of the barbarians on Roman territory rather than their social structure and history, the information considering Vandal society and their life beyond the Limes is of very little use. It is still a very dubious project to try to connect the historically known Vandals with the archaeo-logical ones.

How did the Germans outside the Imperial borders conceive themselves? What did a 'tribe' believe marked the difference between itself and 'the others'? And between friend and enemy? The 1st century AD Roman sources give us an answer to this: beliefs, habits, looks and even armament (Tacitus, pp. 43, 46, Léube 1983). Strabo (7.1.3) adds: 'It is a common characteristic of all the peoples in this part of the world that they migrate with ease'. We must thus accept the existence of different tribes that mark their ethnicity, their alliances, enmities, etc., in a way which can be materially detected, and that migration seems to be a part of the nature of this system – a way of keeping it in balance. These elements are necessary if we want to understand and describe the world of the Early Iron Age north of the Roman borders.

'The archaeological Vandals' – i.e. the Przeworsk culture – show many similarities in the material record with the Early Iron Age cultures of North Jutland and of the Eastern parts of Central Celtic Europe. The latter can easily be explained by the geographical nearness of the cultures and the cultural and economic relations arising from this – the Celtic civilization providing the Przeworsk culture with raw materials and technology for metal working, and receiving amber, food, furs and military assistance in return. The first ones are less-obviously comprehended, and it would be tempting to explain them by a genetic relationship. The Przeworsk culture emerges at the beginning of the late pre-Roman Iron Age, showing a lot of new features compared with the preceding Cloche culture; however, the North Jutland area shows a fairly continuous development containing several of these traits at an earlier date. Therefore, it seems likely that we must take the North Jutland culture for the originator. This does not mean that we expect that a 'North Jutland Empire' subjugated central Poland, but that in our view a migration took place from north to south at the beginning of the late pre-Roman Iron Age, and was thus a part of, and perhaps the starting point for, the genesis of the Przeworsk culture.

References

Altschlesische Blätter 1936. Vol. 11, No. 5, Breslau.

Bech, J.-H. 1975. Nordjyske fibler fra periode IIIa. *Hikuin* **2**, 75–88.

Bech, J.-H. 1980. Late pre-Roman Iron Age in Northern Jutland. In *Die Vorrömische Eisenzeit im Kattegatgebiet und in Poland*, L. Kaelas & J. Wigfors (eds), 68–84. Gothenburg: Göteborgs arkeologiska museum.

Bech, J.-H. & Lysdahl, P. 1976. Vendsyssel. In *När Järnet kom*, L. Kaelas (ed.), 191–226. Gothenburg: Göteborgs arkeologiska museum.

Becker, C.-J. 1961. *Førromersk Jernalder i Syd- og Midtjylland*. Nationalmuseets skrifter, Større beretninger VI. Copenhagen: The National Museum.

Becker, C. J. 1980. Vendsyssel während der vorrömische Eisenzeit. In *Die Vorrömische Eisenzeit im Kattegatgebiet und in Polen*, L. Kaelas & J. Wigfors (eds), 54–67. Gothenburg: Göteborgs arkeologiska museum.

Brøndsted, J. 1941. Vort Folks Oldtidsliv og Forhistorie. In *Schultz Danmarks Historie*, Vol. 1, A. Friis, A. Linvald & M. Mackeprang (eds), 109–334. Copenhagen: J. H. Schultz Forlag.

Courtois, C. 1955. *Les Vandals et l'Afrique*. Paris: Arts et Métiers Graphiques.

Dabrowska, T. 1977. Próba ustalenia chronologii wzglednej cmentarzysk kloszowych z obszaru Mazowsza. *Wiadomosci Arcaeologiczne* **LXII**(2), 117–36.

Godlowski, K. 1981. Kultura Przeworska. In *Prahistoria Ziem Polski*, W. Hensel (ed.), 57–134. Wrocław: Zaklad Narodowy im. Ossolinskich. Wydawnictwo.

Haüsler, A. 1983. Die Zeit der Völkerwanderung und ihre Bedeutung für die Geschichte Europas. In *Die Germanen*, Vol. 1 & 2, B. Krüger (ed.), Vol. 2, 647–59. Berlin: Akademie Verlag.

Hülle, W. 1936. Foreword and notes. In *Die Deutsche Vorgeschichte. Eine hervorragend nationale Wissenschaft*, G. Kossina, 7th edn, III–IV, 267–92. Leipzig: Curt Kabitzsch.

Jahn, M. 1922. Zur Herkunft der schlesischen Wandalen. In *25 Jahre Siedlungsarchäologie*, H. Hahne (ed.), 78–94. Leipzig: Curt Kabitzsch.

Jahn, M. 1937. Die Heimat der Wandalen und Norwegen. *Acta Archaeologica* **VIII**, 159–67.

Jahn, M. 1940. Die Wandalen. In *Vorgeschichte der deutschen Stämme*, Vol. 1–3, H. Reinerth (ed.), Vol. 3, 943–1032. Berlin: Herbert Stubenrauch.

Jazdzewski, K. 1980. Die frühesten Staatsgebildte in Oder-Weichselgebiet. In *Die vorrömische Eisenzeit im Kattegatgebiet und in Polen*, L. Kaelas & J. Wigfors (eds), 16–32. Gothenburg: Göteborgs arkeologiska museum.

Kaelas, L. (ed.) 1976. *När Järnet kom*. Gothenburg: Göteborgs arkeologiska museum.

Kaelas, L. & J. Wigfors (eds) 1980. *Die vorrömische Eisenzeit im Kattegatgebiet und in Polen*. Gothenburg: Göteborgs arkeologiska museum.

Kaszewska, E. 1980. Bemerkungen zur Frage Kulturverbindungen zwichen Westpommern und Skandinavien. In *Die vorrömische Eisenzeit in Kattegatgebiet und in Polen*, L. Kaelas & J. Wigfors (eds), 31–40. Gothenburg: Göteborgs arkeologiska museum.

Kossinna, G. 1896. Die vorgeschichtliche Ausbreitung der Germanen in Deutchland. *Zeitschrift des Vereins für Volkskunde* **6**, 1–14. Berlin: Asher.

Kossinna, G. 1912. *Die Deutsche Vorgeschichte. Eine hervorragend nationale Wissenschaft*. Leipzig: Curt Kabitzsch.

Kossinna, G. 1929. Die Wandalen in Nordjutland. *Mannus* **21**, 233–55.

Kostrzewski, J. 1965. *Zur Frage Siedlungstetigkeit in der Urgeschichte Polens*. Wrocław: Zaklad narodowy im. Ossolinskich-Wydawnictwo.

Léube, A. 1983. Die Gesellschaft – Entwicklung und Strukturen. In *Die Germanen*, Vol. 1–2, B. Krüger (ed.), Vol. 1, 523–43. Berlin: Akademie Verlag.

Martens, J. 1984. The material and immaterial in culture. *Kontaktstencil* **26–27**, 1–14.

Moberg, C.-A. 1941. *Zonengliederungen der vorrömischen Eisenzeit in Nordeuropa*. Lund: Gleerup.

Nerman, B. 1924. *Die Herkunft und frühesten Auswanderungen der Germanen*. Stockholm: Kungliga Vitterhets Historie och Akademiens Avhandlinger **34**(5).

Nerman, B. 1930. Vandalernes äldste hem. *Fornvännen* **25**, 365–70.

Nieweglowski, A. 1981. Zur Forschung des Bestattungsbrauchtums der spätlatènezeitlichen Przeworskkultur. *Archaeologia Polona* **XX**, 81–122.

Peschek, C. 1939. *Die frühwandalische Kultur in Mittelschlesien*, Vol. 1–2. Leipzig: Kurt Rabitzsch.

Petersen, E. 1932. Keramik der Ostdeutsch–Polnischen Spätlatènezeit in ihren Beziehungen zu Nordischen Tongefässen. *Acta Archaeologica* **III**, 47–57.

Pliny the Elder. *Historia Naturalis*.

Richthofen, B. von 1930. Zur Herkunft der Wandalen. *Altschlesien* **3**, 21–36.

Schmidt, L. 1934. *Geschichte der deutschen Stämme*. Munich: C. H. Bech.

Strabo. *Geografia*.

Tacitus. *Germania*.

3 Theory, profession, and the political rôle of archaeology

BRIAN DURRANS

There is a conspicuous 'political' trend in archaeology which is concerned with the influence of ideology on interpretations of the past. Cutting across this kind of political consciousness – but not yet clearly integrated with it – is the experience of archaeologists in dealing with issues more obviously (because more immediately) to do with allocating, exercising or resisting power in society. Monuments like Stonehenge or the Parthenon Marbles raise questions which are political in this sense – about access (to whom?), protection (from whom?) and what they represent (in whose interests?). Similarly, problems like the looting, destruction or neglect of archaeological evidence bring to the fore not just the motives of those implicated in such things, but also the system of social division and exploitation which generates the motives themselves.

In one way or another capitalism is the backdrop for most archaeological work currently undertaken throughout the world. One of its most distinctive tendencies is to integrate cultural activities subtly and closely with economic and political processes while giving those involved the impression that they are operating in isolation from one another. Contemporary academic work thus reflects in an advanced and specialized form the same contradiction that Marx identified at an earlier stage in the development of modern capitalism.

Given this context, and despite a growing 'politicization' of the subject, it is understandable that many archaeologists, like other academics, fail to recognize how intimately archaeology is linked with economic and political aspects of society. This relationship is becoming more thoroughly documented and analysed within the traditional definition of the subject through studies of the history of archaeology, and more thoroughly experienced from outside that definition through legislative, fiscal or political limitations on archaeological practice. What is then experienced negatively as political abuse or restriction, which many rightly perceive as coming from 'outside' the subject as traditionally defined, not only legitimizes the idea that archaeology does indeed operate hermetically, but then allows this idea to set the agenda for how archaeologists should work. The real issue is therefore missed: instead of addressing ourselves to the interactive relationship between archaeology and other aspects of social reality, we substitute the idea of a beleaguered fortress. The corollary is that the siege should be lifted in the sense that, whatever the circumstances, an independent specialist centre should be free to disseminate its knowledge to consumers in return for bankable prestige for worthy work against the grain of narrow commercialism. This way of doing business can seem reasonable, even noble, despite being modelled on the paradigmatic transaction of advanced capitalism.

A tentative or hermetic politics of archaeology might be defended on two grounds. First, we might claim that because many archaeologists operate in sharply divided societies in which job security or promotability can rarely be taken for granted if one expresses radical views, it is a sensible tactic to pursue political arguments in a covert way, expressed as far as possible in the recognized professional idiom. Alternatively, we could suggest that from an assessment of contemporary politics, the most useful way in which archaeologists can contribute to a wider political movement is by exposing the ideological bias of archaeology, thereby encouraging people to recognize and therefore transcend ideology in their own lives (for example, Leone *et al.* 1987). Either argument is reasonable insofar as it concedes the grounds on which a third approach might be based. Concern about a career – or even, these days, about just a job – acknowledges the influence of economic power on archaeology. Seeking to make the specialized work of archaeologists politically relevant presupposes a degree of social integration of their subject and practices. These recognitions, alongside respect for the distinctive expertise and intellectual aspirations of archaeologists, are essential ingredients of any viable politics of the subject.

Of course, there are different degrees of hermeticism in how archaeology is viewed in relation to its social context. Few would recognize themselves in the 'beleaguered fortress' caricature outlined above, although the widespread influence of its logic justifies criticism of an extreme example. However, is it not still parochial to view politics as a sort of moral spreadsheet on which objections can be registered against various iniquities, whether organized archaeology is to be confronted with them or not? Such a view of politics is the product of the liberal conscience; but the liberal conscience, regardless of how persuasive it may be within the rules of its own discourse, is itself the product of bourgeois democracy. In this area, the liberal conscience is peculiarly myopic. The cause of certain kinds of freedom elicits great, necessary and progressive inspiration, but the analysis of why those freedoms are denied in the first place, and of what structural changes in the organization of societies might secure and defend them, requires an approach that inevitably raises questions about bourgeois democracy itself.

Such problems would probably not arise, or would be handled differently, in a profession whose members generally had more-personal acquaintance with routine forms of organization in large-scale movements for social change (the participants in which may be so familiarized by personal experience with the connection between different aspects of political activity that they can forget that for those not so steeped in it, the links are not always so clear). Similarly, archaeologists might be more expected to view archaeological theories and assumptions in a broader social context when they themselves take part in activities which cut across, transcend or even challenge their professional commitments.

Perhaps limited experience of wider organization can help to explain why even radical archaeologists have been influenced by narrow, liberal ideas about the way in which their subject actually develops and the context in which it does so. Although a creditably more reflexive and internationally aware archaeology gains momentum, this limitation may weaken future opportunities for archaeologists to influence their subject and their societies. As people's egos are tied to their work, and the development of archaeology properly involves rejecting some interpretations or methods, a degree of professional irritation is to be expected. However, disagreement over the politics of archaeology, extending to fundamental questioning of the subject's epistemological status, has often been conducted in an acrimonious and narrow way; even when they themselves have been partly to blame, this has unnecessarily alienated many traditionalists with an outstanding commitment and contribution to archaeology. Given the radicals' neglect of the political implications of their own arguments, an outsider or sceptic might be forgiven for interpreting this controversy in Kuhnian terms as simply an archaeological yuppy subfraction rubbishing the old guard. The crux of my argument at this point is that alienating orthodox archaeologists would not matter in the least if archaeology were not the socially embedded discipline that it really is. In their zeal the radicals have been less than radical in their neglect, beyond the issue of apartheid, of the central problems of how to promote social change through changing archaeology – even when they profess to take such an aim seriously (for example, Potter & Leone 1986, Leone *et al.* 1987).

The main problems in this context seem to stem from an inadequate understanding of politics as a unity embracing archaeology, theory and wider social practice. Thus, whereas 'real' politics operates in a way that many archaeologists find crude or distastefully 'reductionist', archaeological politics can appear, by contrast, respectably refined and comfortingly complex (for example, Pratap & Rao 1986, pp. 2–4). This tendency is clearly not confined to archaeology, but is symptomatic of even the most 'socially relevant' academic work carried out under the influence of the values of advanced capitalism. Even theorists whose work is explicitly premised on a deep connection between political practice and unconsciously held positions may write as if they are exempt from their own arguments.

Despite the growth of academic interest in radical and revolutionary ideas, at least since the 1960s, the socially rooted prejudice against implementing them seems as secure as ever. If it is reasonable to assume that social and scientific archaeological knowledge are dialectically related (Gathercole 1984, p. 150, citing Leff 1969), there is also a dialectical interaction between the institutional organization of archaeology and its specific social setting. From its own perspective a movement for social change needs an ideological radicalization in the professions as much as radical professionals need the wider movement as a stimulus to new ideas and an antidote to parochialism (LeRoy 1976).

A weakness in otherwise resourceful and sensitive formulations about the rôle of ideology in society that attempt to escape determinist or voluntarist distortions (for example, Miller & Tilley 1984, Introduction) is that even when setting forth models of (and about) the theory and practice of power, they take no account whatever of the extent to which, inside or outside archaeology itself, such models might be actionable, by whom, and to what ends. Supplying these missing dimensions requires a critique of the ideas on which such models are based, and this in turn implies a concern with the implications that such ideas have in the wider political context in which they are deployed. It further suggests the restriction which lack of contact with wider social movements places on insight (and hence of the alienated experience within capitalism referred to earlier) that those so preoccupied with integrating the theory and practice of archaeology pay so little attention to the interaction of the cognate arguments that they regard as important with the hegemonic ideology of advanced capitalism on which these arguments have a political bearing.

The same criticism can also be applied to polarizing ideology as either 'false consciousness' or a means of challenging existing power through social intervention (for example, Hodder 1986), when there are various intermediate possibilities that can develop in one direction or the other. Nevertheless, whatever their labels or apparent significance, some ideas effectively support establishments whereas others undermine them; they contend with each other in a given society. However, can there be any grounds for choosing between rival ideologies, apart from a previous commitment to one or other of the political positions that they entail?

In a short-term, practical sense that is elaborated below, the answer for most people is probably no. In the longer term it is not only possible to test ideological claims against practical criteria, but standard practice for effective ideological buttressing of existing power or effective opposition to it. How else can a justificatory or critical ideology learn from experience? Such testing need be no more consistent or thorough than in normative science, and for similar reasons: as a practical guide to action or making 'sense' of a certain range of experience, it would be counterproductive for either an ideology or a body of scientific knowledge to be constantly subjected to revision. It is only when its scope for useful application is exhausted by new experiences that an ideology or scientific paradigm, or part of either, is finally displaced. Typically, these new experiences do not come from within the field in which the ideology or theory is conventionally deployed; they often arise from external processes. Under these circumstances, taking a formal political position in relation to the larger issue of power in society may be a reasonable short cut to political activity, which makes it unnecessary to rehearse every step of ideological reasoning before advancing specific ideas that are relevant to a given academic discipline. If that is no guarantee against inappropriate affiliation or applying the tenets of a wider doctrine insensitively, at least it avoids the immobilizing illusion that personal commitment to knowledge and collaborating with others for social change are necessarily antagonistic.

Wide-ranging discussions about the past and present social dimensions of archaeology and its practice (for example, Patterson 1986, Trigger 1985) themselves constitute part of that social dimension. In order to explore the epistemological grounds on which archaeology might continue to be practised, I offer a criticism of the distinction between 'pure' and 'applied' embodied in the conventional definition of archaeology. An epistemology that is confined to theory can be radical only in name; it is Eurocentric and imperialist because it fails to address other archaeological traditions, and it is hegemonic because it offers no perspective on the extent to which it is historically determined.

What archaeologists actually do has so far received insufficient attention in the debate between realists and relativists in 'post-positivist' epistemology (Rowlands 1984, Wylie, Ch. 5, this volume). Wylie, for instance, evokes concatenation of inferences from 'collateral (independent) fields' as a reliable test for knowledge claims, at least when such claims refer to 'quasi-functional causal principles and low-level empirical generalizations'. She goes on to say that it is on just these kinds of claims that science depends for its 'undeniable instrumental success' (Wylie, Ch. 5, p. 100). In other words, although she defines both the claims and the grounds for accepting them in terms that constitute them as part of an epistemology, the grounds themselves derive from practical application. However, if a suitable epistemology for archaeology cannot be constructed without including practical applications of the subject at the level of 'low-level empirical generalizations', then there is no *a priori* reason why practice cannot also be included at the level of social applications of archaeological theory or epistemology itself. Theorizing about the epistemology of the subject has therefore already opened up the possibility of redefining archaeology in a radically new way at the same time as the practical experience of at least some archaeologists has been leading them to a similar position.

However, several influential attempts to reformulate the epistemology of studying the past so as to incorporate the idea of the past having an active value in the present are themselves ideologically restricted. By this I mean that the special advantage that operating in the present gives us in trying to understand what happened in the past – the opportunity to recognize at least something of how past societies developed – has been neglected because the rôle of the past in the present has been treated more as a problem than as an opportunity. If studying the past is not a neutral activity, as almost everyone now accepts, then it has a bearing on how archaeologists and others construct the future; the past is a resource for deriving knowledge to guide social action. Such knowledge may be inadequate, inaccurate, misleading, misinterpreted or misused, but its potential cannot be denied. Yet treating evidence as if the pursuit of knowledge about the past were an end in itself is still widespread in archaeology, even among those who are sensitive to past misinterpretations. Miller & Tilley (1984, p. 4), for instance, claim that:

> Working with models of social action which seem plausible and pertinent in the analysis of our own actions as interpreters may break down the distance that otherwise allows the emergence of implausible mechanised and fetishised models of past peoples.

Leaving aside the double difficulty of whether we can believe what anyone tells us about their own actions, and whether applying a model of the behaviour of late 20th century critical archaeologists is much of an advance on those that have been used before, we are left with the problem that although critical archaeology continues, like any other kind, to interpret evidence of change in the archaeological record, its theoretical elaborations refuse to concede the unique advantage conferred by the directionality of time.

Perhaps one source of unease among critical archaeologists about the directionality of time is its apparent link with narrow objectivist perspectives; but there is no reason why it cannot be combined with more-reflexive modes of interpreting the past. Another possible source is the past experience of contemporary subject peoples being treated as equivalent to earlier 'stages' in the development of human society, so that peoples of the past became associated with the contemporary symbolism of oppression just as those of the present were identified with them. Interpreting what people did in the past may therefore seem subtly imperialistic. However, the most likely reason for the unpopularity of the directionality of time among critical archaeologists is the threat that it poses to scrutinize much more rigorously what archaeologists do, and in a wider context, than they themselves can manage.[1]

As I have already suggested, the idea that archaeology might become coherently orientated towards politics largely as a result of the arguments and academic practice of existing radical theorists is open to question. As with other groups, their grasp of the organizational techniques for enhancing the rôle of their subject in the wider arena of 'real' politics is deficient, not just because, like other archaeologists, their own social backgrounds tend to be deprived in this sense, but also because coherent, academic- and social-issue-oriented political interventions which might have compensated for it have for some years been lacking in this professional context. Moreover, their theoretical criticisms of archaeology are also deficient through their neglect of how movements for social change in their own and other societies have operated in the past, and how further and deeper changes might be effected in the future. Too often students of the past are advised to tackle this problem in purely intellectual terms. For instance (Hanen & Kelley 1983, pp. 114–15):

> Once we come to understand the socio-political and ideological factors affecting the discipline [of archaeology] we are in a position to take the

next step of evaluating the interests served with a view to selection, on carefully justified intellectual and moral grounds, of the directions to be pursued.

and (Colson 1984, p. 183):

> For us to use our history to learn to do a better job, the historical critique has to be able to discriminate, to make judgements about what is valuable and can be built upon and what is valueless or worse and should be discarded or avoided.

Even if some individuals can be expected to understand the sociopolitics and ideology influencing their subject through intellectual enquiry alone, most people, whether trained academics or not, find it easier to change their opinions under the stimulus of practical engagement with others on issues that affect them more comprehensively than for the satisfaction of curiosity (for an appropriate illustration of this principle, see Ucko 1987). Selecting which line to pursue therefore implies social as well as intellectual options. At present, and for most archaeologists and historians, such things are decided on the basis of private, pragmatic and largely implicit assumptions. Once the criteria for such discriminations are made explicit, they become more fully political in the sense that they are open to being shared, and therefore open to negotiation with other people. However, given a shift from individualized to more-collective working in archaeological theorizing, the process need not stop there. It is almost a cliche that the study of the past benefits from interdisciplinary perspectives, and similarly the social implications of theorizing about the social dimensions of archaeology suggest familiarity with wider social processes and may have an equally salutary effect on the subject. Insofar as archaeologists can secure an accurate impression of functioning, development and change in past societies, and at the same time organize themselves professionally to defend their subject and advance its interests, they will create favourable conditions for future public support of, and participation in, their subject and for social advance in general.

Some of the more obvious obstacles to achieving that goal are clarified by a sociological view of the construction of a framework in which archaeological knowledge is produced. In keeping with an intellectual community in a class-divided society, the efficacy of active thinking is often overrated by comparison with that of thoughtful action. It is significant that although no-one seriously advocates abstract criticism by itself as a suitable response to the wider social problems that archaeologically assisted forms of knowledge might help to solve, the idea of abstract criticism does play a special rôle in attempts to deal with the more parochial difficulties in which archaeology finds itself. This rôle is one of illusion: as everyone knows, what counts in academic and professional circles, as at other levels of daily life, is winning not just arguments but positions of influence and control, requiring skills of institutionalized micropolitics. The level of the politics makes all the difference to the consciousness of most of those concerned, because what archaeologists can handle or appreciate in their professional lives is in practice as political as anything on the news, yet their own social background and experience encourage a limited view of how, if at all, they themselves might engage with the politics of the wider world. It is therefore not surprising that some of the sharpest criticism of orthodox archaeology is now coming from those furthest from academic parochialism: from the Third (and Fourth) World and from Blacks and women in the West (Blakey 1983).

Although a greater proportion of contemporary archaeologists may be women or from the working class or ethnic minorities than was the case in the past, the profession as a whole still seems to be dominated by relatively privileged white men. At least in Great Britain and France, the percentage of students from working-class backgrounds in most colleges and universities, even at the high point when the post-World War II bulge went through tertiary education in the late 1960s, never gave them a position of numerical or cultural dominance. The structure of inequality in education therefore restricted (although it did not completely prevent) the influence of even limited forms of working-class experience in trade union and labour movement politics on the archaeological profession at a time when it was of interest to a still small, but in relative terms unusually large, number of students from working-class backgrounds.

Once enrolled, students of varying backgrounds have long been subjected to intense and unprecedented experiences that can shape their attitudes for the rest of their lives. To the extent that their activities in the political field had the character of mass politics outside the student community, this experience would have paralleled that of the organized working class, with commensurate implications for the future views and continued involvement of those concerned. To a remarkable extent this did, in fact, happen during the late 1960s and early 1970s in several Western countries, but the idea of a link between the theoretical direction of their subjects, the content of their courses of study, and the sometimes spectacular discontinuities in the extra-academic 'world outside' (discontinuities which, in retrospect, can seem less dramatic than some of the claims made for them at the time) was never strongly developed. A compartmentalized experience translated implicitly into a view that the world itself is compartmentalized in a similar way, and thus that the social practice of archaeology could be separated from the social experience of archaeologists. To a lesser degree (because the individuals concerned are older and arguably have more attitude-restricting commitments), similar considerations apply to the post-student lives of professional archaeologists. Whether in college departments, government or local service, or in other careers, the opportunity for alternative ideas of politics to intrude on the way in which the subject is practised depends on the extent to which such professionals are exposed to such ideas, and especially to activities that give substance to the ideas themselves, in the course of their work. When economic and political systems are in a state of crisis, demanding reductions in what had been provided in easier, more liberal (or social democratic) times, the opportunities for such experiences are generally increased. As these problems are growing more difficult, it is therefore possible that direct involvement of significant numbers of archaeologists in kinds of political action for which their previous personal and professional experience did not prepare them will itself begin to encourage them to think about their subject in new ways, particularly in terms of the relationship between theoretical formulations and wider politics.

Acknowledgements

This chapter revises some ideas about reflexive archaeology that were presented but inadequately explored in a discussion paper at the World Archaeological Congress under the title 'Capitalism as an archaeological problem'. For comments and criticisms of the earlier paper I am grateful to Howard Creamer, Peter Gathercole, Joan Gero, Dolores Root and Nick Winder. Malcolm McLeod made helpful criticisms of an earlier draft of this chapter. None of these people, of course, is responsible for the outcome.

Note

1   By the idea that time is *directional* I simply mean to re-emphasize, in Eagleton's (1981, p. 51) expression, 'that the past is a discursive construct of the present; but it is not, of course, merely an imaginary back-projection of it. Materialism must insist on the irreducibility of the real to discourse; it must also remind historical idealism that if the past itself – by definition – no longer exists, its *effects* certainly do'. Effects do not precede their causes.

References

Blakey, M. L. 1983. Socio-political bias and ideological production in historical archaeology. In *The socio-politics of archaeology*, J. M. Gero, D. M. Lacey and M. L. Blakey (eds), 5–16. Amherst: Department of Anthropology, University of Massachusetts.

Colson, E. 1984. Defining American ethnology. In *Social contexts of American ethnology, 1840–1984*. Proceedings of the American Ethnological Society Annual Spring Meeting, J. Helm (ed.), 177–84.

Eagleton, T. 1981. *Walter Benjamin or towards a revolutionary criticism*. London: Verso.

Gathercole, P. 1984. A consideration of ideology. In *Marxist perspectives in archaeology*. M. Spriggs (ed.), 149–54. Cambridge: Cambridge University Press.

Gero, J. M., D. M. Lacey & M. L. Blakey (eds) 1983. *The socio-politics of archaeology*, Research report no. 23. Amherst: Department of Anthropology, University of Massachusetts.

Hanen, M. P. & J. H. Kelley 1983. Social and philosophical frameworks for archaeology. In *The socio-politics of archaeology*. Research report no. 23, J. M. Gero, D. M. Lacy & M. L. Blakey (eds), 107–17, Amherst: Department of Anthropology, University of Massachusetts.

Hodder, I. 1986. Politics and ideology in the World Archaeological Congress. In *Politics and archaeology. Archaeological review from Cambridge*, A. Pratap & N. Rao (eds), 113–18.

Leff, G. 1969. *History and social theory*. London: Merlin Press.

Leone, M. P., P. B. Potter Jr & P. A. Shackel 1987. Toward a critical archaeology. *Current Anthropology* **28**(3), 283–92.

LeRoy, G. C. 1976. Literary study and political activism: how to heal the split. In *Weapons of criticism: Marxism in America and the literary tradition*. N. Rudich (ed.), 75–104. Palo Alto: Ramparts Press.

Miller, D. & C. Tilley (eds) 1984. *Ideology, power and prehistory*. Cambridge: Cambridge University Press.

Patterson, T. C. 1986. The last sixty years: toward a social history of Americanist archeology in the United States. *American Anthropologist* **88**(1), 7–26.

Potter, P. B. Jr & M. P. Leone 1986. Liberation not replication: 'Archaeology in Annapolis' analysed. *Journal of the Washington Academy of Sciences* **76**(2), 97–105.

Pratap, A. & N. Rao (eds) 1986. Archaeology and politics. *Archaeological Review from Cambridge* **5**(1).

Rowlands, M. J. 1984. Objectivity and subjectivity in archaeology. In *Marxist perspectives in archaeology*, M. Spriggs (ed.), 108–13. Cambridge: Cambridge University Press.

Trigger, B. G. 1985. Writing the history of archeology: a survey of trends. In *Objects and others: essays on museums and material culture, History of anthropology*, Vol. 3, G. W. Stocking Jr (ed.). Madison: University of Wisconsin Press.

Ucko, P. J. 1987. *Academic freedom and apartheid. The story of the World Archaeological Congress*. London: Duckworth.

Wylie, A. 1989. Matters of fact and matters of interest. In *Archaeological approaches to cultural identity*, S. J. Shennan (ed.), ch. 5. London: Unwin Hyman.

4 An epistemological enquiry into some archaeological and historical interpretations of 17th century Native American–European relations

MICHAEL S. NASSANEY

Introduction

A spectre is haunting archaeology. This spectre is the claim made by some New Archaeologists that the past can be objectively knowable. Dissatisfaction with such claims, and the concordant methods and goals of the New Archaeology, have led some investigators to re-examine the epistemological basis for our understanding of the past (for example, Hodder 1985). Explicit recognition of the relationship between archaeological or historical interpretations and their sociocultural contexts provides a point of departure to construct a critique of objectivism (see Wylie 1985, Ch. 5, this volume). In the course of the critique I will show that 'objective' interpretations of the archaeological record are ideologically charged while serving to empower those with access to the record.

The nature and extent of the social transformations that accompanied a culture contact situation, specifically Native American and European interactions, provide a case study. The history of Native Americans is laden with legends and myths that refuse to die (Campbell & LaFantasie 1978, p. 67). In the case of English relations with the Narragansett of southeastern New England in North America (Fig. 4.1), there has been the creation of a 'dual mythology, two separate myths that parallel each other, yet are so very different from each other' (ibid., p. 67). One myth, which appears most often in historical writings, stresses European domination (for example, Durfee 1849). The other attempts to counter this view by maintaining that the Narragansett successfully resisted European acculturation and their 'traditions . . . persisted and remained virtually intact throughout the following three hundred years of history' (ibid., p. 68). The latter myth is currently being creatively reproduced and supported by ethnic and archaeological interpretations of a 17th century Native American cemetery.

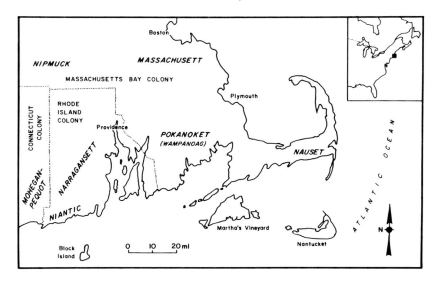

Figure 4.1 Early 17th century aboriginal territories in New England, showing the location of the Narragansett people and neighbouring groups.

Rethinking objectivity: the case of culture contact

In a discipline devoid of both a unified theory and a dominant paradigm for addressing the relationship between human action and material products and precedents, ambiguity is likely to arise in any attempt to explain the meaning of the composition and configuration of an archaeological site or assemblage. Cemeteries, as a particular site type, are often perceived as important archaeological contexts for understanding social and ideological aspects of human behaviour. However, a burial pattern is not necessarily a direct behavioural reflection of social patterns (Hodder 1982). Moreover, the ambiguity of the relationship between material remains and human action can often result in equally plausible interpretations that are mutually contradictory. Archaeologists are left with the unenviable task of having to decide among multiple explanations, each of which appears to be based on objective observations. I maintain that the process of observing a cultural context is essentially one of translation and intersubjective interpretation. Thus, claims of archaeological or scientific objectivity must be called into question.

Although a claim can be made that all archaeological remains are ambiguously patterned, cemeteries seem to be even more confusing in comparison with other archaeological contexts. First, cemeteries represent ritual space – a location in which social contraditions are articulated (Turner 1967). Burial patterns are structured through symbolically meaningful codes which can mask or otherwise distort social relationships. Secondly, material items (e.g. grave goods) have no inherent meaning – they acquire meaning in a cultural context. Thirdly, the events of the past are separate from the culture-centred meanings which we give them. Archaeological interpretations tend to propagate the values of one's own culture. Reconstructions of the past 'directly serve the interests of the present; they are a medium for the self-definition and self-legitimation of those who create . . . them' (Wylie 1985, p. 138). The past becomes a creation which (often unconsciously) serves to legitimate the present and reinforce one's own values; in other words, a fable people have agreed to admit as true (Voltaire, cited in Campbell & LaFantasie 1978, p. 67).

Archaeological interpretation, as part of the production of knowledge, is ideologically charged. The production of archaeological information and its content are organized to mirror the general social production of ideas and the general social relations (of production) that characterize society or segments thereof (Lewontin 1983, p. 14). Although some maintain that such production occurs in an ethically neutral setting (cf. Harvey 1973), it is argued here that the scientific method serves to 'establish . . . [and reinforce] . . . facts in such a way that they fit into theory as currently accepted' (Horkheimer 1972, p. 197). The production of knowledge, as constituted through scientific activity, consists of instances in which a segment of society comes to grips with nature and recreates it in its own image. The result obtains from the mode of production practised in particular forms of society (*ibid.*, p. 197).

The significance and meaning of a configuration of cultural phenomena can only be rendered intelligible by exploring the context of an interpretation's creation. In other words, in the process of appropriating the past, certain elements of the archaeological and historical record are given greater significance than others. Indeed, the subject matter, in all of its richness, is constituted through the very act of observation. As a consequence knowledge of cultural reality is always knowledge from a particular point of view (Weber 1949, p. 81).

Just as artefacts of the past can be studied to understand people of other times, so too can cemetery interpretations themselves be studied as artefacts of the social group producing the interpretations. A critical analysis of mortuary studies becomes, in effect, an ethnography of archaeology (Nassaney 1985). Knowledge of the past is produced within a cultural context and is an artefact of and a tool in that context. Social systems exploit the inherent ambiguities of mortuary archaeology by interjecting sociological and ideological messages that serve to produce and reproduce the existing social order (Leone 1981).

A major dilemma in culture contact studies is the reconciliation of two obvious but seemingly contradictory viewpoints. On the one hand, Native American societies and ways of life changed drastically after European contact; yet at the same time Native American ethnic identities and societies persisted (Berkhofer 1976b, pp. 102–3). The epistemological problem of the relationship between the past and the present in the study of indigenous history is often excused by noting that present enquiry 'has not yet advanced to the point of offering a well-documented objective view' (Fitzhugh 1985b, p. 9). Interpretations of a 17th century Native American cemetery provide a case study to explore how we come to know the past, why we seek to know the past, and the relationships between the past and the present. Interpretations tend to emphasize either continuity or change when they are used to 'explain' indigenous responses to culture contact. Interpretations obtain from particular points of view; each ultimately dependent on specific assumptions and sensitive sociopolitical issues within and between the archaeological community and the 20th century descendants of the cemetery population in question. Recent interpretations of 17th century Native American behaviour in southeastern New England (Nassaney 1986, Robinson *et al*. 1985) warrant a fuller exposition of the archaeological, ethnohistoric and ethnographic contexts that have structured these studies.

Historical context

Seventeenth-century Native American societies of southeastern New England were being invaded. The invaders were explorers who belonged to societies which operated on principles fundamentally different from those of their indigenous hosts, leading to a predictable clash between practices and world views. The first known written account of an aboriginal group on Narragansett Bay dates to AD 1524, although sustained contact with Europeans began nearly 100 years later when the Pilgrims landed at Plymouth, Massachusetts in 1620 (Fig. 4.1). At that time the Narragansett were the paramount tribal group in southeastern New England (Williams 1827), having survived the pestilence of 1616–17 which devastated their rivals to the east, the Pokanokets. In the spring of 1621 the Narragansett sent a snake skin filled with arrows to the colonists as a symbol demanding customary tribute. The colonists responded by returning the snake skin filled with gunpowder, a clear denial of Narragansett authority.

Since the remaining Pokanokets had aligned themselves with Plymouth Colony, the Narragansett sought to create a balance of power and obtain ready access to European commodities by inviting the outcast Roger Williams to settle at Providence (1636) and to establish a trading post to the south at Wickford, Rhode Island (Cocumscussoc; Fig. 4.2). Increasingly, the Narragansett entered a lucrative trading relationship with the British. Many material items of Narragansett culture were being replaced by European items. In short, the Narragansett became linked to the European market system (cf. Wolf 1982). However, there is little agreement over how heartily they embraced their new connections.

A major change in the political climate of southern New England occurred in 1636–7 after the Pequot War. British interest in the wampum production of eastern Long Island, New York, led them to wage war in order to obtain

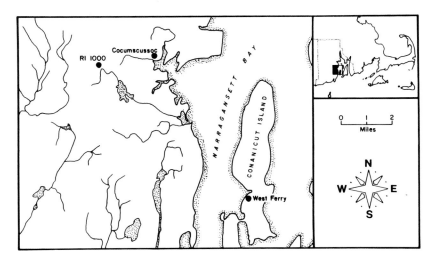

Figure 4.2   Map of the Cocumscussoc vicinity in Rhode Island colony, showing the locations of selected 17th century sites.

the right of customary tribute. The Narragansett remained neutral, having been promised by the Massachusetts Bay Colony that they (the Narragansett) would 'assume the . . . tribute-collecting . . . privileges formerly assumed by the Pequots' (Salisbury 1982, p. 229). However, this rôle was filled by a different British entity: the Connecticut Colony. The Narragansett received only a portion of the Pequot survivors as subjects (*ibid.*, p. 229). The Narragansett position in southeastern New England became increasingly tenuous in 1643, with the execution of Miantonomi, co-sachem and nephew of Canonicus, by Uncas, a neighbouring rival. The act was indirectly supported by the United Colonies. In 1644 the Narragansett submitted voluntarily to King Charles I of Britain (Bartlett 1856, pp. 134–6) 'to protect themselves from further treachery' (Simmons 1978, p. 194). By the 1660s, significant parcels of the eastern portion of Narragansett country had been mortgaged or sold, or both (Bartlett 1856), including the lands south of Cocumscussoc adjacent to the RI 1000 cemetery (see below).

The turning point of the 17th century for southern New England was King Philip's War. The Narragansett were drawn into it when they refused to surrender Pokanoket refugees to the United Colonies (Chapin 1931, p. 78). On 19 December 1675 the Army of the United Colonies entered the Narragansett refuge in the Great Swamp, inflicting massive casualties. The number of Narragansett casualties in the fort is unknown (Campbell & LaFantasie 1978). Nevertheless, numerous Narragansett survivors were sold into slavery or otherwise forced into servitude (Boissevain 1963, and others), as indicated by census figures for the early 18th century (Channing 1886). The remaining Narragansett survivors moved to southern Rhode Island, where they merged with the Niantics and collectively became known as Narragansett (Simmons 1981, p. 37).

The 18th and 19th centuries brought chronic problems to the Narragansett, both politically (internally and externally) and socially. These tendencies culminated with the decision of the state of Rhode Island to initiate detribalization proceedings as a measure to integrate the tribe legally into the community (Boissevain 1963). Claimants to a share of the quit-claim money ($5000) from the state were limited to 324 acceptable members (Boissevain 1963, pp. 497–8).

In this century the American Indian Reorganization Act of 1934 encouraged and enabled the Narragansett to reassert their tribal status (Boissevain 1975, pp. 89–91). At present the Narragansett have re-established themselves as a federally recognized sovereign tribal entity. In doing so, they must continuously reaffirm their ethnic identity. In the process of retribalization they have sought to convince the public that the Narragansett tribe still exists and that a number of persons have a right to be known as Narragansett. The means by which this identity has been asserted have taken many forms (see Boissevain 1963, 1975, Hicks & Kertzer 1972, Simmons 1978, 1981), including a Narragansett concern with writing their history from a native point of view.

Narragansett cosmology and mortuary ritual

Information about 17th century Narragansett cosmology and mortuary ritual can be gleaned from Roger Williams' *A key into the language of America* (1827), first published in London in 1643, 'the first English language ethnography of an American Indian people' (Simmons 1978, p. 197). As with any historical document, however, Williams' work is subject to critical interpretation. A provocative analysis of *A key* suggests that although a negative view of the Indian as expressed in much of the colonial literature was determined by Puritan convictions, 'the perspective from which Williams penned his positive response to the native was shaped by the spirit of Renaissance humanism' (Teunissen & Hinz 1976).

With these qualifications in mind, Roger Williams informs us that the chief religious practitioner was the powwow, shaman or medicine man. He presided over cultural rituals and rites performed in the event of drought, famine, sickness and war (Simmons 1978). This activity was addressed to the creator, *Cautantowwit*, who resided to the south-west. After death the human spirit was destined to return to *Cautantowwit*'s house 'where it continued in an afterlife similar to life on earth' (Simmons 1978, p. 192). Death marked the beginning of the soul's journey to the afterlife. The journey was a rite of passage, not unlike birth. According to the Narragansett, individuals were buried in a flexed or foetal position to symbolize the transition from one world to the next.

The prescriptions of mortuary ritual were directed by a respected tribal member who was designated the tribal mortician, or *Mockatassuit* (Williams 1827). The tribal mortician was responsible for the preparation of individual corpses for their post-mortem journey. The preparation, although incompletely described, appears to have been highly ritualized. Individuals were placed or wrapped in mats or blankets and buried with artefacts appropriate to their rôle and status (Simmons 1970). The replacement of Indian objects by European goods to accompany the dead is poorly understood. It has been suggested that the latter 'were deemed to be in great favor but short supply' in the afterworld, and therefore were being sent up in increasing quantities (Simmons 1970, p. 44).

Legitimating the quotidian: the RI 1000 cemetery

In the summer of 1982 several human burials were exposed by a bulldozer operator in southeastern New England. Further investigations disclosed a partially disturbed 17th century Native American cemetery (Robinson & Gustafson 1982). Consultation among the Rhode Island Historical Preservation Commission, the Narragansett tribe and the landowner led to the complete excavation of the cemetery the following season (Nassaney 1984, Robinson *et al.* 1985). The Narragansett were influential and significant contributors during the planning, recovery and (evidently) interpretive phases of the archaeological project. For example, 'the Chief Sachem and [Tribal] Council designated a tribal member to work with the project on a daily basis during fieldwork and as liaison during analysis' (Robinson *et al.* 1985, p. 113). On more than one occasion the tribal representative called on the tribal medicine man to oversee the removal of sacred objects, which were then appropriated or curated in a manner consistent with native custom. (In each case the objects were known to have 'great power'.) Furthermore, the Narragansett were provided with copies of manuscripts before their reading at conferences. Thus, Native American consultation was a significant factor throughout the duration of the project. According to Robinson *et al.* (1985, p. 113) 'the participation of the Narragansett Chief Sachem and Tribal Council have *facilitated synthesis of perspectives* on seventeenth-century history and the dynamics of culture contact' (emphasis added).

The cemetery, designated RI 1000, contained the skeletal remains and grave associations of 56 individuals. Diagnostic artefacts appear to have been manufactured between AD 1630 and 1670 with few exceptions (Turnbaugh 1984), and were deposited in the ground with the interments beginning after 1650. The cemetery was organized by rows aligned perpendicularly to the general south-west orientation of the individual graves (Fig. 4.3). Individuals were placed in a flexed position, facing east, with the tops of their heads to the south-west. Associated grave goods were usually found to the east of the individual, between the head and the waist. Thus, the cemetery is characterized by a systematic orientation of graves and homogeneity in burial posture.

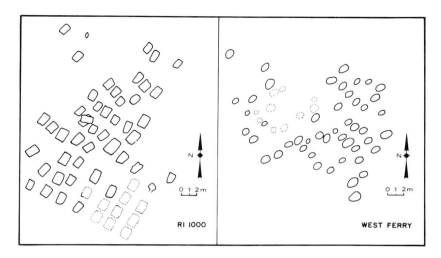

Figure 4.3 Comparative plan views of the RI 1000 and West Ferry cemeteries. Dotted lines represent hypothetical locations of burials disturbed in 1936 (West Ferry) and 1982 (RI 1000). (West Ferry plan redrawn from *Cautantowwit's House* by William S. Simmons, by permission of University Press of New England. Copyright 1970 by Brown University.)

Recent investigators (for example, Robinson *et al.* 1985) have interpreted the composition and configuration of RI 1000 as an expression of Native American resistance to European domination. Continuity is emphasized over change. This position deflects away from the strategies which Native Americans used to accommodate themselves to European arrival, settlement and eventual domination. The following evidence is presented in support of this viewpoint (see Nassaney 1986, p. 7). First, many European grave goods from RI 1000 exhibit evidence of modifications such as repair, reworking and reuse. These modifications and inferred activities are interpreted as indications of a Narragansett conservatism with regard to European material goods. Secondly, it is suggested that Narragansett involvement in European commodity exchange was confined to wampum production. It is claimed that the production of wampum would not have altered the seasonal round or traditional economic activities of Narragansett society. Evidence of wampum production is represented in the archaeological record by finished beads and artefacts of production (Turnbaugh 1984). Fewer artefacts associated with wampum production were found at RI 1000 than at the West Ferry site, a slightly earlier Narragansett cemetery nearby (Fig. 4.2). The significance of the decreased quantity of artefacts associated with wampum production is not clear, although one might interpret this pattern as evidence of decreased production. In addition, finished beads in graves might be thought to express the desire to remove wampum from circulation. The frequency and context of these remains could be interpreted as effective strategies used by the Narragansett to resist European domination.

The organization of the cemetery is also interpreted as evidence of Native American autonomy through the argument that persistence of Narragansett religious beliefs and mortuary practices would be reflected in homogeneity in the attributes of burial posture and orientation. Therefore, similarities in burial posture between RI 1000 and the earlier West Ferry cemetery are considered indicative of the persistence of native religious beliefs (Robinson *et al.* 1985, p. 109). Furthermore, the closer spacing of individuals at RI 1000 is interpreted as 'increased efficiency in the use of space' suggesting 'a more rigorous attention to detail, perhaps an intensification of mortuary practice' (*ibid.*, p. 124).

Thus, a picture emerges of a 17th century Native American community reluctantly involved (at best) with European commodity production while seeking to maintain traditional (i.e. pre-contact) cultural practices and ethnic group solidarity in the face of a markedly changing world of interethnic relations. Although the Narragansett may not have heartily welcomed all aspects of British colonization, their survival strategies were complex, heterogeneous, and often subtle. I suggest that interpretations of the past which fail to consider the varied and sophisticated responses of the Narragansett may fill a politically expedient rôle, but one that is anthropologically and epistemologically naive.

I argue that the assumptions underlying an emphasis on resistance, continuity and persistence ultimately derive from attitudes related to the process of retribalization in this century, whereby the Narragansett have had to convince the public that the tribe is not extinct and that a number of people have the right to be known as Narragansett. The re-creation and renewal of a tribal identity may also be part of a general political strategy towards social justice developed in the mid-20th century in the context of Civil Rights, including the women's and ethnic movements (Robert Paynter, pers. comm.). It is not clear whether this strategy for recognition is unanimous or spearheaded by a segment of the population. Simmons (1981, p. 48) notes that the renewal of Narragansett 'identity is a source of recognition and pride to its adherents and . . . is a symbol of as well as a basis for a range of social commitments which unite them'. However, Simmons (1981, p. 48) ends with a provocative statement:

> Maintenance of this identity now involves an increased interest in cultural authenticity, and requires an increasingly *deliberate denial* of the history of inter-racial and intercultural synthesis which has long been taking place. [Emphasis added.]

Part of this denial is manifest in an ideology which attempts to reproduce social relations in the past as a mirror of social relations in the present – i.e. as a means of legitimating the present. This ideology has embedded within it a view of the past based on the following assumptions and premises: (a) the

Narragansett Tribe of Indians, Inc. (Boissevain 1975, p. 99) is a group directly descended from the Native Americans interred at RI 1000; (b) the Narragansett people are biologically and genetically 'pure'; and (c) presently the Narragansett are culturally autonomous; thus, their ancestors resisted European domination and avoided acculturation. This ideology can be examined from several different perspectives. I maintain that these assertions influence the way in which the archaeological record is interpreted by emphasizing (and removing from context) specific data classes and ignoring others. The relationship between an archaeological interpretation which emphasizes continuity and the ideological goals of the modern tribe is subtle indeed. Although the relationship may not be causal, neither is it coincidental. Rather, it obtains from a 'synthesis of perspectives on seventeenth-century history' (Robinson et al. 1985, p. 113) as 'interpreted in collaboration with Indian descendants' (Fitzhugh 1985a, p. 103). It is my contention that these interpretations exploit a limited set of the entire range of data available to archaeological and anthropological researchers. By ignoring certain dimensions of the ethnohistoric and archaeological database, interpretations are produced which serve native interests. Healy (1984, p. 126) notes that strong political persuasions may require that interpretations adhere rigidly to what might be termed the 'party line'. Divergence from this accepted dogma may result in restricted access to the archaeological record in the future. Having examined the relationship between the proposed interpretations and their sociocultural contexts, we can begin to suggest alternative readings of the archaeological record based on a different set of assumptions.

Another way of telling

Archaeological enquiry is often plagued by a situation in which multiple tenable explanations obtain for an archaeological distribution. I suggest that an alternative reading of the archaeological record at RI 1000 can enhance our knowledge of 17th century cultural interactions and the manner in which 20th century investigators appropriate the past. I maintain that continuity and change are not mutually exclusive processes, but rather that they articulate in a dialectical relationship. Accommodation and resistance constitute complementary and organically connected strategies of ethnic persistence in the face of cultural change (Genovese 1974, p. 78). Moreover, a group need not maintain cultural isolation and biological purity to assert cultural autonomy and ethnic solidarity.

The dialectic of accommodation and resistance is discussed in McLoughlin (1982) in the context of cultural interaction and syncretism between the Cherokee and Euroamerican missionaries in the southeastern USA. He notes (1982, p. 335) that effective resistance among the Cherokee included elements borrowed from the culture that they fought to resist (see Berkhofer 1976a, p. 159). The level of borrowing may take place quite unrealized, for example, 'in [the] acceptance of the broader perspective on science, geography, and human history' (McLoughlin 1982, p. 336). One might also add the unconscious borrowing of fundamental concepts related to the self, society, scale of decision-making and geometrical order – all of which could be expressed archaeologically in a mortuary context (for example, see the discussion on grave shape below). Finally, I might add that cultural strategies of accommodation and resistance are often temporally and spatially variable.

The success of a survival strategy can only be evaluated within a particular context. As an example, the Tunica of the Lower Mississippi Valley represent an extraordinary case of cultural accommodation (Brain 1983, McEwan & Mitchem 1984). With a long (pre-)history 'as commercial agents in the salt trade, they were able to use their economic prowess to their advantage in dealing with the French in both salt and horses' (McEwan & Mitchem 1984, p. 274). Tunica survival in the 20th century suggests that their strategy of 'exploiting rather than fighting [i.e. resisting] the economic opportunities which accompanied the arrival of the French was crucial to their success' (ibid., p. 275).

If we view the RI 1000 cemetery remains from the point of view of cultural accommodation – that is, that the Narragansett chose to incorporate European elements in their world view to rationalize a changing social order – then a different interpretation of the archaeological record emerges. An argument to support this perspective can be constructed from the following evidence. First, it is noted that a greater proportion of individuals received grave goods at RI 1000 than at the West Ferry cemetery. These grave goods are interpreted as evidence of new wealth that was given continuity and rationality in the context of mortuary practice. However, changes in the economy of Narragansett society may have been more dramatic than some investigators have led us to believe. Wolf (1982) has described the mechanisms of an expanding European mercantilism which provided individual Native Americans with new opportunities for socio-economic mobility outside of their traditional economic rôles (see also Brenner 1984, Robinson et al. 1985, pp. 124–6). Thus, the process of acquiring the goods themselves represents fundamentally different intracommunity relationships. Although the goods may have been evenly distributed, careful examination shows that grave goods carried neither equal value nor similar symbolic meaning, as attested by the grave lots themselves and their ease of acquisition. Both male and female rôles are expressed (Turnbaugh 1984) and, more importantly, certain constellations of items may be interpreted as symbols of status and authority, perhaps available to limited segments of society.

In 17th century southern New England native entrepreneurs were using imported European material goods as burial accompaniments to mark symbolically political rôles and relations of inequality (Brenner 1984). Although some goods were clearly utilitarian in function and had been repaired and reworked, certain artefacts such as latten spoons show little evidence of wear (Turnbaugh 1984), suggesting that they were acquired explicitly for placement with the dead. Thus, the quantity, distribution and nature of grave goods can be used to infer changing material relationships within the community.

Secondly, changing material relationships may be associated with transformations in the relationships between the self and society, the scale of decision-making and structural concepts of order. Economic relations of production were being transformed. For example, documentary evidence exists for the use of voluntary Indian labour by Rhode Island settlers as early as the middle of the 17th century (Sainsbury 1975). Roger Williams mentioned in a letter to Winthrop (10 July 1637, cited in Dorr 1885, p. 210) that Indians served as guides, messengers and scouts. Other economic rôles included the construction of stone fences, search for and capture of renegades, cattle herding and bounty hunting for wolves (Rider 1904, Sainsbury 1975). Thus, the introduction of a cash economy had significant ramifications. A capitalist mode of production (Wolf 1982) is often accompanied by an 'economic mentality' (Geertz 1963) and a different conception of order. Identifiable correlates of an economic mentality include (ibid., p. 120):

> increased flexibility of land tenure, growth of individualism and slackening of extended family ties; greater class differentiation and conflict; . . . weakening of traditional authority and wavering of traditional social standards.

The economic processes of uneven accumulation within class societies are mediated through a 'hegemonic ideology – "hegemonic" because it compels . . . [segments of society] . . . to define themselves within the ruling system even while resisting its aggression' (Genovese 1974, p. 77).

Given the social and political climate of 17th century southern New England, it is probable that some Narragansett entrepreneurs welcomed the new economic opportunities which promoted cultural change. However, not only were pre-European *economic* pursuits being modified, but changes in group identity were also occurring.

In 1644 the Narragansett signed a document placing themselves under the protection of King Charles I (Bartlett 1856, pp. 134–6). Then in 1663 the Narragansett sachems and Ninegret (Niantic sachem) renewed their submission to the King. The attempt to use the power of the monarchy as a counterweight to the Puritans is a politically sophisticated move 'represent[ing] an effort to fit themselves into the new order whites had created' (Sehr 1977, p. 51). Again, tactics of submission are interpreted as part of a larger strategy, not of outright resistance but rather of carefully executed political understanding. The Narragansett were not alone in their tactics of submission. To the east, individual Wampanoags used the Plymouth Colony courts in the 1660s to protect their diminishing land resources by registering title to specific lands (Weinstein 1983, p. 81). The strategy of employing the European legal system to their benefit represents a fundamentally different understanding of land-use rights and an accommodation to the European presence.

The configuration of the RI 1000 cemetery also expresses changing conceptions of spatial order. Simmons (1970) consistently noted that the West Ferry graves were oval in plan, with concave bottoms. In contrast the RI 1000 graves were clearly rectangular, exhibiting right-angled corners and flat bottoms (Fig. 4.3). Different implements were apparently used to excavate the graves in each of these cemeteries. It is not clear whether the rectangular graves at RI 1000 were merely the result of using square European shovels or whether they represent a conscious attempt by the Narragansett to imitate European grave shape. In any event, the spatial configuration of the cemetery expresses a new conception of order adopted by the Narragansett.

As indicated above, the scale of Narragansett decision-making also seems to have been affected during the period discussed. Although it has been assumed that decisions were made for the good of the group, it would appear that individual actors were making decisions to effect personal gain. Within a cash economy the non-random distribution of grave goods suggests differential access to European commodities. The acquisition and disposition of these goods express individual strategies aimed at satisfying the wants, needs and expectations of a new social milieu.

It is important to emphasize that individual social strategies were variable, not homogeneous. Social actions were motivated by different perceptions of the nature of cultural encroachment and the appropriate means of rationalizing this changing world view. In times of rapid social change, certain leaders may emerge and undertake to alter or revitalize a society in some way (Kottak 1982, p. 353). In the cross-fire of dynamic social strategies and ambiguous representation of symbolic messages, the tribal mortician may have anticipated the end of his own claim to traditional legitimacy. As conversions were rampant among surrounding aboriginal groups (e.g. John Eliot's conversions among the Massachusett), the Mockatussuit may have felt threatened by the new social order. Consequently, he may have sought to consolidate and revitalize a changing Narragansett society through increased attention to one of the few available private contexts still remaining – mortuary ritual space. The systematic spatial configuration and the homogeneity in the placement of individual interments at RI 1000 were a means of expressing ideal (egalitarian) social relationships in aboriginal society. Although certain objects (e.g. grave goods) may have served to distinguish individual actors by marking political inequalities, the living simultaneously sought to organize individual graves and the cemetery so as to mask asymmetries in access to material resources. Thus, the systematization and intensification of mortuary ritual is interpreted as a means of revitalizing a rapidly changing (perhaps declining) set of beliefs.

The turmoil of King Philip's War (1675–6) marks a turning point in the history of Native American–English relations in southern New England. Interestingly, 'the Narragansett did not immediately enter [the] War, but attempted to maintain neutrality' (Robinson *et al.* 1985, p. 111). Narragansett means of survival and persistence as an ethnic group in the years immediately following King Philip's War are of crucial importance. Several investigators (for example, Boissevain 1963, Channing 1886) have documented biological accommodations which the Narragansett made to declining group size. Unfortunately, no clear count exists of the number of Narragansett surviving King Philip's War. What is fairly certain is that many of the Narragansett who were not sold to the West Indies worked as indentured servants and in other domestic tasks in the Narragansett country. Channing (1886, p. 10) notes that 'slavery, both negro and Indian, reached a development in colonial Narragansett [place name] unusual in the colonies north of Mason and Dixon's line. In 1730 South Kingstown [area immediately south of RI 1000] contained 965 whites, 333 negroes, and 223 Indians'.

Boissevain (1963, p. 494) summarizes the plight of the Narragansett beginning in the early 18th century:

> Obviously, this servitude in homes and plantations had the effect of speeding up the Indians' acculturation. Besides this it initiated a thoroughgoing racial mixture between the Indians and Negro slaves. This mixture has been so profound that there is at present hardly a Narragansett family living in the area of their homeland that does not reveal some Negroid traits. Mixture with the White colonists also took place, making the present day Narragansett a group composed of mixed types and extremes. Already in 1880 this was noted and the tribal members were described as 'from glossy black to shining white'.

However, she concludes (*ibid.*, p. 500) that 'in the 80 years since detribalization [1880], the Narragansett have not lost their identity', a conclusion which is not altogether inconsistent with the view that identities are creatively produced and reproduced in the process of dynamic social interaction.

Summary and conclusions

The way in which we interpret the past cannot be divorced from the way in which we perceive the present, especially when access to political and economic power is at stake. The major goal of an ethnography of archaeology is to explicate the linkages between archaeological interpretations and their sociocultural contexts. I have tried to show how the current 'party line' interpretation of a 17th century Native American cemetery in southern New England, in its emphasis on resistance, continuity and persistence, is influenced by 20th century Native American conceptions of themselves and archaeologists' concern with the creation of an 'objective' view of the past, free from the biases of the dominant society. By bringing a different set of assumptions to the data, an alternative interpretation can be suggested which: (a) is consistent with the larger archaeological, ethnohistorical and ethnographic datasets presented herein; (b) is potentially acceptable to the Narragansett *and* to the archaeological community; and (c) attributes the Narragansett with a creative rôle in dealing with the new social context of European encroachment, without confining their strategies to stubborn resistance or passive acceptance of an inevitable fate (cf. Merrell 1984). Certainly 'Indians . . . resisted European domination, often tenaciously and heroically, but they . . . also succumbed to it . . . (M)ost of the changes in their way of life since European colonization have been responses to a loss of power' (Trigger 1986, p. 263). Survival under the documented conditions is itself evidence that the Narragansett have successfully learned to live with the world around them. The alternative perspective which I advocate should stand as a critique of the current explanation of indigenous responses to change – a critique which is itself subject to further analysis and contextualization.

An issue which I have yet to address concerns the 20th century Narragansett motivations and tactics to create a particular past; a past which often 'deliberately denies' certain aspects of the Colonial encounter. Certainly, the rôle of the state, which establishes the criteria for indigenous sovereignty and legitimacy, must be considered (Robert Paynter, pers. comm.). For example, the adoption of pan-Indian traits (feathers, moccasins, Plains Indian dress, etc.) in the 1930s represents a form of invented tradition (Hobsbawm & Ranger 1984) which served to authenticate Narragansett identity and to foster an image of 'Indian-ness'. The state's insistence on continuity and persistence makes it difficult (if not impossible) for Native ethnic groups to assert their legitimacy without sufficient evidence; most notably through unambiguous outward signs of Indian-ness which are interpreted as signs of cultural continuity. Thus, the Narragansett and other Indian groups are forced to define and symbolize their ethnicity on the basis of criteria established by the dominant society. In a very real sense all of our pasts contain substantial elements of invented tradition, since the writing of history and the creation of a past is part of the continuing process of negotiation that occurs in any social relationship.

Ultimately, as anthropologists and social scientists we cannot evaluate the truthfulness of an interpretation. Any claim to objectivity fails to recognize the ideological constraints placed upon any and all modes of enquiry and explication. Rather, archaeological and historical interpretations emphasize different points of view for political and economic purposes. Interpretations are best evaluated with regard to their usefulness toward achieving specific ends, and in the ways in which they can be used to promote a greater sensitivity to and understanding of the human condition and the motivations for human action.

Acknowledgements

I owe considerable appreciation to numerous scholars and colleagues for contributing their ideas and constructive criticism over the past few years. Dena Dincauze has been especially supportive of my research since the first time that I mentioned an interest in the Contact period. Brinkley Messick introduced me to the meaning of interpretation, the limits of objectivity and the nature of the anthropological enterprise. The final versions of the manuscript were carefully scrutinized by Neal Salisbury; an historian with a rare appreciation for the archaeological record. Bob Paynter, Martin Wobst and Ken Sassaman always showed a willingness to discuss critical ways of thinking about the past. Several reviewers provided encouragement throughout the preparation of the manuscript; most notably William Simmons, William Turnbaugh, Mary Ann Levine, Glenn LaFantasie and Brooke Thomas. The comments I received at the World Archaeological Congress, especially from David Lowenthal, Alison Wylie and Stephen Shennan, helped me to understand the wider implications of epistemological enquiry. I have also benefited from Stephen Shennan's editorial comments, which served to focus and strengthen my arguments. I thank Paul Robinson for inviting me to direct the excavations of the RI 1000 cemetery and for provoking me to write this chapter. Without the technical assistance of Ken Sassaman the figures would still be on the draughting table. Lastly, I have adopted the concept of accommodation from the work of Timothy Sehr (1977). I hope that I have used the term in the way in which he intended it to be used. In any event, I alone am responsible for the current of thought that lies within these pages.

References

Bartlett, J. R. 1856. *Records of the colony of Rhode Island and Providence plantations in New England*, Vol. 1. Providence: A. C. Greene.
Berkhofer, R. F., Jr 1976a. *Salvation and the savage*. New York: Atheneum.
Berkhofer, R. F., Jr 1976b. The political context of a new Indian history. In *The American Indian*, N. Hundley (ed.), 101–26. Santa Barbara, California: Clio Press.
Boissevain, E. 1963. Detribalization and group identity: the Narragansett Indian case. *Transactions of the New York Academy of Sciences*, (*Second Series*) **25**, 493–502.
Boissevain, E. 1975. *The Narragansett people*. Phoenix, Arizona: Indian Tribal Series.
Brain, J. P. 1983. Tunica triumph. In *Geoscience and man*, Vol. 23: *Historical archaeology of the eastern United States*, 45–62. Baton Rouge: Louisiana State University Press.
Brenner, E. B. 1984. Strategies for autonomy: ethnic mobilization in seventeenth century southern New England. PhD dissertation, Department of Anthropology, University of Massachusetts, Amherst.
Campbell, P. R. & G. W. LaFantasie 1978. Scattered to the winds of heaven – Narragansett Indians 1676–1880. *Rhode Island History* **37**, 66–83.
Channing, E. 1886. The Narragansett planters: a study of causes. *Johns Hopkins University Studies in Historical and Political Science*, (*Fourth Series*) **3**, 1–23. Baltimore: John Murphy.
Chapin, H. 1931. *Sachems of the Narragansett*. Providence: Rhode Island Historical Society.
Dorr, H. C. 1885. The Narragansetts. *Rhode Island Historical Society Collections* **7**, 135–237.
Durfee, J. 1849. History of the subjection and extermination of the Narragansets. In *The complete works of the Hon. Job Durfee*, T. Durfee (ed.), 203–48. Providence: Gladding & Proud.
Fitzhugh, W. W. 1985a. Commentary on part II. In *Cultures in contact: the European*

impact on native cultural institutions in eastern North America, A.D. 1000–1800, W. W. Fitzhugh (ed.), 99–106. Washington, DC: Smithsonian Institution Press.

Fitzhugh, W. W. 1985b. Introduction. In *Cultures in contact: the European impact on native cultural institutions in eastern North America, A.D. 1000–1800*, W. W. Fitzhugh (ed.), 1–15. Washington, DC: Smithsonian Institution Press.

Geertz, C. 1963. *Agricultural involution: the process of ecological change*. Berkeley: University of California Press.

Genovese, E. D. 1974. *Roll, Jordan, roll: the world the slaves made*. New York: Pantheon.

Harvey, D. 1973. *Social justice and the city*. London: Edward Arnold.

Healy, P. 1984. Archaeology abroad: ethical considerations of fieldwork in foreign countries. In *Ethics and values in archaeology*, E. L. Green (ed.), 123–32. New York: Free Press.

Hicks, G. L. & D. I. Kertzer 1972. Making a middle way: problems of Monhegan identity. *Southwestern Journal of Anthropology* **28**, 1–24.

Hobsbawm, E. & T. Ranger (eds) 1984. *The invention of tradition*. Cambridge: Cambridge University Press.

Hodder, I. 1982. The identification and interpretation of ranking in prehistory: a contextual perspective. In *Ranking, resource and exchange: aspects of the archaeology of early European society*, C. Renfrew & S. J. Shennan (eds), 150–4. Cambridge: Cambridge University Press.

Hodder, I. 1985. Postprocessual archaeology. In *Advances in archaeological method and theory*, Vol. 8, M. B. Schiffer (ed.), 1–26. Orlando: Academic Press.

Horkheimer, M. 1972. *Critical theory* (translated by M. J. O'Connell *et al.*). New York: Seabury Press.

Kottak, C. 1982. *Anthropology: the exploration of human diversity*, 3rd edn. New York: Random House.

Leone, M. 1981. Archaeology's relationship to the present and the past. In *Modern material culture: the archaeology of us*, R. A. Gould & M. B. Schiffer (eds), 5–14. New York: Academic Press.

Lewontin, R. C. 1983. Science as a social weapon. *Occasional Papers* 1. University of Massachusetts, Amherst: Institute for Advanced Study in the Humanities.

McEwan, B. G. & J. M. Mitchem 1984. Indian and European acculturation in the eastern United States as a result of trade. *North American Archaeologist* **5**(4), 271–85.

McLoughlin, W. G. 1982. *Cherokees and missionaries, 1789–1839*. New Haven, Connecticut: Yale University Press.

Merrell, J. H. 1984. The Indians' new world. *William and Mary Quarterly* **41**, 537–65.

Nassaney, M. S. 1984. Composition and configuration: spatial–temporal attributes of a seventeenth century Native American cemetery. Paper presented at the 49th annual meeting of the Society for American Archaeology, Portland, Oregon.

Nassaney, M. S. 1985. Mortuary perspectives in an ethnographic setting: towards a critical analysis of cemetery interpretation. Paper presented at the annual meeting of the Society for Historical Archaeology, Boston, Massachusetts.

Nassaney, M. S. 1986. Objectivity and critical analysis of mortuary remains: a North American case study. In *Archaeological 'objectivity' in interpretation*. World Archaeological Congress, vol. 1 (Mimeo).

Rider, S. S. 1904. *The lands of Rhode Island as they were known to Canonicus and Miantunnomu when Roger Williams came in 1636*. Pawtucket, Rhode Island: Chronicle Printing.

Robinson, P. & G. Gustafson 1982. A partially disturbed 17th Century Indian burial ground in Rhode Island: recovery, preliminary analysis, and protection. *Bulletin of the Archaeological Society of Connecticut* **45**, 41–50.

Robinson, P. A., M. A. Kelley & P. E. Rubertone 1985. Preliminary biocultural interpretations from a seventeenth-century Narragansett Indian cemetery in Rhode Island. In *Cultures in contact: the European impact on native cultural institutions in eastern North America, A.D. 1000–1800*, W. W. Fitzhugh (ed.), 107–30. Washington, DC: Smithsonian Institution Press.

Sainsbury, J. A. 1975. Indian labor in early Rhode Island. *New England Quarterly* **48**, 378–93.

Salisbury, N. 1982. *Manitou and Providence: Indians, Europeans, and the making of New England, 1500–1643*. New York: Oxford University Press.

Sehr, T. J. 1977. Ninigret's tactics of accommodation: Indian diplomacy in New England 1636–1675. *Rhode Island History* **36**, 43–53.

Simmons, W. S. 1970. *Cautantowwit's house: an Indian burial ground on the island of Conanicut in Narragansett Bay*. Providence: Brown University Press.

Simmons, W. S. 1978. Narragansett. In *Handbook of North American Indians*, Vol. 15: *Northeast*, B. G. Trigger (ed.), 190–7. Washington, DC: Smithsonian Institution Press.

Simmons, W. S. 1981. Narragansett identity persistence. In *Hidden minorities: the persistence of ethnicity in American life*, J. H. Rollins (ed.), 35–52. Washington, DC: University Press of America.

Teunissen, J. J. & E. J. Hinz 1976. Roger Williams, Thomas More, and the Narragansett utopia. *Early American Literature* **11**, 281–95.

Trigger, B. G. 1986. Ethnohistory: the unfinished edifice. *Ethnohistory* **33**, 253–67.

Turnbaugh, W. A. 1984. *The material culture of RI-1000, a mid-17th-century Narragansett Indian burial site in North Kingstown, Rhode Island*. Report to the Rhode Island Historical Preservation Commission, Providence. Kingston, Rhode Island: Department of Sociology and Anthropology, University of Rhode Island.

Turner, V. 1967. *The forest of symbols: aspects of Ndembu ritual*. Ithaca: Cornell University Press.

Weber, M. 1949. 'Objectivity' in social science and social policy. In *The methodology of the social sciences* (translated and edited by E. A. Shils & H. A. Finch (eds), 49–112). Glencoe, Illinois: Free Press.

Weinstein, L. L. 1983. Survival strategies: the seventeenth-century Wampanoag and the European legal system. *Man in the Northeast* **26**, 81–6.

Williams, R. 1827. A key into the language of America. *Rhode Island Historical Society Collections* 1. Providence: John Miller.

Wolf, E. 1982. *Europe and the people without history*. Berkeley: University of California Press.

Wylie, A. 1985. Putting Shakertown back together: critical theory in archaeology. *Journal of Anthropological Archaeology* **4**, 133–47.

Wylie, A. 1989. Matters of fact and matters of interest. In *Archaeological approaches to cultural identity*, S. J. Shennan (ed.), ch. 5. London: Unwin Hyman.

5 Matters of fact and matters of interest

ALISON WYLIE

The problem of epistemic limits

'Post-positivist' archaeology is dominated by a renewed, and newly open-ended concern with questions about the epistemic limits of enquiry: what can be understood of the human past and what the status is of knowledge claims about the past. Of course, this was a central issue in the campaign waged by the New Archaeology against traditional forms of practice, but the terms of the debate have shifted significantly. The current point of departure is disillusionment with the New Archaeologists' own 'strongly positive' optimism that all aspects of the past are accessible if only archaeological data were used effectively as a testing ground for hypotheses about the cultural past. It is by now generally accepted that matters of fact, including both past matters of fact and evidential facts about the surviving record of the past, are constructs whose specific form and content depends very largely on the theoretical and ideological presuppositions that researchers bring to enquiry. Serious questions thus arise about whether the available evidence is sufficiently secure to sustain the ambitions of the New Archaeology either in practice or in principle.

The current debate is dominated by a concern to come to grips with this particularly broad and *principled* version of the problem of epistemic limits. In the hands of critics of the New Archaeology, on the one hand, it is the basis for denying that anything of the preoccupation with scientific objectivity and generality can be salvaged as a regulative ideal appropriate to archaeology (see Miller 1982, Hodder 1982a). Where, on the other hand, the 'contextual' nature of factual claims has been recognized even by such a visible proponent of the New Archaeology as Binford, it has been the occasion for renewed efforts to articulate and defend objectivist principles (for example, Binford 1982). In this chapter I examine the process by which the problem of limits has re-emerged, focusing on Binford's response to it, particularly as articulated in debate with contextualists like Hodder, whom he accuses of 'paradigmatic posturing'. Despite vehement opposition, Binford and his opponents both engage elements distinctive of the positions that they oppose at strategic points in their argument. This is indicative of significant limitations in both positions, and I conclude that neither is tenable in pure form. In a more constructive vein, several clear guidelines emerge for articulating a position that comprehends the valid core of objectivist and contextualist insights and suggests a new strategy for addressing the questions about epistemic limits that are central to post-positivist archaeology.

Theoretical and methodological foundations

The problem of epistemic limits originally arose, as indicated, in reflection on traditional research practice which was perceived to be in the grip of a pervasive and paralysing 'anxiety . . . about the task of coming to know what literally does not exist' (to borrow Dray's 1980, p. 29 clause) compounded by an anxiety about the special difficulties of coming to know a human, cultural subject matter that 'literally does not exist'. On the Binfordian analysis this took an extreme (sceptical) form in traditional archaeology because of commitment to two dubious premises: a narrowly empiricist conception of the research enterprise which precluded, as illegitimate, any inferential extension of knowledge claims beyond empirical description of the record, and a self-defeating conception of the cultural subject as consisting of essentially unreconstructable (intangible and idiosyncratic) norms or conventions. Of course, his response was to reject these premises outright and to propose a more congenial alternative conceptual framework for research. Its essential components are:

(a) a theoretical proposal that cultural phenomena must be understood in materialist (ecosystem) terms; and
(b) a two-part methodological proposal that researchers must, first, develop a body of independently secured explanatory principles linking archaeological material with specific causal antecedents and, secondly, systematically test interpretive hypotheses against the archaeological record of the past that they purport to describe or explain.

The former is, in essence, an orienting (quasi-metaphysical) conception of the subject domain which was defended as explanatorily powerful with regard to the archaeological record and as inherently plausible, especially given the authority of aligned anthropological theories. The methodological proposals are defended on the grounds that law-governed explanation and systematic testing are essential components of properly 'scientific' practice, as characterized by positivist theories of science, and appeal to this particular conception of science is defended as because it is the best account available (i.e. most widely accepted, see Watson *et al.* 1974) of the success-making practices of developed (highly theoretical) science. However, the real import of this theory of science is that it underwrites the methodological proposals of the New Archaeology by corroborating the necessary assumption that the epistemic conditions that they require for implementation – the existence of a stable factual ground against which theory can be decisively tested – actually obtain.

I note these empirical and theoretical arguments for the conceptual core of the programme because they are frequently obscured by the rhetoric of reaction against 'traditional' research, and are only now coming into focus as the direct object of debate. In the first instance, the main popular appeal of these proposals was certainly pragmatic; if true, or at least plausible as an account of the conditions and subject of enquiry, they do dramatically broaden the horizons of research. They suggest that the cultural past is, in principle at least, an archaeologically knowable subject. Binford, of course, drew the much stronger, and polemically more compelling conclusion that they provide grounds for rejecting not only the pervasive scepticism that he imputed to traditional research, but also any more nuanced acceptance of limitations like the Hawkes–Piggott 'ladder of inference', according to which different aspects of past cultural contexts are accessible to different degrees, depending on how closely and uniformly determined they are by material (therefore more reliably reconstructable) conditions of life (Hawkes 1954, Piggott 1965). He insisted that, given the ecosystem model, 'there is every reason to expect' that cultural systems are sufficiently integrated (and their material record multiply determined) that 'data relevant to most if not all the components of past sociocultural system [sic] are preserved in the archaeological record' (Binford 1972, pp. 94–5). Binford and the New Archaeologists who embraced his analysis thus declared the philosophical problem of epistemic limits a non–issue (Binford & Binford 1968).

Despite its appealing optimism, this programme has run into two sorts of difficulty which have, together, resurrected the problem of limits. In the first place the methodological component of the programme is widely perceived to have failed to deliver on its promise at a *practical* level. In particular, attempts to design research as a test of explanatory hypotheses have routinely yielded either trivial success with non–controversial or uninteresting hypotheses, or dramatic failure to establish anything determinate about more-significant hypotheses. This problem has concerned Binford since at least 1978 when, in the introduction to *For theory building in archaeology*, he first sketched the diagnosis that it arose because his followers and students, who he now describes as the 'lost second generation' of the New Archaeology, were so preoccupied with testing procedures that they failed to see that these are insufficient, in themselves, to guarantee any transcendence of the limitations of traditional research.

On the face of it Binford would seem to be concerned, in these reflective assessments, simply to minimize the import of the practical difficulties, to assert that they do not reflect on the potential of the programme as a whole, but only on the inadequacies of attempts by the lost generation to bring it into practice. However, there is significantly more to Binford's argument than this when you consider his elaboration of the reasons why testing is inherently limited. He argues that what the lost generation failed to appreciate, most fundamentally, is that observations on the record can tell for or against a test hypothesis (in Binfordian terms, they stand as diagnostic 'symptoms' of particular 'dynamics' or cultural variables) only under interpretation; factual claims are themselves interpretive hypotheses. Recently Binford has put this insight in more general, Kuhnian terms (Kuhn 1970); he observes (Binford & Sabloff 1982) that the essential shortcoming of the New Archaeology was its failure to appreciate the extent to which all research and all knowledge claims are 'paradigm-relative'. Of course, he is resolute that this simply affirms his assessment that the testing programme failed because it was initiated prematurely. If archaeological data stand as evidence only under interpretation, then the lost generation should not have attempted to use it as test evidence before establishing a body of properly scientific interpretive principles – a 'Rosetta Stone' for reliable archaeological code-breaking – capable of securely linking the data to antecedent conditions (1983, p. 12).

In fact, Binford's Kuhnian insight has even more radical implications than this. It reveals a conceptual level of difficulty with the programme (the second sort of difficulty alluded to above) that has compromised its integrity from the outset; the practical problems of implementing specific directives simply serve to bring this deeper difficulty to a head. Kuhnian arguments figure in the programmatic literature of the New Archaeology long before their introduction by Binford; ironically enough, they provide the basis for a criticism of traditional researchers that parallels exactly Binford's objection to the lost generation (see Hill & Evans 1972). As 'narrow empiricists', the New Archaeologists argued, traditional researchers failed to appreciate the theory-ladenness of observational claims; they assumed that the import or 'meaning' of the record is exhausted by whatever they establish about it through direct observation, and are thus forced to conclude that the record can provide no epistemically respectable access to the (unobservable) past. The New Archaeologists invoked Kuhnian insights to establish that this is simply implausible. If observation inevitably incorporates a theoretical component that transcends experience, then the data of observation is as rich evidentially as background theory can make it. Given this, it seemed that 'the practical limitations of our knowledge of the past are not inherent in the nature of the archaeological record; the limitations lie in our methodological naivete, in our lack for principles determining the relevance of archaeological remains to propositions regarding processes and events of the past' (Binford 1972, p. 96).

However, it is self-evident that if this Kuhnian argument proves anything, it proves too much. If the data are, indeed, as extensively plastic as is presumed by the loosely Kuhnian argument appropriated by the New Archaeologists, then it is not clear how they could ever be expected to provide a decisive test of the truth, falsity or empirical adequacy of knowledge claims about the past. The Kuhnian insight may *seem* to support the first of Binford's methodological proposals – it may seem to broaden research horizons dramatically – but, as he has recently acknowledged, it does this at the expense of the second, testing proposal which it directly undermines. Binford's recent turn to Kuhn brings at least this inherent difficulty with the programme into clear focus, although it has even deeper critical implications which Binford has been unwilling to concede. If it is correct in what it claims about the 'theory-ladenness' of *all* observation, which Binford seems to accept when giving his worries about testing their general formulation, then it follows there can be no independent (and decisive) factual test of theoretical claims, whether the subject of these claims is accessible to direct observation or not. Binford's Kuhnian insights would seem, therefore, to undermine his first methodological proposal as much as it does his second, testing proposal. He gives no reason why the worries that he raises about the uncertainty of testing in an archaeological context should not be extended to the 'actualistic' contexts in which the interpretive principles necessary for using the data as evidence will be established.

   The full import of Binford's Kuhnian diagnosis of the problem of testing is, therefore, that it brings into view a fundamental conceptual flaw in the original programme; its ambitions were defined in terms of a theory of science which presumes the existence of a stable, factual base, and yet various New Archaeologists, now including Binford, embrace the conclusions of philosophical critics who purport to demonstrate that this fundamental presupposition is untenable. If the Kuhnian insight is taken seriously, then the practical problems with testing become symptoms of deeper, more-intransigent problems; it suggests that the possibilities for effectively using archaeological data as evidence of the cultural past may be seriously limited in principle. With this, the metaphysical anxiety of traditional archaeology reasserts itself in newly compelling terms.

The objectivist response

Binford is, of course, adamant that the original ambitions of the New Archaeology are in no way compromised by Kuhnian objections, despite endorsing them in quite general terms and despite a strong tradition of external criticism that has treated them (or, more specifically, parallel arguments from sociology of science and neo-Marxist theories of science; see Miller 1982, and contributions to Hodder 1982a) as decisive proof against the 'positivism' of the New Archaeology. The reason for this is that, although he cites Kuhnian insights as authoritative when giving general reasons why testing, on its own, could not but fail, Binford clearly presumes that, in practice, the Kuhnian threat can be circumscribed, that it is a local – not a global – problem; he treats the contextualist insight as limited in breadth (in the range of disciplines and types of knowledge to which it applies), and in depth (the pervasiveness of context- or theory-dependence within any given field is limited). Given this, he is quite confident that interpretive principles ('middle range theory') can be established, through 'actualistic research', or imported from other fields (presumably those regularly engaged in the relevant sorts of actualistic research), that are capable of securing the interpretive inferences by which archaeological data acquires 'meaning' as test evidence; that is, he is confident that his original solution to the problem of limits can be sustained, if only researchers get their priorities straight. Consider first the rôle that the assumption of limitation in breadth plays in Binford's defence of this renewed objectivism.

When Binford characterizes the problem of testing in Kuhnian terms, his concern is that the process of testing seems unavoidably and viciously circular; the import of archaeological data seems to be a function of whatever theory of cultural dynamics the archaeologist uses to make and justify the hypotheses that he or she means to test against this data. However, when he considers the kinds of linking principles on which researchers actually rely in ascribing 'meaning' to their data, he observes that a great number of their interpretive principles are formulated and established quite independently of any of the cultural theories or reconstructive hypotheses that they might want to test archaeologically; in fact, many do not concern cultural phenomena at all. I would argue that the real significance of this, to which Binford gives surprisingly little emphasis, is that even if component inferences concerning the evidential import of the record are insecure in themselves, the circularity and arbitrariness of inference that worries him is decisively broken when researchers exploit a concatenation of inferences that are based on principles drawn from a range of collateral (independent) fields. Interpretive inferences based on quite different interpretive principles can be counted on to be mutually constraining, even self-correcting (i.e. error in one is unlikely to be replicated by parallel errors in all the others; the likelihood that they will arbitrarily converge on a single test hypothesis dwindles very quickly as the range of sources on which they are based is expanded). Of course, the corollary to this is that a consilience of independently grounded inferences provides uniquely strong evidence (evidence which is at least not single-context-dependent) that the interpretive hypothesis on which they converge is approximately true. This sort of consideration, an inverse of the 'conjunction objection', has been central in philosophical arguments against radical (usually anti-realist) theses of context-relativity (Hardin & Rosenberg 1982, Meehl 1983, Smith 1981).

In fact, Binford usually exploits a more straightforward, and more controversial, qualification of the Kuhnian thesis. He seems to assume, *contra* the general implications of Kuhnian contextualism, that the problem of vicious circularity in theory-dependence does not, in fact, afflict the whole range of research disciplines or bodies of background knowledge from which interpretive principles are drawn (or at least, it does not afflict them all equally); some such principles are uniquely secure, in and of themselves (i.e. independent of whatever additional constraint or reinforcement collateral principles might provide). In particular, he seems to assume that Kuhnian worries really only arise when the subject of enquiry is observationally inaccessible, as in archaeology. He has no doubt that the causal connections holding between 'static' variables (of the sort measurable in the archaeological record) and 'dynamic' variables (of the sort that are presumed to have produced them) will be self-evident, and that researchers will have no trouble in establishing reliable (independently grounded) linking principles between them, when they are observed in 'actualistic' contexts where both components are directly accessible.

This is surely untenable as a general principle; indeed, it is untenable for reasons that Binford himself introduced when he objected that the traditional practice of simply citing correlations among variables cannot be considered explanatory, because it fails to demonstrate any causal connection among these variables (see, for example, his critique (1968) of Sabloff & Willey (1967)). The relevant corollary to this view about explanation is that, even when all interacting variables can be observed, a very rich theoretical judgement is required to single out one particular 'dynamic' variable as the *cause* of a given 'static' effect, from among all those associated with the effect. Even richer judgements are required to establish that the regularities observed in 'actualistic' contexts (causal or otherwise) can be generalized, projected on to unexamined, past or future, contexts. However, even granting that 'actualistic' research cannot be considered, as a whole, to be exempt from Kuhnian worries, simply because all the relevant variables are observable, there do seem good (although more complicated) reasons to suppose that context- and theory-dependence is not so monolithic that all such theory-dependent or theory-rich judgements are purely arbitrary. Considered as historical theses, Kuhnian claims have proven difficult to sustain for all levels and kinds of knowledge claim; there does seem to be a relatively stable core of observational claims, quasi-foundational causal principles and low-level empirical generalizations, particularly in the biophysical sciences, which persist through successive episodes of theory change and which find continuous application in practice. The undeniable instrumental success of science depends on this sort of knowledge. Even if it is never in principle immune to revision, it is routinely treated as reliable (although perhaps incomplete) truth; so much would be called into question if it were in error that it is not typically considered open to revision.

This is just the sort of knowledge Binford seems to have in mind when he insists that the 'ascription of meaning' to archaeological data can be secured, and when he defends the potential of actualistic research. The linking principles that Binford cites in this connection inevitably concern relatively stable, well-understood biophysical conditions or processes; they include principles about the physical properties of the materials found in the archaeological record and the processes by which they can be modified, and ecological and dietary principles concerning the survival requirements of human populations. He frequently appeals to radiocarbon dating in this connection (for example, Binford 1983, p. 135), observing that such an ascription of temporal 'meaning' to archaeological material depends on knowledge of 'processes that are in no sense dependent for their characteristics or patterns of interaction upon interactions between [in his example] agricultural manifestations or political growth' (*ibid.*, p. 135) and, I would add, that seem above question with regard to their scientific authority (at least, where they are controversial, their reliability in application to archaeology has been established by appeal to quite uncontroversial principles of dendrochronology). Another case to which Binford frequently refers when he means to illustrate the potential of actualistic research undertaken by archaeologists is his study of the relationship between butchering practices and faunal remains on Nunamiut sites. He insists, in rebuttal of Gould, that what he establishes here are 'uniformitarian assumptions' about the 'economic anatomy of caribou and sheep' (*ibid.*, p. 19), not merely contingent propositions about human adaptive responses to environmental circumstances of different kinds. He evidently views these 'eco-utilitarian' linking principles as a secure basis for interpretation, because they concern non-cultural, therefore non-contingent, material constraints on behaviour that, once established, will fall into that broad category of pragmatically uncontroversial empirical knowledge which we routinely presume to be projectible, regardless of our theoretical presuppositions (either about humans or about the natural world).

It would therefore seem undeniable that there is a considerable body of background knowledge and collateral theory that archaeologists could exploit to establish hypotheses about the factors responsible for the archaeological record, consistent with Binford's objectivist ambitions. The difficulty is that, by example at least, the range of inferences that these principles support is limited to reconstruction of the biophysical conditions which human agents manipulated and to which they responded in inadvertently producing the archaeological record. They do not allow for any very rich ascription of *cultural* significance to the data; they do not provide a basis for reconstructing the non-material (social and ideational) context in which these human agents operated. This means that they do not provide access to precisely those social and ideational dimensions of cultural systems that Binford insisted should become accessible, *contra* limited sceptics like Piggott and Hawkes, when archaeologists develop a sufficiently rich interpretive framework.

When Binford does address the problem of how to secure ascriptions of specifically *cultural* (as opposed to biophysical) meaning, he typically turns to a second, completely different, sort of background knowledge than that which he used to defend the general potential of middle range theory. He stresses the need to consider interpretive problems in light of 'a new set of relationships at a higher level of organization than that of the feature itself' (Binford 1983, p. 12) and advocates ethno-archaeological research which supplements the analysis of material formation processes with an understanding of 'how the operation of different system types generate diagnostically different statics' (*ibid.*, p. 223). Actualistic research is thus expected to produce not just microprinciples, as it were, that particularly link remains with particular past conditions, but macroprinciples that specify 'diagnostic criteria' by which functionally and adaptively distinctive types of cultural *systems* can be 'unambiguously' recognized in the archaeological record.

Two difficulties with this sort of linking principle are immediately obvious. The first is that they (or, properly, their use in interpretive inference) risk just the sort of circular theory-dependence that Binford is concerned to circumvent; because they concern specifically cultural processes (of adaptation, in this case) and they are not in principle 'intellectually independent' of assumptions about the cultural subject (the source of test hypotheses, if not themselves direct object of testing) as are the low-level biophysical principles. In fact, these principles would seem to be a component (or specification) of Binford's own ecosystem 'paradigm', the theoretical core of the New Archaeology research programme. Apparently they do not enjoy anything like the entrenched security associated with the principles concerning dietary requirements, technological efficiency, the availability of palaeoenvironmental resources, and the growth of trees. So far as Binford has developed them, they articulate just the sort of comprehensive theoretical principle which, on a Kuhnian analysis, compels acceptance by conversion and wholesale replacement in periods of paradigm crisis, as distinct from principles that occupy the relatively stable infrastructure of empirical knowledge that such theory is meant to explain.

The second difficulty is that, even if the system-level linking principles were established on an equal footing with those comprising the less non-controversial component of middle range theory (the biophysical principles) they do not solve Binford's original problem unless a very stringent version of the encompassing ecosystem theory of culture is accepted. They do not, themselves, provide any access to the truly 'middle range' of human, social–cultural phenomena that lie between the material conditions realized or manipulated in producing an archaeological record, and the encompassing 'systemic contexts' in which these conditions are confronted and transformed by human agents. Thus, they could only be considered to solve Binford's interpretive problem if all of the mediating variables at issue – actions, intentions and beliefs – reduce to or are a function of the material and adaptive parameters that Binford insists can be reconstructed on the basis of the micro- (biophysical) and macro- (system-level) principles that Binford believes actualistic research can establish.

Given his withering condemnation of an 'ethnographic' preoccupation with 'lifeworld' phenomena, Binford does seem prepared to make this claim. He insists, invoking the ecosystem theory as a non–controversial given, that sociocultural systems can be expected to take the distinctive forms and have the distinctive content (and archaeological records) that they do by virtue of adaptive response to selective pressures operating at a systemic level; 'there will be selection for and against certain culturally organized means of articulating with the environment' which will presumably manifest itself in archaeologically identifiable systemic types (Binford 1983, p. 223). Also, in his diatribes against ethnography, Binford is prepared to deny categorically that variables other than systemic, organizational ones – variables like the cognitive systems, beliefs, rationalizations or ideologies – have any autonomous causal efficacy either in the constitution of the encompassing systems in which they operate or in the production of an archaeological record of these systems. Binford's assessment seems to be that these features of life are merely interchangeable means of enculturation which ensure that the behaviour of individual agents fulfils the functional needs of the system. They contribute to the production of a material record that is distinctive, not of the agents' idiosyncratic beliefs or means of meeting system demands, but of the demands that the system – its modes of organization and adaptation – impose on them.

If this conception of the cultural subject can be sustained, then the problem of epistemic limits is once again banished. Of course, the difficulty is that, since it constitutes the theoretical core of Binford's paradigm, it must be admitted that his entire programme – not just a few crucial linking principles, but the orienting ambitions and methodology of the programme – is paradigm-dependent in just the sense that he considers objectionable. What he considers to be knowable or methodologically accessible (i.e. his definition of the limits of enquiry) is transparently a function of his preferred conception of the subject matter. Alternative conceptions, which his critics endorse, yield quite different and much less confident assessments of the limits of enquiry and very different directives for enquiry.

Paradigm relativity

To meet this new threat of circularity, Binford must shift to a different strategy or level of debate; he must show that his paradigm assumptions can, themselves, be established on 'objective', 'intellectually independent' grounds, consistent with his epistemic commitments, so that the circularity of interpretive or methodological dependence on them is not vicious. To this end he exploits a quite different sort of limitation of the Kuhnian thesis than that of breadth. He presumes a limitation in the depth or pervasiveness of paradigm-dependence. He insists that his critics persist in raising problems with his programme only because their approach is 'pseudo-scientific'; they proceed, not by turning to the relevant 'experience' to assess the claims at issue, but by exploiting 'high school debate team' techniques of polemic and assertion of opinion. If only they were willing to engage properly scientific methods of theory evaluation, then they would recognize the (obvious) cognitive and empirical superiority of the assumptions on which his own programme rests. In arguing this, Binford takes it that, although observation cannot be assumed to have theory-autonomous significance, its content is not entirely or arbitrarily determined by theoretical presuppositions. Observation can overturn even the most entrenched expectations in a way that quite decisively challenges the presuppositions that are said to inform it. Thus, it can provide a basis for systematic, empirical adjudication of paradigm-level disputes (Binford 1982, p. 136).

The obvious move for Binford to make at this juncture is to demonstrate, in objective, what he calls 'experiential' terms, that his conception of culture has incontrovertible empirical support that its rivals simply cannot claim. Instead, his usual strategy is to reaffirm the general (epistemological) thesis that 'ideas generated in paradigmatic context', like the paradigm assumptions on which his position rests, *can*, in principle, be established rationally and empirically, in a manner that is not strictly context-dependent. When he does argue directly for the merits of his own theoretical presuppositions, he reverts to his initial assertion that the normativist paradigm is self-evidently false and his self-evidently correct. For example, he asks (rhetorically) 'why assume [by analogy to the normativist conception of cultural phenomena] that the earth is flat' when we can 'learn through our objective means of evaluating our ideas that the world is round?' (Binford 1983, p. 137).

I make out two possible interpretations of this analogy. One is that Binford means to suggest that it is, and has always been, simply self-evident that normativist theory, like flat-Earth theory, is false (or would prove to be false if tested). This is obviously untenable in what it claims about both the source and the subject of the analogy; it is clear that, historically, flat-Earth theory and normativism have been anything but self-evidently false throughout the periods in which they have enjoyed various degrees of currency. Alternatively, Binford may intend that archaeology, like the Earth sciences, is now at a point where it is *no longer* tenable to hold the normativist equivalent of a flat-Earth paradigm; in both contexts theories that were formerly unquestioned have been decisively proven to be wrong, and those who persist in endorsing them are just stubborn obscurantists, bent on obstructing the progress of science. This last is a more plausible reading but, if it is what Binford intended, why has he rested his case on an intimation of self-evident truth and not iterated the evidence that he suggests, by appeal to the demise of the flat-Earth paradigm, must long since have established the falsity of normativism and the truth of his own ecosystemic paradigm? If the analogy holds, then there must be a body of readily identifiable evidence that is as decisive in refuting normativist theories of culture (and in establishing his materialist alternative) as the 'experience' of finding it possible to sail *around* the world was in refuting flat-Earth theory.

However, it is striking that, rather than identifying such a body of evidence, and thereby providing substantive support for these rhetorical claims of self-evident superiority, Binford routinely elaborates on the objection that his opponents are just obstructionists, and in this he decisively shifts the ground of debate from a consideration of cognitive, empirical to pragmatic merit. What they refuse to acknowledge is not the truth of his paradigm, but its superiority as a uniquely 'fruitful' way of conceptualizing the subject matter; a 'functional approach viewed in systems, not psychological terms, is thought to be the most productive form of research' (Binford 1983, p. 223). Presumably the constructive point is that his paradigm promises to get the research enterprise off the ground, and thus better serves the interests of archaeological science than its competitors. More usually the arguments are negative. Binford recommends his own paradigm by implicit contrast with its chief competitor, the normativist approach, and, in some cases, by contrast with simplistic ecological determinism which, he claims, have failed to yield any 'fruitful ideas' in anthropology (Binford 1983, p. 222). He takes special exception to the normative paradigm on the grounds that, in addition to being unproductive, it is actually counterproductive; it forecloses the possibility of undertaking what he considers a properly objective scientific evaluation of paradigm ideas by conceiving the subject in terms that make it essentially unanalysable (or, in archaeological contexts, unreconstructable). In the end it is by default of *pragmatic* inadequacies that Binford claims the unassailable superiority of his ecosystem paradigm. He would deny this, of course, but only by persistently conflating evaluative (pragmatic) with cognitive (objective and empirical) considerations (see, for example, Binford's 1983, p. 137 discussion of 'false paradigms' as false both in the factual sense and in the sense of misleading).

It is a profound irony that the pragmatic argument for accepting an ecosystem theory of culture is the most fully developed, compelling one that Binford provides; his dependence on it undermines the very methodological point that he intends to make, inasmuch as it turns on precisely the sort of rhetorical appeal to extrinsic interests (to evaluative, non-epistemic considerations) that he rejects as patently counterproductive in the hands of his opponents. The real significance of this is not just that it exposes Binford's own posturing for what it is, but that it makes explicit the circularity that I suggested above has lain at the very core of his programme since its inception; the cultural subject of archaeology is conceived of as just that sort of materially-determined system which we can expect to reconstruct with scientific reliability from material remains.

In defence of qualified objectivism

Although it would mean dropping any claim to objectivity, Binford could claim that his defence of a functionalist conception of culture has much to recommend it simply because it should be compelling, if not irresistible, to his relativist or contextualist opponents. If, as they suggest, there can be no empirical grounds for choosing between paradigms that are not themselves paradigm-specific – if the debate inevitably turns on non-cognitive, pragmatic considerations – then it would seem that a paradigm that promises a 'fruitful' and methodologically respectable research programme must take precedence over one that undermines or even forecloses the possibility of productive archaeological enquiry. Binford's conception of the cultural subject could be rejected only if his critics were able to show that it cannot or does not actually secure the practical advantages claimed for it, or that other pragmatic considerations (e.g. political considerations) weigh in favour of reconstructing the archaeological research enterprise around non-Binfordian (non-scientific) ends.

However, it is striking that those whom Binford accuses of paradigmatic posturing take the critical stand they do take, not on the basis of pragmatic counterargument, but because they think that his paradigmatic claims about cultural phenomena are untenable *as empirical claims*. They question his methodological ambitions because they feel compelled, for empirical reasons, to embrace a 'normativist' conception of the cultural subject. In the first instance they find it *prima facie* implausible that human action could be adequately comprehended in strictly eco-materialist terms given its distinctively intentional nature; Binford's theory cuts against well-entrenched principles of common sense and an extensive tradition of social scientific theory which, together, presume human subjects to be agents. In addition, normativist critics go on to substantiate the intuitions which lead them to question Binford's commitment to an ecosystem paradigm. Hodder (1982b), for example, provides extensive and detailed ethnographic documentation of the point that cognitive variables of the sort that Binford considers dependent can play a dramatically active, causal rôle in shaping human behaviour with regard to material things and, thus, in shaping the archaeological record. Moreover, he shows that the interaction between these variables can be quite arbitrary and context-specific so that, in fact, it may be impossible to discover any projectable principles of connection holding among them that would allow their reliable reconstruction from archaeological data, even when living contexts in which all the interacting variables are directly accessible are considered.

I do not find Hodder's generalization of this point compelling; the arbitrariness that he discovers does not establish that no such principles hold or that the search for them is necessarily futile. However, this aside, the second irony is that, insofar as this normativist rebuttal is compelling, it is because it disconfirms Binford's general (paradigmatic) assumptions about the cultural subject in a way that vindicates Binford's limited objectivism. It substantiates Binford's programmatic conviction that paradigm assumptions can be critically evaluated on rational and empirical grounds, very effectively exploiting the possibility – essential to any objectivism – that the evidence may not, in fact, vindicate the claims brought to test against it.

Nassaney's (Ch. 4, this volume) critique of conflicts in the interpretation of Narragansett burial sites is an example of a normativist argument which embodies this irony. He adopts just the sort of anti-objectivism that Binford opposes, arguing that, where a range of interpretations concerning the nature of the Narragansett contact situation all 'appear to be based on objective observations', it is unavoidable that 'claims of archaeological objectivity must . . . be called into question' (*ibid.*, p. 77). After a review of these interpretations, he concludes that 'ultimately, as anthropologists and social scientists, we cannot evaluate the truthfulness of an interpretation'; conflicting interpretations simply represent 'different points of view' that can only be assessed on evaluative (non-cognitive) grounds (*ibid.*, p. 90). However, in the analysis framed by these introductory and concluding comments, Nassaney develops a series of arguments to the effect that the dominant interpretation, which characterizes contact-period Narragansett as passive victims of exploitation, cannot be sustained empirically. He insists that this interpretation has seemed plausible only because its proponents 'exploit a limited set of the entire range of data available to archaeological investigators' (*ibid.*, p. 85), and adds that, 'by ignoring certain dimensions of

the ethnohistoric and archaeological database' researchers have systematically reproduced a conception of Narragansett experience which serves very
effectively to legitimate their status and claims as a tribal group in the present
(*ibid.*, p. 85).

Whether or not Nassaney's account proves, in the end, the most broadly
plausible one available, his argument for it certainly does not turn on a
consideration of its ideological usefulness. Quite the opposite is true. It
exemplifies just the sort of appeal to evidence that, despite its limitations,
Binford insists can settle questions about the nature of cultural systems and,
more specifically, about the actual course and conditions of human action
within these systems. As in the cases cited above, Nassaney's own practice
directly counters his programmatic claim that the evidence available to
archaeologists provides no grounds for choosing among competing hypotheses (i.e. the initial claim that the competing hypotheses are underdeter-
mined by the available data); his analysis is an object lesson in the potential of
this evidence to impose quite stringent (albeit not determinate) constraints
on theory construction, despite being fragmentary and theory-dependent.

Conclusions

Several things follow from the unexpected turns that I have identified in the
current debate between objectivists and their critics. The obvious thing is
that they reopen the question about epistemic limits. If actualistic research
establishes that some of the variables that Binford repudiates as a meaningful
subject of enquiry *do* play a causal rôle in structuring the encompassing
cultural system and the archaeological record that it produces but are not
correlated with unique (i.e. diagnostic) archaeological 'effects', then it must
be admitted that some aspects of the past will inevitably remain inaccessible
and some dimensions of the archaeological record inexplicable. It is,
therefore, simply indefensible to assume, *a priori*, that all aspects of the past
are accessible if only the appropriate actualistic research is undertaken; the
available evidence makes it clear that there is no determinate Rosetta Stone
code to be cracked that will provide comprehensive access to the past.

However, note that in using 'experiential' evidence to establish this
conclusion, the question of limits is raised in completely different terms than
has been typical of past discussions; it is cast as a contingent, empirical
question, not a question to be settled once and for all on the basis of
programmatic argument and the assertion of paradigm commitments as
inescapable or self-evidently correct. The current debate thus suggests that
actualistic research should be treated, not as a means of underwriting
predetermined ambitions, but as a means of realistically defining and
delimiting these ambitions. Indeed, it demonstrates that actualistic research
can determine, in concrete terms, what specific aspects of the past and what
range of problems about cultural systems archaeologists can profitably
investigate, given the nature of the specific record and subject in question.

Moreover, it is evident that actualistic research provides not only the linking principles necessary for reconstructive inference, but also the basis for a nuanced assessment of the relative security of the explanatory–interpretive claims based on these principles. Also, where both the assessment of security and the interpretive inferences themselves are contingent on the state of our interpretive resources, it is clear that any assessment of limits will be open to (continuing) revision; what can be known of the past and the security of this knowledge will change as the relevant background (or 'middle range') knowledge and associated technologies develop. Indeed, the process of reflectively, critically reviewing limits, construed in this sense, may itself be an important source of change. It may function as a catalyst for developing resources in areas where inference seems to be unnecessarily limited or insecure. The lesson that emerges is, therefore, that wishful 'positive' thinking will not exorcize metaphysical anxiety about coming to know a cultural subject that does not exist, but that this does not, in itself, entail wholesale scepticism. It is, at least in part, a contingent, empirical question how broadly or narrowly this anxiety can be circumscribed.

In arguing for this reformulation of the problem of limits, I hope, first, to counter the tendency on the part of all parties to the debate to assume that if knowledge claims about the past are not established with certainty, then they are nothing but arbitrary speculation. Secondly, I hope to have established that although Binford was right to reject any *a priori* delimitation of the scope of enquiry, he was wrong (indeed, it was inconsistent with his own objectivist commitments) to respond in kind by asserting that all aspects of past cultural systems are accessible *a priori*, given commitment to his ecosystem conception of the subject. A limited objectivism of the sort that he seems to defend in principle, and which his critics exploit in practice, requires that the problem of limits be addressed by developing an empirically specified 'ladder of inference', one in which the relative degrees of security attainable by different sorts of interpretive inference are assessed against the background knowledge on which it necessarily depends.

References

Binford, L. R. 1968. Some comments on historical vs processual archaeology. *Southwestern Journal of Archaeology* **24**, 267–75.

Binford, L. R. 1972. *An archaeological perspective*. New York: Seminar Press.

Binford, L. R. 1978. *For theory building in archaeology*. New York: Academic Press.

Binford, L. R. 1982. Objectivity – explanation – archaeology 1981. In *Theory and explanation in archaeology*, C. Renfrew, M. J. Rowlands & B. Abbott Segraves (eds), 125–38. New York: Academic Press.

Binford, L. R. 1983. *Working at archaeology*. New York: Academic Press.

Binford, L. R. 1985. Brand X versus the recommended product. *American Antiquity* **50**, 580–90.

Binford, L. R. & S. R. Binford (eds) 1968. *New perspectives in archaeology*. Chicago: Aldine.

Binford, L. R. & J. A. Sabloff 1982. Paradigms, systematics, and archeology. *Journal of Anthropological Research* **38**, 137–53.

Dray, W. 1980. *Perspectives on history*. London: Routledge & Kegan Paul.

Hardin, C. L. & A. J. Rosenberg 1982. In defense of convergent realism. *Philosophy of Science* **49**, 604–15.

Hawkes, C. 1954. Archaeological theory and method. *American Anthropologist* **56**, 155–68.

Hill, J. N. & R. K. Evans 1972. A model for classification and typology. In *Models in archaeology*, D. L. Clarke (ed.), 231–73. London: Methuen.

Hodder, I. 1982a. Theoretical archaeology: a reactionary view. In *Symbolic and structural archaeology*, I. Hodder (ed.), 1–16. Cambridge: Cambridge University Press.

Hodder, I. 1982b. *Symbols in action*. Cambridge: Cambridge University Press.

Kuhn, T. 1970. *The structure of scientific revolutions*, 2nd edn. Chicago: University of Chicago Press.

Meehl, P. E. 1983. Consistency tests in estimating the completeness of the fossil record. In *Testing scientific theories*, J. Earman (ed.), 413–73. Minneapolis: University of Minnesota Press.

Miller, D. 1982. Explanation and social theory in archaeological practice. In *Theory and explanation in archaeology*, C. Renfrew, M. J. Rowlands & B. Abbott Segraves (eds), 83–96. New York: Academic Press.

Nassaney, M. S. 1989. An epistemological enquiry into some archaeological and historical interpretations of 17th century Native American–European relations. In *Archaeological approaches to cultural identity*, S. J. Shennan (ed.), ch. 4. London: Unwin Hyman.

Piggott, S. 1965. *Approach to archaeology*. Cambridge, Massachusetts: Harvard University Press.

Sabloff, J. & G. R. Willey 1967. The collapse of Maya civilizations in the southern lowlands: a consideration of history and process. *Southwestern Journal of Anthropology* **23**, 311–36.

Smith, P. 1981. *Realism and the progress of science*. Cambridge: Cambridge University Press.

Watson, P. J., S. A. LeBlanc & C. L. Redman 1974. The covering law model in archaeology: practical uses and formal interpretations. *World Archaeology* **6**, 125–32.

6 *The rôle of 'local knowledge' in archaeological interpretation*

JEAN-CLAUDE GARDIN

(translated by Marianne Dumartheray and Stephen Shennan)

'Universal' semantics and 'local' semantics

The distinction between a 'universal' and a 'local' order of knowledge in the context of archaeological description was introduced more than ten years ago (Gardin & Lagrange 1975). It was suggested that the inferences observed in our arguments could be divided into two groups: (a) those which we use as though they were natural, evident and not subject to argument – those, in short, which go without saying – and (b) those that we judge to be more relative, acceptable only in certain contexts, questionable even, so that we feel obliged to define the rationale behind them. The distinction between the two is not categorical, nor was it ever formulated explicitly in these terms; nevertheless, well-established usage in the archaeological literature is that reference notes are given in support of inferences of the second type whereas no such critical apparatus is thought to be necessary in the first case.

A way of rationalizing this procedure consists in postulating the existence of a 'universal semantic' tacitly justifying inferences of the first type, alongside a set of 'local semantics' which provide an explicit foundation for inferences of the second type. Thus, in one of the examples analysed (*ibid.*, pp. 12–54) a bas-relief which shows 'a person holding a large bird of indeterminate nature on his gloved hand' is related to the theme of hunting, by a chain of inferences which might be schematized as follows: 'large indeterminate bird on gloved hand → falcon → hunting'. The knowledge presupposed if one is to accept this interpretation is nowhere explicitly stated: it is supposed to stem from that 'universal' semantic which goes without saying, by implication. Conversely, the rest of the interpretation is anything but obvious: the identification of the human figure as the sultan of a Seljuk dynasty which reigned at Konya in Anatolia during the 13th century is the product of a chain of inferences which are subject to doubt. In fact, they are contradicted by other interpretations, and the author takes care to justify them by references to all sorts of 'local' facts. These facts are local in the sense that they all refer to the specific cultural context of the monument, defined in terms of the usual dimensions of space, time and relevant human groups (in this case *Anatolia* during the *13th century* peopled by *Turks* from *Central Asia* under the *Seljuk* dynasty). No-one would ever use these same facts to support the interpretation of a similar scene found in a ruined Aztec temple.

The stating of this duality is not a great discovery, especially as the border between the two types of knowledge is quite vague. Very often inferences of the first type are natural only to specialists in the universe of discourse under consideration, so that the so-called universal semantic only deserves its name with reference to that particular universe, very much a local one. Nevertheless, in my view progress in archaeological interpretation can only be achieved through reflection on the duality in question; the goal is then not in the least speculative or philosophical, but decidedly practical, as I will try to show.

Setting-up schemas and rules for inferences

I have shown elsewhere (Gardin 1979, pp. 175–202 (1980, pp. 101–20)) a method which I find convenient for representing the architecture of interpretative constructions in archaeology. This is in the form of chains of propositions:

$$\{P_0\} \longrightarrow \{P_1\} \longrightarrow \{P_2\} \longrightarrow \cdots \longrightarrow \{P_n\}$$

These propositions are linked to one another by rewriting operations $\{P_i\} \rightarrow \{P_j\}$.

(a)   The propositions $\{P_0\}$ are descriptive propositions indicating the properties or attributes which the author of the construction has chosen to characterize the material under study and its natural or archaeological environment.

(b)   The propositions $\{P_n\}$ are explanatory: the author states hypotheses or conclusions which he or she thinks he or she can establish concerning the meaning of the material in question with regard to whatever sphere is appropriate: for example, attribution to known 'groups' (in the most abstract sense of the word: types, cultures, styles, etc.), hypotheses concerning utilitarian or symbolic functions, reconstruction of historical events, etc.

(c)   The propositions $\{P_1\}$, $\{P_2\}$, . . ., $\{P_{n-1}\}$ are those which make up the line of argument linking $\{P_0\}$ to $\{P_n\}$, or $\{P_n\}$ to $\{P_0\}$ depending on the way in which the author has chosen to present it: (i) the empirico-inductive (EI) approach, if one starts from the empirical observations $\{P_0\}$ in order to reach interpretative conclusions $\{P_n\}$; (ii) the hypotheticodeductive (HD) approach, if the interpretative hypothesis $\{P_n\}$ is presented first and one then goes on to demonstrate that it is corroborated by the observed data $\{P_0\}$.

Thus, in every interpretative construction we can distinguish: (a) the 'initial' propositions, i.e. those which have no explicit antecedents in the

Table 6.1 The analysis of interpretative constructions.

Mode	Initial propositions	Constituents Terminal propositions	Rewriting operations
empirico-inductive	P_0	P_n	$P_i \rightarrow P_{i+1}$
hypotheticodeductive	P_n	P_0	$P_i \rightarrow P_{i-1}$

argument: observations $\{P_0\}$ in an EI construction, hypotheses $\{P_n\}$ in an HD construction; (b) the 'terminal' propositions, which have no explicit consequences in the argument: conclusions $\{P_n\}$ in the EI case, empirical data $\{P_0\}$ in the HD case; (c) the 'intermediate' propositions $\{P_i\}$ given to establish a bridge from $\{P_0\}$ to $\{P_n\}$, or vice versa. The rewriting operations $\{P_i\} \rightarrow \{P_j\}$ can thus take one or the other of two forms: $\{P_i\} \rightarrow \{P_{i+1}\}$ for empirico-inductive arguments, $\{P_i\} \rightarrow \{P_{i-1}\}$ for those which are hypotheticodeductive (Table 6.1).

These operations of rewriting express plainly the architecture of the reasoning process. Questions may then be raised about the legitimacy of each operation: what knowledge does the author rely on when stating that IF $\{P_i\}$ is established, THEN one may pose $\{P_j\}$?

I called the analysis of archaeological literature carried out in this way 'logicist', because it proceeds in the manner of a logical calculus, but without laying claim to all its rigour (Gardin 1979, pp. 32–8 (1980, pp. 13–16)). The rewriting operations $\{P_i\} \rightarrow \{P_j\}$ in particular cannot be considered to be *rules* of reasoning, applicable under all circumstances, after the manner of a formal rule: they express at the most recurrent discursive practices in the archaeological literature, when we observe that more than one author uses the same propositions $\{P_i\}$ as the starting point for the same inferences $\{P_j\}$.

One way of understanding the quest for objectivity in archaeological interpretation is to elucidate what separates a 'discursive practice', thus defined, from a 'rule of reasoning'. This is the objective that we set ourselves when we recently took one further step towards a formalization of the process of interpretation in archaeology, by means of artificial intelligence. One of the aims of artificial intelligence is to reproduce on the computer the complex reasoning processes current in various areas of specialized discourse. To this end, computer tools called 'expert systems' have been developed using a general formalism which is remarkably similar to that of our logicist schematizations (Gardin 1983). Without going into too much detail here, let us recall that an expert system includes the following elements:

(a) a 'knowledge base', which contains in a condensed form the knowledge communicated to the computer, in two forms: (i) the database, made up of observational data equivalent to our propositions $\{P_0\}$; and (ii) the rule base, which holds 'production rules' of the type IF . . . THEN, corresponding to our rewriting operations 'IF $\{P_i\} \rightarrow$ (THEN) $\{P_j\}$';

(b) an 'inference engine' which constitutes the actual computer part of the system. Its rôle is to find whether there exists in the rule base one or more propositions $\{P_n\}$ which can be linked to one or more propositions $\{P_0\}$ in the database by the application of some or all of the production rules, either in the $\{P_0\} \rightarrow \{P_n\}$ direction ('forward chaining') or $\{P_n\} \rightarrow \{P_0\}$ ('backward chaining').

If we dare to speak in this case of 'rules', where before we confined ourselves to 'practices', it is because the rôle of the inference engine is not merely to reproduce constructions which already exist, as was the case with the logicist schematization process. Its function is ultimately to produce new ones, as the initial knowledge base becomes larger. In this perspective we should consider the operations of rewriting drawn from schematizations as possible inference rules that are potentially applicable in the context of other arguments. An expert system is thus a means of conducting experiments in the area of interpretation. Archaeologists are only just beginning to see the interest of this. One thing we have learnt from our own experiments along these lines (Gardin *et al.* 1987) is the overwhelming preponderance of 'local' as opposed to 'universal' semantics in archaeological reasoning. It is this fact and its consequences which I shall explore here.

The local character of the rules of inference

Let me begin with an observed fact. When we schematize an interpretative construction and attempt to set up as rules the rewriting operations used in this schematization, then we discover that this 'regulation' process is most often impossible, for a simple reason: one immediately finds all kinds of counterexamples which contradict the rules. The process is the following.

(a) The schematization uncovers the elementary constituents of the argument, in the form of inferences $\{P_i\} \rightarrow \{P_j\}$. These are masked by the rhetoric of natural language; yet, stripped down, they represent the basic operations of interpretation.

(b) We then proceed to the 'regulation' of these inferences, meaning that we transform local rewriting operations into general rules of reasoning. That is, instead of limiting ourselves to noting that a particular author has carried out in a specific context an operation of the type 'IF p THEN q', we add the hypothesis that in doing so he or she followed a process of reasoning of the *modus ponens* type: 'IF p AND $p \rightarrow q$ THEN q', where '$p \rightarrow q$' would be an inference rule of more-general applicability.

(c) It then remains to put these potential rules to the test: the game consists of systematically searching out interpretative constructions where the application of a given rule $p \rightarrow q$ leads to an incorrect interpretation. An attempt is made, if you like, to 'falsify' the rule, but in a very specific sense of that word: the aim is not to establish that the rule is *wrong*, but only to show that, inasmuch as it is not general, it is *incomplete*.

It is the ease of this exercise that allows us to assert 'the overwhelming preponderance of local semantics' in archaeological interpretation (examples and references in Gardin *et al.* 1987). However, the connection between these two propositions must be agreed upon: the *incomplete* character of the rules of inference underlying our reasoning, and the *local* limits of their validity. As already stated, the *raison d'être* of logicist analysis, or its extension in artificial intelligence, is not to show that given interpretations are false, but rather that they rest on implicit assumptions which the authors regard as obvious or natural, and in this sense 'universal', even though we easily find reasons to challenge them.

I mentioned above the simple example of a chain of inferences apparently depending on this natural order of things, in connection with the interpretation of a 13th century bas-relief from Anatolia: large undetermined bird on gloved hand $\rightarrow$ falcon $\rightarrow$ hunting. However, elsewhere in time and space there exist similar representations where the chain would be completely different: 'large undetermined bird on gloved hand $\rightarrow x \rightarrow$ magic, circus, etc.', depending on the identity of the intermediate term: pigeon, parrot, etc. The 'gloved hand' is thus not a sufficient basis for inferring that the 'large bird' is a 'falcon', or that the scene is therefore concerned with 'hunting': the corresponding rules would be local, or incomplete, or both.

(a) *Local* to begin with, because there exist cases where, starting from the same given knowledge ('large bird on gloved hand'), one arrives at different conclusions ('hunting', 'magic' or 'circus').

(b) *Incomplete* as a result, until we add further information to the premises in order to get rid of the uncertainty and to direct the interpretation towards what is judged to be a satisfactory conclusion, in each particular case.

(c) However, as soon as this requirement is satisfied our rules cease to be incomplete even though they remain local. The further information serves the function of specifying the context in which a particular rule is applicable; that is, it defines the extension of the rule in some way. The rule therefore remains local although it is true that one could formally describe it as general within its own limited domain.

It should now be clear that, when pressed to such limits, the analysis of the inferences used in our constructions leads to the conclusion that the majority of the rules which could support them are, in fact, local in character. This is by no means a catastrophic conclusion, however, and it remains to demonstrate the decidedly positive consequences which flow from it if the need for a reorientation of archaeological interpretation along new lines is accepted.

'Locality', objectivity and subjectivity

Let us agree first of all on one point: the 'locality' of our rules does not necessarily mean that they bear the stigma of subjectivity. It is customary in archaeology, and more generally in the human sciences, to contrast two types of relativism in the area of interpretation: (a) an 'objective' one which has to do with the diversity of the systems of thought and behaviour prevalent in the societies we study; and (b) a 'subjective' one which is supposed to arise from our tendency to interpret human conduct through the medium of our own categories, instead of calling on those of the societies in question. An echo of this dichotomy may be seen in the World Archaeological Congress Second Announcement of the theme from which this book derives, where one finds the contrast drawn between 'the culturally specific rules of behaviour of ancient societies . . . to which we do not have access' and the conceptual frameworks of the 'modern world', which we use in reconstructing the history of those same societies for want of anything better. In my view one of the most promising aspects of the perspective outlined above is the fact that it induces us to overcome this distinction – without denying it – to the benefit of a unitary view of archaeological interpretation, where all constructions meet up in the same destiny, determined by trying out the rules of inference from which each one draws its specificity. The introspective exercises of logicist analysis mediated by the use of expert systems seem to me at the moment to be the most efficient way of carrying out this process of experimentation. The result is that the methodological debate is no longer concerned with the objective or subjective character of the interpretations, nor the ideological or cultural determinisms which produced them, but with a practical question which is more urgent: *when we translate the system of inferences underlying a particular construction into explicit rules, can we apply those rules to the interpretation of new archaeological facts, in circumstances which allow us to judge the empirical validity of the result?*

This apparently innocent question may be taken as a sort of touchstone for the whole interpretative edifice of archaeology, since it seems to me to sum up all of the conditions which are necessary and sufficient for its progress.

(a)   The strongest of these conditions is the possibility of empirical validation, where one establishes that a particular interpretative construction is in agreement with new facts, and is thus effective in this sense. Any discussion of the objectivity of our constructions is bound to get nowhere if these constructions do not lend themselves, one way or another, to tests of their validity (Gardin 1974, pp. 107–14, 1979, pp. 213–25, 1980, pp. 127–34)). This point of view is not a reflection of a personal ideology (neo-positivistic, scientist, or whatever), but a tautological consequence of the very notion of objectivity, however it is defined (Gardin 1981, pp. 11–15).

(b)   It follows from this that we can perfectly well put up with certain inferences whose origin or foundation seems enigmatic, arbitrary, impressionistic, or any other pejorative adjective of this type. If these inferences nevertheless turn out to be productive in the sense just outlined, one must presume that they express 'objective' connections between the phenomena in question, at least so long as we have not observed any empirical facts to the contrary. Inferences of this type are extremely common in the traditional discourse of archaeology, and our interpretative arsenal would be sadly depleted if we suddenly proscribed them on the basis of an ill-advised purism.

(c)   However, it remains true that the game of science obliges us to give these productive inferences a formal basis. It is here that the process of logicist reconstruction comes into its own, or better still the formulation of hypothetical production rules, corresponding to our rewriting operations, as understood in expert systems.

(d)   Such systems enable us to test the rules by applying them to expanded databases in order to generate 'artificial' (in the sense of artificial intelligence) interpretations; it is then up to us to decide, by the usual empirical methods, whether they are acceptable.

(e)   Even if they turn out not to be acceptable, we will in fact have made progress, by circumscribing the field of operation of our rules, using an experimental approach. This brings us back to the assessment of their more or less local character, which I suggested from the outset was a more sensible objective than trying to find 'universal' interpretative systems in archaeology, or indeed in the human sciences as a whole.

The prospection of 'possible worlds'

The roads leading to this objective, by schematizing and trying out rules of inference, may appear tortuous; unfortunately, I do not know any others. However, there is an intermediate step in this direction which consists of first setting up an inventory of those rules which are to be found in the archaeological literature, without immediately trying to determine the limits of their validity. Even this task is a considerable one, but it cannot be skimped if archaeological interpretation is to be made a consistent exercise. Some recent publications seem to have taken on board this need already: monographs exist dealing with a specific category of archaeological material – pottery (Arnold 1985), bone (Binford 1981), etc. – where the authors draw up a systematic inventory of the inferences which they themselves or other people have thought it possible to make on the basis of the properties of the material or its distribution. The inverse approach has fewer followers, but is no less instructive: it consists in starting from a set of interpretative propositions concerned with a particular field or topic (for example, demography, the economy, forms of the state, etc.) and investigating the different means which have been used to provide a basis for those propositions, using archaeological evidence of all kinds. Both types of enquiry serve our cause admirably, except that they do not go quite as far as one would wish in the way in which the results are presented. It would be preferable for them to be expressed concisely by schematizations showing the routes through the graph which link the particular category of $\{P_0\}$ under consideration (pottery, bone, etc.) to some propositions $\{P_n\}$ in the first case, or the particular category of $\{P_n\}$ in question (demography, economy, etc.) to some propositions $\{P_0\}$ in the second case (whatever the direction of the argument in the texts chosen, whether EI or HD; see above). We have been trained instead to deck out our findings in a rhetorical finery which is supposedly 'natural'. The result is a discourse which is unnecessarily long-winded, from which the precious substance must be extracted at great expense. In the final analysis this substance is nothing more, but also nothing less, than the 'cognitive graph' referred to above. This reveals the extraordinary tangle of ways open to 'reason' (?) for going to and fro between the two poles of our constructions, $\{P_0\}$ and $\{P_n\}$.

I have just cast doubt on the use of reason – the word, but also the thing itself – in a situation of this nature. Some will be quick to see in the tangle in question, a consequence of the 'complexity' of human phenomena: if we reason so freely in our interpretations, it is because we are not as lucky as our colleagues in the exact sciences, whose objects are much more simple than ours. I must admit that I do not share that view, but let us suppose, for the sake of argument, that it is true. We will still not convince our colleagues of their 'luck' until we have given them a clear view of the *necessary* entanglement of our chains of reasoning, in the face of objects more resistant than theirs to the experimental method.

This is precisely the object of the inventories mentioned above. They are an example of the study of 'possible worlds' that are so important in various domains of contemporary thought – logic, linguistics, pragmatics and semiology (Gardin 1985a, b). Each route through the cognitive graph represents, in effect, a particular vision of the world; in simpler words, a system of relationships between empirical phenomena, postulated by a particular author in a given universe of observations. For some disciplines connected to the human sciences, such as literary studies, it has been argued that there are as many different visions of the world as there are observers. Furthermore, the multiplicity of interpretations of works of literature is sometimes made into a norm, without even admitting that such a course raises questions about the status of what is in every way a curious 'science' (Gardin 1982). In other fields – history, for example – the rules of the game are tougher, and historians themselves sometimes take the trouble to assemble vast inventories similar to ours, to illustrate the same entanglements (for example, Joll 1984, in his remarkable compilation of the different types of explanations advanced by professional historians for the origins of World War I). All of these attempts reflect, in one way or another, the same desire to go more deeply into the problems raised by the foundations of our arguments, whether scholarly or everyday, scientific or literary. By placing them all on the same footing, or at least in the same perspective, I wish to broaden the vision that some archaeologists have of the place of ethnography in our discipline. It is to this task that I now turn.

Local knowledge and ethnography

I think that we can take it as accepted today that our archaeological inferences can only be founded on ethnography. The transfer mechanism and the assumptions which are supposed to justify it can be summarized as follows. The complexity of the overall graph of interpretations linking our $\{P_0\}$ and $\{P_n\}$, even in the case of an analysis restricted to a single narrowly defined category of $\{P_0\}$ or $\{P_n\}$, demonstrates immediately an important fact: the diversity of the routes through the graph arises – apart from the circumstances which determined the choice of a particular set of $\{P_0\}$ or $\{P_n\}$ – from the corresponding diversity of ethnographic facts called upon by each author to support the various inferences $\{P_i\} \rightarrow \{P_j\}$ between the two poles of the construction. The situation becomes clear when our authors take the trouble to point out explicitly the correlations $\{P_i\} \rightarrow \{P_j\}$ observed in living societies which, according to them, justify the transfer of similar inferences to the ancient societies that they are studying. However, the point to remember is that this 'ethnographic' reference is necessarily present, in other forms, at the basis of *all* inferences $\{P_i\} \rightarrow \{P_j\}$.

(a)   A first example is arguing by analogy in the comparative phase of our constructions, where we propose a similar transfer from one archaeological context to another; this formally plays the same rôle and poses the same epistemological problems as the ethnographic transfer. A concise way of expressing the equivalence is by means of an aphorism: today's ethnographic foundations are tomorrow's archaeological ones, just as the ethnological observations of yesterday provide the basis for the historical constructions of today (for example, Herodotus, father of ethnology for some, father of history for others).

(b)   The same view holds for so-called natural inferences, which, as we have seen, rest on analogies or precedents which are implicit, which are supposed to be universally known, and thus are not worth citing. Detailed analysis reveals that many of these inferences which 'go without saying' in fact have foundations which are just as cultural, and in this sense ethnographic, as those of the inferences discussed above.

(c)   It is also the case with interpretations which follow particular paradigms that are more- or less-widely shared at particular moments in the history of ideas. This is true whether these paradigms are apparently purely technical ones (ecological, materialist, etc.) or are more obviously marked by ideology (sociobiology, Marxism, etc.). It is not hard to see that this 'shared knowledge' which guides the interpretative constructions of a particular group of authors has the same status and function as the ethnographic knowledge explicitly employed in other

LOCAL KNOWLEDGE AND ETHNOGRAPHY   119

constructions. Indeed, we are entitled to regard the groups of archaeologists defined in terms of their adherence to this or that paradigm as
just as open to ethnographic observation as the Scythians or the Bantu,
when it comes to rationalizing their interpretations of the behaviour of
the one or the other, or of one by the other, whether alive or dead.

The advantage of this point of view is that it provides a unified operating
framework for studying the mechanisms of archaeological interpretation,
which is our present concern. A number of controversial subjects then take
on only a secondary importance – objectivity versus subjectivity, absolute
versus relative truth, multiculturalism versus multiple ideologies, ethnographic knowledge versus 'common sense', etc. More thought is given instead
to related questions of more-immediate import, such as the following.

(a) Is the proposed interpretation amenable to empirical confirmation or
     falsification? If the answer to this is 'no', then what are the criteria
     proposed for deciding in some way or another between conflicting
     interpretations? (See, for example, Hodder's 1984 propositions in this
     respect.) If it is suggested that there are none, then how is it possible to
     distinguish a 'scientific' interpretation in archaeology from a less
     scientific, or even an unscientific, one if the collection and observation
     of the data have been equally rigorous in both cases?
(b) If the reply is 'yes', then what are the elementary operations
     $\{P_i\} \rightarrow \{P_j\}$ which come into play in the interpretation? What are their
     foundations, implicit or explicit? Finally, but most importantly, once
     these have been established, what is the 'range' of each of the corres-
     ponding IF . . . THEN rules, in any of the following senses: (i) its
     extension, i.e. the necessary and provisionally sufficient conditions for it
     to be admissible; (ii) its *resistance* to the test of new facts, measured by
     the weight of the accumulated constructions which it can bear as the
     edifice of interpretations grows larger; (iii) or, seen from a different
     angle, its *posterity*; and (iv) in short, its *value* measured in terms of one or
     other of the preceding criteria.

It is quite likely that systematic assessments of this sort will most often
lead to an assertion of the 'local' character of our rules. Nevertheless, this
does not compromise the project of a 'scientific' interpretation of archaeological facts. On the contrary, I would say that such a project, if we support
it, can only be achieved via an acknowledgement of the 'local' nature of the
orders which govern human behaviour, as others have emphasized (notably
Geertz 1983) in innumerable variations of the sweeping statement: 'what is
general is insignificant'.
Some people are worried about the reductionist overtones of the programme just outlined. Far from denying this, I see it as a virtue, since I am
more worried about the opposite tendency in archaeology: namely, a
continuing flow of inflated discourse in which 'anthropological' inferences

have replaced the aesthetic or psychological commentaries of the past, but where the game of interpretation commends itself no more in the first case than in the second, for lack of reasonably solid rules to make it exciting.

Conclusion

The different points of view which have been presented are so many aspects of our operational approach to the study of reasoning processes in archaeology, in which the emphasis is laid on the two necessary components of every interpretative 'construction': (a) the *semiological* system used to represent empirical facts in the database $\{P_0\}$; and (b) the set of rewriting operations used in the argument to back up the hypotheses or reach the conclusions $\{P_n\}$, in a computer-science perspective. The encounter with artificial intelligence a few years ago was useful in this respect, since here too a very similar pair of terms is used, 'representation and processing of knowledge', with which my two terms may easily be connected: (semiological) representation and (computer) processing. However, the danger is that people should think of our enterprise as a development of artificial intelligence applied to archaeology. Nothing could be further from our intentions: the setting up of expert systems is, in fact, secondary, and the main objective remains the elucidation of the mechanisms of archaeological interpretation and of its foundations – with or without expert systems. To be sure, there will be a great proliferation of artificial intelligence applications in archaeology in the next few years, because of the prestige of computers in the humanities. This phenomenon, which can already be detected, is reminiscent of the growth of mathematical exercises in the past 20 years. These have remained precisely that – exercises – contributing little to the progress of our knowledge of past societies (Doran 1986). However, the encouraging feature beyond these fleeting infatuations is the emergence, or re-emergence according to Wylie (ch. 5, this volume), of the 'problem of epistemological limits', which several archaeologists are posing today in much the same terms as we do. One of Wylie's merits is to remind us that our emphasis on the epistemological limits of interpretation is nothing new: 20 or 30 years ago Stuart Piggott and Christopher Hawkes raised the same questions in fairly similar terms (references in Wylie, ch. 5, this volume). The only thing that is new is the firm intention of some people today actually to *deal with* these questions, rather than simply continuing to raise them; indeed, some people have made this the main objective of 'Archaeology Tomorrow' (Gallay 1986).

It is clear that for this purpose we need something less vague than the concept of 'natural logic' in order to check our inferences, both from a formal and from an empirical viewpoint (Gardin 1987). The transformation of our traditional discursive practices into rules of inference of the type we have been discussing is a step in this direction, so long as we take care at the same time to assess the boundaries of such rules. As for the criteria upon which our assessments should be based, I see no other possibility than one or other of the two following, each of which has its supporters, both in archaeology and in other disciplines.

(a) Either the allegiance of a particular scientific community at a particular time to some specific theory and the inferences which constitute its key features (for example, Hodder 1984), following the principles of interpretation presented by hermeneutics for the humanities as a whole (for example, Ricoeur 1976, 1981).
(b) Or the more down-to-earth mechanisms of validation of the type which have been accepted for several centuries in the natural sciences, and are applicable in archaeology as in any empirical discipline, whether it be one of the humanities or not (Gardin 1979, pp. 77–119, (1980, pp. 127–34). However, this last course implies certain concessions; these have been brilliantly discussed by Gallay in his most recent book (1986), which also deals in its own way with the 'problem of limits' raised by Wylie. The almost simultaneous publication of Gallay's book and the collective work on expert systems in archaeology referred to above (Gardin *et al.* 1987) is a sign of the times. They both provide the tools and the examples required to understand better the nature of our interpretation processes and the way in which they may be confronted with the empirical observations provided by the social sciences – not only archaeology itself, but also history, sociology, economics, etc.; in short, 'ethnology' in the deliberately extended sense which we gave to it above.

References

Arnold, D. E. 1985. *Ceramic theory and cultural process.* Cambridge: Cambridge University Press.

Binford, L. 1981. *Bones. Ancient men and modern myths.* New York: Academic Press.

Doran, J. 1986. Paper presented at the Anglo-French seminar on expert systems in the humanities, Poigny-la-Foret, 13–14 February 1986 (in press).

Gallay, A. 1986. *L'Archéologie demain.* Paris: Belfond.

Gardin, J. C., 1974. *Les analyses de discours.* Neuchâtel: Delachaux & Niestlé.

Gardin, J. C. 1979. *Une archéologie théorique.* Paris: Hachette. (English version 1980. *Archaeological constructs.* Cambridge: Cambridge University Press.)

Gardin, J. C. 1981. Vers une épistémologie pratique en sciences humaines. In *La logique du plausible*, J. C. Gardin, M. S. Lagrange, J. M. Martin, J. Molino & J. Natali (eds), 3–91. Paris: Maison des Sciences de l'Homme (2nd revised edn 1987).

Gardin, J. C. 1982. Lectures plurielles et sciences singulières de la littérature. *Diogène* **118**, 3–14.

Gardin, J. C. 1983. L'aide au raisonnement en archéologie: travaux d'intelligence artificielle. In *Actes de l'école d'été européenne sur les applications des mathématiques et de l'informatique a l'archéologie, Montpellier, juillet 1983* (in press).

Gardin, J. C. 1985a. Fondements possibles de la sémiologie. *Recherches Sémiotiques/ Semiotic Inquiry (RSSI)* **5** (1), 1–31.

Gardin, J. C. 1985b. Sémiologie et informatique. *Degrés*, **13** (42–43), b1–b23.

Gardin, J. C. 1987. La logique naturelle, ou autre, dans les constructions de sciences humaines. *Revue européenne des sciences sociales* (special issue in honour of V. B. Grize, M. J. Borel (ed.)), t. xxv, no. 77, 179–95.

Gardin, J. C. & M. S. Lagrange 1975. *Essais d'analyse du discours archéologique*. Notes et monographies techniques du Centre de Recherches Archéologiques. Paris: CNRS.

Gardin, J. C., O. Guillaume, P. O. Herman, A. Hesnard, M. S. Lagrange, M. Renaud & E. Zadoro-Rio 1987. *Systèmes experts et sciences humaines: le cas de l'archéologie*. Paris: Eyrolles.

Geertz, C. 1983. *Local knowledge. Further essays in interpretive anthropology*. New York: Basic Books.

Hodder, I. 1984. Archaeology in 1984. *Antiquity* **58**, 25–32.

Joll, J. 1984. *The origins of the First World War*. London: Longman.

Ricoeur, P. 1976. *Interpretation theory*. Fort Worth: Texas Christian University Press.

Ricoeur, P. 1981. *Hermeneutics and the Human Sciences*, J. Thompson (ed.). Cambridge: Cambridge University Press.

Wylie, A. 1989. Matters of fact and matters of interest. In *Archaeological approaches to cultural identity*, S. J. Shennan (ed.), ch. 5. London: Unwin Hyman.

CULTURAL IDENTITY AND ITS MATERIAL EXPRESSION IN THE PAST AND THE PRESENT

7 Material aspects of Limba, Yalunka and Kuranko ethnicity: archaeological research in northeastern Sierra Leone

CHRISTOPHER R. DeCORSE

The Limba, Yalunka and Kuranko are ethnic groups occupying adjacent areas in northeastern Sierra Leone. The three groups share several culture traits, but various factors allow the groups to be distinguished ethnographically. Examination of archaeological data, primarily relating to defensive sites occupied during the past 200 years, indicates that material culture provides only a limited indication of these divisions. Material expressions of group cohesion, social identity and ethnicity that do occur are primarily manifest in ritual. This chapter provides an insight into the problems faced by prehistorians in identifying ethnic groups or defining culture areas. Possible directions for future work and implications of the research are considered.

The geographical and culture setting

Northeastern Sierra Leone is located within the forest–savanna ecotone; the southern part of the region is characterized by tropical forest and farm bush, whereas the north is more open and savanna grass and baobab trees are common. Physiographically the area lies on the Koinadugu Plateau, an extension of the Guinea Highlands, and is dominated by intricately dissected plains, hills and mountains. Culturally the area consists largely of Limba, Yalunka and Kuranko (Fig. 7.1), but smaller numbers of Fulani, Mandinka and other ethnic groups are also present. The three larger groups are swidden agriculturalists. Chicken, goats and sheep are commonly kept, but cattle, when owned, are often tended by Fulani herdsmen. There is a high degree of cultural similarity throughout the region, but a variety of linguistic, cultural, political and historical factors characterize the individual groups.

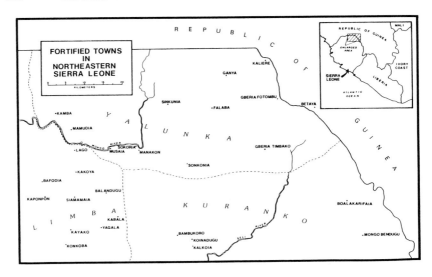

Figure 7.1   Map of northeastern Sierra Leone, showing sites referred to in the text.

The Yalunka, Kuranko and Limba are most easily distinguished on the basis of language. The two former groups are closely related Mande peoples whose languages are, to a degree, mutually intelligible. Greenberg classifies both within the Mande group of the Niger–Congo language family, which also includes more-northerly groups such as the Bambara (Greenberg 1970, p. 8). Many Kuranko live in Sierra Leone, but a significant number are found in the Republic of Guinea, occupying the territory as far east as Beyla. The Yalunka – also referred to as Djalonke, Dialonke and Jallonke – are an extension of a large ethnic group in Guinea. The Limba are set apart from the Yalunka and Kuranko linguistically, and are placed in the West Atlantic subfamily (*ibid.*, p. 8). Other members of this group include the Temne, Bulom, Kissi and Gola, people found to the south. Most Limba live in northern Sierra Leone, but a small number are found in the Republic of Guinea.

Only a limited amount of ethnographic information is available for northern Sierra Leone before the late 19th century, making it difficult to assess the change that has occurred in the various ethnic groups during the past few centuries. Dress, social structure and religion ('secret societies'), as well as language, in southern Sierra Leone tie the Limba to groups who are generally regarded as the first occupants of the region (Rodney 1967, p. 219, Atherton 1969, pp. 139–45, Fyle 1979a, pp. 4–5). By the 17th century it seems that European visitors to the coast were able to distinguish the Limba and related groups (i.e. the 'Sapes': Bullom, Temne, Baga, etc.) from more-recent arrivals (Atherton 1969, pp. 140–1). At least some ritual practices seem to have undergone little change between the 17th century and the present (MacCormack 1979). On the basis of the continuity of stone tool forms throughout the Late Stone Age and the early Iron Age, Atherton has suggested that the Limba may have occupied Sierra Leone during the entire period (Atherton 1969, p. 140).

In the more recent past the Limba have been increasingly influenced by northern Islamic groups, such as the Mandinka and the Fulani, and Christian missionaries (Ottenberg 1983, 1984). Today there is a prevalence of Mandinka names among Limba ruling families, and it has been suggested that many of the Limba settlements founded during the past 200 years were connected with the arrival of Mandinka settlers (Finnegan 1965, p. 15). Work by Christian missionaries did not begin until the 1940s and has concentrated in a few of the larger settlements. Despite these influences, Islam and Christianity have had comparatively little effect on Limba sociocultural practices.

Oral histories suggest that the Kuranko and Yalunka are more-recent arrivals in Sierra Leone, perhaps beginning to migrate south out of the Sudan during the 16th century (Fyle 1976, pp. 109–12, 1979b, pp. 6–8). Oral histories indicate that slave raids were frequently carried out against the Limba by the incoming groups. The impetus for the migration of the Kuranko may have been the disintegration of the Mali Empire in the late 15th century. The Yalunka originally occupied the Futa Jallon in the Republic of Guinea, but they were displaced by the Fulani (Fyle 1979b, pp. 34–9). They may have entered northern Sierra Leone as early as the 17th century, but oral histories place the founding of most towns in the second half of the 18th century.

The Yalunka and Kuranko share certain ritual practices, particularly those of the hunters (Donald 1968; Jackson 1977). However, the Yalunka are more Islamized than the Kuranko (over 90% of the former consider themselves Moslem), and this is reflected in ritual, Islamic prayers and references to Allah having more prominence among the Yalunka. Various styles of dress, musical instruments and other culture traits are common to both groups.

Before the 20th century a series of Limba, Yalunka and Kuranko polities controlled large areas which at times extended well outside the border of present Koinadugu. However, the degree of political cohesion exhibited, particularly within the Limba and Kuranko areas, seems to have been quite variable. It appears that although a settlement might be considered as being subject to another, individual towns retained a great deal of autonomy. It also seems that spheres of influence varied with the power of individual chiefs. For example, Finnegan notes that the town of Yagala was at times subject to Bafodia, and during other periods was controlled by Bumban far to the south (Finnegan 1965, p. 16). Oral histories further suggest that at other times Yagala may have been independent.

Within the Yalunka area the pre-colonial political situation was somewhat different. By 1800, under the influence of the Samura of Falaba, different Yalunka groups had coalesced into what Fyle (1975, 1979b) refers to as the 'Sulima Yalunka Kingdom'. The borders of Sulima came to include all the

Yalunka chiefdoms of modern Koinadugu, as well as Yalunka land in the Republic of Guinea. The Kuranko of Sengbe Chiefdom also came under domination (Fyle 1976, p. 111), resulting in a slightly more complex political organization than among the Limba and Kuranko. Falaba emerged as a regional judicial and administrative centre, with the *manga*, or king of Falaba, as its leader (Fyle 1979b, pp. 49–64). Important cases were tried at Falaba, and all trading and redistribution was supervised by the *manga*. On a continuum of political development, the Yalunka situation was much closer to the 'state', as described by Service, whereas the political organization of the Limba and Kuranko could be classed as 'chiefdom' (Service 1975, pp. 74–80, 104–64).

Material aspects of Limba, Yalunka and Kuranko ethnicity

The data examined here primarily relate to Limba, Yalunka and Kuranko sites dating to the past 200 years. Archaeological research in Sierra Leone is still largely in its exploratory stages, and only a limited amount of research has been done in the northeastern part of the country (Newman 1962, 1966, Cole-King 1976). Larger-scale excavations were undertaken by Atherton at Kamabai and Yagala rock shelters, sites located within Limba territory. A sequence ranging from *c.* 2500 BC until at least the 14th century AD is represented (Atherton 1972, pp. 42–3). As noted above, a fair degree of cultural continuity is suggested by the archaeological data. Although it is tempting to see the Limba as the descendants of this Late Stone Age population, the question requires more study.

Atherton also provided the first archaeological descriptions of fortified towns in Koinadugu District (Atherton 1968, 1983). He commented on some of the unique features of the sites, and obtained a radiocarbon date of AD 1740 ± 100 years on charcoal from a cave used as shelter during the rainy season or during periods of warfare. This agrees with Limba oral histories, which generally extend no further back in time than the late 18th or early 19th centuries, and which recall the founding of several of the larger Limba settlements.

Survey work carried out by the author between December 1978 and January 1981 focused on defensive sites known to have been occupied by the Limba, Yalunka and Kuranko during historic and protohistoric times (DeCorse 1980, 1981). The area examined covers approximately 4500 km² in Koinadugu District, including portions of the Limba Chiefdoms of Wara Wara Yagala and Wara Wara Bafodia; the Yalunka chiefdoms of Musaia Dembelia, Sinkunia Dembelia and Sulima; and the Kuranko chiefdoms of Mongo and Sengbe. The objective of this research was to provide archaeological data from an area that had received only limited attention. More than 25 settlements were examined. Oral histories were collected or were available for many of the sites. Several sites were mapped, surface collections were made and test excavations were undertaken at one settlement.

Although an attempt was made to visit as many sites as possible within the study area, the size of the area covered, time constraints and transport problems resulted in research being concentrated in some areas. The comments and conclusions presented are therefore of a preliminary nature.

Settlements

Defensive sites dating to the past 400–500 years are common in West Africa. Many such sites are found in Liberia, Sierre Leone and the Republic of Guinea, and a variety of defences are represented (Alldridge 1901, p. 219, Malcolm 1939, Haselberger 1964, p. 99, Siddle 1968, Abraham 1975). Kup (1975, p. 26), for example, notes that hilltop forts protected by circular entrenchments are associated with Mande peoples. The Mende of southern Sierre Leone at times surrounded their settlements with more than ten fences or walls, while ditches and towers protected each entrance (Alldridge 1901, p. 230, Malcolm 1939, pp. 48–9). The Susu of northern Sierra Leone, a group closely related to the Yalunka, protected their towns with mud walls which at times were more than 15 ft (4.5 m) thick. In many cases winding entrances through dense brush were also employed (Alldridge 1901, pp. 97, 155, 298–300, Siddle 1969, p. 33). The Limba, Yalunka and Kuranko utilized similar defences, and the remains of many of these still survive.

The defences represented at the sites examined in northeastern Sierra Leone varied due to vegetational and topographical considerations, and possibly due to some culturally determined patterning. Settlements of the Yalunka tend to be located on level areas on low riverine plateaux of interfluves, although hilltop sites are also found. Settlements on level open areas such as Musaia, Manakon and Sinkunia often contained more than 100 houses. Laing estimated that Falaba, capital of the Sulima Yalunka Kingdom and one of the larger settlements, had 400 houses in 1822 and a population of between 6000 and 10 000 people (Siddle 1968). Located in lightly forested areas, the towns were protected by mud walls, or *tatana*. Small portals near the gates enabled men to fire at attacking forces. In some instances the town fortifications were stockades of living trees interspersed with timber or mud walls. Such was the case at Falaba, which was '. . . surrounded by a natural stockade of over 500 huge trees. . . . One of the gates of the town, of which there are seven, is ingeniously cut through the trunk of one of the largest trees' (Blyden 1873, p. 128). Outside the walls a large moat was sometimes dug. Today the ditch at Falaba, though heavily eroded, is still more than 20 ft (6 m) across and 15 ft (4.5 m) deep in places.

The Kuranko sometimes made use of defences similar to those of the Yalunka. Such was the case with the towns of Mongo Bendugu and Masadugu, which had encircling stockades of living trees. However, in the more densely forested areas to the south a different strategy was utilized. Thickets of dense brush which surrounded a town were cultivated as a natural, impenetrable barrier. This distinctive vegetation pattern can be seen clearly on infrared false-colour photographs. Walls or stockades provided

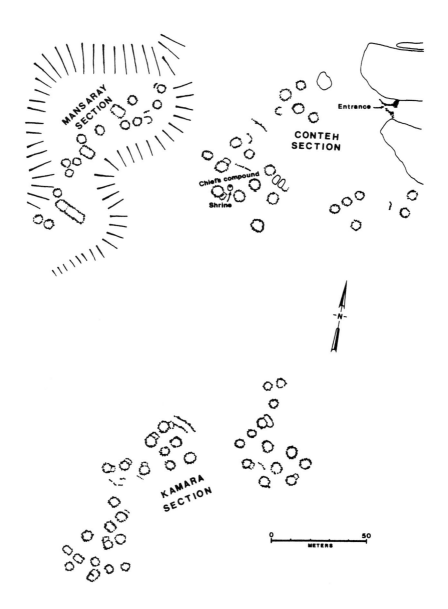

Figure 7.2 A sketch map of the ruins of the Limba settlement of Kakoya, illustrating the clustering of dwellings in clan groups.

additional protection at entrances. The entrance itself was usually a low, narrow doorway which could be closed with a thick wooden slab.

Situated to the west of the Yalunka and Kuranko, the Limba of the Wara Wara Mountains employed a wide variety of defences. In addition to being more-heavily forested, the area is broken by dissected hills of granodiorite, and it presents some of the most rugged topography in the country. The terrain is often broken by outcrops, rock shelters and massive boulders. Some Limba towns, such as Kaponpon, were protected by stockades similar to those already described for the Yalunka. Others employed thickets of thorn bushes, which the Limba call *inthiri*, not unlike the vegetation barriers used by the Kuranko. Other Limba settlements presented some unique features employing the natural inaccessibility of the Wara Waras. Inconveniently situated on top of steep hills, distant from farmland and water sources, these towns were easily defended. Unable to set wooden house-supports into the rock hilltops, the Limba often constructed their houses of stone (Atherton 1983).

Observations of modern Limba, Yalunka and Kuranko settlements indicate that they are often broken into sections which reflect clan groupings. Membership in a clan carries certain ritual and social obligations and, to a certain extent, regulates marriage patterns. A traditional village has several circular clusters of clan groupings, a feature which can be recognized archaeologically, particularly at Limba sites such as Balandugu, Yagala, Siamamaia and Kakoya, where houses were constructed of stone (Fig. 7.2). In cases where houses were constructed of mud, the task of the archaeologist is much more daunting, although the study of modern dwellings and careful excavation does provide clues (MacIntosh 1977, Agorsah 1985). Traces of dwellings are quickly levelled by rain and vegetation, and farming often obliterates the remains. Even at the old Limba town of Bafodia, which was occupied until the 1950s, it was difficult to identify clan groups even though traces of some house mounds remain and informants were able to indicate which areas were associated with each clan.

Architecture

Problems of preservation also make it difficult to examine differences in the spatial arrangement of individual Limba, Yalunka and Kuranko houses. Plans of several modern dwellings and structures, as well as stone-walled dwellings from abandoned Limba sites (Fig. 7.3), illustrate some of the basic similarities found in architecture throughout the region. Structures are usually round and traditionally had thatch roofs of some kind, though the manner in which the thatch was applied and even the thatching material itself seems to have varied, particularly in the Limba chiefdoms south of Koinadugu District. Buildings, whether of stone or of wattle and daub, were plastered with a mixture of mud and cow dung, a technique widely used in West Africa. Dwellings of all three groups generally have two opposing doors, and the space under the eaves is frequently utilized as a work or storage area.

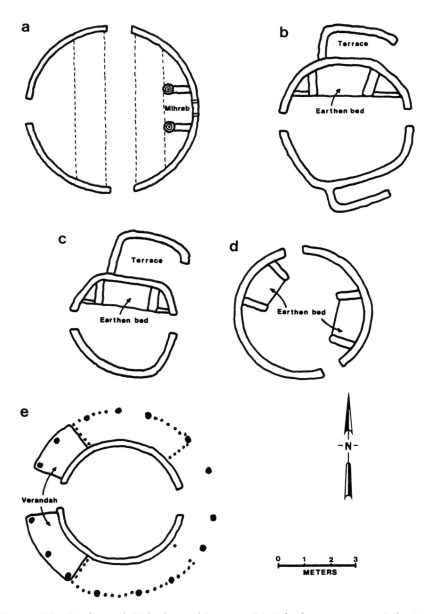

Figure 7.3 Limba and Yalunka architecture: (a) Yalunka mosque at Sokoria; (b–d) stone-walled Limba dwellings at Yagala; (e) a Yalunka house at Kamba.

Limba stone houses are frequently smaller and sometimes have a distinct-ive spatial arrangement. This almost certainly resulted from the terrain where the houses were constructed, rather than from cultural differences or patterns. The mountain-top sites are craggy and boulder-strewn, and houses had to conform to the space available. In some cases dwellings were actually perched on top of some of the larger boulders. Terraces for work areas had to fit in where space allowed. Differences in stone coursing noticed between different sites are probably also due to natural factors; the size of naturally occurring cobbles varies at different locales. Mud-walled Limba houses located in more-open areas are similar to those of the Yalunka and Kuranko. Structures of comparable form and construction can be seen among the Foulbe to the north in the Republic of Guinea (Prussin 1982, p. 63) and in Temne settlements to the south. Differences between the housing of various ethnic groups may exist, but a significant amount of variation also occurs within the individual ethnic groups.

Ritual behaviour

Material aspects of ritual behaviour such as shrines, rock paintings and burial practices can be important indicators of ethnicity. Only a limited amount of information on these practices was collected, but enough is available to indicate their significance, and the data are surveyed here. A variety of devices are used by the Limba, Yalunka and Kuranko to intercede in supernatural events. These may take the form of individual shrines, talis-mans worn on the body and ritual offerings hung above doorways or, occasionally, buried under the floor.

Several shrines and ritual areas were still in use or had been used in the recent past, and informants were able to assist with interpretation. The forms taken by the shrines varied greatly between settlements; many were unique, and most were constructed of insubstantial materials. One example is a shrine located next to the Mongo River, some distance outside the Yalunka settlement of Kamba. A place of offering for spirits associated with the hippopotamuses in the river, the shrine was little more than four sticks supporting a light covering. The shrine to a spirit at Sinkunia, another Yalunka town, was slightly more substantial in appearance. It was located in a dome-shaped hut approximately 3 m across, constructed of poles with a covering of thatch. A fence bounded the space around the shrine. Another example is the founder's shrine at the Yalunka town of Musaia. Oral history indicates that a virgin was sacrificed and buried beneath a young orange tree. Today little denotes the special significance of the tree except that the fruit-laden branches remain unpicked. A Limba ancestral shrine at Yagala was marked by nothing but a small broken iron pot and a large piece of quartz.

Because of the wide variety represented, and the fact that many of the shrines described above are made of very perishable material, their import-ance as archaeological indicators of ethnicity is limited. However, there are

Figure 7.4   A Yalunka shrine in front of the chief's house at Kamba. An Islamic prayer area lies in the background. The gun barrel is approximately 2.5 cm in diameter.

certain shrines which deserve special comment. Shrines associated with the chief's house can be seen in many settlements. In the Wara Wara Limba chiefdoms a platform of flat stones approximately 6 ft (2 m) across is prepared and a round stone is placed in the centre. In some cases a flat stone slab may be placed upright. In Yalunka and Kuranko areas similar shrines consist of a stone or pile of stones, a wooden post (*sarakawodena*) and a piece of iron. The last of these is frequently an old sword or trade gun (Fig. 7.4), but other items may be used (for example, at the paramount chief's

compound in Musaia an old engine block lies next to a large pile of stones).
Trotter (1898, p. 40) may have been referring to this type of shrine when he
noted that two guns were buried in the centre of villages to mark the end of
the Sofa War.

Shrines and ritual areas are also associated with hunters' societies and
puberty rituals. Hunters among the Kuranko erect a special shrine outside of
their settlement to the hunting deity Mande Fabourre, a first man–first
hunter figure. This is made of mud and consists of a low platform
surmounted by an anthropomorphic figure (sometimes little more than an
amorphous pillar) 2–3 ft (60–90 cm) in height. This is usually covered by a
small thatch roof. When sacrifices are made, blood is spilled on the figure,
and traces of this can often be seen. The hunters are organized into groups at
the subchiefdom level. Shrines are associated with certain territories, and
they are not necessarily found outside every Kuranko settlement. Shrines of
this type were not observed at any Limba or Yalunka settlement, although
apparently the latter group did construct similar shrines in the past. Yalunka
hunting rituals still focus on sites where the shrines were located, although
no evidence of these can be seen today.

Puberty ceremonies involving the circumcision of males and the excision
of females are important throughout the entire area. Each group has its own
particular practices, but the 'borrowing' of certain customs can be seen in
marginal areas. Material aspects of this ritual behaviour include special dress,
sacrifices, tools and specially designated areas, but little which is of use to the
archaeologist. Circumcision of males and the excision of females traditionally take place outside of the settlement, in special areas which are
sometimes left unbrushed. Temporary shelters were sometimes erected for
the initiates, but no other special features mark the sites. Locating and
identifying these ritual sites without the aid of informants or oral histories
would be difficult, though distinctive vegetation patterns might provide
some indication of their location. What would be preserved archaeologically
at such sites would be difficult to associate with a particular group. An
exception is ritual paintings made in connection with Limba excision rituals
(DeCorse in press). However, such paintings seem to be confined to a very
localized area and do not appear in all Limba chiefdoms.

The most substantial ritual structures found in the region are mosques.
These are usually variations of the square mosque prescribed by Malekite
law, but local adaptations can be seen, such as the small round mosque at
Sokoria (Fig. 7.3a). Archaeologically such a structure might prove difficult
to differentiate from a dwelling. At times the sacred Moslem space is reduced
to a simple square of stones with a pebbled surface (for examples among the
Foulbe, see Prussin 1982, p. 62). Among the Yalunka and Kuranko these
prayer areas sometimes lie adjacent to traditional shrines, indicating the
syncretic nature of religious beliefs.

Artefacts

Of the artefactual material recovered from surface collections and excavations, ceramics are by far the most common. Ethnographic studies of Fulani pottery by David & Hennig (1972) and Bedik–Fulbe pottery by Atherton (1983) indicate some of the problems and possibilities in using pottery in studies of ethnicity, and a similar situation is seen here. Ethnographic observations of modern Limba and Yalunka potters provide an indication of how pottery was probably produced in the past. Pottery manufacture seems to have always been exclusively a female occupation (Thomas 1918, p. 111, Atherton 1969, p. 108). Vessels of 'all kinds' were still being produced in the north-east in 1918 (Thomas 1918, p. 41), but today work is largely confined to undecorated cooking pots.

Traditionally clay for potting was obtained from two sources – geological deposits and the interior of large termite mounds – sources which are still used today. Dry clay is pounded into a powder using a stone or wooden pestle, and is then sifted by hand or sieved. Informants indicated that temper was not intentionally added to the clay. When the clay is used, water is added and the paste is pounded to the right consistency. A pot is started by moulding a slab of clay over the bottom of an old pot or calabash. Coils are then used to build up the remainder of the pot. The surface is smoothed with a calabash paddle. In ethnographic cases decorations were confined to occasional raised bands, incising, stabbing or stamping. These decorations were applied when the newly formed pot had become leathery. The completed pots were fired in the open under a pile of brush.

The type of manufacture described above is common to much of the interior of Sierra Leone and probably to many of the neighbouring parts of West Africa. Analysis of archaeological collections indicates similar methods were used in the past. Evidence of a moulded base and coil construction could be seen on many fragments. The paste of all sherds examined from archaeological sites contained fine to very coarse sand inclusions, with occasional fragments grading up to 4 mm. This is similar to ethnographic examples. Tempering with millet stalks, shell or other organic material has been reported from other parts of Sierra Leone, but does not appear to occur in Limba, Yalunka and Kuranko areas. Four per cent of the sherds excavated from Wara Wara Rock Shelter contained large fragments of laterite, granule to pebble in size (0–1 cm), which may have been intentionally added as temper. Such inclusions were not found in any ethnographic or archaeological examples from other sites in Koinadugu District, or from any other part of the country. However, this could be due to the small size of the comparative collections.

Certain vessel forms and decorations may be associated with certain ethnic groups, but insufficient work has been carried out in Sierra Leone to make a complete assessment. No highly distinctive ritual pots, such as those found in some areas of West Africa, were noted in northern Sierra Leone. However, some local variation in utilitarian forms were noted in both ethnographic and archaeological examples. There also seem to be styles of decoration that are common to some areas (or even to individual towns), yet other decorative techniques clearly cross-cut ethnic groups and some motifs can be found as far afield as southern Sierre Leone, Mali and Ghana. It may prove difficult to separate variation due to local artistic traditions and ethnic factors from those resulting from temporal changes. For example, pottery forms and decorative styles from Bafodia Old town (occupied from the late 18th century to 1950) are quite different from those recovered from the original settlement at Kawoya located nearby.

Discussion and conclusions

The Limba, Yalunka and Kuranko, although sharing certain cultural practices, are regarded by themselves and outsiders as distinct ethnic groups. Examination of their material culture, although providing information about social organization, ritual practices and technology, offers only limited indications of these divisions. Culturally influenced choices greatly affect methods of house construction, use of space, settlement patterns and numerous other aspects of material culture, yet climatic, topographical and historical factors are also of importance. Archaeologically, Limba, Yalunka and Kuranko sites look very similar. In fact, the Yalunka and Kuranko sites have more in common with Limba settlements than with those of more-closely related Mande groups living in the Sudan. Several writers have noticed similarities in house construction and settlement patterns from widely disparate parts of Africa which share certain climatic or topographical characteristics (Denyer 1978). These factors were probably more important in determining the types of defences and methods of house construction used by the Limba, Yalunka and Kuranko than ethnicity.

Some indication of the slightly more centralized political system within the Yalunka area is suggested by the archaeological data. Yalunka settlements (especially Falaba) are much larger than any Limba or Kuranko sites. This was largely determined by using documentary sources, but this is something that could be examined archaeologically.

Technology also presents a confused picture of ethnicity among the Limba, Yalunka and Kuranko. Pottery, the only industry discussed in detail here, varies in form and decoration both temporally and geographically. This variation does not readily reflect ethnic differences. Other manufactured items may be more useful. For example, iron-smelting furnaces reported in the Kuranko area earlier in this century (Dixey 1920) are different from any observed archaeologically in the Yalunka area. Although this may have potential, any patterning along ethnic lines would be confused by the movement of skilled craftsmen between groups. This was definitely the case in northern Sierra Leone, where oral histories indicate that blacksmiths were so highly valued for their skill that they were singled out for capture in raids into neighbouring areas. Women, the manufacturers of pottery, were also frequently taken as wives or slaves.

The most important archaeological indicators of ethnicity within the study area are material aspects of ritual behaviour. These exhibit more variability than other categories of material culture, and to some extent seem to be associated with particular ethnic groups. To follow Wiessner's (1989) approach to style, shrines play important social and symbolic rôles among the Limba, Yalunka and Kuranko, and provide a suitable means of expressing individuality or ethnic identity, or both. In contrast, other aspects of material culture examined have very minor social and symbolic rôles and have a limited amount of 'comparative' value. However, the shrines described exhibit a high degree of variability and none appears to be present in every settlement of a certain ethnic group. Preservation again poses a problem, as exemplified by the Kuranko hunting shrines. Relatively small, impermanent and located some distance outside of settlements, it is unlikely that such sites would be easily discovered without the aid of informants.

It is notable that various types of aesthetic expression, an area which is often noted as an indicator of ethnicity or social identity, is very limited throughout northern Sierra Leone (DeCorse & Benton in press). Representative and geometric painting is uncommon, and there are no traditions of carving or sculptural ornamentation. Traditional types of embellishment seem to have been mostly confined to simple geometric designs found on iron weapons, shrine posts, storage boxes and occasional house supports. These limited areas of aesthetic expression provide little indication of 'individuality' or 'social cohesion' and further complicate an archaeological assessment of ethnicity.

The research reviewed here underscores the work of others which has clearly demonstrated the difficulty in using material culture to ascribe ethnicity or even to define broader cultural groups (for example, Vansina 1961, Atherton 1983). In fact Atherton, in his review of ethno-archaeology in Africa, suggests that archaeologists would be better off if they avoided 'a fruitless quest for paleosociopolitical epiphenomena such as ethnicity' (Atherton 1983, p. 96). This may be good advice. However, given the important rôle of archaeology in the study of culture history and ethnic origins, and the increasing political and legal implications of such research, it seems a difficult area of study to ignore.

What seems clear from the ethno-archaeological research that has been undertaken is that culture traits, artefacts or attributes are often poor indicators of ethnicity when considered individually. However, the study of overall artefact, attribute and trait patterns may prove more helpful in defining ethnic groups. Work in this direction can be seen in the 'local rule' model evolved by Agorsah (1983) for his work on the Nchumuru in Ghana, where regularities in spatial distributions provide a distinctive archaeological signature. Quantitative studies of artefacts and their patterns by historical archaeologists suggest possible directions for future research. Methods of pattern recognition developed by South (1977) have been employed in a variety of historic period sites. A good example of their potential is provided by work by Lewis, Moore, Armstrong, and others, on slave plantation sites.

In these cases the researchers were able to demonstrate the unique character of African–American culture, even though no artefacts of clearly African origin were recovered (Singleton 1985). Further research along these lines may make it possible to define ethnicity more clearly among groups such as the Limba, Yalunka and Kuranko.

References

Abraham, A. 1975. The pattern of warfare and settlement among the Mende of Sierra Leone in the second half of the nineteenth century. *Institute of African Studies, Fourah Bay College Occasional Paper No. 1.*

Agorsah, E. K. 1983. Social behaviour and social context. *African Studies Monographs* **4**, 119–28.

Agorsah, E. K. 1985. Archaeological implications of traditional house construction among the Nchumuru of Northern Ghana. *Current Anthropology* **26**(1), 103–8.

Alldridge, T. J. 1901. *The Sherbro and its hinterland.* New York: Macmillan.

Atherton, J. H. 1968. Valecne jeskyne kmene Limba. *Novy Orient* (October), 237–8.

Atherton, J. H. 1969. The Later Stone Age of Sierra Leone. PhD dissertation, University of Oregon.

Atherton, J. H. 1972. Excavations at Kamabai and Yagala rock shelters, Sierra Leone. *West African Journal of Archaeology* **2**, 39–74.

Atherton, J. H. 1983. Ethnoarchaeology in Africa. *African Archaeological Review* **1**, 75–104.

Blyden, E. W. 1873. Report on the expedition to Falaba, January to March 1872. *Proceedings of the Royal Geographical Society* **17**(2), 117–33.

Cole-King, P. A. 1976. *Sierra Leone: development of the new national museum and preservation of antiquities.* Paris: Unesco.

David, N. & H. Hennig, 1972. The ethnography of pottery: a Fulani case seen in archaeological perspective. *McCaleb Module in Anthropology No. 21.*

DeCorse, C. R. 1980. An archaeological survey of protohistoric defensive sites in Northeastern Sierra Leone. *Nyame Akuma* **17**, 48–53.

DeCorse, C. R. 1981. Additional notes on archaeological fieldwork in Northeastern Sierra Leone. *Nyame Akuma* **19**, 14–17.

DeCorse, C. R. in press. Rock paintings from northern Sierra Leone. *Bollettino del Centro Comuno di Studi Preistorici.*

DeCorse, C. R. & C. J. Benton in press. Yalunka child drawings: the draw-a-man intelligence test in cross cultural perspective. *West African Journal of Educational and Vocational Measurement.*

Denyer, S. 1978. *African traditional architecture.* New York: Africana.

Dixey, F. 1920. Primitive iron-ore smelting methods in West Africa. *Mining Magazine* **23**(4), 213–16.

Donald, L. H. 1968. Changes in Yalunka social organization: a study of adaptation to a changing cultural environment. PhD dissertation, University of Oregon.

Finnegan, R. H. 1965. *Survey of the Limba people of Northern Sierra Leone.* London: Her Majesty's Stationery Office.

Fyle, C. M. 1975. The origin and integration of the Solima Yalunka State. *Africana Research Bulletin* **6**(1), 3–36.

Fyle, C. M. 1976. The Kabala Complex: Kuranko–Limba relationship in the nineteenth and twentieth centuries. In *Topics in Sierra Leone history: a counter-Colonial interpretation*, A. Abraham (ed.), 106–19. Freetown: Leone.

Fyle, C. M. 1979a. *Almany Suluku of Sierra Leone c. 1820–1906*. London: Evans.

Fyle, C. M. 1979b. *The Sulima Yalunka Kingdom*. Freetown: Nyakon.

Greenberg, J. H. 1970. *The languages of Africa*. Bloomington: University of Indiana.

Haselberger, H. 1964. *Bautraditionen der westafrikanischen Negerkulturen*. Wien: Herder.

Jackson, M. 1977. *The Kuranko*. London: C. Hurst.

Kup, A. P. 1975. *Sierra Leone: a concise history*. Vancouver: David & Charles.

MacCormack, C. P. 1979. Sande: the public face of a secret society. In *The new religions of Africa*, B. Jules-Rosette (ed.), 27–37. Norwood, New Jersey: Ablex.

MacIntosh, R. J. 1977. The excavation of mud structures: an experiment from west Africa. *World Archaeology* **9**(2), 92–101.

Malcolm, J. M. 1939. Mende warfare. *Sierra Leone Studies* **21**, 47–52.

Newman, T. M. 1962. *Archaeological survey of Sierre Leone*, MS.

Newman, T. M. 1966. Archaeological survey of Sierra Leone. *West African Archaeological Newsletter* **4**, 19–22.

Ottenberg, S. 1983. Artistic and sex roles in a Limba chiefdom. In *Female and male in West Africa*, C. Oppong (ed.), 76–90. London: Allen & Unwin.

Ottenberg, S. 1984. Two new religions, one analytic frame. *Cahiers d'études africaines* **96** XXIV(4), 437–54.

Prussin, L. 1982. Islamic architecture in West Africa: the Foulbe and Manding models. *Via* **5**, 53–69.

Rodney, W. 1967. A reconsideration of the Mande invasion of Sierra Leone. *Journal of African History* **8**(2), 219–46.

Service, E. R. 1975. *Origins of the state and civilization: the process of cultural evolution*. New York: Norton.

Siddle, D. J. 1968. War-towns in Sierra Leone: a study in social change. *Africa* **38**(1), 47–56.

Siddle, D. J. 1969. The evolution of rural settlement forms in Sierra Leone circa 1400 to 1968. *Sierra Leone Geographical Journal* **13**, 33–44.

Singleton, T. A. (ed.) 1985. *The archaeology of slavery and plantation life*. New York: Academic Press.

South, S. 1977. *Method and theory in historical archaeology*. New York: Academic Press.

Thomas, W. T. 1918. Industrial pursuits of the Yalunka people. *Sierra Leone Studies* (June), 39–42.

Trotter, J. K. 1898. *The Niger sources*. London: Methuen.

Vansina, J. 1961. Les zones culturelles de l'Afrique. *Africa-Tervuren* **7**(2), 41–6.

Wiessner, P. 1989. Style and changing relations between the individual and society. In *The meanings of things: material culture and symbolic expression*, I. Hodder (ed.), ch. 2. London: Unwin Hyman.

8 Multiculturalism in the eastern Andes

ANN OSBORN

This chapter focuses on cultural variations encountered among the U'wa (known in literature as Tunebo), presently inhabiting the eastern slopes of the Colombian eastern Andes, where the mountain chain curves into Venezuela (lat. 7°N, long. 72°W). Cultural variations exist among these people who, nevertheless, recognize themselves as belonging to the same society. The oral tradition, including chanted mythology of one clan-like group, the Kubaruwa, belonging to this cultural complex, suggests that there was a linking of U'wa groups over a territory stretching along the eastern *cordillera* of the Andes, from northeastern Venezuela into southwestern Colombia (Fig. 8.1).

In this chapter it is shown how notions about ethnicity are expressed in material culture, in beliefs about the body and in a geocosmological construct involving distance and direction. My main concern is to demonstrate how each U'wa group is different from its U'wa neighbours – in this society it is the institutionalized nature of these differences that mark each group as being a similar people with varying and complementary facets of what is socially a unified thought structure. It is when these elements are radically different and transgress the belief system that ethnic distinctions are made.

By and large, anthropologists agree on the criteria by which a tribe may be described: a common territory, a tradition of common descent, common language, common culture and a common name, all of these forming the basis of joining small groups (Gould & Kolb 1964, p. 729). For Amerindian societies the criteria should be questioned, particularly before the European conquest, when current Amerindian social and cultural organization may not have been of the discrete–cultural entities type: boundaries being fluid rather than fixed, as implied above.

The manner in which the culture under discussion hung together is more akin to polythetic classification, treated in a paper by Needham (1975, p. 350):

> . . . classes can be composed by means of what Vygotsky calls complex thinking: specifically, in a 'chain complex' the definitive attribute keeps changing from one link to the next: there is no consistency in the type of bonds, and the variable meanings carried over from one item in a class to the next with no 'central significance', no 'nucleus'.

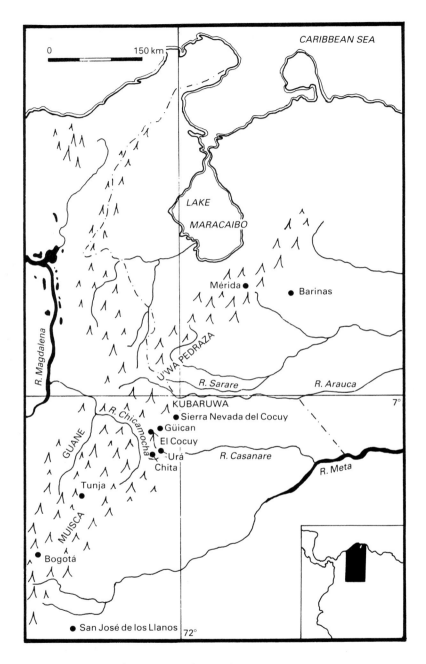

Figure 8.1 The northeastern Andes.

Needham goes on to note that these features are what Wittgenstein termed 'family resemblances'. Family resemblances are what the U'wa have in common with cultures strung out along the eastern Andes. Clarke (1968) makes a strong case for polythetic classification in archaeology, and Bray (1984) has suggested a similar concept over time and across the Caribbean Colombian lowland from Panama into Venezuela.

U'wa history and beliefs are embedded in oral tradition, which includes chanted mythology. This chapter is based in part on U'wa myths and contemporary shamans' interpretations of them, as well as other ethnographic data collected in the field and on archaeological survey work in an attempt to follow the situation backwards in time. Present U'wa society consists of six groups which are in different states of deculturalization, and which number some 2000 people. The Kubaruwa, on whom this chapter is based, number 500. In living memory two further groups have become extinct; one of these inhabited the highland area adjacent to the snow-capped peaks of the Sierra Nevada del Cocuy in Colombia (the highest permanent snow peaks of the northeastern Andes), whereas the other group lived in the temperate zone lying at middle altitudes, which is an extension of the Sierra Nevada spreading into lowland Venezuela. Political organization between these groups is decentralized. No one group was able to dominate another; rather, each had a particular place in power relationships based on religious beliefs, performing ceremonies for others and having rights to the exploitation of particular goods, including food. Fixed ownership to land did not pertain either to individuals or to groups: land was held in usufruct and a group's agricultural land was separated from that of other groups by forest, paramo or steep slopes. It was not the land itself that was of prime value, but rather what grew on it, and specific edible foods were owned by specific groups and not by others. Each group had three or four master shamans and a number of apprentices; in everyday life shamans compete against each other but cooperate in the presentation of myth and ritual. In the past, and to a certain extent today, master shamans have political alliances with master shamans of other adjacent groups; in fact the position of a master shaman is held in part on the support of a master shaman of another group. Political meetings take place between groups on the completion, by one group, of a myth cycle performance and 'judicial' cases are presented to the gathering. These are presented in a religious language and guise; physical or verbal agression is not permitted due to the religious nature of the event and the presence of deities. In principle anyone can present a case or argue against one. Finally a consensus of opinion is achieved through the master shaman's indirect intervention.

Today, as in the past, shamans remark that this system did not unite all groups or only a few in exceptional circumstances. Aguado (1956 (1582), Vol. I, p. 333) notes that Indians of U'ra, Chita and Cocuy fought together against Hernán Pérez de Quesada, but the neighbouring groups of Güican and Chiscas are not mentioned. Again, in the late 19th century the Pedraza group attacked Venezuelan road builders, but the adjacent groups did not support them.

In addition to the political meetings mentioned above, political relationships were maintained as a secondary result of religious pilgrimages. These appear to have been confined to the eastern Andes, following routes mentioned in chanted mythology (see below), although at the same time shamans travelled with the aim of teaching or learning over areas that extended beyond the Andean range. Hence, there was a continual exchange of knowledge taking place. The European conquest with its accompanying missionary activity, together with the subsequent expansion of other ethnic groups, broke this up very rapidly. For example, a Kubaruwa master shaman in the late 19th century, lamenting the isolation of the remaining U'wa, travelled into the so-called Guane and Muisca areas in an attempt to re-establish relationships, and other shamans travelled to the Pedraza area and to Barinas for the same reason. These pilgrimages together with the exchange of ideas linked many groups and only ceased with people who could not, or would not, be identified in the chain of relationships thus created.

In the past, and documented in chant prosody, federations existed within the U'wa and U'wa related groups. The number of groups belonging to a federation depended on the purpose of the relationship; for example, eight appears to have been the number of groups composing a political and ceremonial federation. It is worth emphasizing again that these alliances were open-ended in the sense that peripheral groups maintained dual- or triple-alliances with others in mountain and hill areas.

To illustrate the differences that exist between groups based on 'family resemblances', as indicated above and underpinned by a convergence of similar beliefs, I shall concentrate here on a number of pivotal themes. These are language, chanted mythology – particularly where this deals with place names – the agricultural-cum-ceremonial system, food and material culture. By selecting these I am concerned as much with ethnicity as with indicating how, if patterns are discerned, the variations of those belonging to one people may be recognized in the archaeological record.

Language

The language spoken by the U'wa is generally agreed to be a variant of Chibchan, a linguistic stock spoken from Honduras in Central America to northern Ecuador (Gonzáles de Pérez 1980). Language is often taken as an indicator of a common culture, although for some South American societies this has been shown to be questionable (Sorensen 1967). According to Matheson (1972, p. 93), the language spoken today resembles that spoken at the time of the European conquest called 'Chibcha proper' and spoken by the Muisca (or Chibcha proper) inhabiting the Bogotá plateau of the eastern *cordillera*.

Dialectical differences, although intelligible to other U'wa groups, are one of the ways in which U'wa distinguish one group from another. Headland

(1976, p. 18), writing on the current language, has distinguished three dialects. Again, everyday language differs from that of chant, the latter being esoteric and poetic, and modified by metre and delivery. To an unaccustomed ear the forms sound quite different, as two observers have remarked at different periods of U'wa history (Rivero 1956 (1739), pp. 57–8, Rochereau 1959, pp. 15–16). Furthermore, some aspects of chant language, that of the deities (and U'wa become deities when chanting), also differ between groups. For example, groups have different named protagonists in chant episodes, although their actions may be similar, and different sets of groups have their own centres where key mythological events are considered to have taken place. For the current U'wa these took place around the Sierra Nevada; for those now-extinct groups on the far side of the Sarare depression, mythology, with regard to place names and events, presumably centred on the highest peaks of Merida. I shall return to chant and place names below.

Within the Chibcha language groups of the eastern *cordillera*, U'wa was probably an affix indicating 'themselves', their own people; Kubaruwa, Bethuwa and, historically, Achagua: 'A nation extending from Barinas to San Juan de los Llanos and from there to Popayan . . . more than 20 nations or provinces (belonging to the Achagua) were subsumed under one language' (Rivero 1956 (1739), p. 21). The concept of a cultural continuum from the eastern flank of the *cordillera* crossing over to the western side fits my own data surprisingly well, although to extend it to Popayan in southern Colombia and the central *cordillera* may be an exaggeration. The same author also gives one of the few references to Tunebo inhabiting the highland area of the Sierra Nevada (Rivero 1956 (1739), p. 237). Rochereau (1959, p. 15), a missionary well-versed in U'wa language, noted that 'U'ua' is their own name for themselves (rather than Tunebo), meaning the intelligent people who know how to talk. The ability to discuss, reason and argue their point is another way in which these people distinguish themselves from others. Rochereau's remark is significant due to its implication of greater intelligence. U'wa do believe that they are a clever people, within their own culture, and maintain that others are ignorant of it. With this goes the belief that others cannot learn their language, their chant and even less, understand these or begin to interpret them.

In Kubaruwa chanted texts place names belonging to 16 groups are chanted, repeating two sets of four. They perform for all groups, but emphasize the federation to which they belong. The leading chanter will murmur to himself 'now the Karouwa' or the Bethuwa, and lead the chant of that group's place names. On this evidence, both in myth and in chant prosody, place names are divided by refrains separating one group's names from the next, and after a sequence of six groups, a temporary halt is made; on this evidence I suggest that there were once two sets of eight ceremonial groups forming federations – the groups at either end were those that linked the sets of eight. With reference to the eight groups of the Sierra Nevada, these were again subdivided into four, those with a highland to middle country range, and those of a middle country to lowland range. Elsewhere (Osborn 1985, pp. 120, 137), I have termed the groups of the Sierra 'the U'wa' and other adjacent and linking groups and group clusters 'U'wa related'. This distinction 'proper' and 'related' is consistent with terminology used by others referring to peoples of the eastern *cordillera*: Chibcha (or Muisca) 'proper' language or people being those who inhabited the Bogotá highland plateau at the time of the European conquest. Although I maintain that each cluster of groups would have considered themselves to be the 'proper', as the remaining groups do today.

In the literature the U'wa appear under a multitude of names, and inhabiting many micro-environments. One of the results of this is that people belonging to such a society were not recognized as such, due to the cultural variations between them. The other is that they were not recognized as a people, due to being encountered in different geographical areas (altitudinal zones) at different times of the year. In addition, the groups clustered around the Sierra Nevada may not have moved at the same time as they farmed different altitudinal zones.

This, and the associated agricultural-cum-ceremonial system, is a variant of that concept introduced into Andean studies by Murra (1972) and known as 'verticality' (first coined by Troll 1968, in the context of Andean ecological zones).

The agricultural-cum-ceremonial system

Four altitudinal, hence ecological, zones are exploited by the traditional U'wa. I shall continue by taking the Kubaruwa as my reference. This is a group that farms both the tropical lowlands at the foot of the Sierra Nevada and the higher temperate lands. The four zones are moved between seasonally, and in each of them similar crop assemblies are grown (maize, coca, plantains, manioc, numerous other roots and tubers, a variety of edible leaves, and chard-like plants and nuts of certain trees or palms), but in each zone a particular crop is emphasized, as the U'wa believe that they are composed of the foods they eat. These, in their seasonal and ceremonial context, are documented below, together with seasonal residence.

The wet to dry season spanning the September equinox

Residence at this time is in the temperate uplands at an altitude of 1300 m with the farming range from 1000 to 2000 m approximately, and taking place within a radius of 3–4 km from the village. The residential unit is a village of some 70 houses grouped around a ceremonial house. The dwellings are arranged in three parts on a number of natural platforms. From August to November eight pair performances (16 times) of the Aya chant take place and each performance is punctuated by a maize harvest. The first harvest is around the houses and then harvests continue from the valley bottom to above the village. Here men tend to work for and live with their wives' kin.

The dry season spanning the December solstice

The group now move together down to an altitudinal zone ranging from 900 to 500 m, with farming taking place within a radius of 3 km. The tendency in the lowlands is for men to work for their mothers' kin. Honey and beeswax are collected, sweet potatoes eaten and the main coca crop tended before the solstice. After the solstice small groups of men travel to the plains or the highlands to trade sisal bags, wax and, in the past, cacao, for shells, salt and cloths. At the same time *yopo* (*Anadenanthera macrocarpa*) is collected on the edge of the plains. The chants performed, together with the appropriate activity, are the Hives, Salt (no longer performed) and Hallucinogen. In the past men of other groups travelled into Kubaruwa territory to exchange goods, and during the performance of the Hives, sexual licence was permitted. Residence here is dispersed through the forest and not as in the above season and place, in an open village, when travelling men build temporary shelters on the edge of the plains, but sleep in caves in the highlands.

The dry to wet season spanning the March equinox

In March the people move back up to the upland village to plant the Aya maize, and then they return to the lowlands. It is now the main hunting season, and the chant performed is ostensibly about animals. Food eaten includes avocado pears, *chontaduro* (*Guilielmo gasipaes*), game and fish. People who have not lost land to the Whites move down to a third zone of permanent residence. This is at an altitude of 500 m, with the houses spread along levée land. The main manioc crop is grown here, as well as coca.

The wet season spanning the June solstice

Residence during this season is for the most part in the upland village. It is the *kara* nut (*Metteniusa edulis*) season, during which time the Kara chant is performed (in the past, eight pair performances) with the people fasting from normal food, eating only *kara* during performances.

Above, I have described the agricultural-cum-ceremonial system, as practised by middle-country groups who farmed horizontally across the valleys and vertically on the mountain, exploiting the temperate and tropical zones. The highland groups farmed up and down the mountain between cold country, from an altitude of 3000 to 2000 m in warm country. Those which have the closest identity are the groups that moved together, exploiting similar altitude zones, and between which formal marriage alliances took place. When marriage was exogamous, a group married its nearest neighbour to either side of it (group B married into A and C and vice versa; group D married into C and E; group F married into E and G), so that marriage alliances ultimately linked many groups. I shall return to marriage in the context of breeding, as it involves food eaten by different groups, and part of the U'wa concept of ethnicity.

Given the different altitudinal range, particularly between the highland and middle-country groups, their different crop assemblages (the highlanders are remembered as potato eaters), the distinct settlement patterns within a group, variations in language and mythology, it is hardly surprising that these groups were not recognized as the same people.

Radical ethnic differences are made by the U'wa between people who practise the above system and those who do not. The latter are classified as *dri'kuma*: 'beyond the pale', non-consumable, dangerous, and can mean poisonous. For example, this term is applied to those neighbouring Indian plains dwellers amongst whom the emphasis in the subsistence pattern may be on fishing and hunting, rather than on agriculture: they eat animals that do not exist within the mountains, hunt with poisoned arrows and eat bitter *manioc*. This distinction applies also to white cattle farmers. These differences are still very real for the Kubaruwa, and they are perceptible to the ethnographer as well as evident in the archaeological record due to the different lifestyles. Apart from the distinctions given above, a uniform one is that other people (or peoples) are physically violent and attempt to steal U'wa 'wealth', e.g. women.

Material culture

Under this heading I shall select a number of aspects that are likely to be preserved in the archaeological record; constructions – domestic and ceremonial houses and menhirs; men's and women's personal adornments and pottery. In each of the above there exist variations between groups which are at the same time unified by their belief system.

Domestic housing in the highlands was constructed, and in some cases still is, of stone or frailejon stems (*Espeletia* sp.) with grass roofs. In the middle country, houses are of local wood with a leaf thatch reaching to the ground, and house plans vary within the same group, from rectangular to oval (Headland 1973, p. 249). In the same group the ceremonial house is rectangular, whereas in a neighbouring group, it is round. What is consistent and recognizable is the presence of two doors, one at either end, facing obliquely east and west, respectively; the houses are built on a sunrise–sunset axis. The east front is made of a line of posts with the door in the centre. The west end of the house curves around, with a smaller door built in the curve. This door is not made for light to enter, whereas the east door and front acts as a sundial. At the solstices the Sun's rays fall at the south or north corner of the house front, and the rays move along, falling through the posts, until equinox time, when they enter the door opening. Some houses are lined up eastwards to a particular mountain peak that serves as an additional time marker. In highland ceremonial sites, menhirs are aligned on the same east–west axis.

During a reconnaissance in the highlands round the Sierra Nevada, I was able to locate two of these ceremonial centres with stone alignments. A third site is known to me in the temperate zone, near the Kubaruwa's village at an altitude of 1200 m. No survey or excavation work has yet been done; since all of the structures have been partially destroyed, it is difficult to come to any firm conclusions other than the following. The stones are roughly hewn, measuring approximately 120×180×12 cm, and set up in two pairs of parallel rows flanking a central area. The stones are aligned ENE towards a ridge with twin peaks between which the Sun moves from solstice to solstice (Osborn 1985, plates 5 & 6, fig. 3). With the exception of the temperate-zone site, where sherds were not found, the menhir complexes and the other eight sites all share the following features. They are located at an approximate altitude of 2700 m on platforms overlooking impressive canyons. These platforms are at the confluence of two rivers, whose sources are in the Sierra Nevada. Other water sources are abundant, including salt and thermal springs (all deified in U'wa mythology). Sherds and other artefacts are concentrated in an area of some 80 m². Beyond this, agricultural-cum-living terraces were found, all following the lie of the land.

The surface collections made from the sites amounted to more than 4000 archaeological items, chiefly sherds, most of which were well preserved and relatively large. Approximately 20% of the sherds are decorated. A preliminary description of the sherds by Cardale Schrimpff is published as an appendix in Osborn (1985). Sherds from four different sites that were formerly inhabited by the U'wa are illustrated. The pottery falls into two main groups. One of these is stylistically so similar to pre-Muisca or Herrera phase pottery from neighbouring areas to the south that it can be confidently considered to be contemporary. A relatively early position for this pottery was first postulated by Broadbent (1969, 1971). Further work has been carried out by several authors (for example, Cardale Schrimpff 1981a, b, Castillo 1984, pp. 212–14 – who refers to the pottery as 'incised ceramic complex'). Correal & Pinto (1983, pp. 180–6) have established that the wares were in use from the second half of the first millennium BC or earlier to the earlier part of the second half of the 1st millennium AD.

Moving northwards, it is clear that some of the sherds found by Silva Celis (1945, figs 8–11) in his excavations in U'wa belong to this same complex, and related wares have been found by Bray and colleagues in an area west of the Sierra Nevada del Cocuy, inhabited in historical times by a people known as the Guane, with dates covering the first half of the 1st millennium AD. Stylistically the Sierra Nevada sherds would appear to belong to the latter part of the Herrera sequence.

The second group of pottery shows marked similarities with both Muisca pottery to the south of U'wa territory and with the pottery of the Guane, the U'wa's neighbours to the west. The Muisca occupation of the altiplano dates from the latter part of the 1st millennium AD (Castillo 1984, pp. 220–2,

Cardale Schrimpff 1981b, pp.12–18) and radiocarbon dates obtained by Sutherland (1971, p. 242) and Bray (pers. comm.) for Guane pottery suggest that it was roughly contemporary.

Family resemblances in ceramic styles are also found in the Barinas area of Venezuela (Zucchi 1975). All of these areas figure in Kubaruwa mythology, in which place names are recorded from the north-east to the south-west of the Sierra Nevada del Cocuy. This geocosmological axis across the eastern Andes relating to the Sun's movements is repeatedly emphasized in U'wa mythology; its directional aspects may well have spatial and ethnic significance for these people.

What I wish to stress here is that the U'wa sites and their artefacts were found on the basis of a myth chant – the Flight of the Swallow Tailed Kite. In chanted mythology these birds recount place names as they fly, beginning in the Barinas area of Venezuela and, although further investigation is required, artefacts found there appear to relate to the Sierra Nevada area (Wagner 1979). The birds then cross the Sierra Nevada and fly westwards into the Guane and Muisca areas, passing over some of the areas excavated and mentioned above. The picture that this presents is of a cultural spread along the eastern *cordillera* and, for the eight groups discussed in this chapter, focusing on the Sierra Nevada. It appears that cultural identity was strongest around the Sierra Nevada, and with distance from it this decreased. Sherds found in the surface collections from the Sierra Nevada sites support my argument that each U'wa group had its own identity. Although the sherds belong to the two periods mentioned above, each site produced a particular variant of them. In other words, each group had its own pottery style within the two periods, with some specific features that were associated with a particular site found only on that particular site. Sutherland (1971, p. 254) confronted by the 'bewildering amount of cultural variety' found in his excavations, made the analogy with a language stock with dialects in different places. I liken it to the U'wa kinship practices which link groups spread over a relatively wide area.

More-recent U'wa sherds present the same problem, particularly when we remember that a group lives at different altitudes, and that at each altitude every household maintains a set of domestic pots. Although today these are scantily decorated, in the past, when different ceremonies and other related activities took place in different altitudinal zones, the ceremonial pots involved were elaborately decorated. Overall, however, the sherds, like the other artefacts and customs, share a family resemblance.

A final example of an item of material culture that varies today from one group of contemporary U'wa to the next is that of the necklaces worn by men and women; these variations probably have a long history, since fragments of shell plaques still used for the women's necklaces were found in the surface collections.

According to oral tradition all U'wa wore necklaces, and some remaining U'wa groups still do. The women's necklaces are of snail shells and beads, both from the plains. As mentioned above, they are exchanged by the men with the Guahibo whom they classify as non-U'wa and *dri'kuma*. This trade is carried out over the ethnic boundary, and necklaces are fertility symbols. It is precisely because of this that they are obtained from non-related people: *in lieu* of exchanging women, they receive female fertility symbols. Radically different ethnic groups did not marry and nor, by extension, do they eat the same food assemblages. This theme of food will be enlarged on below.

On the other hand, teeth necklaces worn by men are from animals that are only present in their own territory. In Kubaruwa men wear peccary and fox teeth, and make *yopo* inhalers of the shinbone of the lowland deer. Their neighbours make necklaces from the bones of the lowland turkey. The master shamans of some groups wore ocelot-teeth necklaces.

The unifying features are to be found at the level of the thought system which is expressed in the material culture. Pottery styles and other artefacts vary between groups, as an expression of their distinctiveness. In this society and from an emic or native point of view, identity is emphasized through a series of graded differences between one group and the next, rather than by comparing themselves with others (Wiessner 1989).

Food, fertility and race

Referring to U'wa, Kubaruwa say that they are 'all mixed'. The deities did this first when those of the upper world (in geocosmological terms equivalent to the highlands) mixed with those of the lower world (equivalent to the lowlands). This miscegenation brought about conditions suitable for U'wa existence. Similar statements are made in the context of the Kubaruwa no longer marrying with the group to their north-west, the Rik'uwa, since the latter married in the wrong direction. Again, although formal marriage alliances took place between three groups, extramarital alliances took place with members of other groups. These took place when men travelled into Kubaruwa lowlands to exchange goods, at the time of the Hive festivities. These men were allowed to copulate with Kubaruwa women. U'wa believe that a child is produced by the woman's menstrual blood, and may have a number of genitors, produced by different men's semen (nourished by honey, akwa and foods classified as *rora*, see below). Today there are Kubaruwa who can trace parentage back to the now-extinct highland groups, who were in the marriage chain, but out of the direct marriage alliance. The object is to conceive a child with a blend of certain characteristics, belonging to different but related groups.

Above, we saw (see also Osborn 1982, 1985, p. 82, 1986) that U'wa believe that they are composed of the foods they eat, with particular procreative foods eaten at periods in the development cycle which relate to the seasons. The greatest number of births to the Kubaruwa take place during the Aya, also the leading maize season, since maize nourishes maternal milk. At 'baptism' the child is introduced to 'blowing' foods (so-called because they are used during blowing purification rituals) – salt, peppers, mice and small fish. These foods are in the same category for different reasons, but are grouped together because they all contain harm or extract it. During the onset of menstruation a girl is introduced to sweet potato (*Ipomoea* sp.), beer and armadillo meat – the first to nourish her breasts, the second to strengthen her blood. During the first four months of conception the male and female contribution of semen and menstrual blood are nourished first by hallucinogen and, secondly, by *rora*, a term meaning inherent life, 'seed', and referring to different categories of seasonal foods. Both contributions are nourished by honey. After the fourth month of pregnancy copulation stops and the foetus is nourished by *kara* nuts – thus the basic ingredient of a Kubaruwa.

I stated above that all U'wa eat the same foods, but different groups replace particular nourishing foods eaten by the Kubaruwa with others, such as beans or chontaduro nuts; in the case of hallucinogen, Virola or Myristi-caceae may be taken instead of *yopo*. People having the closest ethnic identity eat the same food assemblages. During the seasons they eat different, but related, foods and for similar reasons perform different, but related, chants about these.

Throughout the annual cycle U'wa eat preserved foods. With reference to the middle-country Kubaruwa, in their mountain village this is *kara* nuts and maize, and, in the lowlands, beans, fish and game. Each of these is called *rora* and is made from the first and last harvest or catch. They are eaten, and stocks are replenished in storage tanks, before leaving the particular altitudinal zone. From crop to crop the seed is therefore carried across the seasons: it is not lost and, furthermore, the foods are not cooked, as cooking would kill the element of fertility. The maize and *kara* nuts are fermented in bundles under water in a tank (reminiscent of the *mitoys* of the Venezuelan eastern *cordillera*), and fish and game are dried and hung.

The Kubaruwa are classified as a Ruya lower world female-oriented clan and are divided residentially into two sections – the eastern section, Ruya-oriented people, and the western section, Kubina upper world male-oriented clan. Marriage can be either endogamous and exogamous to the clan, and there is a tendency for people of endogamous marriages to reside between the east and west sections, forming a centre, where today the ceremonial house is situated, and is the only place where all clan members meet on ceremonial occasions. When an exogamous marriage alliance occurs, eastern Kubaruwa women marry men from the adjacent Kaibaka clan (a clan classified as Kubina-male), and women of the western section marry Rikuwa men. According to the sex of one of the children resulting from such a union, it becomes the 'preserved seed' of its father. The object is to acquire different seed from other people to alter and balance the properties of one's own group. Also, in the past women copulated for procreation with a number of men, some non-clan members, the object being to produce a child having different properties. A child born of such a 'mixture' becomes a Kubina and a potential master shaman (even today a master shaman will use his various fathers to justify his position by mentioning his mixed ancestry).

This demonstrates well the notion of separateness and co-operation – they rely on other related people in certain instances, in the same sense that chanted mythology is performed for other groups.

Clearly they believe in mixing U'wa genetic stock. The essence of a particular strain is believed to come from particular foods. The logic continues through to non-related people. They eat different food items which the U'wa do not eat; for example, the neighbouring Indians, who eat bitter manioc and animals not found on U'wa territory. Similarly, the non-Indian farmers on the plains are known to eat foods such as beef, rice, coffee and onions, which are not grown or consumed by traditional U'wa. It follows from this, and what was stated above, that the strongest ethnic boundary is that made on the basis of food.

When off their home ground the U'wa will eat these non-traditional foods, but on their return home they must undergo a purification ritual; this lasts for one night when returning from the nearest white town and for eight nights when returning from a distant place such as Bogotá. It follows that traditional attitudes towards whites are to credit them as 'people' beings, but not to mix with them. For example, 'whites' have *rora*, inherent seeds, and when discussing this with the Kubaruwa the following comment was offered: 'The army general who killed a lot of whites was a good man for he left a few to be the seed (*rora*) of their race'.

Other people's food is not grown, because it was not put into the U'wa universe by their deities. The universe is conceived as a house represented by the menhir complexes and visualized as a mountain. Inside the mountain houses are other houses, stacked like Russian dolls. On the outside of the house, people are not U'wa.

Concluding remarks

I have attempted to show that, for the Indians of the eastern Andes, ethnic boundaries within the mountain zones are not fixed and rigid. Physical features, such as rivers or mountains, are of less importance in marking the divisions between groups than are cultural differences. Conversely, radical ethnic differences were drawn by U'wa groups between themselves and others inhabiting non-mountainous areas.

In this chapter I have attempted to demonstrate the parameters along which ethnicity is made explicit, parameters which run through all aspects of life. Cultural identity between different groups of U'wa is strengthened or weakened according to the degree of geographical closeness or distance between these groups. Such cultural aspects as language, habitat and religious beliefs, including attitudes to food, will be more closely similar between neighbouring groups, although there will always be recognized and institutionalized differences. These differences between one group of U'wa and the next will increase with distance, but they still fall within the same general cultural parameters. It is not until radical differences are met, in

terms of language, habitat, food habits and world view, that ethnic and
territorial boundaries are drawn.

As to why this society evolved, with its fragmentation into many ethnic
groups maintaining their own individuality and at the same time being able
to recognize similarities, this was most likely due to a combination of
reasons. Those that I would stress are the prevalence of disease, which may
have racked pre-Colombian society and as a preventive measure resulted in
the physical separation of people. Disease, in part, is perceived as coming
from sexual relationships, particularly with non-related people, sent by their
own deities, and contained in the food of others. Another reason that I would
draw attention to was the ability facilitated by family resemblances to
negotiate peaceful relationships by way of the similarities and re-group with
relative ease after conflict.

I do not believe that in pre-Conquest times radical differences were
drawn between people living in different areas of the northeastern Andes. It
seems much more probable that the Spanish conquest, with its disruption
of native beliefs, was a prime factor in the development of sharper boundaries. These would have evolved as communications between the different
regions were disrupted, leading to increasing isolation between groups. As
time passed this situation was exacerbated by the dispersal and disappearance of many of those groups that had once formed links in a
more-or-less continuous chain.

For the ethnographer or the archaeologist the moral to be drawn from the
U'wa is clear: monolithic classificatory divisions such as 'the XYZs are this
or that' should be avoided for societies of this sort. Such monolithic
classifications stem from our own concepts of society and nation–states, and
our need to be able to communicate in terms understandable to colleagues in
other disciplines. However, when dealing with the type of society described
in this chapter, in place of standardization we find institutionalized variation
between the beliefs and practices of the member groups. These groups
recognize themselves as members of the same society, and they interpret the
variations in aspects of their culture as part of a wider U'wa pattern in which
these variables have a similar significance and are susceptible to similar
interpretations.

Acknowledgements

The research on which this chapter is based was made possible with a contract from
the Fundación Arqueológicas Nacionales del Banco de la República, Bogotá.
Fieldwork with the Kubaruwa was conducted intermittently from 1972, financed in
part by the Wenner-Gren Foundation and The Social Science Research Council of
Great Britain. I acknowledge gratefully the support of all these. I also wish to thank
Peter Riviére, Marianne Cardale de Schrimpff and Stephen Shennan for their
comments on earlier drafts of this chapter. Finally, I am grateful to the World
Archaeological Congress for the financial assistance which enabled me to attend it.

References

Aguado, F. P. 1956 (1582) *Recopilación Historial*, Vol. I, 333. Bogotá: Biblioteca de la Presidencia de la República.

Bray, W. 1984. Across the Darien Gap: a Colombian view of Isthmian archaeology. In *The archaeology of Lower Central America*, P. W. Lange & D. Stone (eds), 335–8. Albuquerque: School of American Research, University of New Mexico Press.

Broadbent, S. M. 1969. Prehistoric chronology in the Sabana de Bogotá. *The Kroeber Anthropological Society Papers. No. 40.* Berkeley: The Kroeber Anthropological Society.

Broadbent, S. M. 1971. Reconocimiento Arqueológicos de la Laguna de 'La Herrera'. Bogotá. *Revista Colombiana de Antropologia* **XV**, 171–208.

Cardale Schrimpff, M. 1981a. *Las Salinas de Zipaquirá, su explotación indígena.* Fundación de Investigaciones Arqueológicas Nacionales. Bogotá: Banco de la República.

Cardale Schrimpff, M. 1981b. Ocupaciones Humanas en el Altiplano Cundi-Boyacense. *Boletín museo del Oro*, Año 4, September–December 1–2. Bogotá: Banco de la República.

Castillo, N. 1984. *Arqueología de Tunja.* Fundación de Investigaciones Arqueológicas Nacionales, Bogotá: Banco de la República.

Clarke, D. L. 1968. *Analytical archaeology.* London: Methuen.

Correal, G. & Pinto, M. 1983. *Investigación Arqueológica en el Municipio de Zipacón Cundinamarca.* Fundación de Investigaciones Arqueológicas Nacionales, Bogotá: Banco de la República.

Gonzáles de Pérez, M. S. 1980. *Trayectoria de las Estudios sobre la lengue Chibcha o Muisca, Bogotá.* Instituto Caro y Cuervo Series menor XXII.

Gould, J. & Kolb, W. J. 1964. *A dictionary of the social sciences.* New York: Free Press–Macmillan.

Headland, P. 1973. Tunebo. In *Aspectos de la Cultura Material de Groupos Etnicos de Colombia*, Vol. I, 247–65. Meta: Ed Townsend.

Headland, P. & E. Headland 1976. Fonológica del Tunebo. In *Sistemas Fonológicas de Idiomas Colombianos*, Vol. III, 19–26. Meta: Ed Townsend.

Matheson, E. (ed.) 1972. *Comparative studies in American Indian languages.* The Hague: Mouton.

Murra, J. V. 1972. El control de un máximo de pisos ecológicos en la economía de las socidades andinas. In *Visíta de la Provincia de Léon de Huánuco en 1562 par Iñigo Ortiz de Zúñiga Visitador*, J. Murra (ed.), Vol. II, 429–68. Huánuco: Universidad Nacional H. Valdizán.

Needham, R. 1975. Polythetic classification: convergence and consequences. *Man* **10**(3), 349–69.

Osborn, A. 1982. Mythology and social structure among the U'wa of Colombia. DPhil thesis, University of Oxford.

Osborn, A. 1985. *El Vuelo de las Tijeretas.* Fundación de Investigaciones Arqueológicas Nacionales, Bogotá: Banco de la República.

Osborn, A. 1986. Eat and be eaten, Animals in U'wa (Tunebo) oral tradition. In *Attitudes to Animals.* World Archaeological Congress, Vol. 1 (mimeo).

Rivero, J. 1956 (1739). *Historia de las misiones de los llanos de Casanare y los Ríos Orinoco y Meta*, No. 23. Bogotá: Biblioteca de la Presidencia de Colombia, Ed. Argra.

Rochereau, H. J. 1959. Colección de Textos Tegrias. Bogotá: *Revista Colombiana de Antropología VIII*, 15–24.

Silva Celis, E. 1945. Contribución al Conocimiento de la Civilización Lache, Bogotá. *Boletín de Arqueología* **II**(5), 371–424.

Sorensen, A. P. 1967. Multilingualism in the northwest Amazon. *American Anthropologist* **69**, 670–84.

Sutherland, R. D. 1971. Preliminary investigation into the prehistory of Santander, Colombia. PhD thesis, Tulane University.

Troll, C. (ed.) 1968. The geo-ecology of the mountainous regions of the tropical Americas. *Proceedings of the Unesco Symposium*, 1–3 August, Bonn: Dummler.

Wagner, E. 1979. Arqueología de los Andes Venezuelanos. In *El Medio Ambiente Páramo*, M. L. Salgado (ed.), 209–18. Caracas: CEA-IVIC, Unesco.

Wiessner, P. 1989. Style and changing relations between the individual and society. In *The meanings of things: material culture and symbolic expression*, I. Hodder (ed.), ch. 2. London: Unwin Hyman.

Zucchi, A. 1975. *Caño Caroni, un groupo prehispanico de la selva de los llanos de Barinas.* Caracas: Universidad Central de Venezuela, Facultad de Ciencias Economicas y Sociales.

9 *The property of symmetry and the concept of ethnic style*

DOROTHY K. WASHBURN

Introduction

One of the most pervasive assumptions in archaeology has been the inference of the existence of ethnic groups from spatially and temporally limited constellations of similar artefacts. However, with the shift from culture history to more-explanatory approaches, many of these standard correlations of artefactual similarities and differences are being reassessed. The field of ethno-archaeology has been developed as a means to test these assumptions about artefactual correlates of behaviour, although too often these studies have been viewed as 'cautionary tales' or as unique instances which are not necessarily applicable to other areas or periods.

I suggest that one of the problems with our inability to develop satisfactory explanatory models is that archaeologists have been studying all kinds of features rather indiscriminately. Many of these features are object-specific; because we do not find them present in exactly that form in any other similar cultural situation, we have difficulty in formulating general behavioural 'laws' about how such features either actively create or passively reflect human activities.

In fact, much recent ethno-archaeological fieldwork is now undertaken to reassess many of the new explanatory generalizations (Hodder 1977). For example, Hodder has shown, in his study of Tugen, Pokot and Njemps material culture that many items are tribally exclusive despite the fact that there is considerable interaction between the tribes. In fact, he argued that it is 'where there is greater competition over land and more fighting and raiding for resources, [that] identities are most clearly displayed [in material culture]' (Hodder 1982, p. 31).

Wiessner investigated the features which showed intragroup and intergroup relationships among the Kalahari San, and defined two types of stylistic variation in features used to carry information about social and personal identity: emblematic and assertive. She found that different attributes carry different information. For example, the size of projectile points carries information about linguistic group affiliation, whereas the shapes of point tip, body and base carry information about individual expression (Wiessner 1983, p. 270).

However, these and many other studies have focused on items and attributes which appear to the analyst to vary over space and time. This variation is assumed to carry social information (Close 1979), although Wiessner does point out that homogeneity '. . . can be as important a social indicator as variability' and that the analysis '. . . should not be restricted to attributes that vary, but [be] extended also to those that have many possible alternate forms . . .' (*ibid.*, p. 270).

No consensus yet exists regarding which aspects of these features are critical for object recognition, identification, categorization and use, thereby precluding the development of general theory. Without a doubt, constellations of stylistic features are used in identity activities. I contend, however, that, rather than looking at whether or not specific and unique details of the design on ear flaps or the shapes of projectile point barbs correspond to ethnic boundaries, we first need to investigate the features which are at a more basic level than these object-specific features. These features are the basic component properties of form. They are combined to form the object-specific features that we have been recording and seeing as stylistic.

I am suggesting that in a given object there are basic level features and object-specific features which an individual uses in the recognition and categorization process. Archaeologists and ethnographers for the most part have been focusing on the object-specific features. In an object like a mug, the presence of features such as handles and flat bottoms are such object-specific features (Kempton 1981). In an object like a design the presence of certain motifs like the star motif (Hodder 1982, fig. 81) is such a pattern-specific feature.

In contrast, by moving to the more basic level of feature analysis, we shift from culturally specific and object specific features to properties of features that are considered by all individuals in all cultures. The organization of the parts into the star motif and the repetition of the stars in a pattern are described by the basic-level features of vertical and horizontal reflection symmetries. There are as well other basic-level universal features of form, such as orientation, texture, line and colour, which are combined and manipulated into motifs and artefacts that are unique to the culture. Constellations of these specific ways of elaborating an artefact are seen as stylistic by the analyst and as pleasing and 'ours' by the makers and users.

In sum, (a) basic-level features are combined and manipulated to form object-specific features, and (b) consistencies in the appearance of basic-level features formulate the regularities that we see as stylistic. That is, culture-specific (i.e. ethnic) styles result from specific combinations and manipulations of basic-level, universal features of artefactual form such as symmetry, orientation, colour, texture, line, etc. Certain states (for example, particular symmetry classes) of these basic-level features are more salient to a particular group than to others.

Put simply, we need to know what features the individual looks at when making identity and category decisions. Once these are identified, we can proceed to study how these features have been specifically elaborated and manipulated into a unique constellation of recurrent features. Through examining the patterns of use of these significant features in decision-making situations we can begin to consider hypotheses which relate these features to other activities in culture. My preliminary results from analysis of Bakuba raffia cloth patterns and Laotian skirt patterns indicate that investigating the universal form feature of symmetry can enable us to understand why certain object-specific features display ethnic identity.

The perception of symmetry

The process of perception involves two stages: form recognition and form categorization. This chapter focuses only on aspects of form recognition. In the process of form recognition, the eye checks such universal properties as topology (Chen 1982), line spacing and spatial frequency (Levinson & Frome 1979), orientation (Rock 1973) and symmetry (Julesz 1975, Corballis & Roldan 1975).

The *Gestalt* psychologists, arguing that the organization of form is basic to the perceptual process, contended that 'good' forms were regular, symmetrical, simple and stable. Although at the time that these principles were presented there were no systematic ways to test this structured view of perception, the ensuing years have witnessed the testing and confirmation of many of their propositions (see discussion in Dember & Warm 1979). Attneave (1954) and Hochberg & McAllister (1953) recast the *Gestalt* principles of perceptual organization into the quantitative framework of information theory such that symmetrical figures are seen as 'good' because their redundant structure reduces uncertainty. That is, a figure with bilateral symmetry (mirror reflection across two identical halves of the figure) can be predicted from inspection of only one half of the figure. In fact, Locher & Nodine (1973) have shown in eye-tracking experiments how the eye fixates on only one half of the perimeter of symmetric shapes, but must track the entire boundary of asymmetrical forms. So important is organized form to the human perceptual system that individuals even tend to 'see' a slightly asymmetric form as symmetric; that is, they mentally disregard minor imperfections in shape (Freyd & Tversky 1984). It is not surprising, therefore, that symmetry is one of the fundamental properties of form that the perceptual system examines in the object recognition and categorization process.

I have been studying the property of symmetry, one aspect of the feature of plane pattern layout, to determine its rôles in pattern recognition and categorization (Washburn 1977, Washburn & Crowe 1987). This is the property which describes the geometrical structure of repeated patterns. Crystallographers and geometers have shown how it is present in all regular patterns and can be measured consistently (Speiser 1927, Grünbaum & Shephard 1986).

For patterns in the plane there are three basic axial layouts: finite designs which are generated around point axes; one-dimensional designs which are generated along a single line axis; and two-dimensional patterns which are generated along multiple line axes. Four basic geometric motions generate repeated patterns in the plane: translation, rotation, mirror reflection and glide reflection. For one-dimensional patterns, most commonly known as bands, there are seven classes, or motion combinations which repeat the unit parts along the line axis. For two-dimensional patterns there are 17 motion combinations which repeat the unit parts along the axes. Further details on symmetry analysis can be found in Washburn & Crowe 1987.

Although one can study the symmetry of three-dimensional objects such as chairs or projectile points, I have focused on the analysis of the symmetries which repeat elements in the two-dimensional plane. Patterns which result from such symmetries in the plane are typically found on tile, painted and incised ceramics, textiles, carved wood and basketry, and as such constitute a large fraction of the decoration on artefacts. Given that many of these artefactual forms resist decay, are found in quantity in archaeological sites, and have been used extensively as the basis of style and discussions of style relationships, it would seem that further refinement of our understanding about pattern, in both its physical and cultural senses, can help us to understand the information contained in the similarities and differences of this widespread mode of cultural expression.

Experimental psychologists have shown the importance of universal form features, such as symmetry, in the process of form recognition. Anthropologists now need to develop methodologies to study how they are specifically manipulated in different cultural situations.

Several anthropologists, and others, have noted clear consistencies for certain kinds of symmetry within the decorative system of a given cultural group (Ascher & Ascher 1981, Crowe 1980, Donnay & Donnay 1985, Kent 1983, Van Esterik 1981, Washburn 1983, 1986, Washburn & Matson 1985, Zaslow & Dittert 1977). I describe here two sets of preliminary studies which show that these consistencies are actual expressed preferences, not simply coincidental correlations or artefacts of the analyst's classification scheme, for certain kinds of structural arrangements in patterned design. Although previous studies have shown a correlation between frequency of certain symmetries and tribal affiliation, interaction and boundaries, it has been the adoption of methodologies from experimental psychology which has enabled us to demonstrate that different symmetries are differentially preferred in different cultures.

The individuals who participated in the case study

Two groups of subjects were tested for symmetry preferences: Laotian refugees resident in Rochester, New York, and Bakuba raffia-cloth weavers and embroiderers from Mweka District, West Kasai, Zaire.

The Laotian subjects were women from villages and cities in southern Laos who either formerly wove cloth used as skirts or who wore those skirts in Laos and in the refugee camps in Thailand, where they lived before they came to the USA. None of the subjects now weaves cloth, since most are busy working and none has the large loom required to produce this skirt fabric. All wear these skirts at least on special occasions, and all continue to acquire these skirts from relatives who are still living in Laos or Thailand.

The Bakuba subjects came from four tribes of this central Zaire kingdom: the Bushong, the Bangende, the Bashoba and the Bakete. The subjects were male weavers of the background raffia cloth and female embroiderers of the designs on this background cloth. At the turn of the 20th century all of these tribes produced raffia cloth and decorated it with embroidered and plush geometric patterns. At this time raffia cloth was produced as one form of tribute from the subject tribes to the ruling Bushong, and was stored in vast storehouses in the king's compound in the capital city of Mushenge. Today it is only produced to sell to art dealers and the occasional missionary or personnel associated with foreign mining interests. Nevertheless, production of decorated raffia cloth, as well as carved cups and boxes, continues to flourish among some of the Bakuba tribes. The patterns are accurate, but simplified, versions of the turn-of-the-century tribute cloths. The weavers and embroiderers are very knowledgeable carriers of the design system applied to these objects.

The preference tests

Two types of tests were administered to determine whether symmetry was an attribute involved in preference decisions. The format and procedure of these tests were modelled after preference tests administered by experimental psychologists with two notable differences.

We first showed our subjects patterns constructed of culturally familiar motifs before testing them with patterns constructed with abstract shapes. We considered the familiarity-of-motif factor important for introducing the subjects to preference tests.

In the first series of tests, the symmetries of actual Lao and Bakuba patterns were modified on computer-generated designs (MacIntosh Mac-Paint program) by rearranging the motifs in various different symmetrical structures (Fig. 9.1). Not all symmetry classes could be produced with all motifs, but as many different rearrangements of the familiar motifs were produced as possible.

In the second series of tests, two kinds of abstract motifs were arranged in all the one- and two-dimensional plane-pattern one-colour symmetry classes. The first tests used right triangular motifs because they allowed formation of all of the pattern classes, yet were a recognizable if not specifically indigenous design motif (Fig. 9.2). We then administered tests containing more-abstract comma-shaped motifs arranged in all of the pattern classes (Fig. 9.3). We used this unfamiliar motif to control for bias introduced by preferences for familiar motifs.

Figure 9.1 Computer-generated patterns varying the symmetry of a Bakuba motif.

In order to test whether the respondents were basing their preference choices on the criteria of symmetry, we had to eliminate other possible features such as texture and colour. Computer-generated patterns of simple outline shapes allowed us to focus the individual's attention on the different symmetries, because all other features could be eliminated or kept constant.

The testing protocol required that all of the symmetry patterns, each on a

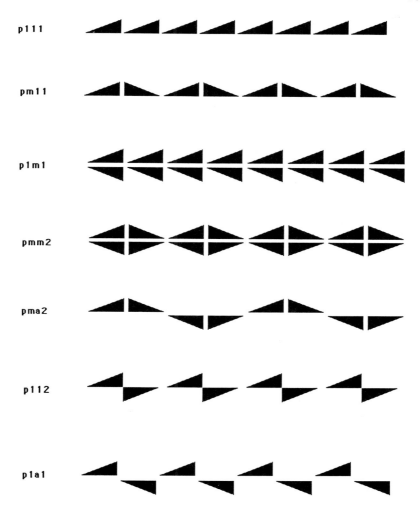

p111

pm11

p1m1

pmm2

pma2

p112

p1a1

Figure 9.2 The seven classes of one-dimensional design in the right triangle motif.

separate 8×10 inch (20×25.5 cm) page, be laid out in front of the subject, who was then asked to indicate preferences in rank order.

Individuals were asked to indicate their symmetry preferences by choosing among all the seven one-dimensional motion classes and the 17 two-dimensional motion classes, rather than simply to indicate preference for symmetric or asymmetric forms.

It is notable here that almost all of the psychological preference tests for symmetry have merely tested for preference for symmetry versus asymmetry (cf. Corballis & Roldan 1974). In these tests symmetry was illustrated

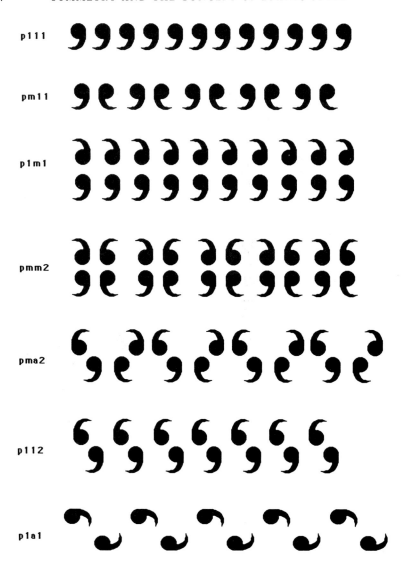

Figure 9.3   The seven classes of one-dimensional design in the comma motif.

by a series of figures with vertical bilateral mirror reflection, and asymmetry was indicated by a series of asymmetric shapes. The tests were administered to the typical test group – white, middle-class college sophomores – who overwhelmingly preferred symmetrical patterns. Further, it is interesting that symmetry, in almost all cases, was presented as being in only one form –

Figure 9.4 Lao skirt body design with *cmm* symmetry and border design with *pmm2* symmetry.

Figure 9.5 Lao skirt border design with *cmm* symmetry.

bilateral reflection. Although this is the symmetry that most often comes to mind among Western subjects (Fox 1975), there are, technically, seven different symmetries for one-dimensional band designs and 17 different symmetries for two-dimensional overall patterns. Our tests thus tested for preference for a specific class of symmetry, rather than simply for symmetry or asymmetry.

Results

Laotian skirts have two fields of design: the skirt body which, if decorated by tie dying, generally contains two-dimensional patterns, and the hemline border in which are woven a series of one-dimensional bands, one of which usually predominates (Fig. 9.4). Sometimes two-dimensional patterns are squeezed in the band space on these skirt borders (Fig. 9.5).

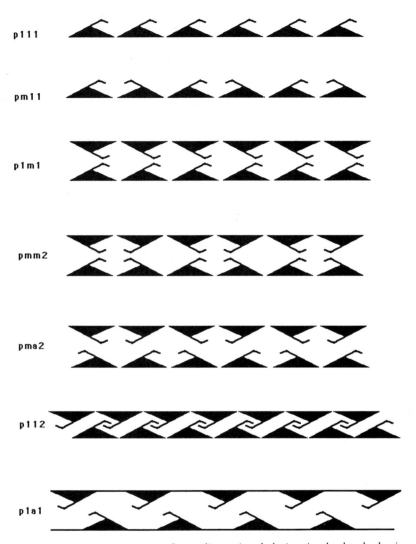

Figure 9.6   The seven classes of one-dimensional design in the hooked triangle
motif.

When shown the computer-generated one-dimensional band patterns
created using familiar Lao design motifs, the Laotian women consistently
expressed preference for the patterns where the motifs were structured by
the symmetry classes *pmm2* as well as *pma2*, *p112* and *p1m1*. Although the
diamond motif could only be arranged by *pmm2* symmetry, a triangular

Figure 9.7   Lao skirt border design with *p112* symmetry (upper and lower band).

hooked unit could be rearranged in all seven one-dimensional symmetries (Fig. 9.6). When shown the seven computer-generated pattern symmetries of this motif, the women consistently chose the pattern arranged by class *p112*. In fact, this symmetry arrangement represented the most common way that this particular motif is arranged on Laotian one-dimensional skirt border patterns (Fig. 9.7). When shown patterns composed of abstract right triangles and commas, the Lao women again selected the patterns composed by these same symmetries.

In order to determine whether these preferences represented a general Lao use of these structural arrangements, I compared these structural preferences with the predominant symmetries on Lao textiles personally owned by Laotian women in Rochester (Table 9.1). Although it is not possible to state unequivocally that this privately owned sample accurately represents the relative popularity of design structures on southern Laotian textiles, the similarity of the relative frequencies of structures on these textiles with the preferred structures in our tests is notable.

The most popular symmetry on the skirt body was *cmm* (69%); the most popular symmetry on the border was *pmm2* (73%). *pmm2* is the one-dimensional class formed most frequently by series of diamonds arranged in a linear band; *cmm* is the two-dimensional class formed most frequently by a layout of diamond shapes in an overall diamond grid (Fig. 9.4).

In contrast, designs on Lao textiles made for Western consumption (i.e. tablecloths, table runners, place mats, etc.) are constructed by symmetries which are not used on skirts, shawls and other articles made by the Laotians

Table 9.1   Symmetries of Laotian skirt patterns.

Symmetry class	Skirt body No. (%)	Skirt border No. (%)
two–dimensional		
cmm	18 (69)	8 (10)
cm	6 (23)	
pmg	1 (4)	
p4g	1 (4)	
pmm		1
one–dimensional		
pmm2		58 (73)
p111		4
p1m1		3
pm11		3
pma2		1
p112		1

for their own use. Of eight articles examined, all were decorated with patterns arranged by symmetries not typically used on the two-dimensional design field. Two-dimensional symmetry classes *pmm* and *pgg* were not recorded on any Lao skirt body, yet they were frequently used to decorate tablecloths and throws for sale to Westerners. The one-dimensional symmetry

Figure 9.8   Lao-made throw with one-dimensional bands of *pmm2* symmetry.

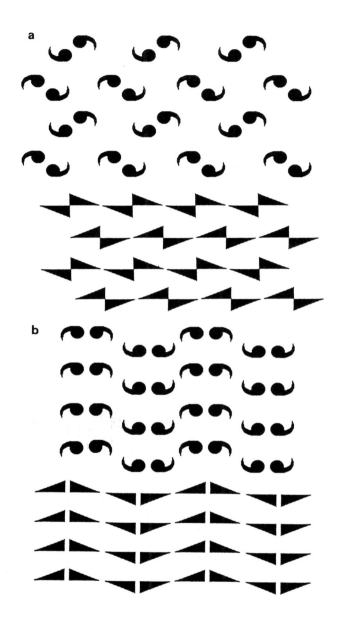

Figure 9.9 Abstract patterns of right triangles and commas with (a) *pgg* symmetry, and (b) *pmg* symmetry.

Table 9.2   Symmetries of Bushong raffia cloth patterns.

Symmetry class	1900 No. (%)	1950 No. (%)
pgg	21 (54)	20 (16.5)
p2	5 (13)	15 (12)
p1	3 (8)	31 (26)
p4m	3 (8)	10 (8)
p4g	3 (8)	1 (1)
pmg	2 (5)	31 (26)
pg	1 (2.5)	7 (5.5)
cmm	1 (2.5)	1 (1)
p6m		4 (3)
cm		1 (1)

class *pmm2* which dominated on the skirt border designs does not appear in two-dimensional design fields on Lao skirt bodies, but it does appear in two-dimensional design fields on tablecloths and throws. Here rows of diamond motifs are alternated with rows of other motifs (Fig. 9.8).

The remarkable agreement between the relative frequencies of symmetrical layouts on privately owned textiles and the preferences for layout symmetry expressed by the Laotian women when examining abstract pattern arrangements reinforces our conclusion that the property of symmetry is an important feature of Laotian pattern style.

Bakuba weavers and embroiderers shown the drawings, first of right triangles and then of the more abstract commas, consistently expressed preference for patterns generated by *pgg* and *pmg* symmetries (Fig. 9.9a & b). These responses were compared with the relative frequency of all of the 17 two-dimensional symmetry classes on a sample of cloths in museum collections. This analysis was limited to Bushong cloths since a documented sample of cloths from the turn of the 20th century and the 1950s was available only for the Bushong from these two periods.

The turn-of-the-century collection showed a preference (54%) for class *pgg* symmetry. When these symmetrical preferences are compared with those on raffia patterns made by the Bushong during the 1950s (Table 9.2), it is clear that although the overwhelming preference for *pgg* was being diluted by increasing use of *pmg* and *p1* symmetries, there continued to be consistent and limited use of less than half of the possible 17 two-dimensional symmetry classes. Further, it is notable that the addition of the *p1* symmetry arrangement is largely a function of the simplification of the original patterns into less-complex compositions in order to speed production and enhance sales. This comparative study reinforces the importance of the feature of structural symmetry by showing the continuity in use of the same symmetries, despite the myriad political and economic changes that the kingdom has experienced since its first contact with missionaries and explorers at the end of the 19th century (Washburn 1987).

Discussion

Several observations can be made from these results. (a) Both groups of subjects consistently preferred a small number of symmetries relative to the total number of plane pattern symmetry classes available on both actual and abstract computer-generated renditions of patterns. (b) Both groups claimed that these preferred symmetrical arrangements were the ones that they would choose to use to structure patterns on cloths that they would make for their own use. (c) These same symmetries were also found to be most prevalent on museum and personal collections of these textiles.

Although none of our participants discussed symmetry in terms of its mathematical properties, or even used the term 'symmetry', it was clear that this property figured largely in their consistent selection of certain symmetries, even when we abstracted the patterns.

On several occasions our Lao participants remarked that one of the computer-generated patterns which displayed a frequently preferred symmetry would be 'just right' for an all-over design on a skirt body or a band design on a hem border. They also indicated symmetries on computer-generated patterns that would be acceptable for use on textiles, such as place mats, shawls, etc., made for sale to non-Lao. These items were often decorated with motifs in 'easy to make' arrangements that were not the traditionally preferred symmetries.

Even when the texture differences (plush and embroidery and smooth background cloth) and colour contrasts (tan and yellow and black) on the Bakuba cloths, which are hallmarks of the Bakuba style (Washburn 1987), were eliminated in the computer-generated patterns, many people still found some motif arrangements so familiar that they gave them the appropriate pattern name. The best Bushong patterns were those in which not only the basic-level features of colour, line, and texture were manipulated by contrast, but also those where these basic-level features were used to highlight motifs that were arranged consistently in a limited number of symmetrical layouts. Such patterns were recognized immediately as Bushong, and they were consistently assigned to named pattern categories by my informants.

In this chapter I have suggested that anthropologists need to focus their analyses of design features, not on object-specific features, but on the basic-level universal features which are combined and manipulated to create the object-specific features that we recognize as markers of ethnic style. I have shown how to test for salience of one of these properties. In particular, I have shown in two preliminary analyses, where symmetry was the only feature which varied, that people in an ethnic group consistently prefer certain pattern structures.

Acknowledgements

This research was conducted in collaboration with Andrea Petitto, cognitive psychologist in the Graduate School of Education, University of Rochester, New York. The computer drawings were executed by student assistant Lois Katzman.

Translation services were capably provided by Fong Tran in Rochester, New York, and by Kulondi Malu and Mbope Mulambila in Zaire. Fieldwork was conducted among the Bakuba in June and July 1985, and among the Lao in Rochester, New York, in spring 1985 and autumn 1986.

The turn-of-the-century Bushong cloths were collected by Emil Torday in 1909, and were analysed through the courtesy of the Museum of Mankind, London. The collection of Bushong cloths from the 1950s was obtained for the Brussels International Exposition in 1958, and was analysed through the courtesy of the Musée Royal de l'Afrique Centrale, Tervuren.

This research was funded by a grant from the National Science Foundation, BNS 85–08523.

References

Ascher, M. & R. Ascher 1981. *Code of the Quipu*. Ann Arbor: University of Michigan Press.
Attneave, F. 1954. Some informational aspects of visual perception. *Psychological Review* **61**, 183–93.
Chen, L. 1982. Topological structure in visual perception. *Science* **218**, 699–700.
Close, A. E. 1979. Identification of style in lithic artifacts. *World Archaeology* **10**, 223–37.
Corballis, M. C. & C. E. Roldan 1974. On the perception of symmetrical and repeated patterns. *Perception and Psychophysics* **16**, 136–42.
Corballis, M. C. & C. E. Roldan 1975. Detection of symmetry as a function of angular orientation. *Journal of Experimental Psychology* **P1**, 221–30.
Crowe, D. W. 1980. Symmetry in African art. *Ba Shiru* **11**, 57–71.
Dember, W. N. & J. S. Warm 1979. *Psychology of perception*, 2nd edn. New York: Holt, Rinehart & Winston.
Donnay, J. D. H. & G. Donnay 1985. Symmetry and antisymmetry in Maori rafter designs. *Empirical Studies of the Arts* **3**, 23–45.
Fox, J. 1975. The use of structural diagnostics in recognition. *Journal of Experimental Psychology: Human Perception and Performance* **1**, 57–67.
Freyd, J. & B. Tversky 1984. Force of symmetry in form perception. *American Journal of Psychology* **97**, 109–26.
Grünbaum, B. & G. C. Shephard 1986. *Tilings and patterns*. San Francisco: Freeman.
Hochberg, J. E. & E. McAllister 1953. A quantitative approach to figural goodness. *Journal of Experimental Psychology* **46**, 361–4.
Hodder, I. 1977. The distribution of material culture items in the Baringo District, Western Kenya. *Man* **12**, 239–69.
Hodder, I. 1982. *Symbols in action*. Cambridge: Cambridge University Press.
Julesz, B. 1975. Experiments in the visual perception of texture. *Scientific American* **232**, 34–43.
Kempton, W. 1981. *The folk classification of ceramics*. New York: Academic Press.
Kent, K. P. 1983. Temporal shifts in the structure of tradition: Southwestern textile

design. In *Structure and cognition in art*, D. K. Washburn (ed.), 113–37. Cambridge: Cambridge University Press.

Levinson, J. Z. & F. S. Frome 1979. Perception of size of one object among many. *Science* **206**, 1425–6.

Locher, P. J. & C. F. Nodine 1973. Influence of stimulus symmetry on visual scanning patterns. *Perception and Psychophysics* **13**, 408–12.

Rock, I. 1973. *Orientation and form*. New York: Academic Press.

Speiser, A. 1927. *Theorie der Gruppen von endlicher Ordnung*, 2nd edn. Berlin: Springer.

Van Esterik, P. 1981. *Cognition and design production in Ban Chiang painted pottery*. Papers in International Studies, Southeast Asia Series, No. 58. Athens, Ohio: Ohio University Center for International Studies.

Washburn, D. K. 1977. *A symmetry analysis of Upper Gila area ceramic design*. Papers of the Peabody Museum of Archaeology and Ethnology, Cambridge, Harvard University, No. 68.

Washburn, D. K. 1983. Symmetry analysis of ceramic design: two tests of the method on Neolithic material from Greece and the Aegean. In *Structure and cognition in art*, D. K. Washburn (ed.), 138–64. Cambridge: Cambridge University press.

Washburn, D. K. 1986. Symmetry analysis of Yurok, Karok, and Hupa Indian basket design. *Empirical Studies of the Arts* **4**, 19–45.

Washburn, D. K. 1987. *Native categories of material culture: named patterns on Bakuba raffia cloth*. MS.

Washburn, D. K. & D. W. Crowe 1987. *Symmetries of culture*. Seattle: University of Washington Press.

Washburn, D. K. & R. G. Matson 1985. Use of multidimensional scaling to display sensitivity of symmetry analysis of patterned design to spatial and chronological change: examples from Anasazi prehistory. In *Decoding prehistoric ceramics*, B. Nelson (ed.), 75–101. Carbondale: Southern Illinois University Press.

Wiessner, P. 1983. Style and social information in Kalahari San projectile points. *American Antiquity* **48**, 253–76.

Zaslow, B. & A. Dittert 1977. *Pattern mathematics and archaeology*. Anthropological Research Paper No. 2. Tempe: Arizona State University.

10 Patterns of learning, residence and descent among potters in Ticul, Yucatan, Mexico

DEAN E. ARNOLD

The relationship of style to society constitutes one of the most problematic, yet important, topics of archaeological research. Archaeologists have advanced several models relating style to social behaviour. The most controversial of these models is a kin-based model in which patterns of descent and residence account for transmission of style from generation to generation (Deetz 1965, Longacre 1970, Hill 1970, see Hayden & Cannon 1984, Kramer 1985, for reviews). Questions have been raised about the validity of this model as a behavioural model, as opposed to its value as an ideal, cognitive model, and whether archaeologists can infer kin-based learning patterns based on descent and residence (Allen & Richardson 1971, Hayden & Cannon 1982, 1984). Can a model based on descent and residence account for the transmission of ceramic style from generation to generation? One ethnographic test of this model revealed questionable ethnographic validity in at least one case (Stanislawski 1977, Stanislawski & Stanislawski 1978).

This chapter reports a preliminary test of the hypothesis that a kin-based model can account for the transmission of ceramic style. It is shown that a kin-based model of transmission of the potter's craft is valid in a modern peasant society in which pottery production is almost exclusively oriented to the tourist trade, and that this kin-based model also has material correlates in the residence patterns.

In the late 1960s[1] Ticul pottery was made primarily for carrying and storing water and for coin banks. It was sold by the potters themselves in the markets and fiestas of the Yucatan, and bought by local peasants. The craft was primarily organized at the household level in the production mode of what Peacock (1982, pp. 8–9) called a 'household industry' or 'individual workshop'. However, in 1984 the craft had changed radically from the late 1960s, with greatly altered vessel shapes and decoration. Vessels were produced almost exclusively for flower pots and the tourist industry, and they were marketed primarily by middlemen in the capital city of Merida and the resort city of Cancun. The mode of production continued at the household level, but had also evolved into a 'nucleated workshop', with substantial production occurring outside the household in what could best be called 'manufactories' according to Peacock's typology (Peacock 1982, p. 9). However, little change occurred in the population of potters, with the same families making the pottery in 1984 who did in the late 1960s.

The population of potters in Ticul

In the summer and autumn of 1984 the pottery making population of Ticul consisted of 167 active potters.[2] Twenty-one additional people (mainly children) were learning the craft. Potters were still largely concentrated in nine square blocks. Of the total sample of 435 past and present potters, 44% (192) were female and 56% (243) were male. Only 12% (48, N=427) were children. Sixty-seven per cent (276, N=410) were married, and 27% (110) were single. Six per cent (24) were widowed or abandoned.

Even though 44% (243) of the sample were female, pottery making is heavily influenced by males. Women potters who marry non-potters only practise the craft with their husbands' permission, and many abandon the craft after marriage. Women who are not potters, but who marry potters and move into a potter's household, may learn how to make ceramics only if their husbands wish them to learn.

Residence patterns of potters reflect the male influence on pottery-making. Twenty-five per cent (85, N=344) were male heads of household and another 28% (97) lived and worked with their father or paternal grandfather. Seven per cent (23) worked in workshops. Twenty-nine per cent (98) lived and worked with their husband.

Land is inherited patrilineally; females inherit only personal items like earrings and jewellery. If houselots are sufficiently large to be subdivided, then they may be subdivided for the sons before the death of the father, but fathers may sometimes buy land nearby for their sons and rent it out to others until their sons marry. When a potter needs to obtain money, he may sell part of his land (if necessary), but he will almost always sell to a relative. Land thus tends to remain within the extended family.

Newly married couples ideally reside in the household of the groom's father for at least a short period. In some cases the couple do not move elsewhere, but remain permanently in the household of the groom's father. In other cases conflict may result between the bride and her in-laws and the couple may move into or near to the household of the bride's parents. A man may also give land near his own household to his newly married daughter, and she will live there with her husband. A newly married couple may move away from both parents, but not until some time is spent living with the groom's parents immediately after the marriage. Neolocal residence is largely impossible unless the couple have the financial resources to buy, rent or construct a house or one has a secure job with a good salary (e.g. a schoolteacher) to begin marriage away from both parents.

Table 10.1   Learning patterns of Ticul potters by kin type.

Patrilineal relatives	Matrilineal relatives	Affinal relatives	Other
Fa	Mo	Hu	self
FaFa	MoSi	HuMo	
FaBr	MoBr	HuFa	non–relative:
FaFa	MoSiSo	HuBr	(a) workshop
FaMo		HuFaBr	(b) other
FaSi		HuFaFaSiSoDa	step–father
FaBrSo		SiHu	step–mother
		SoWiFa	Da
		SoWiMo	Si
		Wi	Br
		WiFa	
		WiMo	
		WiBr	
		WiFaBr	
		WiMoBr	
Total = 7	Total = 4	Total = 15	Total = 8
	Total learning types = 34		

Fa, father; Br, brother; Mo, mother; Si, sister; So, son; Hu, husband; Da, daughter; Wi, wife.

The analysis of learning patterns reveals 34 different types (Table 10.1). When these patterns are ordered by frequency (Fig. 10.1), 42.8% of the potters in the sample (for whom data were available) learned the craft from their father. Eighty-three per cent learned from members of their immediate family (mother, father, husband or wife). Most of the potters in the remaining 17% of the sample learned the craft from other relatives who had also lived in the same household.

However, these learning patterns consisted exclusively of verbal data mapped on to genealogical diagrams. Since archaeologists deal with the material correlates of behaviour, it was necessary to obtain a material, observable and quantifiable measure that expressed the potter's descent, residence and learning patterns in material terms. To meet this criterion, I chose the distance between potters' households. This distance was not the shortest distance between two households, but was 'social' or 'interaction' distance, which is the distance that people must walk to interact with people in another household. Thus, two houselots which share a back fence would have an interaction distance of 1½–2 blocks because household members never interact across the back fence. Interaction distance was an important measure because transmission of the craft involves communication to the next generation. The smaller the distance between two given households, the more likely communication between them is.

Households were defined as a houselot surrounded by a stone fence, with a

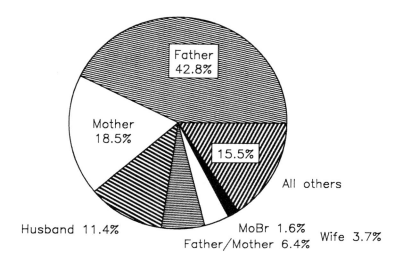

Figure 10.1 Learning types among Ticul potters (N=374). Each section of the chart indicates the percentage of the sample of Ticul potters learning from that particular type. The 'all others' category indicates all other single types of people from whom potters learned the craft (see Table 10.1).

gate or door to the street. Adjacent houselots of close relatives may have gates between them, but access to adjacent houselots of other people occurs only via the street.

Inter-household interaction distance was calculated in units of tenths of a block. There are rarely ten households to a linear block; usually there are between four and eight. The minimum distance value used was 0.1 block, which indicated residence in the same houselot. If the houselots were side by side or directly across the street from one another, then the distance was expressed as 0.2 block. Larger distances were expressed as the actual distances between households. Although there may be errors in calculating distances of more than 0.2 block, this error was probably no more than 0.1 block.[3]

Three types of inter-household interaction distance (Fig. 10.2) were calculated for each potter's household: (a) the distance to the potter's father; (b) the distance to the person from whom the potter learned the craft (i.e. his or her 'teacher'); and (c) the distance to the nearest pottery-making family outside of the potter's own household.

When one examines the frequency distribution of the inter-household distances in the sample, the highest frequency distances to fathers and teachers occurred at 0.1 block (Fig. 10.2). These distances indicate that most of the potters learned the craft in the household in which they live, and that their father lives in the household in which they themselves live. The next most frequent inter-household distance occurs at 0.2 block and indicates

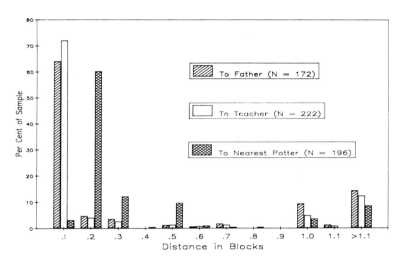

Figure 10.2 Inter-household distances of the entire sample of potters in Ticul, Yucatan (*N*=344). The category '>1.1 blocks' is spread between 1.2 blocks and 15 blocks.

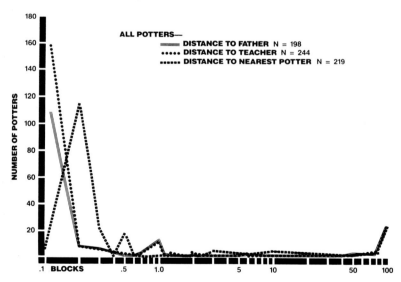

Figure 10.3 Graph of the distances between households and their frequencies for the entire sample of potters in Ticul in 1984. The horizontal axis is a logarithmic scale. Data are missing for the difference between the totals indicated here and the total sample of 435 potters.

that potters live next door to or across the street from their father and learned the craft from a person in those households.

These distances were plotted on a logarithmic scale (Fig. 10.3) because the frequency distribution showed the friction effect of increasing distance between households. The resulting curves revealed the following: first, the curve of the interaction distances of a potter to his or her father and to his or her teacher were almost identical, and secondly, the curve of the distance to the nearest potter's household was very different from the curve to the potter's father and his or her teacher. All of these data thus suggest that a patrilineal–patrilocal model accounts for the learning patterns of Ticul potters.[4]

In order formally to test the hypothesis that a patrilineal–patrilocal model accounts for the learning patterns of Ticul potters, a correlation coefficient was calculated for the interaction distances of potters to their father and to their teacher. The results ($r=0.751$, $N=156$, $P<0.001$) reveal a strong relationship between the inter-household distance to a potter's teacher and his or her father.

Since potters' households cluster together in a nine square block area, residence proximity may also be a factor in learning the craft. To test formally this alternative hypothesis that potters learned the craft from the nearest potter outside their household, a correlation coefficient was calculated for the distance from each potter's household to that of his or her teacher and to the nearest pottery-making household. The results ($r=0.381$, $N=148$, $P<0.001$) indicate a weak relationship between the distance to a potter's teacher and the nearest potter's household. These results suggest that the distance to one's father influences the transmission of the craft more than just distance to the nearest potter. The clustering of Ticul potters in a relatively small area thus reflects the concentration of the craft in the hands of four extended families more than residence proximity defined by occupation or some other non-kin-based factor.

Once one eliminates the inactive and deceased potters from the sample and includes only the active potters in Ticul ($N=167$; see Fig. 10.4), the distance curves corroborate the patterns found in the total sample of potters. Most potters are living in or next door to the same household as their fathers and their teachers.

Correlation coefficients of the interaction distances for the sample of active potters also corroborate the results of the entire sample of potters. The correlation of the distance of each potter's household to his or her father's household and of the distance to the household of his or her teacher ($r=0.656$, $N=116$, $P<0.001$) reveal that a patrilocal–patrilineal model also accounts for the learning of the craft among potters who were actively making pottery. Conversely, the correlation of the distance of each potter's household to his or her teacher and to the nearest pottery-making household ($r=0.608$, $N=129$, $P<0.001$) suggests that residence proximity is also an important factor in learning the craft, but that this proximity reflects patrilineal land inheritance and a patrilocal or virilocal post-nuptial residence pattern.

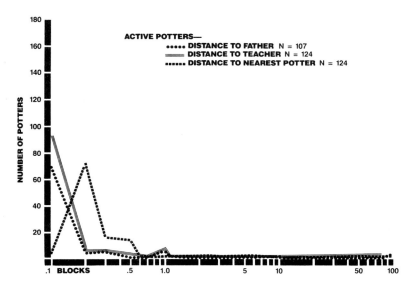

Figure 10.4 Graph of the distances between households and their frequencies for the population of active potters in Ticul in 1984. The horizontal axis is a logarithmic scale. Data are missing for the difference between the totals indicated here and the sample of 167 active potters.

Discussion

How does one explain the strong relationship between the patrilineal–patrilocal model and the transmission of the craft from generation to generation? In traditional societies (like Ticul) pottery-making is learned through imitation and practice, rather than by direct teaching. The learning of the craft involves learning a series of complex motor-habit patterns for fabrication, combined with cognitive knowledge of raw materials (like clays, non-plastic additives and fuels) and knowledge of processes like fabrication and firing (see Arnold 1971, 1985a). Of these, motor habits are the most difficult to learn. Motor habits are unconscious, culturally patterned but habitually used activity patterns that cause particular muscles to be strengthened (Arnold 1985a, p. 147). Motor-habit patterns thus require repetition over a period in order to be effectively utilized.

Given the length of time necessary to learn pottery-making using traditional knowledge and techniques, the most effective and efficient learning of pottery-making occurs during childhood while muscular patterns are developing. Childhood learning is effective because the child is exposed to the craft over a period and motor-habit patterns can be reinforced during the many years before adulthood. Learning the craft as a child is also efficient because learning to make pots does not compete with activities for subsistence, as it does when adults learn the craft. Learning traditional pottery-making is thus best accomplished in the household during childhood, where the skills and knowledge can be practised and reinforced every day (Hayden & Cannon 1984, p. 328). As one might expect, then, the transmission of pottery fabrication follows the kin-based rules of household composition and recruitment and will be more resistant to changes than the transmission of decorative patterns. Decorative patterns are derived less from motor-habit patterns than from cognitive knowledge, and are thus more easily modified than the basic motor habits involved in vessel fabrication.[5] Indeed, although decoration has changed radically in Ticul, the basic motor habits of vessel fabrication (see Arnold 1985b) have changed little. Thus, the long period of learning the craft, the locus of the process in the household and the advantages of learning during childhood explain why Ticul learning patterns are still kin-based in spite of the orientation of the craft towards the production of tourist pottery. However, once production moves outside the household the kin-based learning pattern will be broken because children will no longer grow up learning the craft. Thus, as pottery production becomes occupationally based in workshops outside the home (which is beginning to happen in Ticul) and potters learn the craft in these workshops, then kin-based patterns of household composition and recruitment will no longer play a rôle in transmitting the craft from generation to generation.[6]

Implications for archaeology

This study has demonstrated that a kin-based model is a valid model for relating learning and residence patterns in a population of potters. This conclusion has important implications for the identification of social groups in the archaeological record.

In order to relate style to society, archaeologists need to have a clearly formulated reason to explain why style is related to one kind of social group or another. Rather than beginning with the ethnic group and trying to find a relationship with the material evidence, archaeologists should begin looking for the relationship of style (or artefacts) and society on the micro-level with the population of the artefact producers. If any social patterns or social identity are reflected in the artefactual evidence, then they would certainly occur in the population of artefact producers.

For ceramics, then, the locus of the relationship between style and society lies primarily with the population of potters. Although the use and shape of the pot have signficance for the larger society of which the population of potters is a part, the primary relationship of ceramics and society exists with the population which produced the ceramics. Indeed, ethno-archaeological evidence from Ticul and from Quinua, Peru (Arnold 1983, 1984) suggests that there are material and stylistic correlates of the local community of potters. The population is thus the interface between the ceramics, on the one hand, and the larger society, on the other. If any aspect of society manifests itself in the ceramics, then it is mediated in some way by the population of potters. Furthermore, the population of potters is the interface between the ceramics and the environment. The population of potters inputs energy to obtain raw materials from the environment, fabricates and fires ceramic vessels, and exchanges them for food. The finished products then serve as channels of nutrient flow from the environment to the society. In a more evolved state of the craft, ceramics serve as a channel of ideological or social structural information between members of a society (Arnold 1985a, p. 127) using symbols created by a particular population of potters.

The unit of analysis in studies that relate artefacts to social groups should be the population of artefact producers. Artefacts (or style) may or may not correspond to a particular ethnic group, but if a relationship exists, it is probably much weaker than that between the artefacts and the local population which produced them. Although there is some relationship between ceramic fabrication methods and groups larger than the local population (see Reina et al. 1978, pp. 204–6, Arnold 1981, pp. 38–9), the search for material correlates with social groups will be more productive on the micro-level of the local community of artefact-producers than on the macro-level of the ethnic group.

Acknowledgements

Research in Ticul from June to December 1984 was funded by an American Republics Research Grant awarded under the Fulbright Program. I wish to thank Jose Luis Sierra Villareal, Director of the Centro Regional del Sureste del Instituto Nacional de Antropologica e Historia, Salvador Rodriguez, Director of the Escuela de Ciencias Antropologicas, Universidad de Yucatan, and the entire staff of the Centro Regional del INAH and the Escuela de Ciencias Antropologicas for their hospitality, collaboration and co-operation in facilitating and supporting this research. I also wish to thank all my potter-friends in Ticul for their help and co-operation. Finally, I am grateful to Patricia Ward, Dean of Arts and Sciences of Wheaton College, and Ward Kriegbaum, Vice President of Academic Affairs of Wheaton College, for providing funds from the Faculty Development Fund to attend the World Archaeological Congress. Funds for preparing the illustrations for publication came from the Wheaton College Alumni Association.

Notes

1   This chapter is based on research conducted in Ticul, Yucatan, Mexico from 1965 to 1970 and in 1984. I studied pottery-making in Ticul first in 1965 when I spent six months there focusing on ceramic ethnotechnology (Arnold 1971, Arnold & Bohor 1975, 1977). Between 1965 and 1970 I returned to Ticul six times. This research gave me enough data to know that all of the potters were members of four large extended families concentrated in a nine square block area. These data suggested that the kin-based factors of descent and residence were operating to recruit potters and transmit the craft from generation to generation.

In 1984 I returned to Ticul for six months in order to document the changes in the ceramics, and in the population of potters, that had occurred since the late 1960s. In order to achieve this goal I wanted to describe the social characteristics of the community of potters. I thus concentrated on obtaining complete genealogies of the potters, and on mapping the location of their households. I also collected data concerning the person from whom the potter learned the craft. I assembled genealogies of potters' families to the limits of the memory of a few informants, and then I cross-checked these with other informants for accuracy. Information I collected in the late 1960s was also useful in verifying many genealogies.

2   Complete genealogies of Ticul potters span four to six generations and include a total of 435 potters who had practised the craft at some time during their life. These potters include active, inactive and deceased individuals. There are gaps in the data, however, because information was not obtained about all of the deceased and inactive potters. The sample is thus biased heavily towards the potters who were alive and active in 1984, and the conclusions in this chapter are therefore preliminary.

3   In some cases, where non-potters came from locations outside the concentration of potters' households and learned the craft after marriage, distances to households had to be estimated. Usually, where precise locations were not available, informants only provided the name of the *barrio* from which they came: 'San Juan', 'Mejorada' or 'Santiago'. In these cases interaction distances were calculated from the plazas of these *barrios* in order to have some precise quantitative data of the relative distances involved, rather than having no data at all.

4   Only the distances of potters who lived in Ticul were used for the calculation of the correlation coefficients. The 25 potters who live outside Ticul and are inactive (except for one or two active potters in Merida) were not included in this analysis. Originally the correlations were calculated with all of the values present, but the resulting coefficients were unusually high (>0.9). Since the maximum distances between the households in Ticul were 15 blocks, the outlying values of >99.9 blocks (which indicated that the potters had moved outside the community) were eliminated.

5   Changing fabrication techniques is difficult (because of the motor-habit patterns involved) unless potters use a forming technique (like two-piece moulds) which requires little skill.

6   Some workshop potters in Ticul do not come from the pottery-making families and did not learn the craft from relatives, but learned it as teenage apprentices in commercial workshops outside the household.

References

Allen, W. L. & J. B. Richardson III 1971. The reconstruction of kinship from archaeological data: the concepts, the methods, and the feasibility. *American Antiquity* **36**, 41–53.

Arnold, D. E. 1971. Ethnomineralogy of Ticul, Yucatan potters. *American Antiquity* **36**, 20–40.

Arnold, D. E. 1981. A model for the identification of non-local ceramic distribution: a view from the present. In *Production and distribution: a ceramic viewpoint*. H. Howard & E. L. Morris (eds), 31–44. Oxford: BAR International Series 120.

Arnold, D. E. 1983. Design structure and community organization in Quinua, Peru. In *Structure and cognition in art*, D. K. Washburn (ed.), 56–74. Cambridge: Cambridge University Press.

Arnold, D. E. 1984. Social interaction and ceramic design: community-wide correlates in Quinua, Peru. In *Pots and potters: current approaches in ceramic archaeology*, P. Rice (ed.), 133–61. Monograph XXIV. Los Angeles: Institute of Archaeology, University of California.

Arnold, D. E. 1985a. *Ceramic theory and cultural process*. Cambridge: Cambridge University Press.

Arnold, D. E. 1985b. *Maya potters after 20 years: archaeological implications*. Paper presented to the Maya Ceramics Conference, Washington, DC, 4 December 1985. (Paper in press in published papers of the conference, BAR International Series.)

Arnold, D. E. & B. F. Bohor 1975. Attapulgite and Maya Blue: an ancient mine comes to light. *Archaeology* **28**, 23–9.

Arnold, D. E. & B. F. Bohor 1977. Ancient clay mine at Yo' K'at, Yucatan. *American Antiquity* **42**, 575–82.

Deetz, J. 1965. *The dynamics of stylistic change in Arikara ceramics*. Illinois Studies in Anthropology No. 4. Urbana: University of Illinois Press.

Hayden, B. & A. Cannon 1982. The corporate group as an archaeological unit. *Journal of Anthropological Archaeology* **1**, 132–58.

Hayden, B. & A. Cannon 1984. Interaction inferences in archaeology and learning frameworks of the Maya. *Journal of Anthropological Archaeology* **3**, 325–67.

Hill, J. N. 1970. Broken K. Pueblo: prehistoric social organization in American Southwest. *Anthropological Papers of the University of Arizona, No. 18*. Tucson: University of Arizona Press.

Kramer, C. 1985. Ceramic ethnoarchaeology. *Annual Review of Anthropology* **14**, 17–102.

Longacre, W. A. 1970. Archaeology as anthropology: a case study. *Anthropological Papers of the University of Arizona No. 17*. Tucson: University of Arizona Press.

Peacock, D. S. P. 1982. *Pottery in the Roman World: an ethnoarchaeological approach*. London: Longman.

Reina, R., E. Reina & R. M. Hill 1978. *The traditional pottery of Guatemala*. Austin: University of Texas Press.

Stanislawski, M. B. 1977. Ethnoarchaeology of Hopi and Hopi–Tewa pottery making: styles of learning. In *Experimental archaeology*, D. Ingersoll, J. E. Yellen & W. MacDonald (eds), 378–408. New York: Columbia University Press.

Stanislawski, M. B. & B. B. Stanislawski 1978. Hopi and Hopi–Tewa ceramic tradition networks. In *The spatial organization of culture*, I. Hodder (ed.), 61–76. London: Duckworth.

11 Some ethnospecific features in central and eastern European archaeology during the early Middle Ages: the case of Avars and Hungarians

CSANÁD BÁLINT

Introduction

The biggest attraction for the archaeologist is to provide source material for acquiring knowledge about historical events and processes. In the archaeology of the early Middle Ages this ambition is stronger in the eastern half of Europe than in the western half, for two reasons. In the former, written sources – if they exist at all – are disproportionately fewer than in the latter. In respect of some large areas of eastern Europe it is not even known exactly what peoples lived there through centuries, whereas long texts provide information about the Merovingians, for example, including their dress and medicine. This is why many west European medieval archaeologists can afford to devote their attention mostly to the typological or art–historical analysis of objects. Apart from the constraint mentioned, east European archaeology has also endeavoured for the past 20 years to become a truly historical discipline for ideological reasons: in a marxist reaction to the earlier, almost exclusively typological, interest, it set itself the task of becoming acquainted not only with political, but even with economic and social processes. In addition, under the indirect influence of the post-World War II political changes, a stronger demand arose in most countries of central and eastern Europe for a new approach to the past of their own nation. In addition to several positive achievements, this endeavour also had a negative aspect; for example, the relics of the Eastern Germanic peoples temporarily 'disappeared', and for some time the people of the steppe were regarded as the enemies of historical progress. In such circumstances research on ethnic questions became an especially difficult and sometimes delicate task in the archaeology of the early Middle Ages in central and eastern Europe.

The area of interest

In respect of the ethnic identification of archaeological finds, the early medieval archaeology of the Carpathian Basin is in a most favourable situation. Reports by written sources that new peoples migrated from the east can be linked in four instances to archaeological material: around AD 420 the Huns, in AD 568 the Avars, around AD 670–680 the so-called Middle- or Late Avars, and in AD 895 the Hungarians. The numerous archaeological sites of the Avars and Hungarians and their material culture, which distinguishes them sharply from each other and from their neighbours, provide a basis which has not yet been sufficiently exploited for studying the less numerous finds of the east European steppes, whose dating is much more uncertain. The joint investigation of the Carpathian Basin and the east European steppes is also indispensable because of the kinship between their people and because of their cultural similarities. However, several major questions concerning the archaeological legacy of the peoples of the central and east European steppes continues to be open. What are the Avars? What are the Hungarians?

On the ethnospecific rôle of objects

The conventional methods of archaeology include the search for parallels. Innumerable examples show that this method has not become obsolete today, even though we live in a period of demanding methods of a high level and of scientific approaches. It remains very much a current practice to sketch the migration of a people by documenting the spread of finds as well as the parallels and typological prototypes. It can be said of few of the peoples of central Europe that they have lived uninterruptedly in one place for thousands of years, as have, for example, the Caucasian and Baltic peoples, and the Permian Finno-Ugrians. The case of the Huns is a fortunate one, since their movement from central Asia to Catalaunum is defined, somewhat roughly in respect of ethnic accuracy, but nevertheless with rare clarity as far as the direction of migration is concerned, for example by the sites of sacrificial cauldrons and precious stone-inlaid diadems (see Bóna 1979a, pp. 300–5, Werner 1956, pp. 57–61, Zaseckaja 1982). However, the archaeological confirmation or demonstration of a migration, the analysis of an ethnically heterogeneous cemetery (or one which is thought to be heterogeneous) generally demands thorough research, since the ethnic and cultural influences which affected the given population were certainly not translated directly into the language of objects and burial customs. Consequently, whether we investigate the ethnic affiliation of particular types of objects or archaeological cultures, it is highly advisable in every case to conduct a thorough analysis before coming to a final conclusion. In this way we may hope to avoid conclusions of the type which, for example, explains the presence of ornaments of Byzantine type, arms and domestic objects of

Germanic type together with Avar mounted burials, in terms of the existence of a Byzantine–Germanic garrison in the early Avar period (Salamon & Erdélyi 1971; for a critique see the excellent but, for non-Hungarians, totally neglected book review by Tomka 1973).

The relics of the Avars, who conquered the Carpathian Basin and acquainted Europe with the stirrup, can be distinguished sharply and incontestably from those of the local peoples. However, the investigation of their internal ethnic connections with respect to their central Asian roots (see Bálint 1978, pp. 203–6, Bóna 1971, pp. 289–91), and the related steppe peoples who joined them or were conquered by them is still only beginning (Csallány 1953, Simonyi 1957; for a critique Bóna 1981). Conversely, the possibility of confirming the existence of an Eastern Slavic group drifting here from the east appeared to be more promising; for example, the so-called *Maskenfibel* is found, a 7th century ornament form which was certainly alien to the Avars, and which has analogues from the Central Dnieper, considered to be of Slavonic origin (for the latter, see Rybakov 1937, Werner 1950). The assumption soon followed that the early Avars carried along with them Eastern Slavic women. However, the territorial distribution of this fibula is so broad (from the Baltic to the Balkans, from the Crimea to the Carpathian Basin; see Bálint 1981) that it cannot automatically be considered to be an Eastern Slavonic type. This fibula is most frequent around the lower reaches of the Danube and, in any case, despite the efforts made by Soviet archaeologists, the Central Dnieper cannot simply be assumed to have been a purely Eastern Slavonic territory in the 7th century (Bálint 1981). Consequently, it seems dubious to link the fibula in question, and the trapezoidal pendants and star-spangled earrings found with them, to the Eastern Slavs, when in fact they were a universal fashion, and it is in any case only an assumption that the Eastern Slavs drifted to the Carpathian Basin with the early Avars (Bóna 1965, pp. 57–8).

The ethnic background of the wheeled earthenware kettles found in the Carpathian Basin has been contested for a long time. It is only a very recent typological–chronological analysis that finally makes the clarification of the question possible (Takács 1986). In the absence of a thorough knowledge of the Carpathian Basin material, this cooking vessel had earlier been defined as being Pecheneg, on the basis of motives which cannot be considered to be purely scientific. Some even considered it to be Romanian (for criticism see Fodor 1977). Their massive and universal presence in the Carpathian Basin in the 10th century makes it clear that we are facing here a type of object linked to certain ethnic and/or economic groups of the Hungarians. Since such objects can also be found in large numbers on the eastern slopes or to the south-east of the Carpathians, in territories which were then held by the Pechenegs, no exception can be taken to their Pecheneg definition either (since the possibility of local origin there can be excluded). It is equally permissible to assume Pechenegs in the earthenware kettle group of the Raba-Marcal region, in the north-west region of the Carpathian Basin, since we indeed know of Pecheneg settlements in that region at that time (see the map in Györffy 1939). As for the ethnic affiliation of the hand-shaped earthenware kettles, which have been known only for a few years, this is much simpler, since it is primarily a function of chronology. In Hungarian research there were arguments about whether they were of Late Avar or Hungarian origin. The only thing which had to be clarified here was whether the currently small number of finds could be dated before or after AD 895, i.e. the Hungarian conquest (the problems being caused by the difficulties of dating early medieval domestic pottery). Although data are now available which point to the first alternative, the solution is nevertheless not quite so straightforward; however, further discussion of this topic falls outside the scope of this chapter.

It is my conviction that no object is ethnospecific as such. Let us take the example of the sabretach-plate, the most beautiful and famous type of object of the conquering Hungarians. It is linked in the Carpathian Basin exclusively to the Hungarians, although there is a possibility that it was not used by every ethnic group or tribe among them. Nevertheless, it is risky automatically to seek ancient Hungarians in the owners of some specimens found outside the Carpathian Basin, because of chronological, cultural and geographic differences. Or let us look at the most important piece of dress of the free Hungarian man of the 10th century, the studded belt. Belt studs with a similar kind of decoraton also occur in large numbers in Bulgaria, but for both historical reasons and the fact that other objects of a Hungarian character, as well as Hungarian burial customs, are lacking, we do not wish to explain this in terms of a migration of Hungarian men. For similar reasons no Hungarian scholar would assume that Hungarian women who married and emigrated to Slavic areas are represented by the two-member pendants found outside the southern frontier of 10th century Hungary. Such cases as this do not, in my view, reflect ethnic differences, but rather a fashion mediated by the Hungarians. This conclusion may be supported by the fact that even the Chinese and Byzantine emperors reorganized their army following the example of the Hiung-nu (Asian Hunnic) or Avar dress and equipment, whereas the Huns of the Attila period also created a fashion among the contemporary Germanic leading stratum (Bóna 1979b, pp. 299–300), just as the Bulgarians did among the Byzantines. Thus, it is not necessary to exclude the possibility of such an adoption in the case of the belt studs or two-member pendants, which were easy to produce.

A further example to demonstrate that the presence of certain types of objects in a region does not necessarily have the value of a source for ethnic identity is that based on the S-ended hair rings which were widespread in central Europe and may be produced by anybody, but which were assumed to represent Slavic ornaments in the 10th century Carpathian Basin. In fact, this was simply a piece of fashion goods, a straightforward object of commerce (Kralovánszky 1959). That Slavs occupied almost the whole of the distribution area of the S-ended hair ring cannot in itself be regarded as compelling proof of their ethnospecific status for the Slavs. Although Slavs lived in the gigantic triangle enclosed by the Oder, the Dnieper and the

Peloponnese, the Sorbs of the Elbe region, for example, had no common elements with the material culture of the Severians of the Balkans. Thus, it is not possible to speak of Pan-Slavic types of objects as such. Finally, it must be remembered that certain objects dispose of a genuine ethnospecific force only in the immediate vicinity of their own ethnocultural entity, i.e. a significant relationship can be found only between a culture and its closest neighbours ('the others').

As far as the heterogeneous peoples of eastern origin in the early Middle Ages are concerned, the uses and fashions of certain objects were influenced by many kinds of social and ethnic factors which are mostly still not known. Thus, it is a grave error to conclude on the basis of the absence of some type of object from an area that the area was occupied by an ethnic group not possessing that type (as did Vinski 1970, p. 61, in respect of the 10th century Hungarians). The archaeological culture of a people has to be investigated in its totality and not through random objects, which brings us on to our next question.

On the ethnospecific rôle of archaeological culture

The archaeological legacy of the four Eastern immigrations mentioned in the introduction can be considered ethnospecific on the whole, and as having a character distinguishing them from their neighbours. However, if one seeks the traces of these peoples they are almost immediately and completely lost east of the Carpathians. This presented a particular problem for the search for the ancient history of the Hungarians. It took a long time to discover that the earlier ancient homelands and migrations of the Hungarians who conquered the Carpathian Basin in AD 895 and disposed of characteristic objects, ornamentation and burial customs, could not be defined simply by putting on the map the sites where objects or burial habits similar to those of the 10th century Hungarians were found. The reason for this was demonstrated by a survey of broader scope, pointing out that the culture of the peoples moving into the Carpathian Basin changed in every period compared with their earlier culture, under the influence of the ethnic elements found on the spot and new cultural trends (see Bóna 1979). It is perhaps the conquering Hungarians about whom we know most with regard to the mainsprings of this process. In their case a fundamental material contribution to the emergence of a richer and more-varied ornamental style and animus than those of the archaeological cultures of the Eurasian steppe of the Early Middle Ages was represented by the previous metal treasures seized in the European marauding raids and smelted down at home (Dienes 1968). It seems that the massive utilization of the latter resulted in a sort of social levelling in the decoration of the dress and the use of ornaments. By way of a comparison, in Khazaria and in the Turkic Empire only a small stratum of society could use precious-metal ornaments, whereas among the 10th century Hungarians even commoner women occasionally wore silver in considerable quantity.

In the case of the formation of the Avar archaeological culture more assumptions have to be made. We have to take into consideration not only their Inner- and Middle-Asian origin, and new influences which affected them in South Russia, but also, of course, the huge Byzantine gold tax received over nearly 50 years in the Carpathian Basin. (According to the most recent estimates, the latter amounted to 4.5 million solidus=18.55 tons; see Bóna 1984, p. 324). This mass of precious metal provided the raw material for a jewellery and ornamentation so different from that of the relations of the Avars left behind in the East that the original elements of their material culture can only be demonstrated in a few cases (see Bóna 1984, pp. 327, 333). The immigration of the Middle Avars – an event which some German and Slovak scholars continue to doubt – can be confirmed only with difficulty by tracing its eastern ancestry, because the early Avars found in the Carpathian Basin could have had a substantial influence on the groups who had recently moved in from Khazaria. The merging of the Middle and Late Avars was accompanied by a new foreign policy, which first turned inward and finally towards the West, and by the increasing importance of a new agricultural way of life, as well as the use of the multitude of Roman bronze statues standing on the territory of Pannonia. All of this led to the development of a new and rich popular (not aristocratic) material culture (Bóna 1984, p. 333).

It should be mentioned here that a consideration of the 8th–10th century Bulgarian archaeological material is not without lessons in this respect, either. Owing to the small number, rapid assimilation and close Byzantine contacts of the Bulgarian Turks immigrating in AD 681, it is understandable that their connections with the Khazarian material appear to be infrequent and weak at first glance; so much so, that if for some reason we lacked the unequivocal sources reporting their conquest of the Balkans, doubts might easily arise concerning the immigration of the Bulgarian Turks. It is instructive to play with this question: did a people in fact resettle from Khazaria to the Balkans in the last third of the 7th century, or can the identity and analogies which can be demonstrated between the two regions be attributed to trade, to craftsmen who had moved there and to other 'influences'? Also, was burial with a horse merely a social phenomenon lacking any ethnic content? Fortunately, in this case at least, no such doubts exist; however, this example helps to show something of the methods and the nature of the arguments concerning the central European archaeological cultures of the early Middle Ages.

Here I wish only to mention the difference of views which exists between most Slovak researchers and Hungarian archaeology in the assessment of cemeteries found north of the 20th century frontier of Hungary, and which show a substantial identity with those of the Avars. The welcome *rapprochement* of the two views in the appraisal of these cemeteries in the plains, characterized by large numbers of sabres, studded belts, mounted burials, etc., is indicated by the development of Slovak terminology in the past 40 years: 'Slavic', 'Slavic–Avarian', 'Avar–Slavic', 'pre-Great-Moravian' and 'so-called Avar' (see Garam 1987). It is to be noted that in pre-World War II Czechoslovakia such relics were not only called Avar, but the publication of the material of Avar cemeteries excavated in Hungary was even undertaken. Out of the debate, which is approaching a final consensus, I wish to emphasize here only that in the view of Hungarian research the smaller differences in the 7th–9th century cemeteries uncovered in the northern part of the Carpathian Basin are not due to ethnic but to tribal differences. The tribal alliances of steppe origin were made up of constitutive elements of different origins by their very nature. Consequently, their archaeological cultures are always internally heterogeneous, to which must be added the effects of settlement on the local population, and possibly its assimilation. However, externally, compared with their neighbours, they always form an entity which can be distinguished from others. It is again the Hungarians of the 10th–11th centuries that offer an example of the analysis of the emergence of an archaeological culture in our region and period.

The so-called Bijelo Brdo culture is the subject of interest. Until fairly recently (Točík 1973) only Hungarian scholars – 'obviously on account of their national bias' – insisted on the definition of this culture as 'Hungarian' when discussing its ethnic affiliation. What is in fact involved is that the ethnic identification of the first relics of the Hungarian conquest arose from the historical attitude of the Hungarian noblemen in the late 19th and early 20th century. At the time Hungarian scholars could imagine only the mounted and armed graves of an oriental nature as the relics of their ancestors, whereas they ascribed to the Slavs the material from the poorer cemeteries which contained in addition to the eastern cultural elements some elements of a local and Byzantine nature. However, this concept was the result of a simplification. The new political situation and the conditions of national consciousness following World War I in Central Europe greatly favoured the strengthening of the latter definition, and its continuing existence was also assisted by current trends in Hungarian society and political developments. After World War II Hungarian archaeology turned to the many-sided study of the question only when its 'slavophile period' had passed (Szőke 1959, see also Bálint 1986 on the relationship between nationalism and archaeology in Hungary).

It is to be noted that after World War II a new period of Hungarian archaeology started. This was characterized by the overestimation of the political and cultural influence of the Slavic elements on the Hungarians of the 10th–11th centuries. This was not an exclusively Hungarian phenomenon. Interestingly enough, similar views appeared after Liberation in all of the central European countries which had been affected by Fascism. In Hungary this period ended around the 1950s. To us it is already clear today that the so-called Bijelo Brdo culture was the product of the commoners among the conquering Hungarians, blending their own culture with those found on the spot. It is obvious that Slavs also rest in cemeteries of such a type, but their proportion changes considerably from area to area. Owing to their small numbers, it is not possible to distinguish them on the basis of the objects, or even anthropologically, since the majority of the conquering Hungarians were also of the Europid anthropological type. It is an important characteristic of the so-called Bijelo Brdo culture that within the region of its presence there is no essential difference at all in the material and burial customs of the different areas. If one compares this situation with that in similar cultural–ethnic regions, it represents a difference from that of the Late Avars, Khazaria or the Turkic Khaganate. Within these empires – perhaps only the Turks representing an exception – little research has been done on the features distinguishing some areas from others. In respect of the burial customs some regional differences can be found in the choice of meat to be put in the grave, in the inclusion or exclusion of the vessel and, as far as Khazaria is concerned, in variants of the mounted burials, in burials in catacombs, and their orientation. Finally, in the Turkic Khaganate some variations may be seen in respect of the harness and possibly some ornaments (Savinov 1972). It is therefore possible that the uniform nature of the so-called Bijelo Brdo culture, on the one hand, and the small differences – which need to be the subject of further work – in the archaeological legacy of the empires mentioned, on the other hand, may also be connected with the degree of social development of the political formations mentioned. In the last resort the so-called Bijelo Brdo culture should be considered the archaeological culture of the Hungarian state (Bálint 1975, Bóna 1986, p. 576), and as such – to this, but only to this extent – it is an ethnic phenomenon. At the same time it is beyond doubt that the Late Avar and the Khazar Khaganates were empires of an oriental nature with a politically and territorially much looser structure.

An opportunity for studying the possible connection between archaeological culture and the state is also offered by Dalmatia and by the Rus' of Kiev, one by its uniformity and the limited territorial distribution of some of its finds, and the other by the opposite situation. As far as Bulgaria is concerned, there is little to be analysed in this respect, owing to the Byzantine influences which were strong from the beginning. Although it may be going too far to postulate a connection with the state as such, a link between the political power sphere and archaeological culture appears possible in the early medieval empires which have been mentioned. Apart from the case of the so-called Bijelo Brdo culture, what other explanation could be found for the fact that Late Avar cemeteries can be found only as far as the Enns, i.e. the Bavarian–Avar frontier? The assumption of a link between political unit and archaeological culture seems to be confirmed also by the fact that the Turkic Empire was established in AD 552 without any noteworthy migration or displacement of population, while at the same time a large number of artefacts of a Turkic type, and burial customs, occurred and spread without important local antecedents. At least this case is perfectly clear: the birth of the archaeological culture of the Inner Asian Turkic empire coincides with the formation of their political power.

In conclusion, I hope that I have succeeded in drawing attention to the difficulties and possibilities of linking certain objects – archaeological culture

– to ethnicity, and to the need for circumspection on the part of central and east European early medieval archaeology in the investigation of ethnic questions.

References

Bálint, Cs. 1975. *Süd-Ungarn im 10. Jahrhundert*. Budapest: Akadémiai (in press).
Bálint, Cs. 1978. Vestiges archéologiques de l'époque tardive des Sassanides et leurs relations avec les peuples des steppes. *Acta Archaeologica Academiae Scientiarum Hungaricae* **30**, 173–212.
Bálint, Cs. 1981. Über einige östliche Beziehungen der Frühawarenzeit (568–*circa* 670/680). *Mitteilungen des Archäologischen Instituts der Ungarischen Akademie der Wissenschaften* **10–11**, 131–46.
Bálint, Cs. 1986. A magyar régészet és a nacionalizmus. In *Hungaro-Polonica*, Gy. Cs. Kiss & I. Kovács (eds), 166–73. Budapest: Soros Alapítvány.
Bóna, I. 1965. Opponensi vélemény Cs. Dr. Sós Ágnes: A Dunántul IX. századi szláv népessége c. kandidátusi disszertációjáról. *Régészeti Dolgozatok* **7**, 32–59.
Bóna, I. 1971. Ein Vierteljahrhundert Völkerwanderungszeitforschung in Ungarn (1945–1969). *Acta Archaeologica Academiae Scientiarum Hungaricae* **23**, 265–336.
Bóna, I. 1979a. Die archäologischen Denkmäler der Hunnen und der Hunnenzeit in Ungarn im Spiegel der internationalen Hunnenforschung. In *Niebelungenlied*, E. Vonbank (ed.), 297–342. Bregenz: Vorarlberger Landesmuseum. Ausstellungskatalog Nr 86.
Bóna, I. 1979b. Régészetünk és Kelet-Európa. *A Magyar Tudományos Akadémia II. Osztályának Közleményei* **28**, 39–48.
Bóna, I. 1981. Das erste Auftreten der Bulgaren im Karpatenbecken. *Studia Turco-Hungarica* **5**, 79–112.
Bóna, I. 1984. A népvándorláskor és a korai középkor története Magyarországon. In *Magyarország története*. Előzmények és magyar történet 1242-ig, Gy. Székely & A. Bartha (eds), 265–373. Budapest: Akadémiai.
Bóna, I. 1986. Daciától Erdőelvéig. A népvándorlás kora Erdélyben (271–896). In *Erdély története a kezdetektől* 1606-ig, L. Makkai & A. Mócsy (eds), 107–234, 565–82. Budapest: Akadémiai.
Csallány, D. 1953. A bácsújfalusi avarkori hamvasztásos lelet. Adatok a kutrigur-bolgárok (hunok) temetkezési szokásához és régészeti hagyatékához. *Archaeologiai Értesítő* **80**, 133–41.
Dienes, I. 1968. Hungarian metalcraft in the time of the conquest. *The New Hungarian Quarterly* **9**, 210–16.
Fodor, I. 1977. Der Ursprung der in Ungarn gefundenen Tonkessel. *Acta Archaeologica Academiae Scientiarum Hungaricae* **29**, 323–44.
Garam, É. 1987. Die spätawarenzeitlichen Pferdebestattungen. *Alba Regia* in press.
Györffy, Gy. 1939. Besenyők és magyarok. *Kőrösi Csoma-Archívum* **1**, Ergänzungsband.
Kralovánszky, A. 1959. Beiträge zur Frage der Ausstattung, Chronologie und ethnischen Bestimmung der sog. Schläfenringe mit S-Enden. *Studia Slavica* **5**, 327–61.
Rybakov, B. A. 1937. Drevnie rusy. *Sovetskaya Arheologiya* **17**, 23–104.
Salamon, Á. & I. Erdélyi 1971. *Das völkerwanderungszeitliche Gräberfeld von Környe*. Budapest: Akadémiai.

Savinov, D. G. 1972. Ètnokul'turnye svjazi naseleniya Sajano-Altaja v drevnet-jurkskoe vremja. *Tjurkologičeskij Sbornik* 339–50.

Simonyi, D. 1957. Die Bulgaren des V. Jahrhunderts im Karpatenbecken. *Acta Archaeologica Academiae Scientiarum Hungaricae* **8**, 227–50.

Szőke, B. 1959. A bjelo brdoi kultúráról. *Archaeologiai Értesítő* **86**, 32–47.

Takács, M. 1986. *Die árpádenzeitlichen Tonkessel im Karpatenbecken*. Budapest: Archäologisches Institut der Ungarischen Akademie der Wissenschaften.

Točík, A. 1973. Zur Frage der slawisch–magyarischen Kontakte an der mittleren Donau im 10. und 11. Jahrhundert. In *Berichte über den II. Internationalen Kongress für slawische Archäologie*, 32–47, II. Berlin: Akademie.

Tomka, P. 1973. Review of Das völkerwanderungszeitliche Gräberfeld von Környe. *Antik Tanulmányok* **20**, 224–31.

Vinski, Zd. 1970. O postojanju radionica nakita starohrvatskog doba u Sisku. *Vjesnik Arheološkog Muzeja u Zagrebu* **4**, 45–81.

Werner, J. 1950. Slawische Bügelfibeln des 7. Jahrhunderts. In *Reinecke-Festschrift*; 150–72. Mainz: Schneider.

Werner, J. 1956. *Beiträge zur Archäologie des Attila-Reiches*. Munich: Bayerische Akademie der Wissenschaften.

Zaseckaja, I. P. 1982. Pogrebenie u sela Kyzyl-adyr orenburgskoj oblasti (K voprosu o gunno-hunnskih svjazah). In *Drevnie pamjatniki kul'tury na territorii SSSR*, A. M. Mikljaev (ed.), 54–77, 151–61. Leningrad: Gosudarstvennyj ordena Lenina Ermitaž.

12 *Ancient ethnic groups as represented on bronzes from Yunnan, China*

WANG NINGSHENG

Introduction

From 1955 to 1960 more than 40 tombs were excavated at the site of Shi-zhai-shan in Yinning County, Yunnan Province, China. This region was the centre of the ancient Dian kingdom, which was conquered by the Western Han Empire (206 BC–AD 24) in 109 BC. In this year, according to the famous Chinese historical records *Shi Ji*, the Emperor bestowed a golden seal on the king of Dian as a symbol of the monarch–subject relationship between them. In tomb 6 at Shi-zhai-shan archaeologists discovered this golden seal, or a replica of it, inscribed with four Chinese characters meaning 'The Seal of the Dian King' (Fig. 12.1), a find which has been regarded as one of the most important achievements of archaeology in China.

Figure 12.1 The golden seal of the Dian king (after Yunnan Museum 1959, pl. 107:3).

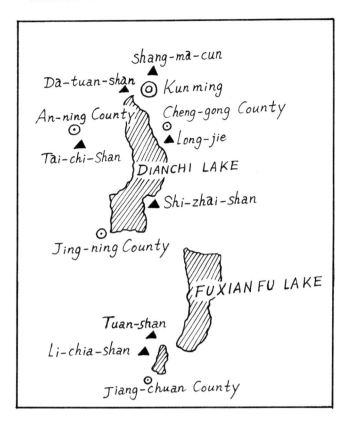

Figure 12.2 The distribution of bronze culture sites around Dianchi Lake.

Since then many similar sites have been discovered and excavated in Jiangchuan County, Chenggong County, Anning County and the suburbs of Kunming. All of these sites, located around Dianchi Lake and the neighbouring area (Fig. 12.2), have produced material (mostly grave goods) with common cultural features. In general it belongs to a late stage of the Yunnan bronze age culture, although a few iron objects had begun to appear at some sites. I have dated this phase to 500–100 BC (Wang 1981); this corresponds to the dating of the Dong-son culture (Karlgren 1942), with which the Yunnan bronze age culture has close connections.

About 5000 elegant and magnificent bronzes have been found at these sites, including weapons, tools, musical instruments, ornaments, plaques of different shapes and uses, wine vessels, containers and drums, which are widely distributed in south China and south-east Asia generally. All of these bronzes were decorated with designs and pictures, and they were inlaid with jades, agates or turquoises. In particular, on a kind of container used for holding cowrie money, the ancient artists cast many sculptures depicting people's daily lives and religious activities of the time, including battle scenes, ceremonies and such activities as weaving. On the plaques and other articles there were also many realistic scenes (Yunnan Museum 1956, 1959, 1975, 1983). These scenes throw new light on the history, art and society of the Dianchi Lake region in the period 500–100 BC.

Many Western scholars have focused their research on the art style of Yunnan bronzes, the relation of the style to the Dong-son culture and the influences on it from central China and the bronze age culture of the steppes (Pirazzoli-t'Sersevens 1974, Bunker 1974, Dewall 1967, 1974, Watson 1968), but the author's interest lies in the study of the ethnic diversity of the Dian kingdom (see Wang 1979, *contra* Feng Han-Yi (Feng 1961)).

A brief outline of the economic and social life of the Dian kingdom

It is necessary to begin with a brief introduction to the economic and social life of the Dian kingdom, in order to provide a background for these ethnic studies (for details, see Feng 1963, Wang 1981).

Agriculture was the main means of subsistence. Planting was carried out with bronze hoes (many examples of which have been discovered), and with bamboo and wooden implements which are depicted on the bronzes. Rice was probably the main crop. Scenes on the bronzes indicate that all agricultural work was a task for women, and that some agricultural ceremonies were presided over by priestesses or female chiefs.

Livestock rearing was also practised, including buffalo, zebu cattle (or something similar), pig, horse, dog, domestic fowl, goat and sheep. All of these, but particularly oxen, are depicted on the bronzes, two of which show herding. In addition, hunting and fishing also went on. Many plaques show hunters chasing or catching their prey, including tigers, leopards, wild boar and deer (Fig. 12.3).

Bronze metallurgy was of a very high standard, and pottery manufacture, basketry and jewellery-making also went on, including the making of buttons of jade and agate, used as belt ornaments and found in some of the tombs. On the lid of one bronze cowrie-shell container was a scene depicting eight women weaving and preparing the thread under other women's supervision.

People engaged in trade and commerce both within the Dian kingdom and beyond it. Cowrie shells (*Monetaria annulus*), and possibly also oxen, were used as the medium of exchange. On a bronze plate incised with pictograms the prices or value of certain items (including horses, oxen and slaves) were marked with symbols of numerals and cowrie shells.

Relatively little is known about the form of social organization which prevailed. In the centre of the villages there was often a meeting-house and public square where religious ceremonies took place. A ranked hierarchy

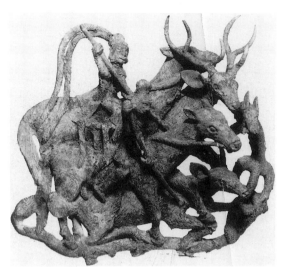

Figure 12.3 Bronze plaque of hunting scene (after Kao Gu Xue Bao 1975:2, pl. 18:1).

Figure 12.4 Lid of a cowrie-shell container showing a battle scene (after Yunnan Museum 1959, pl. 48).

Figure 12.5   Lid of a cowrie-shell container showing a ceremony with four people killed as sacrifices (after Kao Gu Xue Bao 1956:1, pl. 5).

probably existed. People of different status are depicted on the bronzes, including individuals on litters carried and attended by servants or slaves. Their only rôle was to take a leading part in battle (Fig. 12.4) and in ceremonies. Sometimes they were captured and tortured, made to work or killed as sacrifices at ceremonies (Fig. 12.5).

According to *Shi Ji* (ch. 116) a large tribal league or federation had appeared in Yunnan before 109 BC. The Dian kingdom was the strongest of its members, and often acted as a leader. A scene on one of the bronzes shows 17 individuals of different ethnic groups pulling horses, oxen or sheep, or carrying other gifts. It appears to depict tribute-bearers coming to pay their respects to the Dian king.

About the family and marriage at the time we know nothing. From some scenes we can see that women played important rôles in certain ceremonies and attended public meetings with men, but the significance of this is not known.

The ethnic classification of human figures on the bronzes

About 300 male and female human figures with different hairstyles and costumes are depicted on the bronzes. On the basis of these figures it is possible to obtain a vivid picture of ethnic diversity in the Dianchi Lake

Figure 12.6   Ethnic group I: 1, 2, male; 3, female.

region, which was and still is the centre of Yunnan. Obviously this is of very considerable interest for research on the ethnohistory of south-west China.

On the basis of the differences in hairstyle and costume, the figures may be classifed into four ethnic groups, some of which may themselves have been composites of smaller groups.

Ethnic group I

This group represented the majority of the population in the Dian kingdom, to which the king and other members of the ruling group belonged. Although the different tribes of this group were distinguished by minor variations in their appearance, their common characteristic was a bun bound with a band, and a coat without buttons. Both sexes had similar hairstyles, but men often wore their bun on the top of their head, and the women wore theirs on the back of the head. Men's coats often had a tail-shaped cloth, and they sometimes wore a felt cloak over the coat (Fig. 12.6).

Ethnic group II

These were enemies of Dian. From many scenes on the bronzes we can see that they were fighting with ethnic group I and were killed, captured or enslaved by them. Within the Dian kingdom this ethnic group had only a small population and a low status. Both sexes of this group were characterized by wearing their hair in plaits (Fig. 12.7).

Ethnic group III

This group was another minority in the Dian kingdom. Some of them worked as slaves, but others had a higher status; for example, they took part

Figure 12.7   Ethnic group II and a comparison with Yi people (Lolo): 1, male; 2, female; 3, a Lolo woman.

in battles and ceremonies together with ethnic group I, and were thus presumably their allies. They were characterized by wearing their hair in a knot-bun on the top of the head. The hairstyles of male and female adults were the same, but some young women liked to let a tuft of hair fall from the knot-bun. The women are often depicted wearing a long and tight skirt (Fig. 12.8).

Ethnic group IV

This was the smallest group in the Dian kingdom. Only a couple of females could be found among the approximately 300 human figures. They were characterized by wearing their hair in a snail-shaped bun (Fig. 12.9).

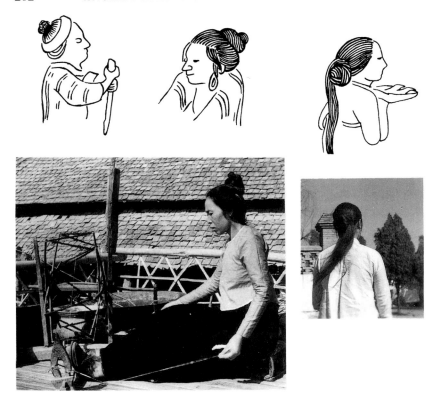

Figure 12.8 Ethnic group III and a comparison with Dai people: 1, male; 2, 3, female; 4, 5, Dai women.

Besides the above-mentioned four ethnic groups, there are a few remarkable and strange human figures. Each has a high nose, wears long trousers and carries a long sword (Fig. 12.10). All these are entirely different from the native people of Yunnan, and we have called them the 'Westerners'. A record in Hua Yang Guo zhi says that some foreigners came from India and other western countries during and before AD 400.

The question obviously arises of whether or not the differences in hairstyles and costumes can indeed be used to classify ethnic groups. In my view the answer is yes. Although today people may casually change their dress according to their needs in different cases, we cannot say the same for the people of the past, especially in ancient China. The ancient Chinese and their 'barbarian' neighbours were accustomed to distinguishing, and indeed to insulting and humiliating, each other on the basis of their hairstyles, costumes and other external features; for example, 'wearing hair in disarray', 'wearing short hair', 'wearing a coat with the buttons on the left side', 'with a

Figure 12.9 Ethnic group IV and a comparison with Miao people: 1, female; 2, a Miao woman.

Figure 12.10. 'Westerner' figures depicted on a plaque.

tattooed face', 'with a tattooed body', etc. Some such features even became the name of the ethnic group itself. Thus, the ancient population of northern China were known by the name *tiu*, after the heavy beard which they were accustomed to wearing. They must initially have been given this name by the people of south China, who liked to keep their faces smooth. Even today the Dai people of Yunnan still call all the Han people *tiu*.

Since the ancient Chinese and their neighbours kept very strictly to their external cultural tradition and regarded hairstyles and costumes as important symbols of ethnic groups, the variety of attire of the human figures on the bronzes must be a reflection of the ethnic diversity of the Dian kingdom.

The identification of ethnic groups on the bronzes

It is difficult to identify the human figures present on the bronzes with known ethnic groups. Nevertheless, if we compare the external and other cultural features of the four groups described above with those of ancient peoples recorded in Chinese texts and with present minorities in Yunnan, we can provide some clues for further research.

Ethnic group I no doubt contained the Dian, as we have suggested. However, there was another ethnic group name in *Shi Ji*: 'the kinds of Me-Mo', which contained the Dian, Me-Mo, Lao-Qin, etc. Since Dian was only the name of the kingdom, which may have orginated from a large tribe, it is better to identify ethnic group I with 'the kinds of Me-Mo', and not just with the Dian. According to *Shi Ji* (ch. 116) this group was 'scattered around Dianchi Lake and the neighbouring region and occupied large fertile lands. They wore their hair in a hammer-shaped bun, lived on agriculture and had large settlements'. All of these descriptions correspond to what we see on the bronzes. The 'hammer-shaped bun' is exactly that of ethnic group I described above. The members of this ethnic group were the ancient inhabitants of Yunnan, and many of their cultural features may be traced back to the Neolithic inhabitants of the area (Wang 1980).

It is difficult to ascertain the relationship between ethnic group I and present minorities in Yunnan. Their hairstyle and costume cannot be found anywhere today. As to the other cultural features, some (for example, the felt cloak and the belt or girdle decorated with buttons of jade, etc.) can be seen in Lalo, or Yi and its related groups; others (head-hunting, pile-dwellings decorated with two birds on the roof, etc.) are to be found among the Wa. The custom of using bronze drums in festivals or ceremonies was still practised by many different minorities, such as the Wa, Miao, Yao, Chuang, Bouyei, Shui, etc. The 'kinds of Me-Mo' have probably merged into many different groups, all inheriting the old cultural tradition, so that it is impossible to say which of the present minorities is the offspring of ethnic group I.

Ethnic group II can be identified as 'the kinds of Kun-Ming'. According to *Shi Ji* (chs 116, 123), this people is 'characterized by plaits' and 'hostile' to

Dian. Originally they were nomadic, and they moved to Yunnan from north-west China at some time before 500 BC. In my view, some of the influences from the Bronze Age culture of the steppes which are found at Shi-zhai-shan and other sites in Yunnan may be attributed to the movement of this group. Among the present minorities in southwestern China only certain Tibet–Burma speaking groups, for example the Lolo, wore their hair in plaits (Fig. 12.7), so we believe that they are closely related to ethnic group II.

Ethnic group III's cultural tradition seems to have been inherited by the Tai people, known as Dai in Yunnan. According to a record in *Man Shu* – a famous ethnography of the 9th century AD – among the tribes called 'golden tooth', 'silver tooth', etc., believed to be the ancestors of the Dai, 'the females like to wear blue skirts to wrap their body tightly'. This is reminiscent of the woman figures of ethnic group III who were wearing similar long tight skirts, which are still today the typical dress of Dai women. Furthermore, the two kinds of women's hairstyle of ethnic group III can still be seen on Dai women in west Yunnan (Fig. 12.8).

Very little can be said about ethnic group IV, since so few figures are depicted on the bronzes. However, the snail-shaped woman's bun can only be seen among the Miao people (Fig. 12.9), which suggests some relation-ship between them.

Conclusion

In the past it was believed that only one group – the Dian – lived in the Dian kingdom, but we can now see that it was characterized by considerable ethnic diversity. The hypothesized relationships between the figures on the bronzes, ancient peoples recorded in texts and present ethnic minorities in Yunnan (LeBar 1964, Pulleyblank 1983) are presented in the following scheme.

Ethnic group as repre-sented on the bronzes	Ancient people recorded in Chinese texts	Present minorities in Yunnan
ethnic group I	'the kinds of Me-Mo'	Wa (Mon-Khmer speaking)
ethnic group II	'the kinds of Kun-Ming'	Yi (Lolo, etc.) (Tibet–Burma speaking)
ethnic group III		Dai (Tai-Kadai speaking)
ethnic group IV		Miaou (Miao-Yao speaking)

References

Bunker, E. C. 1974. The Tian culture and some aspects of its relationship to the Dong-son culture. In *Early Chinese art and its possible influence in the Pacific Basin*, N. Barnard (ed.), 291–338. Authorized Taiwan edition.

Dewall, M. V. 1967. The Tien culture of southwest China. *Antiquity* **46**, 8–21.

Dewall, M. V. 1974. Decorative concepts and stylistic principles in the bronze art of Tien. In *Early Chinese art and its possible influence in the Pacific Basin*, N. Barnard (ed.), 291–372. Authorized Taiwan edition.

Feng, H. Y. 1961. Yunnan Jinning Shi-zhai-shan Chutu Wenwu de Zushu Wenti Shitan. *Kaogu* **1961** (9), 469–87.

Feng, H. Y. 1963. Yunnan Jinning Shi-zhai-shan Chutu tongqi Yanjiu. *Kaogu* **1963** (6), 319–29.

Karlgren 1942. The date of the early Dongson culture. *Bulletin of Far-eastern Art* **14**, 1–28.

LeBar, F. M. 1964. *Ethnic groups of mainland Southeast Asia*. New Haven: HRAF Press.

Pirazzoli-t'Sersevens, M. 1974. *La civilisation du royaume Dian a l'époque Han*. Paris: Publications de l'Ecole Française d'Extrême-Orient XCIV.

Pulleyblank, E. G. 1983. The Chinese and their neighbors in prehistoric and early times. In *The origins of Chinese civilization*, D. V. Keightley (ed.), 411–66. Berkeley: University of California Press.

Wang, N. S. 1979. Yunnan Jinning Shi-zhai-shan Qingqi Tuxiang Suo Jian Minzu Kao. *Kao Gu Xue Bao* **1979**, 4.

Wang, N. S. 1980. Shi Lun Shi-zhai-shan Wenhua. In *Zhongguo Kaogu Xuehui Di Yi Ci Nianhiu Lunwen Ji*, 278–93. Beijing: Wenwu Press.

Wang, N. S. 1981. Dian Ken de Jingji Shenghuo he Shehui. In *Yannan Qingtongqi Luncong*, 42–67. Beijing: Wenwu Press.

Watson, W. 1968. Dongson and the kingdom of Tien. In *Reading on Asian topics*, 45–71. Lund: Scandinavian Institute of Asian Studies, Monograph Series 1.

Yunnan Museum 1956. Yunnan Jinning Shi-zhai-shan Gu Yizhi Ji Muzang. *Kao Gu Xue Bao* **1956**, 1.

Yunnan Museum 1959. *Yunnan Jinning Shi-zhai-shan Gu Muqun Fajue Baogao*. Beijing: Wenwu Press.

Yunnan Museum 1975. Excavation of ancient cemetery at Li-chia-shan in Chiang Chuan County, Yunnan Province. *Kao Gu Xue Bao* **1975**, 2.

Yunnan Museum 1983. *Yunnan Qingtongqi*. Beijing: Wenwu Press.

13 The archaeology of the Yoruba: problems and possibilities

OMOTOSO ELUYEMI

Introduction

The main objective of archaeology as a discipline is to extend the horizons of known history. The aim of a Yoruba archaeology is to use archaeological materials to interpret the socio-economic and ideological history of Yoruba people (Fig. 13.1). Currently Yoruba history is in a disorganized state because there are many writers of history, using many irreconcilable sources and therefore arriving at different, at times contradictory, conclusions. These historians include individuals trained locally during the colonial era who have remained pupils of colonial historians. There are also traditional historians who derive their data from purely oral traditions. Archaeologists are new to the Yoruba historical scene. At this period of their national consciousness the Yoruba need a balanced documented history of their people, based on archaeological, ethnographic and historical data; in particular, it is important to solve the problems of chronology which are at present difficult to tackle in Yoruba history.

Archaeological data

Of key importance is the site of Ile-Ife, the cradle of the Yoruba people, regarded by traditional historians as 'the spot where God created man, white and black, and from where they dispersed all over the world' (Fabunmi 1975, p. 14). Major excavations started in Ile-Ife in 1910 and still continue today. Frobenius (1913, pp. 89–90) was so overwhelmed with the beauty and artistic finesse of the Ife antiquities that he recognized 'the existence of an extremely ancient civilisation', whose origin he attributed to the legendary island of Atlantis. More recently Eluyemi (1980, pp. 28–9) has suggested that artefacts excavated at the site of Oke Ora, near Ile-Ife, indicate much in common between the Ife people (the aborigines of the Yoruba) and the Ife people of our own time: continuity seems to be seen in material culture from the ancient city to the present at Ile-Ife. Yoruba oral traditions suggest that what is Ife is Yoruba, since Ife was the melting pot of the Yoruba ethnic entity.

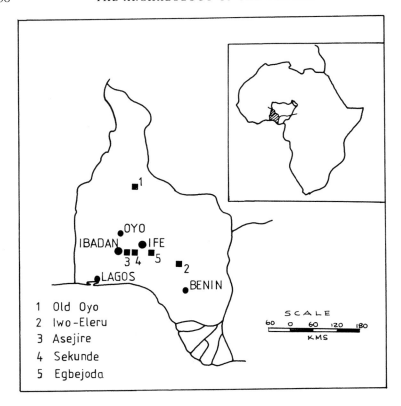

Figure 13.1   The Yoruba archaeological region.

Unfortunately, investigation of such questions of continuity on a larger
spatial scale is difficult at present, because of the lack of excavated sites: the
extent of areas of identity or uniformity is impossible to assess. Nevertheless, some of the other sites which have been excavated provide relevant
indications of continuity, and also of the significance of oral traditions. For
example, the excavations of Isoya (Eluyemi 1977, pp. 97–115) confirmed
some Yoruba historical traditions which had hitherto been considered
unreliable, and the burials from the site were characterized by known
Yoruba practices. Thus, a burial chamber where the coffin of a Yoruba chief
was lying on another skeleton demonstrated the tradition that when an *oba*
(king) was buried, his grave goods usually included a servant to minister to
him. Furthermore, the burials exemplified the practice by which Yoruba
burials are oriented 'homewards'; that is, with the head of the deceased
pointing towards Ile-Ife.

Shrines and the African gods

Is it ever possible for an archaeologist working in a Yoruba environment to proceed from the people's traditions to the reality of history? Can we ever be objective in our historical examination of the African shrines and gods? The possibilities of a combined approach to the Yoruba past using all available sources of evidence are well illustrated by the example of shrines. Archaeological investigation can demonstrate their antiquity; although even here problems arise because the priest removes or unearths the god annually for the annual family festival. Interpretation of the activities which went on there on the basis of archaeological evidence alone is even more problematical. Here current and recent practice and oral tradition can provide a comparative basis for interpretation, and for overcoming the problem that priests and archaeologists live, in effect, in different worlds. Unless and until the archaeologist is initiated into the ideals of the shrine, he remains 'a sheep' at the gathering of the African priests.

In West Africa many communities have institutions known, for want of a better name, as secret societies. In Yorubaland and Igboland, as well as among the Rivers communities of Nigeria, the society is called *Ogboni*. Many broad principles and beliefs which bound together different nationalities in West Africa, such as the Yoruba, the Edo, the Igbo and the Akan, and which permit free interaction, are to be observed in the *Ogboni* house.

Every *Ogboni* house keeps many antique bronze, stone, wood, metal and terracotta objects that await the analysis of the archaeologist; for example, the *ogbo*, a wooden cudgel supposedly used by original members of the society, or the *edan*, a pair of bronze or brass figures which are the symbol of all *Ogboni* societies. However, to be able to comprehend the belief, culture, social behaviour and symbols of worship of these bodies is an extremely difficult task. How reliable is the information given to the archaeologist, who is not himself a member of the society and therefore cannot witness the ceremonies of the house-in-session, never mind seeing the antique objects of worship? Without understanding the tenets of the Yoruba *Ogboni* society no researcher can really comprehend the early sociocultural history of the Yoruba people.

However, despite these observations there can be no doubt of the possibility of a Yoruba archaeology so long as it makes full use of traditional local knowledge, and no doubt of its importance if we are to understand the history of one of the largest ethnic nationalities in Nigeria.

References

Eluyemi, O. 1977. Excavations at Isoya near Ile-Ife (Nigeria) in 1972. *West African Journal of Archaeology* **7**, 97–115.

Eluyemi, O. 1980. *Oba Adesoji Aderemi: 50 years in the history of Ile-Ife*. Ile-Ife: Adesanmi Printing Press.

Fabunmi, M. A. 1975. *The traditional history of Ife*. Ile-Ife: Adesanmi Printing Press.

Frobenius, L. 1913. *The voice of Africa*, Vol. 1 (translated by R. Blind). London: Benjamin Blom.

14 *Ethnicity and traditions in Mesolithic mortuary practices of southern Scandinavia*

LARS LARSSON

A considerable amount of work has been carried out in the area of Mesolithic research with the object of distinguishing between different cultural groupings in Europe during various phases of the period (Kozlowski 1975, 1980, Rozoy 1978). This work has been more or less implicitly correlated with different tribal or folk groups, and therefore is of a directly ethnic character. The studies have been based on the material culture as it reveals itself in tool forms and production techniques. However, a manifest source-critical problem arises here, as the tools' shapes and the manufacturing methods are very dependent on the accessibility, form and structure of the raw material.

Recently particular attention has been directed to the study of southern Scandinavian Late Mesolithic (6000–3000 BC) society (Andersen 1975, Brinch Petersen *et al.* 1982, Larsson 1983), involving intensive investigation of limited areas of Jutland and Zealand (both Denmark) as well as Scania (southernmost Sweden). These investigations have been so comprehensive that they represent what is probably the best factual foundation in the entire European area, in terms of the study of problems related to ethnicity during the Mesolithic. The treatment of material from the three regions is not merely restricted to the lithic finds, but also includes the organic material, as the preservation conditions are unusually good.

The material culture of the so-called Ertebølle Culture, which comprises the whole span of the late part of the Mesolithic in south Scandinavia, at first sight appears to be extremely homogeneous. However, a closer scrutiny shows that certain differences exist, which divide the region into two partially geographically separated areas (Fig. 14.1). This division is based on the distribution of specific artefacts which are known not to differ chronologically from one another. For example, bone rings and T-shaped antler axes occur only in the western part of south Scandinavia, while certain stone axes and harpoon types occur in the eastern part (Vang Petersen 1984). It is precisely due to the considerable amount of organic material that certain other characteristics are traceable to the two areas, such as the ornamentation on bone and antler tools (Andersen 1981).

Apart from the latter, quite exceptionally good conditions at what is now the submarine site at Tybrind Vig, western Funen, have even resulted in the

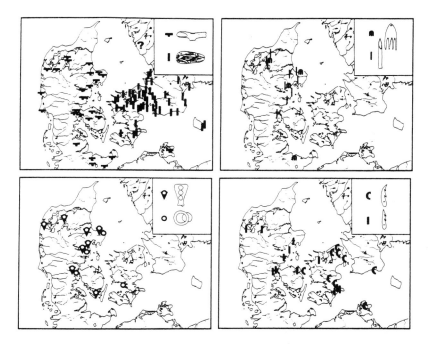

Figure 14.1 The distribution of different artefacts in Denmark dated to the Ertebølle Culture. Upper left, T-shaped red deer antler axes and Limhamn greenstone axes. Upper right, bone combs and bird-bone points. Lower left, scapulae with circular cuts and bone rings or discs made from scapulae. Lower right, straight and curved antler harpoons. (Vang Petersen 1984.)

preservation of a great quantity of wooden implements. Thus, ornamentation on wood – on a pair of paddles – has been established for the first time (Andersen 1985). These proved to feature an ornamentation whose composition differed distinctly from that on bone objects. The ornamentation's composition may well have varied greatly from one material to another. It may also be that ethnic characteristics in decoration were most clearly expressed on paddles and similar well-exposed objects.

The flint material also gives a homogeneous impression at first sight, but certain differences do exist and may be of interest in this connection. One group of tools which has been thoroughly studied is that of flake axes. Microwear analysis shows that they were employed in a range of activities, where their application as axes is only one of several functions (Knutsson 1982). The differences in ways of knapping have been seen as factors linked with chronology. Again, however, a closer study shows that differences occur not only in the knapping technique employed, but also in the shaping, which could not, with any certainty, be connected with the time factor (Vang Petersen 1984). Instead, it has been possible to observe a distinct

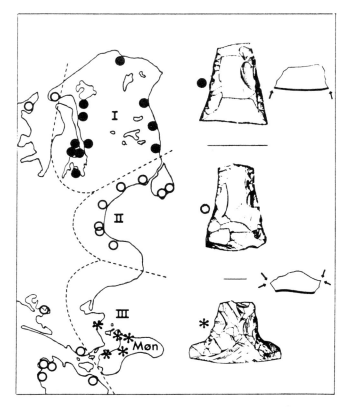

Figure 14.2   Local groups of flake axes in the Late Ertebølle Culture in eastern
Zealand. (Vang Petersen 1984.)

chorological differentiation of axe types in the eastern part of Zealand. At
least three clearly discernible areas have been identified along the coast of the
Öresund strait (Fig. 14.2). At least one special flake axe type has been
established in southernmost Sweden, on the eastern side of Öresund
(Larsson 1984b). Several different areas, each with its own flake axe form,
have therefore been identified within southern Scandinavia.

During the past decade our picture of the Late Mesolithic has been
supplemented by new material from a considerable number of graves. Single
graves from the Late Mesolithic were known earlier, but now they are seen
to appear in veritable cemeteries intimately connected to settlements. One
such was investigated in 1975 at Bøgebakken close to the Danish site of
Öresund (Albrethsen & Brinch Petersen 1977). Five years later, similar
investigations were initiated at the site of Skateholm on the Baltic coast of
southernmost Sweden (Larsson 1984a, 1988). The results of five seasons of
excavations here show that three cemeteries connected to settlements existed

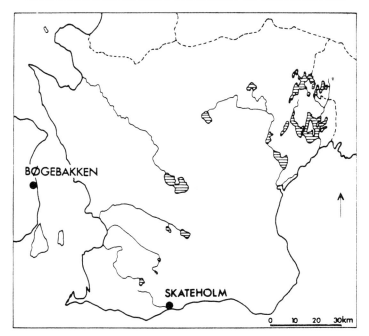

Figure 14.3   The Skateholm site in southernmost Sweden and Bøgebakken in easternmost Denmark.

within an area stretching no more than 400 m, in a former lagoon area. Two of these cemeteries have been investigated, whereas the third was completely destroyed in the course of gravel digging during the 1930s.

One cemetery in Denmark and two in southernmost Sweden cannot, of course, constitute the foundation for any greatly comprehensive discussion on the relationship of burial customs to material culture in southern Scandinavia, but they do provide the basis for an interesting study of interrelationships, in that the three cemeteries are dated to a comparatively short period of some hundreds of years around 4000 BC, as well as being separated by a distance of no more than 80 km, in a straight line (Fig. 14.3). Generally, no great differences exist with regard to the material culture as it is represented in the grave goods at the three sites. However, the assortment of grave goods may well provide interesting information concerning burial customs and conceptions concerning their relationship to individuals, which may in turn be focused on evaluations connected to ethnicity. For example, the same types of artefacts occur at the settlements close to the cemeteries, but there is a marked difference between the Swedish sites and the Danish one in certain cases.

The cemetery at Bøgebakken consisted of 18 graves with 22 individuals. Radiocarbon dates show that burials took place during the timespan

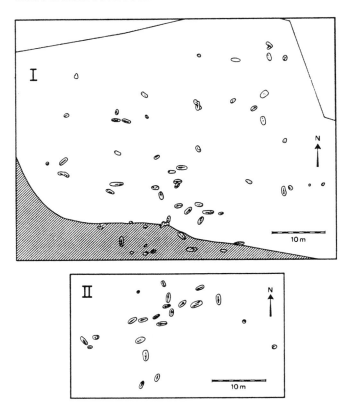

Figure 14.4   The cemeteries of Skateholm I and Skateholm II, southernmost Sweden.

4330±90 BC to 3860±105 BC. The first cemetery encountered at Skateholm – Skateholm I – consisted of a total of 64 graves distributed between 63 humans and seven dogs. Here the period of exploitation is dated to between 4340±95 BC and 3980±125 BC.

There exist, then, two almost contemporaneous cemeteries a comparatively short distance from each other. In addition, both cemeteries have a similar location, i.e. on a southern slope in conjunction with a former lagoon and directly adjacent to a settlement area. The ecological and economic conditions may also be described as similar, even though the bone material from the settlement attached to the cemetery at Bøgebakken indicates a more marked orientation towards marine fishing than is the case for the settlement remains at Skateholm I (Aaris-Sørensen 1980, Jonsson 1988). One might therefore presume that equally great similarities existed between the cemeteries but in fact it is the dissimilarities which are most striking. As to the two cemeteries' formation, that at Bøgebakken is clearly structured within an oblong zone, parallel to the shoreline, whereas that at Skateholm I gives a much more random impression (Fig. 14.4). The radiocarbon dates from the graves of the latter also indicate that large parts of the cemetery's extent of 50×40 m were exploited approximately contemporaneously.

As far as the positions of the dead are concerned, all adults at Bøgebakken, with one exception, were laid on their backs. The exception concerns a woman placed in the crouched position. Such supine burials also occur at Skateholm I, but equally usual are the crouched and sitting positions, and great variations exist even in these. Skateholm I also features two cremations and two inhumation graves containing the skeletal parts of men who were, in all probability, dismembered before burial.

A comparison of the grave goods shows that clear divergences exist even here. Those interred at Bøgebakken have more often than not been furnished with several grave goods; in the case of men, flint knives, and in the case of women, sets of perforated animal teeth are most frequent. Flint knives occur at Skateholm I in only a couple of men's graves, and decorative sets of tooth beads occur in only three women's graves. Here, instead, the most usual grave goods with the men are arrowheads and stone axes, a practice not witnessed at Bøgebakken. Moreover, the majority of graves at Skateholm I held no grave goods whatsoever. Another form of grave goods is red-deer antlers. This occurs in three instances at Bøgebakken, but has not been established at Skateholm I. On the other hand, several individual canine burials were found at the latter site. This form of burial practice had not earlier been encountered in the Scandinavian Mesolithic.

The comparison between two geographically separated societies at Bøge-bakken and Skateholm I provides a basis for the opinion that here we are confronted with a social structure with a largely similar material culture, but within which differences are clearly manifested in terms of conceptions regarding burial customs and the relationship of certain objects to the interred. Thus, it could be interpreted as a case of an ethnicity not demarcated in material terms, but one which primarily expressed itself in conceptions attached to the mortuary practices.

The differences in the cemeteries' structures, positioning of the dead and composition of grave goods support such an interpretation. However, the situation during the Late Mesolithic is not so clear-cut as the conditions above make it appear to be. Other investigations have produced results which give a considerably more nuanced picture of mortuary practices.

Yet another large cemetery has been excavated at Skateholm, designated Skateholm II. This is located only 200 m from the first site, and is similarly situated on the southern slope of a rise which, during part of the Late Atlantic period, constituted a small island. Here, too, the cemetery is immediately adjacent to a large settlement area. Radiocarbon datings from the graves give the values 4480±140 BC to 4140±180 BC. The site's height above sea level, ^{14}C-dates from the occupation layer, as well as artefact forms, all indicate exploitation of the Skateholm II site before the initiation of settlement and burials at Skateholm I (Larsson 1984b). The Late Atlantic transgressions have forced the abandonment of the earlier, lower, site in favour of the later, higher, site. Altogether 22 graves, distributed between 22 humans and two individually buried dogs, were documented within the investigated area at Skateholm II. Thanks to the results from this site, we are provided with the possibility of studying burial customs from an historical perspective within a restricted area, even though the ^{14}C-dates from both sites at Skateholm indicate that interment at each covers a period of some hundreds of years.

Both distinct similarities and distinct dissimilarities are evident between the cemeteries at Skateholm I and Skateholm II. That at the latter, with its clearly defined delimitation within a long-drawn line, oriented parallel to the ancient shoreline (Fig. 14.4), differs from that at Skateholm I, but is similar to that at Bøgebakken. Both the supine and sitting positions occur at Skateholm II, but none of the burials displays a marked crouched position. As to grave goods, several objects occur in the graves, such as flint knives for men and rich sets of decoration for women, a circumstance which, again, is reminiscent of Bøgebakken. On the other hand, stone axes and arrowheads are also found in a similar way to Skateholm I. Grave goods in the form of antlers, however, completely missing in Skateholm I, are present in no less than four graves at Skateholm II.

Taken together, the comparisons between the older cemetery at Skateholm II and the somewhat younger one at Skateholm I provide examples of both tradition and innovation in mortuary practices during the Late Mesolithic. The practice of placing the deceased in a sitting position, as well as furnishing the men with stone axes and arrowheads – the latter in all probability together with a bow – continues. On the other hand, the practice of offering antler beams ceased, whereas the number of grave goods accorded to each, if any, decreases with time. Dogs occur in separate graves, as well as being found, either whole or dismembered, in human graves at both Skateholm I and Skateholm II. The practice of placing the dead in the crouched position may be seen as an innovation.

The investigation at Skateholm suggests that the Late Mesolithic constituted a dynamic era as regards mortuary practices, which naturally makes it difficult to distinguish between what is to be regarded as an ethnic demarcation and what is to be regarded as change dictated by possible transformations in social structure and the effect these had on burial traditions. Both could have influenced that attitude towards the world at large which dictates whether or not new impulses are accepted and which traditional patterns of behaviour are abandoned. The fact that manifest similarities exist between Skateholm II and Bøgebakken, which are not contemporaneous, is striking. Those differences which do exist may be interpreted as being primarily due to various changes in the social structure. The great variation in the positions of those interred, the number of grave goods and the cemetery's apparently random planning at Skateholm I may indicate that a more distinct social subdivision was current within the society represented by the graves there, than was the case at Skateholm II.

That there nevertheless exist elements in the mortuary practices which deserve to be included in a discussion about ethnicity is exemplified by the similarities in the Skateholm cemeteries which, as indicated above, more often than not differ from conditions at Bøgebakken. Even when other single graves from southern Sweden are taken into consideration, it can be seen that differences exist between east Denmark and south Sweden, primarily with regard to the sitting position. That the latter in south Sweden is based on a deep-rooted tradition is shown by the ^{14}C-dates from one of three graves at Kams, on the Baltic island of Gotland, which gave the value 6100±75 BC, i.e. almost 2000 years earlier than the graves at Skateholm (Larsson 1982). At Kams two of the burials, documented *in situ*, were placed in a sitting position.

This account of some elements of the southern Scandinavian Late Mesolithic provides examples of those conditions of a source-critical nature which apply to archaeological material. The inclusion of tradition and innovation in mortuary practices in an ethnic explanatory model is possible, but it also opens up several complicated lines of approach. The account shows that conditions, together with chronological difficulties and an unsound factual foundation, all greatly affect those factors which are directly related to making inferences about ethnicity on the basis of archaeological evidence. On the other hand, the account could be regarded as showing that differences of an ethnic character do exist in Late Mesolithic society, but are apparent in ideas relating to such aspects of mortuary practices, rather than material culture as such.

References

Aaris-Sørensen, K. 1980. Atlantic fish, reptile, and bird remains from the Mesolithic settlement at Vedbæk, North Zealand. *Videnskablige Meddelelser fra dansk naturhistorisk Forening* **142**, 139–49.

Albrethsen, S. E. & E. Brinch Petersen 1977. Excavation of a Mesolithic cemetery at Vedbæk, Denmark. *Acta Archaeologica* **XLVII**, 1–28.

Andersen, S. H. 1975. Ringkloster. En jysk inlandsboplads med Ertebøllekultur. *Kuml* **1973–74**, 11–108.

Andersen, S. H. 1981. Ertebøllekunst. Nye østjyske fund af mønstrede Ertebølleoldsager. *Kuml* **1980**, 7–59.

Andersen, S. H. 1985. Tybrind Vig. A preliminary report on the submerged Ertebølle settlement on the west coast of Fyn. *Journal of Danish Archaeology* **4**, 52–69.

Brinch Petersen, E., H. Juel Jensen, K. Aaris-Sørensen & P. Vang Petersen 1982. Vedbækprojektet. Under mosen og byen. *Søllerødbogen* **1982**, 117–52.

Jonsson, L. 1988. The vertebrate faunal remains from the Late Atlantic site Skateholm in Scania, South Sweden. In *The Skateholm project* Vol. I: *Man and environment*, L. Larsson (ed.), *Regiae Societatis Humaniorum Litterarum Lundensis* LXXIX, 56–88. Lund.

Kozlowski, S. 1975. *Cultural differentiation of Europe from 10th to 5th millennium BC*. Warsaw: PAN.

Kozlowski, S. 1980. *Atlas of the Mesolithic in Europe*. Warsaw: Warsaw University Press.

Knutsson, H. 1982. *Skivyxor*. Experimetell analys av en redskapstyp från den senatlantiska bosättningen vid Soldattorpet. Seminar Paper, Institute of Archaeology, University of Uppsala. Uppsala.

Larsson, L. 1982. De äldsta gutarna. *Gotländskt Arkiv* **1982**.

Larsson, L. 1983. Ageröd V. An Atlantic bog site in Central Scania. *Acta Archaeologica Lundensia* **8**, 12.

Larsson, L. 1984a. Gräberfelder und Siedlungen des Spätmesolithikums bei Skateholm, Südschonen, Schweden. *Archäologisches Korrespondenzblatt* **14**, 123–30.

Larsson, L. 1984b. The Skateholm project. A Late Mesolithic settlement and cemetery complex at a southern Swedish bay. *Papers of the Archaeological Institute, University of Lund* **1983–1984**, 5–38.

Larsson, L. 1988. The Skateholm project. Late Mesolithic settlement at a southern Swedish lagoon. In *The Skateholm project:*, Vol. 1: *Man and environment*, L. Larsson (ed.) *Regiae Societatis Humaniorum Litterarum Lundensis* LXXIX, 9–19. Lund.

Rozoy, J.-G. 1978. *Les derniers chasseurs. L'Epipaléolithique en France et en Belgique*. Charleville: privately published.

15 *Detecting political units in archaeology – an Iron Age example*

RALPH M. ROWLETT

Prehistoric political arrangements pose some of the most subtle problems in archaeology. Even such a basic distinction as that between a chiefdom and a segmented tribe can be difficult to determine clearly (Rowlett 1985). Distinguishing the boundaries of a political system, like distinguishing other aspects of society and culture, can be helpful in delimiting the extent of a system and thus noting additional characteristics. Presented here is an example from the Marnian Variant of the La Tène areal culture (in present-day France, Fig. 15.1), which seems to have some political implication. All cases from this example date from the La Tène Ia horizon, *c.* 480–450 BC as conventionally dated (Hodson 1964, Rowlett 1968, Hatt & Roualet 1977).

The Marnian Variant is well-known to be easily recognized by inspection among other La Tène sub-areal manifestations. The west-oriented graves are full of a black grave fill, and the predominantly inhumed supine skeletons are supplied with a seemingly complete inventory of dress items, equipment, artefacts of personal interest, and food and distinctive pottery for the afterlife. Most of the cemeteries include at least one, and sometimes several, chariot burials. More-recent multivariate factor analyses of internal diversity and co-variation of the rich archaeological burial inventory and settlement–cemetery relations have shown that the internal distribution of artefacts tends to cluster in three or four main geographically integral subcultural groups (Fig. 15.2; Rowlett 1967, Rowlett & Pollnac 1972, Pollnac and Rowlett 1977, Rowlett 1978). These analyses produce geographic groups of contiguous sites in (a) the East Marne, (b) the Marne–Ardennes Group of northern Marne and southern Ardennes, and (c) the Marne–Aisne Group of western Marne and southern Aisne. In south-central Marne a small group which perhaps should be called the West Group (as it is western in the Marnian area), is set apart primarily by some ceramic characteristics and a penchant for minute circular ornamentation on its rangy fibulae and other bronzes. Otherwise, the cultural content of this group is similar to that of the East Marnian, and perhaps belongs to that set.

The objective detection by sophisticated methods of clear-cut socio-cultural groups on the flat, open plain of Champagne, in a cultural context

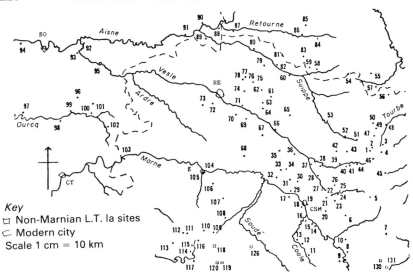

Figure 15.1 La Tène Ia Marnian sites. 1, 'La Gorge Meillet', Marne; 2, Somme-Tourbe 'La Bouvandeau', Marne; 3, Somme-Tourbe 'l'Orgemont', Marne; 4, Somme-Bionne, Marne; 5, Poix, Marne; 6, Marson, Marne; 7, Venault-le-Châtel, Marne; 8, La Chaussée, Marne; 9, Songy, Marne; 10, Pogny, Marne; 11, Fontaine-sur-Coole, Marne; 12, Cernon, Marne; 13, Breuvery, Marne; 14, Mairy, Marne; 15, Sogny, Marne; 16, Ecury-sur-Coole, Marne; 17, Saint-Gibrien, Marne; 18, Châlons-sur Marne 'Côte de Troyes', Marne; 19, Châlons-sur-Marne 'Avenue Strasbourg', Marne; 20, Sarry, Marne; 21, Saint-Memmie, Marne; 22, L'Epine, Marne; 23, Courtisols 'Charmont', Marne; 24, Courtisols 'Grand Ayeux', Marne; 25, Courtisols 'Cote 141', Marne; 26, Courtisols 'l'Homme Mort', Marne; 27, Melette, Marne; 28, Recy 'Graviers', Marne; 29, Recy, 'Voie Chanteraine', Marne; 30, Recy 'Voie Chanteraine', Marne; 31, Juvigny, Marne; 32, Vraux 'Mont Vraux', Marne; 33, Vraux 'Le Boisson', Marne; 34, Grandes Loges, Marne; 35, Livry, Marne; 36, Bouy 'Varilles', Marne; 37, Saint-Hilaire-au-Temple, Marne; 38, Cuperly, Marne; 39, La Cheppe, Marne; 40, Bussy-le-Château 'La Croix-Meunière', Marne; 41, Bussy-le-Château 'Les Govats', Marne; 42, Bussy-le-Château 'Piemont', Marne; 43, Bussy-le-Château 'Mont Dinet', Marne; 44, Saint-Remy-sur-Bussy, Marne; 45, Auve, Marne; 46, La Croix-en-Champagne, Marne; 47, Saint-Jean-sur-Tourbe, Marne; 48, Warge-moulin, Marne; 49, Mèsnil-les-Hurlus, Marne; 50, Hurlus, Marne; 51, Somme-Suippe, Marne; 52, Suippes, Marne; 53, Saint-Hilaire-le-Grand, Marne; 54, Saint-Etienne-sur-Arne, Ardennes; 55, Liry, Ardennes; 56, Fontaine-en-Dormois, Marne; 57, Manre, Ardennes; 58, Saint-Clement 'La Motelle de Germiny', Ardennes; 59, Hauviné, Ardennes; 60, Pontfaverger, Marne; 61, Beine 'l'Argentelle', Marne; 62, Beine 'Petit Cri', Marne; 63, Les Commelles, Marne; 64, Prunay, Marne; 65, Prosne, Marne; 66, Sept-Saulx, Marne; 67, Villers-Marmery, Marne; 68, Bouzy, Marne; 69, Sillery, Marne; 70, Puisieulx, Marne; 71, La Pompelle, Marne; 72, Murigny, Marne; 73, Les Mesneux, Marne; 74, Cernay, Marne; 75, Berru 'Flogères', Marne; 76, Berru 'Le Terrage', Marne; 77, Vitry-les-Reims 'La Neufosse', Marne; 78, Vitry-les-Reims 'Voie de la Haute-Chemin', Marne; 79, Lavannes, Marne; 80, Bazancourt, Marne; 81, Warmeriville, Marne; 82, Heurtegeville 'Mont Sapinois', Marne; 83, Neuville-

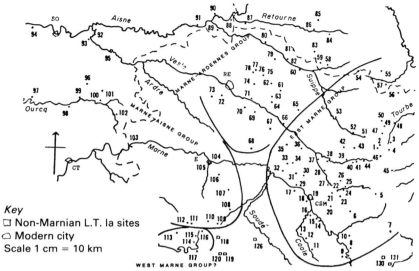

Figure 15.2 Map of Marnian cultural groups.

en-Tourne-a-Fuy, Ardennes; 84, Ville-sur-Retourne, Ardennes; 85, Annelles, Ardennes; 86, Juniville, Ardennes; 87, Poilcourt, Ardennes; 88, Pignicourt, Ardennes; 89, Aguilcourt, Ardennes; 90, Guignicourt, Ardennes; 91, Berry-au-Bac, Aisne; 92, Chassemy, Aisne; 93, Ciry-Salsogne, Aisne; 94, Pernant, Aisne; 95, Limé, Aisne; 96, Arcy-Saint-Restitute, Aisne; 97, Chouy, Aisne; 98, Armentières, Aisne; 99, Trugny, Aisne; 100, Sablonnières, Aisne; 101, Château de Fere-en-Tardenois, Aisne; 102, Caranda, Aisne; 103, Dormans, Marne; 104, Epernay 'Malakoff', Marne; 105, Epernay 'Mont Bernon', Marne; 106, 'Les Jogasses', Marne; 107, Avize, Marne; 108, 'Mont Gravet', Marne; 109, Bergères-les-Vertus, Marne; 110, Etrechy, Marne; 111, Loisy-en-Brie, Marne; 112, Etoges, Marne; 113, Congy, Marne; 114, Vert-la-Gravelle 'Gros Pierres', Marne; 115, Vert-la-Gravelle 'Charmont', Marne; 116, Bannes, Marne.

loaded with vehicles and manifesting far-flung exchange connections reaching even to the Greeks and Etruscans, has been of singular importance for archaeological theory, but the exact meaning of such groups remains less clear. The three main Marnian Groups correspond roughly to the tribal areas of the early historic Remi (Marne–Ardennes Group), the Soissoni (Marne–Aisne Group) and the Catalauni (East Marne Group). The putative West Group would have no recognized counterpart at the historic contact horizon. However, it would be premature to conclude immediately that these groups correspond to politically independent tribal units known nearly half a millennium later. To assume so much is to stifle research into prehistoric times by projecting the facts of history backward too readily.

The meaning of the detected Marnian sociocultural groups can be partially tested in another way, through the strange phenomenon that many of the rich – or at least formerly rich – Marnian burials have been looted. Not only were a high percentage of burials looted before the dawn of modern archaeology, but the looting has several patterned aspects which enable this practice to shed light on other prehistoric behaviour. The nature of this looting must be examined first, as it has implications for several cultural subsystems, not all of which will be explored in this chapter, which is concerned principally with political questions.

Although the early La Tène (Marnian Variant) cemeteries of the Marne and Aisne and southern Ardennes appear at present to be composed of flat graves, prehistorians have not always agreed over whether the graves were originally covered by tumuli, which, if present, would have presumably been ploughed down or eroded away. The arguments have tended to be based more on circumstantial or peripheral considerations than on direct evidence. Some have argued for tumuli because so many Iron Age burials in the Rheinland, Burgundy, southern Champagne and northern Ardennes have been found under tumuli. Those who looked to Champagne for the origin of the tumulus-building Arras Group of Yorkshire, England, have inclined toward this interpretation (Stead 1965, p. 86). Other arguments have turned on the outstanding accuracy with which graves were looted in antiquity. The head and shoulders are usually those areas robbed, since presumably these would have carried relatively valuable bronze torcs and earrings, or even golden ones, and would be more profitable for looting than other parts of the grave, which usually would contain only iron, thin bronze bracelets, or small belt-hooks and pottery. The accuracy with which the graves have been located and the position of the head and the shoulders predetermined is remarkably superior to that which may be achieved through modern survey techniques, prompting some archaeologists to infer tumuli to guide the looters to the exact position of graves and to the exact location of the head.

Some workers ascribe the looting to the Franks of the Migration Period, citing Charlemagne's edicts against grave-looting as evidence of the practice (Berard & Favret 1941, p. 397), whereas others have implicated Gallo-Romans, and even the Gauls themselves as the chief culprits.

Even if tumuli over the graves did give away the grave position to grave robbers, the splendid accuracy of the looters would have required an elongate tumulus, for although the heads in Marne Culture burials point predominantly toward the west, it may be either somewhat north-west or south-west, and a round tumulus would have obscured the exact position of the head. Also, if such tumuli did exist, they cannot have been very high, in order to be ploughed down so readily. Some tumuli, but not dating from La Tène times, do exist in the area of the Marne Culture, and these have not yet been ploughed down.

If tumuli had once been over Marnian graves, then they would not only have had to have been of an unusual elongate shape, but they would have had to have been individual tumuli over each grave, and the burials in the Marnian cemeteries tend to be somewhat scattered and unlike the tumuli of the Aube, Haute-Marne, and Burgundy, where the tumulus itself was a sort of cemetery containing many different burials, most of which were in the body of the tumulus itself.

Not all archaeologists have been convinced by the circumstantial nature of the arguments inferring tumuli to account for the accuracy of the grave-robbing. These prehistorians suggest that it is more reasonable to argue that the remarkable accuracy derives from the Gauls themselves looting the graves when they were comparatively fresh (Dupuis 1926, pp. 47–8). Bretz-Mahler & Joffroy (1959, p. 6) doubt that burial mounds were ever present since, if the mounds had been made of soil, which lies thinly on the chalk plain of Champagne, it would have necessitated removal of the topsoil in a wide circuit around each grave, or, if the mounds had been made of chalk blocks, they would not have been so likely to have been ploughed down.

There is one consideration which provides a basis for thinking that there may have been some heaping of earth over the individual burials in early La Tène times in Champagne – the black earth grave fill. Since this black grave fill was brought in from elsewhere, something else had to be done with the soil and chalk that was dug out of the grave trench. The soil and chalk could have been heaped into a very small mound over graves, just as is done with the surplus earth replaced by the coffin in modern graves.

These low mounds need not have lasted very long, and there is some indication that they did not. Many graves from this area of archtypical Marnian grave sites show accidental superposition, well out of alignment and therefore unconfusable with deliberately superposed double graves, and showing grave goods from slightly later periods. By way of example, the stratified grave Etoges 13 contained two burials of La Tène Ia, though not in alignment, and in Etoges 19, the lowest burial wore a bracelet of La Tène Ia, whereas grave 18, above that one but not in alignment, had a fibula of early Ib form, and still higher and in a slightly different alignment was burial 17, with a late Ib Dux fibula, such as sometimes occurs in La Tène Ic graves. From Pernant (Aisne) Lobjois (1969) reports several instances of non-aligned, superimposed graves, with grave complex 5 being the most notable case.

Other stratified graves are reported from at least six additional cemeteries of the Marne Culture area. Such instances adequately show that, even if the surplus earth from the grave trench had been heaped over the burial, the resultant mound was so low that later in the subsequent century or so, the position of a burial would be so unmarked that a later burial might accidentally be placed over a previous one, and therefore the Marnian cemeteries may be considered as being essentially flat ones.

The inference that the Marnian cemeteries consisted of flat graves, at least when compared with those cemeteries where the mounds are more truly monumental, and not burials under elongated tumuli, leaves open the question of how and by whom was the remarkably accurate looting performed. Although fundamentally the question of grave-looting in early La Tène times is an entirely different question from burial configuration, it is pertinent here because so much of the argument favouring burial mounds has depended on the accurate tomb robbing for its support. In his excavations of the La Tène Ia cemeteries at 'Mont Troté' and 'Les Rouliers' at Manre (Ardennes), Rozoy (1965, 1987) had directed his attention specifically at this problem. As a result of careful observation of the looted graves, Rozoy has found that the mandible has remained in half of the looted graves without crania (total of eight), suggesting that at least part of the tomb violations were motivated by the desire for crania of the deceased, and not merely to loot the artefacts from them, thus leading him (Rozoy 1965, p. 261) to believe that the violations took place by descendants of the deceased within two or three years of burial.

Nevertheless, looted feminine graves are usually torc-less and often the mandible and clavicle, stained green by the corrosion from the torc, remains in the violated grave as evidence of the former presence of torc which had been taken when the grave was open. So it would seem that, regardless of the initial motive for opening the grave, torcs and other valuables were not disdained by those who did so. In the sample studied here, information as to the state of pristinity has been reported for 627 La Tène Ia graves of the Marne Culture in the chariot burying-districts of the Marne, Aisne and Ardennes, 290 (46.2%) of which were looted. From closer inspection it emerges that of the 49 chariot burials on which this kind of information is available, 38 (77.6%) were looted, whereas only 43.5% (252 of 578) of ordinary, chariot-less burials had been violated in remote antiquity. A simple 'difference of proportions' statistical test (Blalock 1960, p. 176) yields the result that the chances are about 1 in 250 000 that this difference of proportions could have occurred by coincidence. The t-value (4.5951) permits rejection at the 0.005 level of the null hypothesis that the proportions of looted versus unlooted graves among the categories of chariot and chariot-less are the result of coincidence. Since it appears most unlikely that the difference in proportions of looted graves is due to chance, it may be inferred that since chariot burials are usually much wealthier in grave goods, as intact burials such as La Gorge Meillet and Somme-Bionne testify, it may be supposed that the chariot burials were the principal targets of grave robbers, because of their greater wealth, i.e. the grave robbers had some knowledge as to what was buried where, and therefore must have been essentially contemporary with the burials themselves.

Considerations as to the accidental superpositions of burials from the same phase (La Tène Ia) or adjacent phases (La Tène Ia and Ib) clearly show that whatever mounding of earth may have existed over the burials of La Tène Ia in the Marne Culture, it did not endure sufficiently long to prevent the accidental disturbance of burials by subsequent ones in the following one or two centuries. Considerations of the grave violations show that, whether the motive was to obtain crania as trophies or to obtain rich grave goods, many violations must have taken place relatively soon after the burials by people who had some first-hand knowledge of who and what were buried where, and this knowledge, rather than presumed presence of tumuli, accounts for the accuracy of some of the looters' soundings and makes the postulation of tumuli unnecessary.

Political units

How does the picture of well-to-do peers and comfortably endowed commoners conform to the great number of re-opened and despoiled graves? Does not the sharp focus of the lootings of chariot burials, with few opportunities passing unnoticed, hint at class conflict, at economic pressures forcing some individuals to brave the spirits of the dead and the swords of the living to seek their share of Marnian wealth in the dark of the night, digging by stealth within a stone's throw of the nearby houses?

Indeed, it is paradoxical that the group with the cemeteries closest to the living, the East Group, is precisely the one with the greatest amount of looting, which must have been contemporary. Although the cemeteries of the other groups are also badly mangled, few are as ravaged as those of the East Marne cemeteries. The proximity of graves to houses seems to have had little influence on the amount of looting that took place, to judge from three sites – Cernon, Poix and Sarry – for which we have house fireplaces indicated plus a complete report of the graves. At Cernon all graves were looted, regardless of their proximity to houses, and at Poix, with a relatively low looting rate, leaving 42% of La Tène Ia graves intact, of the four graves closest to houses, only two – 26 and 28 – are intact, a rate of looting commensurate with the cemetery as a whole. Indeed, the series of graves 53 to 62, farthest from the recorded houses, are the ones which are less looted. At Sarry with nine of 26 (34.6%) intact, of the seven graves closest to the houses – 14, 16, 21, 17, 19, 20 and 34 – only three (42.9%) are unlooted, a rate little better than for those graves away from the houses.

Poix has one of the better rates of looting among those sites of which we have a complete series of graves reported. Nearby Marson, for which we have a report on the first 21 graves (after that, Morel 1898 breaks off to talk only of especially selected graves) 11 of 13 La Tène Ia graves are intact (85.4%). Other cemeteries for which we have some information have even worse rates than Marson, Manre and Poix. Manre 'Mont Troté' (Ardennes) (Rozoy 1987) was 51.2% (22 of 42) intact, 'Les Rouliers' was 70.8% but Sarry is next with 34.6%, Grandes Loges has 25.6% (11 of 43), and Mairy has only 21.4% (21 of 98) intact graves if chariot burials are included, and if these looting-prone burials are excluded, there are still only 23.6% (21 of 89) intact La Tène Ia graves at Mairy. Cernon, of course, has no intact graves. Interestingly, as the percentage of intact graves increases for these sites, so does the distance from the periphery of the East Marne Group. Since, of course, there are large lacunae in the known distribution of sites (particularly toward the eastern limits of the East Group), it is better to rate these communities in an ordinal scale rather than on a purely numerical one based on measured distance, but one has the following result, when the cemeteries are arranged according to approximate distance from the peripheries of the East Group.

Percentage of intact graves	Relative distance from periphery
Marson 85.4%	Marson
Manre 'Les Rouliers' 70.8%	Sarry
Manre 'Mont Troté' 51.2%	Poix
Poix 42.1%	Manre 'Les Rouliers'
Sarry 34.6%	Manre 'Mont Troté'
Grandes Loges 25.6%	Grandes Loges
Mairy 23.6%	Mairy
Cernon 0.0%	Cernon

Thus, we have a very good correlation between the distance from the periphery of the East Marne Group and the number of intact burials for each cemetery. This consistency between distance from the border and the high number of intact graves results in rank–order correlation coefficient r of 0.80.

From the Marne–Ardennes Group, only a small number of cemeteries have been reported in such a way as to permit the count of the number of intact graves by horizon; those that have been yield the following result in order of distance from the periphery of the group.

	Intact graves
Beine 'l'Argentelle' (Marne)	75%
Prosnes (Marne)	50%
Poilcourt (Ardennes)	0%
St Clement 'la Motelle de Germiny' (Ardennes)	0%

Although this small series goes in virtually perfect order, a more rigorous test is provided by the Marne–Aisne Group, wherein at least ten cemeteries provide information on the rate of looting. Remember that these figures include a number of causes of looting; for example, of the three ostensibly violated graves at Pernant (Aisne), only one appears to have been intentionally looted in past antiquity (Lobjois 1969). The Marne–Aisne Group produces the following series arranged in order of distance from the periphery of the group.

	Intact graves
Pernant (Aisne)	94.6%
Ciry-Salsogne (Aisne)	91.7%
Dormans (Marne)	84.6%
Arcy-'Saint-Restitute (Aisne)	77.0%

Chassemy (Aisne)	83.3%
Avize (Marne)	75.0%
'Les Jogasses' (Marne)	25.7%
Etrechy 'Beauregard' (Marne)	65.2%
'Mt Gravet' (Marne)	62.5%
Etoges (Marne)	44.0%

Although this series aligns less neatly than the shorter ones from the Manre–Ardennes and the East Marne Groups, nevertheless it produces a rank-order coefficient r of 0.91, which is also an extremely high correlation for cultural materials. 'Les Jogasses' (Favret 1936, Hatt & Roualet 1981) constitutes the most exceptional site in this series. Nevertheless, for all three of the main Marnian groups distance from the group margin is highly correlated with the rate of looting, even though the patterns are fuzzed somewhat by there being several reasons for which graves were re-opened already in La Tène Ia times.

What can be done is to supplement this approach by noting the relative numbers of intact and looted chariot burials. Although there are only nine intact chariot burials from the entire series of at least 38 Ia phase East Marne chariot burials, the degree of early pristinity is known for at least 37 of them. It happens that eight of the intact burials are well within the interior of the East Group territory; the chariot burial Bouy 'Varilles' F1 is the only intact chariot burial with only one known site between it and the East Marne periphery, and this site is Livry-sur-Vesle, which has produced an anciently looted chariot burial. All of the other chariot burials from the peripheral districts are looted, and some such as the two at the extreme western site of Vraux so badly so as to be undatable. The same holds true for 10 of the 13 La Chaussée burials (Rowlett 1978), as well as for many other sites. There are looted chariot burials in the very centre of the East Marne region, such as the Somme-Tourbe 'La Bouvandeau' chariot burial, and the La Cheppe and Courtisols 'Charmont' chariot burials, but it still remains true that the intact chariot burials come mainly from the interior, and mostly from the heartland of the East Marnian Group.

What can we make of this spatial pattern of burial looting, which shows among other dimensions a marked propensity for selecting adults over children, and rich chariot burials over the graves of other adults? Does this mean that the poor and disinherited were driven toward the peripheries of the region? How, then, do we account for the very westerly Mairy-sur-Marne and the extreme southeastern La Chaussée being two of the most important chariot-burying centres? Surely those charioteers were neither poor nor disinherited. This grave looting obviously constitutes a complex multidimensional, multifaceted phenomenon, which despite, or perhaps because of, its complexity, can yield much information about the Marne Culture subgroups. Certainly there was an element of material acquisition motivating some of the looting, although perhaps some of this acquisitive desire was not so much for outright gain in a purely economic sense, as to obtain a prized weapon or great artefact of immense magical power, the kind of prize for which many Vikings broke into the tombs of previous generations. Rozoy (1965) has also adduced, from the cranial-less and neck-bone-less violated masculine graves at Manre (Ardennes), that these graves were opened perhaps from some kind of filial piety, which instilled desire for physical possession of the cranium of an honoured ancestor. While Grandes Loges does have more intact males (five) than females (one), Poix actually has more intact females (eight) than males (four), as does Sarry (four and one). Mairy has seven intact females to six males, but so many Mairy male graves would be looted because they were in chariots. It does seem reasonably clear that female graves have not been particularly preferred over men's for violation, even if the solid bronze torc and the possibility of gold earrings made females of non-chariot graves a more lucrative target than males. Despite this, males are still looted at the head, just as women are, so there seems to be some additional support to Rozoy's thesis that looting was at least partly motivated by the desire for crania. But why are crania and grave goods more desirable at the peripheries than in the centres of the Marnian Groups?

This remarkable tendency for the greatest looting to occur at the periphery of the group region holds good in the Marne–Aisne and Marne–Ardennes Groups, also, for here too, although the total number of chariot burials datable to La Tène Ia are fewer, the result is equally clear. The five chariot burials on the eastern flank of the Marne–Ardennes Group are violated (data are lacking for the Prunay chariot burial in the British Museum), and although the Sept-Saulx chariot burial's main inhumation was intact, an upper burial had been plundered, suggesting that the looters had mistakenly assumed that they had taken all that that grave had to offer. The western flank of the Marne–Ardennes group must lie in territory that is little explored, but two chariot burials in the easterly Marne–Aisne communities of Les Jogasses 7 and Arcy-Saint-Restitute are looted (there were three others at Les Jogasses looted beyond attribution of a date, but from their positions in the horizontal stratigraphy would presumably date from La Tène Ia), whereas less-marginally placed chariot burials at Chassemy and Sablonnières 842 are intact, as probably was one from Pernant (Aisne), which although disturbed accidentally by modern earth-moving equipment, is so rich in its remains, including the imported bronze situla and basin, that it was almost certainly intact before its dislodgement. The one chariot burial from the West Group, at Vert-La-Gravelle, was looted by antique merchants at the turn of the 20th century, and is thus unusable in the survey.

It would appear that this more spirited looting of the peripheral graves of each group strongly implies that someone from outside each group was doing much of the looting, for although this would not account for all of the looting, it would explain the gradient of rapidly increasing number of looted graves the farther one goes from the central region of each group. Thus, although there would seem to be some intra-group robbing either for objects of value, or magical power, for tokens and souvenirs of honoured ancestors, it also seems abundantly clear that there was also inter-group looting by people belonging to other groups, and whose main targets were those graves that were near the peripheries and thus easiest of access for intruders.

Another sort of intertribal raiding, the stealing of cattle, is well known for the Irish Celts in legendary and documentary sources, as reviewed by Olmsted (1979). Although this material is somewhat remote in space and time (four to five centuries) from the Marnians, who are commonly presumed to be Celtic-speaking, Olmsted (1979) has also pointed out similarities between ancient Irish and continental Celtic legends and lore as reported in classical sources, so perhaps there were other convergences in behaviour as well. Virtually every adult male given a burial with normal ritual, as archaeologically perceived, in the Marne Culture was equipped with a weapon, which must have been intended for some kind of agonistic application.

That grave looting was more easily accomplished on the margins of the group implies strongly that precisely at these frontier outposts the powers of control of the political system were the weakest during La Tène Ia times. The coincidence of the heavily looted communities being where presumably sanctions were least effectively extended, on the borders of the cultural group, which by implication would be a group within which there was much social interaction to maintain stylistic unity, suggests that the limits of the *cultural* group was also approximately the same as the limits of the political group and the social group, as such. It appears then that the Marnian Groups not only constitute a cultural group whose stylistic homogeneity derives from frequent social interaction and shared values of meanings, but that it is also a political group. This is not to say that the political authority of the East Marnian or other Marnian groups did not at times surpass or fail to attain the limit of the cultural group's territory, but does mean that generally these cultural groups more or less constituted political groups as well. Archaeologists are quick to caution that a cultural unit need not necessarily be regarded as a political one, and this could often be so, no doubt, but in this case there is evidence of the effective application of the political power of a particular society as well as evidence of the region of effective cultural dominance of the tastes of the people of that society. This mutual raiding, perhaps along with other forms of competition for land, Mediterranean trading links and the like, seems to explain the sharp cultural boundaries on the open plain in a technological context equipped with good vehicular transport, since these conditions would have promoted in each group the development of artefactual mechanisms to symbolize its within-group organization in opposition to and contrast with those of other interest groups (Hodder 1979). Such a situation would be roughly exemplified in ethnographic times by the structure of culture symbols such as observed by Hodder (1982) in the Lake Baringo district of western Kenya.

References

Berard, C. & P. M. Favret 1941. Le cimetière gaulois des Grandes-Loges (cne de Chalons-sur-Marne). *Bulletin Archéologique du Comite*, 369–405.
Blalock, H. M. 1960. *Social statistics*. New York: McGraw-Hill.
Bretz-Mahler, D. & R. Joffroy 1959. Les tombes à char de La Tène dans l'est de la France. *Gallia* **17**.
Dupuis, J. 1926. Le cimetière celtique de la Motelle de Germiny, territoire de Saint-Clement-à-Arnes et essai de comparaison des cimetières celtiques d'Hauviné et de Saint-Clement-à-Arnes. *Bulletin de la Société Archéologique Champenoise* **20**, 42–51, 52–5.
Favret, P. M. 1936. Les necropoles des Jogasses à Chouilly (Marne). *Préhistoire*, 514–19.
Hatt, J.-J. & P. Roualet 1977. La chronologie de La Tène en Champagne. *Revue Archéologique de l'Est et Centre-Est* **28**, 7–36.
Hatt, J.-J. & P. Roualet 1981. Le cimetière des Jogasses en Champagne et les origines de la civilisation de la Tène. *Revue Archéologique de l'Est et Centre-Est* **32**, 17–63.
Hodder, I. 1979. Economic and social stress and material culture patterning. *American Antiquity* **44**, 446–54.
Hodder, I. 1982. *Symbols in action*. Cambridge: Cambridge Univesity Press.
Hodson, F. R. 1964. La Tène chronology, Continental and British. *Bulletin of the Institute of Archaeology* **4**, 123–41.
Lobjois, G. 1969. La necropole de Pernant (Aisne). *Celticum* **18**, 1–284.
Morel, L. 1898. *La Champagne souterraine*, 2 Vols. Reims.
Olmsted, G. S. 1979. *The Gundestrup cauldron*. Brussels: Collection Latomus.
Pollnac, R. B. & R. M. Rowlett 1977. Community and supracommunity within the Marne culture: a stylistic analysis. In *Experimental archaeology*, D. Ingersoll, J. E. Yellen & W. MacDonald (eds), 167–92. New York: Columbia University Press.
Rowlett, R. M. 1967. The East Marne Group at the debut of the La Tène Iron Age. PhD thesis, Harvard University, Cambridge, Massachusetts.
Rowlett, R. M. 1968. The Iron Age north of the Alps. *Science* **161**, 123–34.
Rowlett, R. M. 1978. Representative assemblage and type selection: a La Tène Marnian example. *Ancient Europe and the Mediterranean: the Hugh Hencken Festschrift*, V. Markotic (ed.), 146–56. Warminster: Aris & Phillips.
Rowlett, R. M. 1985. Archaeological evidence for early Indo-European chieftains. *Journal of Indo-European Studies* **13**, 193–233.
Rowlett, R. M. & R. B. Pollnac 1972. Multivariant analysis of Marnian La Tène cultural groups. In *Mathematics in the archaeological and historical sciences*, D. G. Kendall, F. R. Hodson & P. Tautu (eds), 45–8, Edinburgh: Edinburgh University Press.
Rozoy, J.-G. 1965. Les tumulus sans cranes à La Tène I au Mont Troté. *Bulletin de la Société Préhistorique Française* **62**, 253–61.
Rozoy, J.-G. 1987. *Les Celtes en Champagne*. Reims: Société Archéologique Champenoise.
Stead, I. M. 1965. *The La Tène cultures of eastern Yorkshire*. York: Yorkshire Philosophical Society.

THE GENESIS,
MAINTENANCE AND
DISAPPEARANCE OF
ETHNICITY AND
CULTURAL VARIATION

16 *Who is what? A preliminary enquiry into cultural and physical identity*

CAROL W. HILL

In Memoriam

Harvey Bernard Wyche, 1920–1986
Charles Baltimore Hill, 1909–1987

Dedicated to the ancestors.

Introduction

In anthropology questions of identity are not simply restricted to cultural or psychological structures in the present or the ethnographic past, but also extend to physical identity in the present and in prehistory. For the earlier periods of hominid evolution we are accustomed to constructing genealogical trees and anthropological–biological theories to account for the physical and material changes we observe in the archaeological and palaeoanthropological record. Modern history presents us with physical and material changes which are different from, but perhaps parallel to, the changes observed by palaeoanthropologists. Indigenous peoples of North America are assumed to have a specific physiology and material culture. However, when we discuss modern descendants of precontact and colonial aboriginal populations, we are surprised to find changes in both material and physical identity. Some aspects of change and identity in physical and material culture are explored in this chapter, with reference to the eastern USA in general and Virginia in particular.

The prehistoric and early historic period in Virginia

The diversity of the aboriginal populations of Virginia extends back into the Early Woodland period. The state had at least three different language families: the Siouan, the Algonquian and the Iroquoian. Not only did linguistic differences occur among aboriginal populations, but differences also existed in social organization and, to some extent, in material culture (Egloff 1985, Evans 1955, Hranicky 1973). Each group had cultural connections with other subregions within and beyond the state, evidenced, for example, in the similarity of pottery from the Dan River region in Virginia and North Carolina.

These linguistic and sociopolitical groups responded to colonization in various ways, although all had the same general outcome – loss of sovereignty, including loss of population and land. After their loss of land, remnant populations often scattered. For example, the Pamunkey moved from their centre in Richmond and were allocated a reservation in King William County, as were the Mattiponi. The Pamunkey reservation, a swampy area on Pamunkey Neck, was marginal land of little worth to the colonists. After the Bacon rebellion the Pamunkey were given sovereignty over aboriginal populations lacking a leader, including remnants from Siouan, Iroquoian and other Algonquian tribes.

Another tribe, the Chickahominy, lost their reservation in 1750 and left King William and upper Queen and King counties, relocating in their traditional homeland of Charles City County. The Gingaskin reservation was terminated in 1831, and the Gingaskin left the area, except for a few individuals who merged into the African-American population. The Siouan population was mostly devastated, and individuals were subsumed into a general Eastern Siouan or Iroquoian population. The name Tutelo, a subtribe of the Siouan confederacy, became synonymous for all Siouan remnants, including the Shakori, Keyauwee and the Algonquian Occaneechi of North Carolina. These groups moved back and forth between the borders of Virginia and North Carolina. Iroquoian tribes dispersed into various settlements in southeastern Virginia, and several groups migrated out of the Virginia area; for example, the Tutelo and Saponi tribes, who were adopted into the Seneca and Cayuga Iroquoian tribes in New York and Canada respectively.

Microraces in the eastern USA

The post-colonization history of Native American groups and their descendants provides an extremely interesting insight into the nature of the dynamic processes of ethnic identification.

Mooney estimated 15 000 Native Americans in 1600 (Swanton 1952, Ubelaker 1976), but recent estimates place the figure between 14 000 and 22 000 for the Tidewater Algonquian population. On this basis one could suggest a total aboriginal population estimate of between 32 000 and 50 000 people for the state of Virginia. The aboriginal Algonquian population in Smith's 1607 census was >5724 (2385 bowmen), with a decline by 1750 (Beverly census) to >840 (350 bowmen) (cited in Mooney 1907). The greatest decline in aboriginal population in the post-contact period was between 1616 and 1669. The censuses in the 1900s returned low figures for

American Indians, with an increase in the latter half of the century. The census for 1900 cited 354 American Indians; that for 1940 enumerated 198; and in 1950 1056 were enumerated. Excluding members of Alaskan tribes, the 1980 census enumerated 10 069 Native Americans, of whom 4019 (41.5%) were born in Virginia. More than one-quarter of these Native Americans (29.5%) were resident in rural areas, and of these 65% were born in Virginia.

The significance of such figures raises a number of important questions concerning ethnic formation and maintenance. Inhabiting the eastern part of the USA are enclaves of Native American 'remnant' populations and populations of mixed origins (called here *mestizo*). These groups were by no means always officially recognized: remnant populations were often not recognized as *bona fide* Indians if they did not have a state reservation.

Mestizo populations have distinct origins, some of which are obscure. Often these groups are descendants of several ethnic–racial groups, frequently a Native American substratum with African and European input, who formed self-perpetuating communities. *Mestizo* groups may, or may not, claim a Native American identity; the Lumbees, for example, claim a Native American identity, whereas the Cajans of Alabama adhere to a Cajan identity (Stopp 1972). The literature cites several names for these groups; for example, little races, marginal peoples, cultural isolates, racial islands, biracial or triracial isolates, not to mention historically derogatory names (Hill 1986, Gilbert 1949).

Obtaining an idea of the number of *mestizos* and remnant Native Americans on the basis of the census figures is problematical, as I have already implied. Often the census omitted Native Americans, or enumerated them with Free Negroes or free coloured persons. Historically America had set a precedent for this since the colonial period. The Colony of Virginia in 1705 subsumed Indians in the mulatto category (Lauber 1969, p. 254, citing Hening 1823):

> In one colony, Virginia, the term 'mulatto' was made to include Indians by the act of 1705, which provided that the child of an Indian be 'deemed, accounted, held and taken to be a mulatto' (Lauber).
>
> *Be it enacted and declared, and it is hereby enacted and declared.* That the child of an Indian and the child, grand child, or great grand child, of a negro shall be deemed, accounted, held and taken to be a mulatto (Hening).

Moreover, in Virginia only indigenous peoples who resided on a reservation were deemed to be Indians. Once a person left the reservation, he or she was no longer considered to be an Indian (Bartl 1986, see Rountree 1976 for a discussion of Virginia indigenous peoples' attempts to obtain Native American status in the 1900s). Census-takers were instructed to recognize individuals of white-Indian parentage as American Indians, but not to recognize individuals of black-Indian parentage as Indians 'unless Indian blood predominates and status of Indian is generally accepted in the community' (Bureau of the Census 1931, p. 1399, appendix B). Native American population figures for the East Coast were probably underestimated for the years 1860, 1900 and 1950. The total cited in the historical statistics for these years was less than 500. When raw totals were cited they were often extremely low; for example, North Carolina reported one in 1860, six in 1900 and 31 in 1950. The US total in 1970 was 575, with 234 in New York.

Ostensibly, as we have seen, the *mestizo* population was enumerated with Native Americans, Free Negroes or free persons of colour. Before 1930, but since 1840, Negroes sometimes included two groups: blacks, who looked like full-blooded Negroes (i.e. West Africans), and mulattoes. For the 1870 and 1910 censuses mulattoes included anyone who had a 'perceptible trace of Negro blood' (Bureau of the Census 1931). In the 1890 census blacks included anyone who had between 100% and three-quarters to five-eighths African heritage; mulattoes had three-eighths to five-eighths African parentage; quadroons had one-quarter African parentage; and octoroons had one-eighth, or any trace, of African parentage. The 1890 census enumerated 6 337 980 blacks, 956 989 mulattoes, 105 135 quadroons and 69 936 octoroons. Thus, in 1890 the non-black Negro population consisted of 1 132 060 individuals, or 17.9% of the total Negro population. These breakdowns were discontinued after 1930 on the premise that it was impossible to distinguish accurately between these subdivisions: descendants of two different genetic pools may have phenotypes which do not differ from one another.

The estimated figure of '*mestizo* and remnants' from Gilbert's (1949) research was 65 392. The population in 1950 was 77 407 for 34 aboriginal remnants and *mestizo* groups in 18 states (Pollitzer 1972). Paredes & Lenihan (1973) cite a southeastern Native American population (which includes remnant and *mestizo* groups) of 76 656. These figures indicate a slow growth rate for these two populations, or underrepresentation in the census. Figures for mulattoes in the Negro (black) population are not available after 1930.

On the basis of the social history of the USA, I am assuming that Native American remnants and *mestizo* individuals were often classified in early censuses as white or black. Material culture did not play a rôle in census classification. The decisive criterion was physical characteristics supposedly derived from 'degree of blood'. Place of residence was a secondary characteristic reinforcing exclusiveness among these groups.

Racial categorization and social behaviour

The institutionalization of race and slavery influenced the socialization of all American citizens. Marginal peoples who mated with black Americans were often excluded from the 'marginal community'; for example, the Pamunkey (Powhatan). Alternatively, they were not excluded, but were not publicly recognized; for example, Louisiana Cajans are unsure whether Black Cajans exist (Tentchoff 1980). Alternatively, again, they were recognized but had a lower status within the group; for example, the Brandywine, Nanticoke and Narragansetts. The Nanticoke Indians supposedly congregated into two groups: dark-skinned Harmonies and light-skinned Nanticokes. Narragansetts were also differentiated on the basis of colour, with dark-skinned and light-skinned Narragansetts forming their own associations (Gilbert 1949). The Goins families, reputedly mixed with Africans, and the Denhans, reputedly mixed with Portuguese, were not on the same level within the Melungeon communities as the Mullins, mixed with English, and the Collins, supposedly pure-bred Native Americans (Dromgole 1891).

Other groups were subdivided by geography. The Pineys in some sections were pure-blooded whites, but in other sections were mixed-bloods. According to Gilbert (1949), Taghkanic Basketmakers (Bushwhackers) east of the Hudson were primarily mixtures of Native Americans and Europeans, whereas west of the Hudson they were primarily Native American and African mixtures.

According to Harte (1959) the Brandywine (Wesorts) also differentiated on racial–ethnic lines in mate selection. Harte detected two groups; a core group and a marginal group. The marginal group consisted of Free Negroes who developed kin affiliation with a Brandywine family. Core–core unions were the favoured form. Before 1870 matings between core and marginal families rarely occurred. Moreover, core families married back within the group more often than marginal families did. Cajans of Alabama and Creoles of Louisiana were also supposedly influenced by race in marital selection: Cajan males were more likely to marry mulatto females, whereas ideally Cajan females married white males (Stopp 1972). According to tradition, Creole females, especially quadroons, formed long-lasting unions with wealthy white males (FWP 1941, pp. 212–14). Woods (1972) debated the frequency of the latter among Cane River mulattoes. Although these groups were supposedly inbred communities, if mate selection was influenced by colour, then inbreeding may have been concentrated and differentiated along skin colour hue within the group.

Berry (1963) thought that these groups were transitional between invisibility and attainment of 'white' status. Anthropologists thought as late as 1972 that a majority of these groups would disintegrate due to desegregation and the emigration of young people from hinterlands to urban centres and suburbs. Stopp (1972) foresaw eventual dissolution of the 'Cajans', due to integrated schools and increased job opportunities away from Cajan settlements, as local businessmen 'in the spirit of integration' preferred to hire Cajans instead of local blacks. Stopp does not cite social or psychological factors why Cajans would no longer adhere to a Cajan identity, especially since, according to him, the Cajans voluntarily isolated themselves from both black and white societies. Why would they not maintain this identity in an integrated society? Harte (1959) found that individuals of the Brandywine group still maintained their separate identity even though jobs and residences might occur outside the core area. Differences between Harte's and Stopp's studies may be attributed to social and political changes in the USA between 1959 and 1973. Woods (1972) found Creoles clustering in two cities outside the core area, but not in a third, due to demographic conditions unique to each city.

The personal dimension

It is worth illustrating the nature of the complex historical situation which has just been described, and the past reluctance to acknowledge it, from the point of view of the author's personal experience. My mother once whispered to me as a youngster that we were Cherokee. My grandfather answered affirmatively to the queston of whether he was Cherokee during a discussion of his family genealogy. However, an aunt and her daughter claimed that he was a Black Meherrin, a group with African and Meherrin ancestry. Probably he was both. My grandmother was Cherokee, mixed with European and African ancestry. If my genealogical research is correct, then both families left out an antecedent generation in the recitation of their ancestry.

The present study, in fact, evolved from family history with an emphasis on self-identification. At first we were told that our great-aunt was a Pamunkey Indian, not that our grandfather was a Pamunkey Indian, still less that we were. Textbooks discuss the Powhatan Confederacy with the implication that descendants of the Confederacy are nonexistent. Given the ambiguity of *mestizo* groups in the USA, as outlined above, maintaining such an identity is extremely problematical, especially if one no longer resides in an 'enclave'. Without positive feedback, connection of descendants–members to the group by means of oral history may be extremely nebulous.

Material culture

Information on the material culture of triracial–remnant populations is extremely poor, although it may be suggested that the material culture of these groups differed only in localized traits. Early researchers in the field have cited similarities between various Coastal Algonquian cultures in the eastern part of the USA (Flannery 1939). Reaction to intrusive culture may have been similar in many instances, in that similar aspects of aboriginal culture were maintained. Some groups may have maintained their identity despite the fact that their aboriginal culture was destroyed or abandoned (Hawk 1987, pers. comm.). The question of ideology as opposed to material culture may also play a major rôle in maintaining an identity. The material culture of triracial–remnant groups in the early 1900s was very similar to poor white rural material culture (Berry 1987, pers. comm.). The following is a sketchy synopsis of the material culture of some groups for the period from 1890 to 1915, starting with the Rappahannock (Speck 1928).

The house of one informant was a one-room log house with an open fireplace and whitewashed interior. Inside the house were baskets and other sundries. The baskets were of white-oak splints with rectangular or circular bottoms. Also cited were baskets made of rushes, *Junicus* or *Scripus*, crafted in the twill method on a foundation of willow rods. Supposedly, the Rappahannocks were the only aboriginal group who made grass baskets. Gourds were undecorated. The Rappahannocks lacked featherworking. Pipe-making and pottery manufacture died out after the Civil War. The Rappahannocks did not make cane (Arundinaria) baskets as remnant groups in the southern parts of Virginia did. Their mortars were straight-sided, as were those of the Pamunkey and Gulf-area tribes. Similarly, their gum-wood bread trays were the same as those of the Pamunkey and other Powhatan tribes.

The Pamunkey themselves (on Pamunkey reservation, Speck 1928) had wooden mortars and pestles similar to those of the Nanticoke and dissimilar to those of the Iroquois, Delaware and Cherokee. Mortars were made of gum-wood with either straight sides or sides which tapered towards the bottom. Two types of Pamunkey pottery were described, one with net marks, with pebbly grit; the other smooth, with incisions or impressions and tempered, not with grit or pebbles, but with powdered shells. Smooth ware may have been an innovation in response to European markets. Supposedly, Pamunkey ware was similar to Catawba ware.

Finally, we may note the information provided by Speck (1915) on the Nanticoke of New Jersey. These had basketry similar to other eastern Atlantic Algonquian tribes, made of yellow pine or white oak. Plain splint baskets had circular-bottomed twill weave. Baskets were either circular or rectangular.

Conclusions

The material culture of the various groups and their possible ancestors should be investigated in more detail than was permissible within the time and budgetary constraints of my preliminary research.

One of the major themes of this chapter is that remnant populations may have social networks which have been under-represented in the ethnographic studies of earlier researchers. These social networks must be mapped on to spatial, temporal and material dimensions. Furthermore, changes may occur in any dimension, with a resultant change in social networks. Detailed conclusions cannot be offered until these data are collected. However, tentative comments are possible.

First, social networks may be just as important in describing ethnicity as material culture, since material culture can be shared by several ethnic groups. Secondly, the expansion of ethnic groups may be socially determined by the dominant ethnic group. Thirdly, the formation of distinct cultural groups is not necessarily a long process. Before 1776 there were no remnant populations with various mixtures of 'three geographical races', but in 1948 at least 120 different groups existed, with at least half being indigenous peoples and the other half primarily 'mixed-bloods'; the indigenous peoples were not necessarily residing on lands occupied before the contact period. Biracial mating produced a wide array of phenotypes with different shades of skin colour. The biracial offspring could either form new demes or backbreed into one or both parental populations, with subsequent maintenance or loss of new phenotypes, but with maintenance of biracial ancestry on the immunological and haematological levels.

Fourthly, cultural change can be drastic during periods of contact or subjugation; it can occur without transitional forms and can be artefact-specific within an enduring population. Basketry and pottery traditions within a subjugated group may have different rates of change, due to centrifugal forces within and beyond the cultural group.

Fifthly, the conditions under which cultural and traditional transmission is possible within subjugated, subordinate or coalescing groups need to be investigated, as does the rôle of cultural and educational institutions in promoting ethnic–racial–cultural history.

The histories or recognition of these groups are probably not known by the majority of US citizens, and this factor may result in social death and lack of input in social planning and policy. Hopefully, the study of triracial isolates and remnants will stimulate the way prehistorians interpret culture history, especially demographic modelling of Early Man and stylistic changes and traditions, and produce more detailed ethnohistories on these groups.

Acknowledgements

I wish to acknowledge Ms Baldwin, Reference Librarian, and Mrs Vogel and other staff members of the Deer Park Library for their assistance in obtaining books and microfilm through inter-library loan; family members for financial help and oral history; staff members of the Archives and Genealogy section of the Virginia State Library; Schomberg Center for Research in Black Culture; and special thanks to the Hendersons, Miss Lowery and Ms Nina Trabona.

References

Bartl, R. 1986. Die Beziehungen zwischen Schwarzen und Indianern in Nordamerika. Master's thesis, Faculty of Philosophy, Ludwig Maximilian University, Munich.

Berry, B. 1963. *Almost white*. New York: Macmillan.

Bureau of the Census 1931. *15th census of the United States*. Vol. 1: *Population. Number and distribution of inhabitants*. Washington, DC: Government Printing Office.

Dromgole, W. A. 1891. The Melungeon family tree and its branches. *The Arena* **3**, 745–51.

Egloff, K. 1985. Spheres of cultural influence across the coastal plain of Virginia in the Woodland period. In *Structure and process in southeastern archaeology*, Dickens & Ward (eds), 229–42. Birmingham: University of Alabama Press.

Evans, C. 1955. *A ceramic study of Virginia archaeology*. Bureau of American Ethnology, Bulletin 160. Washington, DC: Smithsonian Institution Press.

Federal Writers Project 1941. *New Orleans city guide*. Boston: Houghton Miffin.

Flannery, R. 1939. *An analysis of coastal Algonquian culture*. Washington, DC: Catholic University of America Press. (AMS Press reprint edition 1983.)

Gilbert, W. H. 1949. Surviving Indian groups of the eastern United States. *Annual Report of the Board of Regents of the Smithsonian Institution for the year ended June 30 1948*. Washington, DC: Smithsonian Institution.

Harte, T. 1959. Trends in mate selection in a tri-racial isolate. *Social Forces* **37**, 215–21.

Hening, W. W. 1823. *Statutes at large*, Vol. 1. New York: Bartow.

Hill, C. W. 1986. 'Triracial isolates'/Native American groups in the eastern United States: a question of settlement, kinship and regional analyses with implications for early man. In *Archaeological 'objectivity' in interpretation*. World Archaeological Congress, vol. 1 (mimeo).

Hranicky, W. J. 1973. Survey of the prehistory of Virginia. *The Chesopien* **11**, 76–94.

Lauber, A. W. 1913. *Indian slavery in colonial times within the present limits of the United States*. Columbia University Studies in the Social Sciences No. 134. (AMS Press edition 1969.)

Mooney, J. 1907. The Powhatan confederacy, past and present. *American Anthropologist* **9**, 129–38.

Paredes, J. A. & K. Lenihan 1973. Native American population in the southeastern states: 1960–1970. *Florida Anthropologist* **26**, 45–56.

Pollitzer, J. G. 1972. The physical anthropology and genetics of marginal people of the southeastern United States. *American Anthropologist* **74**, 719–34.

Rountree, H. C. 1976. The Indians of Virginia: a third race in a biracial state. In *Southeastern Indians since the removal*, W. L. Williams (ed.), 27–48. Athens, Georgia: University of Georgia Press.

Speck, F. G. 1915. *The Nanticoke community of Delaware*. Museum of the American Indian Contributions, Vol. 2, No. 4. New York: Museum of the American Indian.

Speck, F. G. 1928. *Chapters on the ethnology of the Powhatan tribes*. Indian Notes and Monographs, Vol. 1, No. 5. New York: Museum of the American Indian.

Stopp, G. H. 1972. Mixed-racial isolates. *American Anthropologist* **76**, 343–5.

Swanton, J. R. 1952. *The Indian tribes of North America*. Washington, DC: Smithsonian Institution.

Tentchoff, D. 1980. Ethnic survival under Anglo-American hegemony: the Louisiana Cajuns. *Anthropological Quarterly* **53**, 229–41.

Ubelaker, D. H. 1976. The sources and methodology for Mooney's estimates of North American Indian populations. In *The native population of the Americas in 1492*, W.M. Denevan (ed.), 257–9. Madison: University of Wisconsin Press.

Woods, F. J. 1972. *Marginality and identity: a coloured Creole family through ten generations*. Baton Rouge: Louisiana State University Press.

17 Sociocultural and economic elements of the adaptation systems of the Argentine Toba: the Nacilamolek and Taksek cases of Formosa Province

MARCELA MENDOZA and PABLO G. WRIGHT

Introduction

This chapter presents an example of regional variability in the adaptation systems of two Toba ethnic groups of the Argentine Chaco:[1] the Taksek from the north-east of Formosa Province and the Nacilamolek from the north-west of the same province.

Both groups were traditionally equipped with a subsistence technology of hunter–gatherers with horticulture. They organized themselves in nomadic exogamous bands, in which the rule of economic interchange was reciprocity. The bands were led by family chiefs who accumulated political and religious power, sometimes hereditary; and in historical times, especially in wartime, charismatic leaders who grouped several bands appeared, moderated by 'councils' of old men who were members of the bands. Thus, in some areas, a social organization of the 'tribal' type might have been formed (Sahlins 1977). Within this category we could say, perhaps, that the Taksek and the Nacilamolek belong to two different 'subtribes'.

At present these two groups, as all the Toba of the Chaco region, live in sedentary or semisedentary communities which can be considered as 'compound bands' (Service 1973) integrated by individuals of different bands – therefore the marriages within each community continue to respect band exogamy.

Now agriculture is being practised with more intensity, and in some communities we can speak of a certain 'redistribution' of goods as the mechanism of economic interchange, redistribution conceived and sanctioned as a reciprocal relation which is basically a centralization of

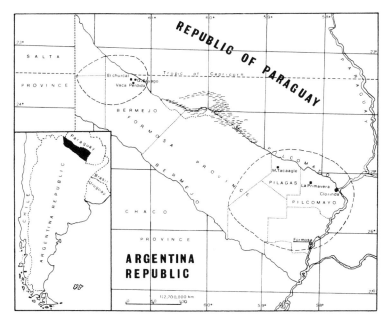

Figure 17.1 Map showing the location of Formosa Province and of the Taksek and Nacilamolek groups (the right-hand and left-hand circled areas respectively).

reciprocities (Sahlins 1983). Leadership is exercised by people connected with the lines of traditional leadership, or with the present syncretic churches (Miller 1967, 1979), from which it can be concluded that kinship continues to be the organizing principle of the majority of social relationships. As regards the cognitive and symbolic systems, we would affirm that both the Taksek and the Nacilamolek share the same basic principles.

We approach the subject of the differences between the adaptation systems of the Taksek and the Nacilamolek assuming that those differences could be explained better if we first studied the environmental variations that occur between East and West Formosa, with a special focus on the modality of interethnic relationships, both with other indigenous groups and with white colonizers.

The Taksek from the north-east of Formosa Province live in a zone within the Provincial Departments of Pilcomayo and Pilagas that is delimited to the north by the right bank of the Lower Pilcomayo River, by the Paraguay River to the East, the Montelindo Stream to the south, and to the west by 59°2′ W longitude (Fig. 17.1). The Nacilamolek are located in the north-west of the Province, within the Provincial Departments of Ramon Lista and Bermejo, close to the right bank of the Mid-Pilcomayo River, between 61°20′ and 61°40′ W, approximately 50 km inland (Fig. 17.1).

In order to deal with the material on which this chapter is based, we took into account the research strategy that Harris (1978, 1983, 1985) proposes to study the existing bonds between the different parts of the sociocultural systems, to make a comparison of some aspects of the infrastructure and structure of the sociocultural systems of the Taksek and the Nacilamolek, and to systematize a series of empirical data obtained in fieldwork among the Toba groups mentioned.

We will follow this scheme and consider the environment, demography and subsistence technology as infrastructural elements and, as the structural elements, the domestic economy and the political economy. In addition to this scheme, we will also mention ethnohistorical data, in order to point out some etic conditions and behavioural processes operating in the history of the region.

Ethnohistory

From the first half of the 16th century there are historical documents provided by the Spanish expeditions which mention the presence of indigenous groups of the Guaycuru linguistic family – among which are the Toba – in the territory of the present Formosa Province (Difrieri 1961, Roitman 1982). The geopolitical and economic projects of the Spanish Crown for the area, related to European commercial capital, privileged the confluence of the Paraguay and Pilcomayo rivers, creating a nucleus of white population there – Asuncion del Paraguay, founded in 1537 – that would support penetration into the Peruvian territories and other regions considered to have great wealth. This European intrusion gave a particular rhythm to the already quite complex anthropodynamics of the indigenous people of the area (Susnik 1972), bearers of Amazonic, Andean and Patagonic–Pampean traditions (such as the Toba). Until the end of the 16th century the relationship between the whites and the Indians was openly hostile (Fuscaldo 1982), but at the beginning of the 17th century a process of sociocultural transformation began in some groups, which also modified interethnic relations, mainly as a result of the multiplication of cattle and wild horses on the Chaco–Pampean Plain. The Toba, and the other Guaycuru, domesticated the horse and started to raise it. Its adaptation to the plain has been characteristic since then for almost 300 years, its essential traits being a 'horse complex', combined with horse raising, hunting–gathering, armed attack and trade (Sahlins 1977).

The armed attack, or *malon*, was certainly the predominant mode of articulation between the Guaycuruan tribes and white colonial society from the beginning of the 17th century to the end of the 19th (Fuscaldo 1982, 1985). We can consider it as an indigenous 'form of production' which was based on the organized plundering of *estancias*, towns, *pulperias*, trading caravans, travellers, vessels, forts and Reductions where other Indians lived, in order to take possession of cattle, arms, clothes, merchandise and captives. These goods were partly consumed, partly redistributed in the commercial circuits of the colonial administration. Thus, although the Indians attacked some towns, they arranged 'peace treaties' with others, where they sold or exchanged what they had taken. Due to these 'agreements' the settlers limited the plundering attacks and encouraged trading relations, creating new consumption needs among the Indians. At the same time the Indians made intra- or interethnic alliances of attack or defence, not only to resist the whites, but also to attack other groups (which they sometimes did, 'sponsored' by the settlers).

In this sense the Taksek were confirmed enemies of the Maka from the left bank of the Pilcomayo River in the Paraguayan Chaco, and they considered themselves rivals of their neighbours to the west, the Pilaga. However, the Nacilamolek were allies of the Pilaga, having mixed marriages and other economic interchanges, and fought against the Chulupi from the left bank of the Pilcomayo. The Nacilamolek also kept frequent alliances with other Toba groups in the north of their territory, in present Bolivia.

On the other hand, in the 17th and 18th centuries the Spanish Crown tried several times to colonize the eastern sector of the present Formosa Province by means of the settlement of military forces, the foundation of towns devoted to agriculture and herding, and the installation of Reductions in the charge of priests from the Company of Jesus. However, these populating strategies turned out to be inefficient because of the decisive defence that the Toba carried out in their territory. Meanwhile, the western sector of the Province remained practically unexplored and was left out of the regional economic circuits until almost the middle of the 20th century. The Nacilamolek had to compete with other ethnic groups there to exploit the biota.

At the end of the 19th century the Argentine government organized the definite 'pacification' of the indigenous groups that inhabit the Chaco plain, through an official policy of advance of the frontier lines and the establishment of settlers (Fuscaldo 1982). In 1879 the city that would be the capital of the present Formosa Province was founded (Romero Sosa 1967) and the first agricultural Formosa colonies were formed. The affluence of foreign settlers increased – mainly European and Paraguayan, and Argentine from other provinces – encouraged by the impulse given to timber activity, and to agriculture (cotton cultivation). Of course, these exploitations meant the division of land and the effective occupation of land belonging to the Indians.

On the other hand, cattle-breeders from the neighbouring Province of Salta started settling in the western zone of the Province, contending for the territory of the indigenous groups. That was probably the only form of white penetration in the north-west until almost the first half of the 20th century, except for the intense trade motivated by the so-called 'Chaco War' between Paraguay and Bolivia from 1932 to 1935. In this period the installation of the railway between Formosa and Salta was fostered, and that gave dynamism to timber exploitation, providing a way out to the production.

Gradually the Toba and other Guaycuruans from Chaco were obliged to sell their work – in a seasonal or intermittent way, as 'rural semiproletarians'

– due to the loss of their hunting territories, their growing dependence on the goods produced by the whites, the extinction of the wild cattle and the superiority of the national army – who began to use Remington rifles from 1870, putting an end to the *malones* (Fuscaldo 1982).

The Toba were the only natives at the beginning of the 20th century who had not been incorporated into the labour market in a permanent way. Many large families migrated seasonally to the sugar plantations and timber mills, but that was temporary. We can say that since 1930 almost all of the groups have depended to some extent on the sale of their work in order to subsist. In this way, because of their incorporation in the productive system of Formosa Province, the Toba still have different types of production relationships, which will be described when dealing with the domestic economy: (a) those based on traditional forms of appropriation – hunting, fishing and gathering; (b) those originating in subsistence agriculture; (c) those that come from the sale of work; and (d) those from the marketing of hunting and handicraft products (Wright 1984–1985, Fuscaldo 1982). This fact generates differences in the level of 'wealth' and 'proletarianization' of the individuals.

Environment

The major ecological variations occur from east to west, which is why the territory of Formosa Province can be divided into the following subregions (*La Argentina* 1959–1961).

(a)   Eastern: humid, with subtropical climate and no dry season. It rains almost all the year round, and the annual temperature oscillates from 20 to 13°C. It is limited to the east by the Paraguay River and to the west by the 700 mm isohyet. The soils, related to zones occupied by fluvio-lacustrine accumulations, are appropriate for agriculture. The natural landscape is the 'Chaco park', with rivers, ponds and marshes.

(b)   Central: semi-arid, with subtropical climate and summer rains from November to March. The subregion is located between the 700 and 500 mm isohyets. It is a plains zone, with characteristics similar to the previous one, but with semidesert soils and salt marshes.

(c)   Western: arid, with subtropical climate and summer rains. It is located between the 500 and 300 mm isohyets. The average annual temperature is 25°C, with a minimum of 2°C and a maximum of 45°C. The natural landscape, in decreasing order, is: the 'Chaco forest', the 'Chaco brush', the steppe of bushes and herbs. Agriculture is only possible where water for irrigation is available. The scarcity of water sources necessitates the construction of dams. The low productive capacity of the soil conditions the herding.

Taking into account the occupation and exploitation activities, the territory can be divided into two zones, limited approximately by 60°W longitude.

(a)   An eastern zone which includes the humid and semi-arid zones, where timber activities – quebracho extraction – have been annihilating the forest and opening fields for agricultural and herding activities.
(b)   A western zone, the arid subregion, very much altered by forest and herding exploitation. In some sectors the primitive forest and even the herbaceous stratum have disappeared, and only the thorny bushes, the bromeliaceous and the cactaceous have been left.

Demography

According to the National Census of 1980, the total number of individuals is 65 852 – without ethnic distinction – in the Provincial Departments where the Taksek live in Formosa Province; 50 875 inhabitants in Pilcomayo Department and 14 977 in Pilagas Department. That total number of natives includes approximately 1750 Toba, which represents 2.65%. The population density for Pilcomayo Department is 9.5 inhabitants per km^2, and 4.9 inhabitants per km^2 in Pilagas.

According to the same source (National Census 1982), the Western Bermejo Department, where the Nacilamolek live, has 7520 native inhabitants of the Province. In a demographic census carried out by the Rural Health Plan of the Public Health Secretariat of the Province in 1982, the number of inhabitants of the three Toba communities that we will consider is 823, which would represent 10.9% of the total. The population density for this Department is 0.6 inhabitants per km^2, which marks a very clear difference from the Eastern departments.

It appears, then, that the eastern zone is more densely populated and that the Toba are less represented there than in the west. These differences correspond to the environmental variations mentioned above, and are still characteristic traits of the population profile of the Eastern and Western Departments.

The population pyramid that can be built from the Taksek population samples (*Estructura ocupacional* 1982) and the Nacilamolek samples (Mendoza & Carrasco 1984) is characteristic of a young population with a high growth rate and with a life expectation of 65 years.

Several traditional methods of demographic restriction exist, which belong to a long-range policy traditionally destined to stop the effects of decrease in subsistence income. Nowadays other practices have been introduced that have a positive effect on the population growth.

(a)   Sanitary control, carried out by Toba personnel trained in nursing, or through periodic official campaigns – it reduces the incidence of infectious diseases and struggles against child malnutrition.
(b)   Provincial schools, set up within or near the communities, which provide at least a daily meal to the pupils.
(c)   Interethnic marriages, with members of other indigenous groups or with whites.

(d)   Neolocalisms, of the young couples that chose a different place of residence from that prescribed by the traditional rule – matrilocalism.

Subsistence technology

In general in the eastern zone of Formosa Province, agricultural–herding exploitations in parcels of up to 50 ha predominate (*Estructura ocupacional* 1982); whereas in the western zone herding is mainly carried out in plots of about 200 ha.

This depends on the regional ecological variations already pointed out, and involves the subsistence activities of the Taksek and Nacilamolek, for the north-east Toba practised mainly subsistence agriculture; whereas this activity has secondary economic importance for the north-west.

Thus, the majority of the Taksek live in agricultural communities run by the Indigenous Communities Institute (ICA), except for Clorinda, where they live in a peri-urban settlement with a surface of 4 ha. Each large family exploits parcels of about 2–30 ha. These parcels are devoted partly to crops marketed in the region (especially cotton and sunflower), and partly to other crops intended for consumption and exchange within the community. It should be pointed out that both types of production are aimed at the family's survival, rather than at profit accumulation. The principal vegetables cultivated for consumption are manioc (*Manihot esculenta* Cranta), sweet potato (*Ipomea batatas*), watermelon (*Citrullus vulgaris*) and melon. In order to prepare the farm and obtain the crops, the following procedure takes place (Wright 1985a).

(a)   Limiting the surface for cultivation (with wires, fences or brushwood). Generally the chosen place is burnt, or raked with oxen or a tractor (lent by the colonial administration).
(b)   Preparing the land: the plough driven by oxen or the tractor is used. The handled plough is the most common.
(c)   Sowing: generally by hand, although there are machines that belong to the administration.
(d)   Raking: the brushwood is cleared at several stages of crop growth. It can be by hand or with tools, such as hoes, spades, etc. Pests are fought with insecticides provided by the ICA.
(e)   Harvesting: by hand, most of the time.

On the other hand, among the Nacilamolek, although many families have small orchards of about 2 ha per family, almost all of the crops are consumed or exchanged within or between villages. The preparation of the land, raking, clearing the brushwood and tilling, begins in spring, i.e. in September. For that purpose sticks are used for clearing the brushwood and spades for raking. The sowing is done by hand when the first rains fall, burying the seed in a hole in the earth. The planting of crops does not follow an order, and generally several types are mixed up. Neither artificial irrigation nor insecticides are used.

The principal cultivated species are maize (*Zea mays*), calabash (*Langenaria siceraria*), pumpkin (*Curcubita maxima* and *C. moschata*), water-melon and melon. The success of the crops depends on the seasonal rains and on whether the crops are damaged by rodents or other pests. In the daily diet the most abundant proteins come from hunting by individuals, using ·22 rifles, maces and dogs. The larger prey are two species of roe deer, tapir, peccaries, carpincho and ñandú. The smaller prey are several armadillos, rodents, iguanas, rabbits, foxes and several birds. Fishing, both individual and collective, is carried out with bow and arrow, and with net. Fishing can be done in the Pilcomayo River, in ponds and in nearby streams. A great variety of edible wild vegetables is collected.

Some families raise pigs and hens, and consume eggs; some others have a few sheep, from which they take advantage of the wool for weaving, and asses. Water is carried in vessels from 'dams', built by the government or by missionaries, or from nearby streams. Firewood is the main fuel, and is carried from the forest that surrounds the village.

This high dependence on natural resources implies that, for the Nacila-molek, winter is considered as the 'hunger season'. During this period, between June and September approximately, the hunters search especially for animals whose skin has commercial value (such as the fox).

Among the Taksek hunting does not play such a relevant economic rôle, although it is still practised, subject to the limitations of a zone which has suffered considerable depredations. The principal techniques are ambush, with traps or by hand (for aquatic birds). The instruments used range from camouflage made with palm leaves, through knives, bow and arrow, to firearms. The species hunted are alligator (*Caiman* sp.) and several already mentioned: nandu, peccaries, cervids, edentates, iguana, rabbits, etc.

Fishing is done with nets, fishhooks, spears or bow and arrow. The fishing expeditions are carried out in places that are nearer than the places used for hunting. Generally, only men go and sometimes they take children with them to train them in the technique.

Water is found in the colony ponds or in scattered wells. When there is a poor harvest, hunting and gathering increase.

Subsistence activities, both for natural species or for cultivated ones, are regulated by 'the masters of animal and plant species', that prescribe 'ecological' rules to guarantee the appropriate exploitation of the resources (Wright 1986). It should be pointed out that these concepts turn out to be as appropriate as those that orient, for example, harvest time or pest fighting.

Domestic economy

The domestic economy of the Taksek and the Nacilamolek is within a 'domestic mode of production', since the production units belong to families, which sometimes combine nuclear elements into large families; the division of labour is according to sex and age; simple technology is used; production is aimed at satisfying the family needs; and the domestic groups have direct access to strategic products.

In this sense it is also a 'subproduction' economy (Sahlins 1983), because the production turns out to be inferior to the possibilities of the environment. This is related to a certain policy of 'demographic restriction' to counteract the possible income decrease.

The Nacilamolek solve this threshold of decreasing performance by semi-proletarianization, in agricultural work or forest exploitation, whereas the Taksek do so by devoting a part of the cultivation surface to crops marketed in the region, and also sell their work in neighbouring farms. In both cases they resort to what Sahlins (1983) calls the 'mobility' and the 'moderation' of the hunter, in order to satisfy the family needs with the technical resources available.

The Taksek settlements are located on Provincial Route 86, along which all the commercial and human traffic flows, linking the rest of the Province and of the country, even the bordering countries. Along the route electricity lines, the telegraph and the telephone run, which have their headquarters in the white towns. This means that there is a variety of services which the Toba can have access to by going to those towns, since no family can afford individual services for its dwelling.

In the agricultural communities the land belongs to the National Treasury. The exploitation surface is distributed to the families and is constantly in the process of subdivision, because of marriage, migration or usurpation by whites outside the colony. When a recently formed nuclear family wishes to occupy a parcel, they must request the agreement of the family chief of the lands that they want to exploit, and also the approval of the ICA authorities.

In a large family the sexual division of labour works in the following way: the men devote themselves to agricultural jobs, from the preparation of the land to the harvest. They also go hunting, fishing and gathering (honey and wild vegetables); they build the dwellings; they make and repair utensils and tools. Occasionally they manufacture brooms, hats and other handicraft objects to be sold. They sell the skins of some animals; and they work for wages temporarily on the neighbouring farms. They also work on a permanent basis for state organizations (ICA, Provincial Police, National Gendarmerie, Provincial School and Public Administration). The women, within the agricultural activities, devote themselves mainly to the harvest, on their own farms or hired temporarily on other farms. They are in charge of the cleaning of the dwelling and its surroundings; looking for water and firewood; gathering wild vegetables; preparing the food; washing and sewing clothes; and washing, educating and looking after the children. Some women are employed as teaching assistants or work in the Provincial Schools. Others are household servants in the white settlers' houses, employees at the ICA or nurses at the Sanitary Controls of the Communities.

The children of 6 or 7 years of age help with the agricultural jobs, and are hired on farms (spending their wages on themselves). They go hunting and fishing with their parents or with groups of contemporaries. They go to the Provincial School of the colony and spend the rest of the time playing – soccer, in particular, is an activity about which boys from 10 years to adulthood are enthusiastic.

On the other hand, the products of hunting–fishing–gathering and a large proportion of the cultivated vegetables are included in reciprocity circuits that go beyond the limits of kinship to reach bonds of friendship, *compadrazgo*, political interest, etc. Part of the harvest – the sunflower and cotton – is sold to white neighbours and to storers that reach to the colonies. The money obtained through local marketing is devoted to cancelling debts, paying credits and paying back the advance payments in merchandise, seeds and tools that the ICA had lent them, and which had to be returned after the harvest. What is left is devoted to satisfying family needs or to exchanging with other settlers.

However, in the Nacilamolek communities money is less available. The daily needs are mostly covered by the reciprocal exchange of hunting meat and wild or cultivated vegetables. These exchanges follow the lines of kinship and leadership. In this sense the producers that return empty-handed know that they will receive from the others who have been luckier.

In the large family – the minimum economic unit of the domestic mode of production – the sexual division of labour works in the way usual in hunting economies. The men go hunting, they go fishing, they gather honey (but not wild vegetables), they prepare the orchard for the harvest and look after the farm, they make and repair tools and utensils, etc. Besides this, they sell their work in rural jobs temporarily and seasonally. They sell the leather of some animals. Sometimes they also carve objects in *palo santo* (*Bulnesia sarmientoi*) to be marketed as 'handicrafts'. In any of these occupations the work is not constant but intermittent, and can be interrupted because of different circumstances (rituals, sports or rains).

The women gather wild vegetables, they sow and harvest the vegetables from the orchard, and are in charge of it when the men of the family are not present, they look for firewood and carry water, they cook the food, they look after the children, they make pottery, they knit vegetable and wool fibres for domestic use and to be marketed as 'handicraft'.

The children are the main assistants to carry water and, especially the girls, participate in other small daily tasks, although they generally have little involvement in the productive process. They spend their time playing and occasionally go with their fathers hunting, fishing or gathering. The girls start being trained before the boys in the typical tasks of their sex.

Political economy

Although political authority among the Toba follows the lines of kinship, the organizing principle of the majority of social relationships, in the northeastern agricultural colonies some individuals stand out because they have an incipient accumulation of capital. This is due to: (a) the inheritance of possessions through direct or collateral kinship; and (b) the fact that they are Provincial Administration employees. This grants them a certain prestige within the community, which is added to the fact that they generally belong to the hierarchical board of the syncretic churches. Besides, because of their relative 'wealth' and religious influence, they are usually in a position to hold successful commercial relations with the whites, which feeds back to their intracommunity prestige.

This sector of natives who own material or symbolic possessions of some social relevance is different from that which includes the 'poor' settlers, who exploit small parcels (of up to 4 ha), and whose social network is far from the knots of prestige and influence already mentioned. That is, the intracommunity social space (and even the intercommunity one) is organized according to the social distance that separates the less influential individuals – less connected with the kinship and reciprocity networks – from those who hold a leading position. This position is achieved through: (a) kinship with a line related to the traditional leadership; (b) association with certain supernatural beings; (c) possession of an appropriate bilingual and bicultural handling in dealings with the whites; (d) belonging to the hierarchy of the syncretic churches; and (e) holding a position in the Provincial Administration. In the internal dynamics of the acquisition of prestige and influence, a blood relationship with the traditional leadership is an excluding condition; perhaps the most accessible condition is that of public employment, or a religious position.

The characteristics that have just been described show that the process of selection of leaders includes elements of adaptation to the present situation. On the one hand, we refer to the need for incorporating basic knowledge of the handling of interethnic relations: bilingualism, practical preparation to do administrative tasks, and other more 'subtle' factors that have to do with decision-making and negotiation. On the other hand, we refer to the active participation within the religious communities, where the highest density of community social interactions take place (Miller 1979), and where the present structural schemes of the Toba society are shown.

In addition, individuals acquire political influence when they participate in the institutions imposed by the provincial administration, but this possibility of having a certain pre-eminence within the community only seems to be confirmed when attributed to certain lines of kinship, or hierarchies in the Toba Pentecostal Churches.

We can point out the incidence of these indigenous organizations at two levels of community life.

(a)   The superstructural level, where they provide a corpus of value orientations accepted by the dominating society, that re-elaborate the traditional symbolic systems.

(b)   The structural level, where they provide a scheme of hierarchical organization that gives new shape to the old shamanic clients and to the kinship groups (Reyburn 1970), for example, in the formation of 'intermediate' groups of the religious bureaucracy, such as the 'Church Commission', 'Groups of Youths', 'Women's Commission', etc. We will deal with this subject more extensively in the discussion.

In the Nacilamolek communities the situation is different because the mode of production does not allow even that incipient accumulation referred to above which is occurring in the eastern communities. In addition, their churches follow the orientation of the Anglican religion. The Anglican missionaries (Wright 1983), who lived among the Nacilamolek from 1930 to 1975 approximately, and who still have close links with them, made a clear distinction between the faith that they preached and the shamanic practices. As a result of this, the leadership associated with shamanism seems to have been separated from religion (Mendoza 1984).

At present the individuals who hold a leading position are not the priests of the church. These individuals are related to the traditional leadership, hold a position in the public administration or are related to a national political party. In all cases they are people – men and women – who show an appropriate bilingual and bicultural handling, and a certain independence of judgement regarding political decision-making with respect to the 'moral' authority of the Anglican Mission. This means that, whereas the Church organization provides the frame for the formation of an intermediate sector between that of the indigenous shepherds and that of the faithful adherents (composed of members of the 'Church Commission'), there are also individuals who are not related to this organization but who have consider-able influence, arising mainly from their ability to handle interethnic relations, and to redistribute their incomes in the community.

Discussion

In order to have a better picture of the sociocultural and economic context of the present Taksek and Nacilamolek, we will frame some hypotheses about what we suppose could have been the sociocultural and economic context of these groups at the end of the 19th century. We take this historic moment as significant because drastic changes in the indigenous mode of production start to occur at this time: the occupation of the hunting lands, the beginning of agricultural and intensive forest exploitation (with Argentine and foreign settlers), and the national government's military expeditions to 'consolidate its sovereignty' in the province.

According to our model, both the Taksek and Nacilamolek were organized in nomadic bands formed by a number of large families, of about 30–100 people. The northeastern bands wandered through a vast territory, which we have calculated at more than 120 km^2, rich in water courses, and in animal and plant species. The northwestern bands went through a smaller territory of about 40 km^2; comparatively more arid, with practically no water courses apart from the Pilcomayo River. We believe that factors such as those that follow could have influenced the delimitation of the economic exploitation area:

(a)   pressure from other indigenous groups on its periphery (principally Mataco, Chulupi and Pilaga);
(b)   absence of white colonists who would compete for the occupation and exploitation of the area;
(c)   adaptative efficacy of the environment exploitation systems;
(d)   efficacy in the control of demographic reproduction; and
(e)   specialization of the bands in two modes of production: first, *ribereno*, with emphasis on fishing in the Pilcomayo River; and, secondly, *montaraz*, with emphasis on hunting–gathering.

The Nacilamolek bands made internal alliances (sanctioned by exogamy), which included coalitions for war, especially against the Chulupi and Mataco. They also allied with the Pilaga to attack these same groups. The frequency of the interethnic wars could be attributed, following Harris (1985), to the need to keep control over the limited resources of the river and the forest.

As was indicated above, the rich exploitation zone of the Taksek started to turn into an agricultural, herding and forest exploitation region, and since 1900 Franciscan missionaries settled there, founding missionary establishments among the Eastern Toba: Mision Tacaagle to the north-east and Mision Laishi to the south-east. Their action promoted the semi-sedentarization of some Taksek, while other bands went on wandering through the teritory, with a hunting–gathering mode of production. Undoubtedly, the fertility of the land favoured the 'civilizing' project of the religious missionaries, and the Taksek gradually incorporated the agricultural and herding work routines. However, in the symbolic field they assimilated only to a very limited extent the Catholicism that the Franciscans proposed to them.

The Taksek did not compete with other ethnic indigenous groups within the area. The true friction zones were on the frontiers, for example on the northern frontier with the Maca, or on the eastern frontier with the Pilaga, although virtually at the beginning of the second decade of this century the ethnic confrontations ceased.

When incorporating agricultural technology in a favourable environment, within a region that is politically oriented towards production for the regional market, the Taksek were not proletarianized as quickly as the Nacilamolek were. The latter had already started to migrate seasonally to the sugar-cane plantations of the Salta Province at the end of the 19th century (Bialet Masse 1968). With the experience of paid work the Nacilamolek acquired as a group a certain competence in the handling of interethnic relations with the whites, at the same time as they began to modify some of their consumption patterns, to practise horticulture on a small scale, and to modify the leadership characteristics that would increasingly demand the individual requirement of bilingual knowledge. In our opinion their experience also prepared them to receive the proposals of the Anglican missionaries who settled among the Nacilamolek in 1930. Both the work at the sugar plantations and the mission calmed down the tribal wars.

Meanwhile depredation of the Eastern eco-environment by the agricultural–herding activities and forest exploitation obliged the indigenous people to migrate temporarily to wood- and sugar-manufacturing workshops, and to the cotton harvest, in order to obtain the European goods that they had become used to consuming as a complement to their traditional products. This economic strategy was also reinforced by actions of a social character (for example, visiting relatives settled in other areas) or of a socio-religious character (such as therapeutic consultations with shamans or participation in meetings with charismatic leaders).

The temporary migrations undoubtedly modified the internal dynamics of Taksek society, just as had happened with the Nacilamolek, and put it in interaction with whites and with other Indians.

Finally, demographic pressure made the Taksek settle in fiscal agricultural colonies administered by the ICA, or in peri-urban settlements without clear rules of land possession. The demographic pressure was comparatively lower in the western territories, due to the already mentioned limitations of the ecosystem and to the absence of political colonizing projects. This allowed the Nacilamolek to keep their hunting–fishing–gathering mode of production for a longer time and to incorporate certain horticultural techniques and habits of work and consumption promoted by the Anglican Mission.

In brief, the major differences among the adaptation systems of the Taksek and the Nacilamolek will be found today in the pre-eminence of an agricultural mode of production – for subsistence and for the market – on the one hand, the prevalence of hunting–gathering complemented by paid work, on the other hand. In the first case the most important complementary economic activities are the sale of temporary rural manual labour and employment in the public administration; in the second case they are subsistence horticulture and the sale of handicrafts.

In the infrastructure we do not find a correlation between the differences mentioned and the biological reproduction strategies of the two groups. At the structural level we observe a greater individualization of Taksek production relations. The nuclear family among the Taksek is turning into the prevailing unit of domestic production, which allows for the possibility of accumulating goods, and a certain 'redistribution' by the 'enriched' family chiefs.

In the sphere of the political economy we do not find fundamental differences between the systems of the Taksek and Nacilamolek, but variations of degree. For example, a greater political–administrative influence of the public power is found in the north-east; and a major secularization of the Nacilamolek leadership in comparison with the institutional incorporation of the Pentecostal syncretic churches in the Taksek leadership. The existence of church organizations could be interpreted as the social expression of the change from a hunting nomadic mode of production to an agricultural and sedentary one, considering that the implied production relations require: fixed settlements, marked social division, redistributing rôle of the leaders and grouping of the domestic units into kinship lines.

At the superstructural level these Church organizations re-elaborate the traditional symbolic system, and they provide a corpus of value orientations that prove acceptable to the dominating society (Cordeu 1984). For example, the positive valorization of continuous work with great effort is a necessary condition to feed back to the typical behaviour of the agricultural and wage-earning mode of production.

Acknowledgements

The field data corresponding to the Taksek Toba were recorded by Pablo G. Wright in campaigns carried out in 1979, 1981, 1982, 1983 and 1985, the later ones supported by the Argentine National Council of Scientific and Technical Research (CONICET). The data on the Nacilamolek Toba come from campaigns carried out by Marcela Mendoza in 1984 and 1985, the last also supported by the CONICET.

Note

1   Although the term 'Toba' names the members of the ethnic group denominated by themselves, the identification and definition of the social units that compose it is a sociogenesis problem not yet solved (Braunstein 1983).

References

Bialet Masse, J. 1968. *Las clases obreras argentinas a principios de siglo.* Buenos Aires: Nueva Vision. (Original 1904.)
Braunstein, J. 1983. *Algunos rasgos de la organizacion social de los indigenas del Gran Chaco.* Trabajos de Etnologia: F. F. y L., U.B.A. 2.
Cordeu, E. 1984. Notas sobre la dinamica socioreligiosa toba-pilaga. *Suplemento Antropologico. Universidad Catolica, Asuncion, Paraguay* 19(1), 187–236.
Cordeu, E. & M. de los Rios 1982. Un enfoque estructural de las variaciones socioculturales de los cazadores-recolectores del Gran Chaco 1982. *Suplemento Antropologico (Asuncion, Paraguay)* 17(1), 131–95.
Difrieri, H. 1961. Poblacion indigena y colonial. In *La Argentina. Suma de geografia* (various authors). Buenos Aires: Peuser.
Estructura ocupacional y dinamica educativa de la Provincia de Formosa 1982. Buenos Aires: ICIS–CONICET–FADES.
Fuscaldo, L. 1982. *La relacion de 'propiedad' en el Proceso del enfrentamiento social (de*

propiedad comunal directa a propiedad privada burguesa). Buenos Aires: Cuadernos de CISCO, Serie estudios 42.

Fuscaldo, L. 1985. El Proceso de constitucion del proletariado rural de origen indigena en el Chaco. In *Antropologia*, M. Lischetti (ed.), 231–51. Eudeba.

Harris, M. 1978. *El desarrollo de la teoria antropologica. Una historia de las teorias de la cultura*. Madrid: Siglo XXI. (Original in English, 1968.)

Harris, M. 1983. *Introduccion a la antropologia general*. Madrid: Alianza. (Original in English, 1971.)

Harris, M. 1985. *El materialismo cultural*. Madrid: Alianza. (Original in English, 1979.)

La Argentina. Suma de geografia (various authors) 1958–61. Buenos Aires: Peuser.

Mendoza, M. 1984. La jefatura Toba: su desvinculacion con aspectos religiosos entre los Toba del Pilcomayo Medio. Unpublished MS.

Mendoza, M. & N. Carrasco 1984. Estudio preliminar sobre el matrimonio Toba en Vaca Perdida (Formosa). *Suplemento Antropologico Asuncion, Paraguay* (in press).

Miller, E. 1967. Pentecostalism among Argentine Toba. PhD dissertation, University of Pittsburgh.

Miller, E. 1979. *Los tobas argentinos. Armonia y disonancia en una sociedad*. Mexico: Siglo XXI.

Reyburn, W. 1970. *The toba indians of the Argentine Chaco: an interpretative report*. Indiana: Elkhart, Mennonite Board of Missions and Charities (3rd Printing).

Roitman, A. 1982. *Bosquejo para una historia de las tribus Toba*. Entregas del Instituto Tilcara: U.B.A., F. F. y L.

Romero Sosa, C. 1967. Historia de la provincia de Formosa y de sus pueblos (1862–1930). In *Academia Nacional de la Historia, Historia Argentina Contemporanea 1862–1930*, Vol. 4, Section 2, 178–9. Buenos Aires: El Ateneo.

Sahlins, M. 1977. *Las sociedades tribales*. Barcelona: Labor.

Sahlins, M. 1983. *Economia de la edad de Piedra*. Madrid: Akal. (Original in English, 1974.)

Service, E. 1973. *Los cazadores*. Barcelona: Labor. (Original in English, 1966.)

Susnik, B. 1972. Dimensiones migratorias y pautas culturales de los pueblos del Gran Chaco y de su periferia (enfoque etnologico). *Suplemento Antropologico Asuncion, Paraguay* **7**, 1–2.

Wright, P. G. 1983. Presencia protestante entre aborigenes del Chaco argentino. *Scripta Ethnologica (Buenos Aires)* **7**, 73–84.

Wright, P. G. 1984–1985. Notas sobre gentilicios toba. *Relaciones de la Sociedad Argentina de Antropologia* **XVI**, 225–34.

Wright, P. G. 1985a. Los conceptos de 'trabajo' y 'marisca' como etnocategorias de los toba de Formosa. Trabajo presentado en el I Congreso Argentino y Latinoamericano de Antropologia Rural, Olavarria, Buenos Aires, Argentina, 4–6 December 1985.

Wright, P. G. 1985b. Iglesia Evangelica Unida: tradicion y aculturacion en una organizacion socio-religiosa toba. Unpublished MS.

Wright, P. G. 1986. Semantic analysis of symbolism of toba mythical animals. In *Cultural attitudes to animals*. World Archaeological Congress (mimeo).

18 *Spatial heterogeneity in Fuego-Patagonia*

LUIS ALBERTO BORRERO

Introduction

Only recently has the process of the human peopling of Patagonia been modelled as a dynamic one in space as well as in time (Cocilovo 1981, Cocilovo & Guichón 1984). Previous models considered the space of Patagonia as being occupied by several different, geographically localized populations (Imbelloni 1938, Bórmida 1953–1954), but they were framed in a *Kulturkreis* line of research, with all of its postulates of differential antiquity according to the geographical position of the 'human waves', and time depth was not dealt with in a satisfactory way. Several anomalies were noted in the osteological record, and the incapacity of those models to account for them was soon obvious (Cocilovo 1981). It was recently observed that they cannot be maintained as an explanation for the process of peopling of Patagonia. Instead, it is now considered that minimal variations in selected variables show a far more complicated process underlying the ethnographic variability observed in the 19th century.

The original populations probably spread slowly through the Patagonian steppes, progressively filling all the available space. The process took at least 12 000 radiocarbon years, which is a short period if judged by global standards of human peopling. When a comparison is made with other Southern Hemisphere cases, such as South Africa (Volman 1984), or Australia (Jones 1979), Fuego-Patagonia stands out as a region used very late.

The process of peopling should not be viewed as a constant southward movement. Instead, a slow multidirectional flow of people should be considered. Decisions of where to move must have been taken with regard to the availability of hierarchically ordered space, and the corresponding structure of critical resources. The gradual extension of hunting ranges and the splitting of bands into new smaller units must have been causes for movement. In this light the southward vector is the result of the full occupation, or lack of desirability, of more Northern space. Thus, it is clear that this process is not to be associated with a simple model of regular migration of people, as Martin's (1973) *blitzkrieg* hypothesis implies.

It is interesting to develop some implications derived from a model of slow filling of the available space. These are concerned with the conditions under which evolution took place in different portions of Patagonia. Essentially the time required for the saturation of space is longer than under the migration hypothesis. Thus, the shift from density-independent to density-dependent adaptations is expected to be more gradual and transitional. Changes in density should promote group differentiation at the regional level, under the associated stimuli of changes in the structure of resources. Intergroup competition is not expected to be a selective pressure at the beginning. I visualize a picture of regional adaptations with different velocities of change responding to alternative sets of selective pressures (see Borrero 1984).

It is important to note that demographic pressure can in no way be considered to be responsible for the observed differences between groups. These differences, as well as the variety of adaptive strategies, result solely from changing accommodations related to the structure of resources. In the process of slow peopling of empty space minimally three phases should be distinguished, not all of them equally amenable to archaeological analysis.

(a) Exploration phase: this concerns the initial spread into empty space. Movements should be limited to natural routes, and the expectation of finding sites that are representative of this phase is necessarily low.

(b) Colonization phase: I refer to the initial consolidation of human groups in given points in space, with more or less specified home ranges (see Schwartz 1970). These population centres are expected to develop in carefully selected regions. Repetitive use of sites, with similar or changing functions, and lack of overlap between territories, should make this phase one of high visibility.

(c) Stabilization phase (see Schwartz 1970): this refers to a moment when all the desirable space is occupied, and new density-dependent selective pressures appear. Cultural drift (Binford 1963) is expected to be at work. Archaeological visibility should be high, but resolution low, due to increasing overlap of territories.

There are selected cases in Patagonia which may be understood as evidence of the exploration phase (see below) but, properly, most of the archaeological record should be referable to the colonization or stabilization phases. In general terms it must be stated that it is not possible to assess the distribution of sites for different periods as random or not, since problems with regional sampling are simply too great to be overcome. This is an important limitation to the systematic analysis of the process of peopling. For that reason this study simply hopes to be of use in delineating tendencies, and pointing out further areas of research.

Cultural differentiation

The cultural history of Fuego-Patagonia should be seen as one of progressive differentiation of populations. Several periods could be constructed, and

Table 18.1 Tentative periodization for Fuego–Patagonia.

	Years BP
t_0	pre-12 000
t_1	12 000–9500
t_2	9500–7000
t_3	7000–4000
t_4	4000–2000
t_5	2000–500

those I am using here are not substantiated better than any alternatives. I only claim that they are useful for my purposes (a slightly different periodization was proposed by Gradín 1980, Table 18.1).

1. By t_1 evidence of the exploration phase is to be expected. Perhaps small sites with slight use in Northern Tierra del Fuego (Massone 1983, Laming-Emperaire et al. 1972) are indicative of this phase. In both cases human occupation appears to be related to poor environments, probably characterized by a low carrying capacity, in a landscape recently abandoned by the Pleistocene ice. In the Deseado Basin (Fig. 18.1) the initial occupation of Los Toldos 3, with the earliest radiocarbon date for Fuego-Patagonia (12 600±600 BP, Cardich et al. 1973), could also be considered as evidence of this exploration phase. In fact, for the Deseado and Fuegian sites a word of caution is needed. It is truly difficult to find the first sites formed by the initial explorers of a given area. Perhaps in a few years a proliferation of dates around 12 000 years ago will carry the implication of a full colonization phase for the Deseado Basin. The situation appears stronger for the Fuegian case, given the early successional stage of the associated ecosystems.

In any case, a previous theoretical t_0 could be defended, which is the time needed for the archaeologically unrecognized exploration phase all along Patagonia. There is good evidence for full colonization of the middle Chico Basin (Fig. 18.1) by t_1. A variety of sites in that area are giving a functionally different and complementary picture. However, the definition of an adaptive system on that database may not be warranted, especially due to the lack of in-depth published reports (Bird 1946).

2. By t_2 a good deal of continental Patagonia was in a colonization phase, with the exception of very marginal lands. In fact, in Patagonia there was a trend towards a moist and warm climate (Markgraf 1983, Lanata n.d.), whereas in Tierra del Fuego there was an alternation of steppe and moorland (Markgraf 1983). In general agreement with the higher productivity associated with the environment prevalent in continental Patagonia, three discrete clusters of sites are observed in the Deseado, Chico and Traful Basins (Fig. 18.1), all characterized by stylistically similar projectile points. Topographic and environmental diversity between the basins mentioned suggests the action of different sets of selective pressures. Accordingly, different

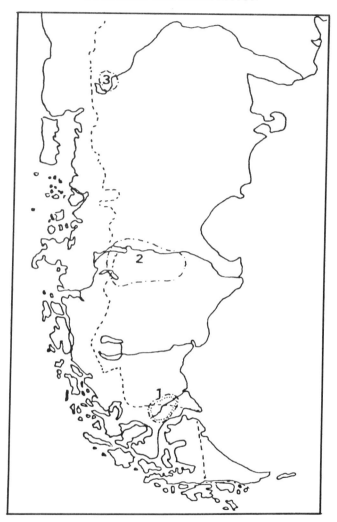

Figure 18.1   Map of Fuego–Patagonia. 1, middle Rio Chico Basin, inner line is for
t_1, outer line for t_2; 2, upper and middle Deseado Basin, t_2; 3, Traful Basin, t_2.

systems were defined at each area (Aguerre 1979, Bird 1946, Curzio *et al.*
1982). Lack of evidence for population differentiation, plus the stylistic
affinities already observed, suggest that these are all developments out of
similar adaptations. I do not think that they represent the migration of a
single group, or even of closely related groups. Instead I argue that they
represent localized segments of populations probably separated by several

generations, all with successfully developed adaptive systems centred in the exploitation of the guanaco, a medium-sized ungulate which was the most important prey in Patagonia. It should be mentioned that no clear time gradient is observed in the geographical arrangement of the dates falling into this period. It must also be stated that one of the systems, that centred in the upper Deseado Basin, is related to a pictographic style executed on cave walls (see Gradín *et al.* 1979) which in no way could be related to the other systems postulated.

The initial occupation of the Tunel site in Southern Tierra del Fuego is defended by its excavators as an expression of an exploration phase (Piana 1984). Interestingly enough, they suggest that this site is perhaps to be linked with the system operating in the Chico Basin (Orquera & Piana 1983).

3. A completely different set of adaptive systems appeared by t_3 in different regions, in general coincidence with the expansion of woods in Tierra del Fuego (Markgraf 1983), and with a cooler trend in Patagonia (Heusser & Streeter 1980). In the Chubut and Deseado Basins the industry known as Casapedrense (Crivelli-Montero 1976–1980) is famous for its lack of projectile points, its blade technology and the special emphasis on guanaco-meat consumption (apparently in greater proportions than previous and subsequent systems; Cardich *et al.* 1973). It is difficult to understand the origin of this cultural unit. Crivelli-Montero argued for the possibility of a diffusion hypothesis, which apparently implied population replacement, but the archaeological record outside Patagonia gave no strong support for this suggestion. Synchronically with the Casapedrense a cultural unit known as 'Toldense Tradition' (different from the Toldense industry) is poorly known, and its relations with the Casapedrense need to be explored further.

In the Southern Fuegian and archipelagic regions the appearance of completely new adaptive systems centred in the exploitation of marine resources (Ortiz-Troncoso 1985, Orquera & Piana 1983, Piana 1984) is further evidence of cultural differentiation. Important differences observed between osteological human collections from Tierra del Fuego and Patagonia led Cocilovo to consider that a cessation of gene flow imposed by the water barrier of Magellan's Strait produced this differentiation (Cocilovo 1981). If it was in some way related to the appearance of the marine-oriented adaptive system, then it could be argued that population differentiation has a history of 5000–6000 radiocarbon years. However, it must be kept in mind that it is not necessary that culture change accompanied changes in the morphology of individuals.

This marine adaptation makes heavy use of marine mammal bones for artefacts, and their diet was centred on sea-lions, molluscs, whales and dolphins.

Expansion of effective adaptive systems is seen as a result of full exploitation of all available space under a given set of adaptive strategies. By efficiency I am referring to the ability to keep up with environmental change (Lewontin 1978). Only gross environmental variations are tracked in this way and, interestingly, the evidence of diversification (the Casapedrense, the marine-oriented adaptation) is spatially less restricted than previous systems. A whole range of adaptive strategies were experienced throughout this period, and the emphasis on one or more strategy by each system in no way precludes the fact that the limits of the Patagonian ecosystems were searched. On the other hand, differences between contiguous groups are to be understood in terms of differences in the secondary strategies (those not involved in guanaco exploitation and consumption for the Casapedrense; those not involved in marine-mammal exploitation and consumption for the Fuegian system). Observed differences between localized groups within each system could be understood in terms of the concept of cultural drift, attesting an embryonic stabilization phase.

4. By t_4 no important ecological changes are registered and no discrete cultural units are easily recognized. The *Protopatagoniense de Tradición Casapedrense* of the Deseado and Chubut Basins appears as a compromise solution for industries that are not easy to define. They have no strong Casapedrense traits, but have some . . .; they have no strong Patagoniense traits, but have some . . . (see Aschero 1983, Gradín 1980).

In Southern Patagonia the Fell IV phase was defined by Bird (1946). Forty years later his definition appears to be fuzzy at best. Its superposition with Phase V has been observed (Gómez Otero 1984, Massone 1981), and I think that the proliferation of groups is reaching a saturation point. In this light the marine-oriented solution, still continuing in the Fuegian islands, appears to be irreversible. Terrestrial strategies in continental Patagonia were similarly exploiting the guanaco, with the supplement of small mammals, birds, rodents, and probably plants. It is expected that there would be an increase in the importance of marine resources as supplementary sources of fat, with a tendency for these resources to be more intensively pursued in southern locations. Some of these supplementary resources must have been incorporated into the adaptive systems as buffers for periodic failures of the prime target (guanaco), especially in winter and early spring.

Functionally different sequential use of cave sites now appears to be an important process. No more clear-cut stratigraphies are indicated, and redundancy in site utilization is suggested.

In the southern archipelagos cultural differences enter a period of stasis. The widespread evidence of maritime adaptations should be attributed to the stabilization phase. For continental Patagonia differences are observed between regions, but these are understandable as the result of minor variations in functional equivalents (see Binford 1963), and are characteristically associated with a stabilization phase.

5. By t_5 different selective pressures appear to be operative. All of Patagonia is in use to some degree, but it is not possible to assume that such occupation means that demographic pressure was at work. It appears that a stabilization phase was achieved in most of Fuego-Patagonia and boundary maintenance, inter-group competition, etc., are all new sources for variation. These changing situations are acting in the absence of marked

environmental change, with a warmer trend accompanied by the retreating of woods, which was particularly important in Northern Tierra del Fuego (Markgraf 1983, Heusser & Streeter 1980).

It is clear that several general adaptive systems could be separated by this time: (a) the territory south of the Santa Cruz River to Magellan's Strait; (b) north of the Santa Cruz River to the Chubut Basin; (c) the steppe region of the middle and lower Limay Basin; (d) the wooded region in Neuquén Province; (e) the north-east Atlantic coast; (f) the north of Isla Grande in Tierra del Fuego; (g) the Beagle Channel; and (h) the Mitre Peninsula. This list is by no means exhaustive. It is probable that some of these regions were occupied by more than one adaptive system at any one time, and a great variety of neighbouring situations should be considered, from symbiosis to competition. The concealed effects of the lack of empty space, boundary maintenance, inter-group competition, etc., should have produced a need for marked stylistic differentiation. Buffers which were utilized at least since t_4, as is the case with the marine resources, now appear to be accessible only to a few groups. It is no longer possible for a given group to maintain extended territories with hinterland and coastal zones. New social strategies must have been selected to cope with this situation. Communal meetings, directly related to rudimentary forms of exchange, or indirectly explained as part of ritual activity, appear as a feasible solution. In any case communal meetings constituted the locus for information exchange and the nexus for social organization. In Tierra del Fuego the appearance of stranded whales was the occasion for male initiation rites between the Selk'nam, meaning that territoriality was interrupted and that groups from the hinterland were allowed to attend. It is interesting to note that the situations of food surplus were the occasion for the periodic meetings, and as such they appear as a replacement for the buffers that are no longer available to the interior groups. Extended exchange networks must also have been of importance, but their analytical study is still waiting to be done.

In general this is the situation attested by the ethnographic record, which is in general agreement with a picture of the full use of all available space. Fuego-Patagonia appears as consolidated in a stabilization phase.

Conclusion

The history of the human peopling of Fuego-Patagonia is a short one. The archaeological record, when compared with a model of human slow movement, reflects a clear trend towards late saturation of space. It appears that adaptations developed in the region were well below carrying capacity, and the reasons for the final collapse of the systems are to be sought in their interactions with the new white colonization. This final phase began slowly in the 16th century, but was accelerated by the mid-19th century. By the beginning of the 20th century most of the ethnographic systems were destroyed, or were transformed beyond recognition.

The explanation of the peopling of this region must be a complex one, in which a variety of factors contributed in different proportions. The simple idea of people expanding throughout the Patagonian space from the very beginning now appears to be unwarranted on anthropological and ecological grounds. The Fuego-Patagonian archaeological record can no longer be used as an empirical reference for migration waves or displacements of huge masses of people.

References

Aguerre, A. 1979. Observaciones sobre la industria Toldense. *Sapiens* 3, 35–54.
Aschero, C. A. 1983. La secuencia de Piedra Parada a través de las campañas 1979–1981. *Arqueología del Chubut. El Valle de Piedra Parada*, C. A. Aschero (ed.), 91–103. Rawson.
Binford, L. R. 1963. 'Red Ochre' caches from the Michigan area: a possible case of cultural drift. *Southwestern Journal of Anthropology* 19, 89–108.
Bird, J. 1946. The archaeology of Patagonia. In *Handbook of South American Indians*, J. Steward (ed.), Vol. I, 17–24. Bureau of American Ethnology Bulletin 143. Washington.
Bórmida, M. 1953–1954. Los antiguos Patagones. Estudio de craneología. *Runa* VI (1–2), 5–96.
Borrero, L. A. 1984. Pleistocene extinctions in South America. In *Quaternary of South America and Antarctic Peninsula*, J. Rabassa (ed.), Vol. 2, 115–25. Rotterdam and Boston: Balkema.
Cardich, A., L. A. Cardich & A. Hajduk 1973. Secuencia arqueológica y cronología radiocarbónica de la cueva 3 de Los Toldos (Santa Cruz, Argentina). *Relaciones* VII, 85–123.
Cocilovo, J. A. 1981. *Estudio sobre discriminación y clasificación de poblaciones prehispánicas del N.O. Argentino*. Publicación Ocasional No. 36, Museo Nacional de Historia Natural, Santiago de Chile.
Cocilovo, J. A. & R. A. Guichón 1984. Relaciones y afinidades biológicas de la población prehistórica de Tierra del Fuego. Paper presented at the V Congreso de Ciencias Históricas Fueguinas, Ushuaia.
Crivelli-Montero, E. A. 1976–1980. La industria Casapedrense (Colección Menghin). *Runa* XIII(1–2), 35–57.
Curzio, D., E. A. Crivelli-Montero & M. J. Silveira 1982. La cueva Traful 1, Provincia de Neuquén, República Argentina. Informe preliminar. *VII Congreso Nacional de Arqueología* (Colonia del Sacramento) 36–45, Montevideo.
Gómez Otero, J. 1984. Posición estratigráfica particular de puntas de los períodos IV y V de Bird en el alero Potrok Aike (Santa Cruz). Paper presented at the Primeras Jornadas de Arqueología de la Patagonia, Trelew.
Gradín, C. J. 1980. Secuencias radiocarbónicas del Sur de la Patagonia Argentina. *Relaciones* XIV(1), 177–94.
Gradín, C. J., C. A. Aschero & A. Aguerre 1979. Arqueología del área Río Pinturas. *Relaciones* XIII, 183–227.
Heusser, C. J. & S. S. Streeter 1980. A temperature and precipitation record of the past 16 000 years in Southern Chile. *Science* 210, 1345–7.
Imbelloni, J. 1938. Tabla clasificatoria de los indios. Regiones biológicas y grupos raciales humanos de América. *Physis* 12, 229–49.

Jones, R. 1979. The fifth continent: problems concerning the human colonization of Australia. *Annual Review of Anthropology* **8**, 445–66.

Laming-Emperaire, A., D. Lavallée & R. Humbert 1972. Le site de Marazzi en Terre de Feu. *Objets et Mondes* **XII** (2), 225–44.

Lanata, J. L. n.d. Paleoenvironments and hunting zones at cueva Traful I. MS in the possession of the author.

Lewontin, R. C. 1978. Adaptation. *Scientific American* **239**(3), 156–69.

Markgraf, V. 1983. Late and Postglacial vegetational and paleoclimatic changes in subantarctic, temperate and arid environments in Argentina. *Palynology* **7**, 43–70.

Martin, P. S. 1973. The discovery of America. *Science* **179**, 969–74.

Massone, M. 1981. Arqueología de la región volcánica de Pali-Aike (Patagonia Meridional Chilena). *Anales del Instituto de la Patagonia* **12**, 95–124.

Massone, M. 1983. 10 400 años de colonización humana en Tierra del Fuego. *Infórmese* **14**, 24–32.

Orquera, L. A. & E. L. Piana 1983. Adaptaciones marítimas prehistóricas en el litoral magallánico-fueguino. *Relaciones* **XV**, 225–35.

Ortiz-Troncoso, O. 1985. Poblamiento temprano del litoral de Sudamérica. Paper presented at the 45 Congreso Internacional de Americanistas, Bogotá.

Piana, E. L. 1984. Arrinconamiento o adaptación en Tierra del Fuego. *Ensayos de Antropología Argentina*, 1–110. Buenos Aires: Editorial de Belgrano.

Schwartz, D. W. 1970. The postmigration culture: a base for archaeological inference. In *Reconstructing prehistoric Pueblo societies*, W. A. Longacre (ed.), 175–93. Albuquerque: The University of New Mexico Press.

Volman, T. P. 1984. Early prehistory of Southern Africa. In *Southern African prehistory and paleoenvironments*, R. G. Klein (ed.), 169–220. Rotterdam and Boston: Balkema.

19 *Cultural and ethnic processes in prehistory as seen through the evidence of archaeology and related disciplines*

P. M. DOLUKHANOV

Approaches to prehistoric ethnic processes

It becomes increasingly clear that the correlation of archaeological and linguistic evidence with that provided by physical anthropology and the environmental sciences is the only path leading to reliable reconstructions of the cultural and ethnic processes of the past. However, the merely mechanical correlation of operational and conceptual entities developed in each of these disciplines is methodologically unacceptable. In each case it is essential to evaluate the cognitive potential of the separate disciplines and the adequacy of the operational–conceptual entities in use. In other words, one should try to see clearly what may and what may not be expected from each of these subjects with regard to the question of palaeoethnicity.

Modern archaeology possesses an hierarchical model expressing the relationships between its basic operational entities. This model, which was explicitly put forward by Clarke (1968), includes as its basic unit the 'attribute', seen as a logically irreducible character acting as an independent variable within an artefact system. Entities such as 'artefact', 'type' and 'assemblage' are placed at higher levels of the model, and higher than all of these is the 'culture', which is seen as a 'polythetic set of specific and comprehensive artefact-type categories which consistently recur together in assemblages within a limited geographical area' (Clarke 1968, p. 232). This hierarchical model is widely accepted and with various modifications is used by numerous archaeologists in different countries.

Considerable controversies arise when attempts are made at the interpretation and explanation of these primarily empirical archaeological entities, and the archaeological culture is at the focal point of these controversies. An opinion that is widely held among archaeologists is that there exists a direct relationship between archaeological cultures, on the one hand, and linguistic and ethnic entities, on the other. There also exists a diametrically opposite view, according to which archaeological cultures are purely archaeological entities without any 'ethnic' content.

Multivariate analysis of some Upper Palaeolithic and Mesolithic lithic assemblages (Dolukhanov *et al.* 1980) showed that the concept of the archaeological culture was inadequate. In some cases the entities interpreted as 'cultures' resulted from the spatial distribution of productive activity directly related to environmental factors. In other cases 'cultures' implicitly involved elements of long-standing traditions that are proper to large social units.

In investigating ethnicity in prehistory, evaluation of the nature of culture change is especially important. For a long time migrations were generally seen as a main mechanism for the transmission of innovations, and as an important factor in culture change. This explanatory model was used especially often to explain the spread of an agricultural economy in Europe and Asia, and attempts were made to model it mathematically in terms of a population wave of advance.

Now the rôle of migration is being increasingly questioned (cf. Renfrew 1973). As far as the neolithization of Europe is concerned, there are reasons to hypothesize that the adoption of agricultural and stock-breeding activities by local Mesolithic populations as a result of acculturation was more important than the suggested migrations. This process was accompanied by the spread of agricultural and pastoral ideologies and symbols, as well as by new cultural and economic patterns. The resulting material manifestations are normally viewed as new cultures.

Modern comparative linguistics faces essentially similar problems. Languages showing regular phonetic and lexical correspondences sufficient for the reconstruction of meaningful units of a protolanguage are regarded as related. In practically all of these linguistic reconstructions migrations are seen as the only possible mechanism of the linguistic spread beyond the limits of a hypothetical 'homeland'. The problem is normally solved by means of a search for a suitable archaeological culture, or for an archaeologically substantiated population displacement. Since such archaeological entities are equivocal in explanatory terms (and archaeological cultures in particular), this procedure seems totally inadequate. Both historical and ethnographic records indicate the possibility of rapid change in language without any migratory processes. Spencer (1979, p. 199) reports that no less than 25% of the Dorobo hunter–gatherer group in eastern Africa altered their language during the 19th century or later, depending on their contacts with neighbouring farmers. In this respect it seems logical to suggest that the Indo-European (IE) protolanguage was originally a kind of *lingua franca* which spread in the process of neolithization and subsequent consolidation (cf. Renfrew 1973, p. 270, 1987).

Palaeoanthropological evidence plays an important part in the process of palaeoethnic reconstruction, but should be treated with extreme caution. On the basis of morphological features seen in skeletal material, anthropologists distinguish 'suprapopulation entities' seen by them as 'races of various taxonomic ranks' (Alexeyev 1978, p. 7). However, it should be pointed out that modern palaeoanthropology only distinguishes with any degree of certainty entities corresponding to major racial subdivisions: europoids, negroids, australoids and mongoloids. Difficulties arise when attempts are made at the identification of anthropological entities of lesser rank with either linguistic or ethnic groups. The main cause of these difficulties lies in the fact that the emergence of these different types of entity is the result of basically different factors. If it is social and cultural factors which are primarily responsible for the formation of both linguistic and ethnic entities, it is social–biological mechanisms which play a major rôle in the emergence of anthropological entities; population dynamics and genetic drift are very important here. Hence, an exact agreement between linguistic, ethnic and physical anthropological entities should be seen as a rare exception.

For the present study it is clearly essential to define what is meant by 'ethnic entity'. Bromley (1984, pp. 15–16) notes that the characteristic features of culture *sensu largo* are of great importance for ethnic differentiation. At the same time he stresses that such features as language, religion, folk art, customs, rituals, behaviour patterns, etc., should not be regarded as 'essential ethno-differentiating indices'. In Bromley's view economic and political factors play a major rôle in the emergence and functioning of ethnicities, whereas *peculiarities* of culture (and of language), as well as psyche, self-consciousness and self-denomination are of still greater importance (Bromley 1984, p. 17). However, I cannot share the view that language should be seen as a component of culture, despite agreeing in principle with the idea of determining ethnicity on the basis of a system of interrelated indices. Language is primarily a system for the storage and transmission of messages; it is an instrument of culture, the principal function of which is the social memory.

I see ethnicity in terms of population entities resulting primarily from the spatial distribution of productive activities and from adaptation to a specific environment; as a result of these factors they show peculiarities in social and economic patterns, in culture and in communication, as well as in corresponding symbolic systems.

Palaeolithic Europe

On the basis of the general considerations outlined above, we shall try to follow some of the main trends in the ethnic and cultural processes going on in western Eurasia during the Upper Pleistocene and Holocene.

According to existing geochronological evidence, the Upper Palaeolithic in Europe and the Middle East was developing roughly between 40 000 and 10 000 years ago, a timespan corresponding to three distinct geochronological units: the Middle Würm Interval (40 000–20 000 years ago), the Glacial Maximum (20 000–16 000 years ago) and the Late Glacial (16 000–10 000 years ago). It is now clear that the first unit, the Middle Würm Interval, was comparatively cool and moist, and included several minor colder and warmer climatic oscillations. The climate in the interval between 20 000 and 16 000 years ago was extremely cold and dry, primarily due to the southern position of the polar front. Numerous pollen-analytical data show that large areas of central and eastern Europe were taken up by periglacial steppe forests that were reasonably rich in biomass. In western and southern Europe forest vegetation was severely restricted; steppes prevailed in the uplands while rare pine forests covered lower mountain slopes (Renault-Miscovsky 1986). The marine microfossil record (Thunell 1979) shows that the winter temperature in the Aegean Sea about 18 000 years ago was 6°C cooler than at present and that the sea was 5% less saline than at present.

According to reliable palaeogeographical evidence, hyperarid conditions prevailed in northern Africa during the interval 'entre la fin des écoulements du Pleistocène moyen et le début de ceux du Pleistocène supérieur' (Alimen 1982, p. 47). A study of the fluctuations in the level of Lake Tchad reveals a regression linked to the climatic desiccation which separated the transgressions of 40 000–20 000 and 13 000 years ago.

Palaeobotanical evidence concerning the climatic situation in the Near East is less homogeneous. Leroi-Gourhan's (1981) data seem to indicate cold and dry conditions which coincided with the regression of the snow-line in the mountains around 22 000–20 000 years ago. At about the same time (c. 20 000 years ago) there occurred a regression of the Dead Sea and Lake Tiberias (Farrand 1971, p. 542), as well as lakes in the southwest Rub' Al Khali (McCure 1978) and in the Konya Plain (Roberts et al. 1979).

The timespan corresponding to the Last Glacial Maximum in Europe saw an uneven distribution of the *Homo sapiens* population, divided into a variety of Upper Palaeolithic cultural groups. On the basis of Gamble's (1986) study one may distinguish two major Upper Palaeolithic provinces in Europe at this time, a northern and a southern one. The first of these consists of the upper Danube Basin, in southern Germany, Austria and Czechoslovakia; southern Poland; and the upper Dniester, upper middle Dnieper, middle Don and the upper Volga, up to the extreme northeastern corner of Europe in the Mezen' and Pechora river basins.

The Upper Palaeolithic sites in this area date from Würm III and the first half of Würm IV (the Glacial Maximum), when their number increased. However, during the Last Glacial, Upper Palaeolithic sites vanished from this province almost completely. The economy of these sites was based on the hunting of large herbivores – mammoth, woolly rhinoceros, bison, horse, red deer and reindeer – and there are indications of a complex settlement pattern including both cold-season and warm-season occupations of different sizes and ranks (Soffer 1985).

The southern province included southern and western Europe, the core of which is represented by the Upper Palaeolithic cave-sites of the Dordogne, the Pyrénées and Cantabria. It has been demonstrated that at least some of these sites were occupied all the year round, and the species exploited included ibex, reindeer and others, including shellfish. Like the northern province, this area was also characterized by a marked increase in population over the level of the Middle Palaeolithic. The rest of Europe was poorly populated: there was practically no population in the north European plain and there are only indications of seasonal occupations in the Apennines and the Balkans.

As far as northern Africa is concerned, there seems to be a prolonged population gap between the Mousterian and Aterian sites of Würm I and II and the appearance of the Ibero-maurusian, which coincided with the Late Glacial climatic amelioration of *c*. 12 000 years ago.

In the Near East the number of Upper Palaeolithic sites is markedly smaller than for the Mousterian. For example, only seven Upper Palaeolithic cave-sites are known from the mountains north of Jerusalem, whereas 18 Mousterian ones are known. The Upper Palaeolithic sites are normally smaller than the Mousterian and no open-air sites have been discovered (Ronen 1975).

In the Caucasus, where Mousterian sites are known from various parts of the mountain country, including some at elevations greater than 2000 m, the Upper Palaeolithic population was restricted to western Georgia and the Black Sea coastal zone. This area, which included the mountains bordering Colchis, which is rich in floral and faunal relict species from the Tertiary, was probably the only area suitable for habitation. The density of cave-sites, the majority of which belong to the developed Upper Palaeolithic, was much higher than at any other period of the Palaeolithic (Meshveliani 1986).

On purely typological grounds it seems possible to show that the Upper Palaeolithic of Transcaucasia and the Near East is close to the southern European province, including the scarcely populated Balkans and Apennines. If this were the case, then one may distinguish two still larger provinces, one including the Mediterranean basin *sensu grosso* and the second eastern Europe, from the upper Danube to the Pechora. However, it should be emphasized that each of the two provinces includes several 'cultures', 'culture groups' or 'technocomplexes' as distinguished by various authors.

It is tempting to see in these two provinces archaeological manifestations of two pre-Indo-European linguistic groups: the Finno-Ugrian and Basque-Caucasian.

An identification of the late Palaeolithic in eastern Europe with a pre-Finno-Ugrian-speaking population is not new. On the basis of the modern distribution of pine, birch and alder (common words in all of the Uralian languages) Laszlo (1961) put forward the hypothesis that the Late Glacial Swiderian culture corresponded to the pre-Uralian communities. However, Laszlo's arguments cannot be considered valid; the wide distribution of pine and birch in the Late Glacial makes such a correlation absurd. Furthermore, alder appeared only later. Nevertheless, the identification of pre-Uralian speakers with the eastern (northern or periglacial) province of the Upper Palaeolithic may be substantiated by a different set of arguments (Dolukhanov 1986).

The problem of the Basque-Caucasian linguistic relationship has been considered for a very long time. On the basis of numerous lexical similarities, Bouda (1949) wrote: 'es ist klar zu erkennen, dass Baskische sowohl mit Südkaukasischen, als auch mit Nordkaukasischen sehr enge sprachliche Beziehungen hat, so dass man berechtigt ist von der Euskaro-kaukasischen Sprachgruppe zu reden'. However, several of the affinities proposed by Bouda have been severely criticized by Klimov (1963). On the other hand, Zytsar' (1955) takes a more moderate position when he writes that the kinship of Basque and Caucasian remains hypothetical.

The hypothesis of a Mediterranean substratum put forward by Hubschmid (1966, p. 89) seems to be highly promising with regard to the explanation of the linguistic situation in the area in prehistoric times:

> in älterer Zeit wurden im Mittelmeergebiet . . . zu mindesten zwei Sprachfamilien angehörten: dem *Eurafrikanischen* (als ältester fussbarer Sprachschicht im Westen) und dem *Hispano-Kaukasischen*. Beide Schichten lebten im Baskischen weiter. . . . Später sind tyrrhenische und vielleicht noch andere Völker, deren Sprache mit dem Baskischen entfernt verwandt sein oder (als Substrat) hispano-kaukasische Elemente enthalten könnte, nach dem Westen gefahren.

In my view the Upper Palaeolithic Mediterranean province, which stretched from Franco-Cantabria in the west to western Transcaucasia in the east, represents the only possible archaeological manifestation of a 'Mediterranean substratum' *sensu* Hubschmid. This substratum probably consisted of a great number of structurally and lexically related languages and dialects, the majority of which are lost, although it is possible that at least several of the written languages of the Ancient Near East (Elamite, Hurrian, Urartian, Hattite or proto-Hittite) belonged to the same substratum. Their relationship to the Caucasian languages has been generally acknowledged (Diakonoff 1967). On the other hand, Zytsar' (1955, pp. 62–3) notes affinities of these languages with the Basque language.

Finally, one should stress the fact that certain linguists have noted similarities in syntax between the Basque language, on the one hand, and the Uralian languages, on the other (Hubschmid 1966, p. 40). This similarity may result from structural affinities of the languages belonging to the two Upper Palaeolithic provinces of western Eurasia.

The origins of agriculture

The introduction of agriculture was the most important achievement of prehistoric people. The spread of the agricultural economy was accompanied by profound changes in the social, subsistence and cultural patterns of the population groups, including an increase in the rate of population growth.

One of the main peculiarities of the evolving food-producing epoch was an intensification of intertribal relationships which included both the ideological and material spheres. This process may be seen in the widespread diffusion of technological knowledge and of newly emerged agricultural and pastoral cults, as well as in the distribution of such materials as obsidian (Renfrew *et al.* 1966).

It may be suggested that such multifaceted contacts would have involved the existence of a *lingua franca*, which could have provided a means of intertribal communication. The proto-Indo-European language could have performed such a function.

The problem of the Indo-European homeland is one of the oldest in both comparative linguistics and prehistoric archaeology. In several publications Gimbutas (for example, Gimbutas 1963, 1965) has identified the first Indo-Europeans with the 'Kurgan People' (the middle Pit Grave culture) in the northern Pontic area, who then spread to the Balkans, Transylvania, central Europe, northern Europe, the Caucasus and the Near East, including northern central Anatolia, in the late 3rd to early 2nd millennium BC. I would suggest that these movements (on a small scale) occurred at a late stage in the development of the Indo-European-speaking groups.

Gamkrelidze & Ivanov (1984) have recently advanced a new hypothesis concerning the origin of the Indo-Europeans. On the basis of the newly elaborated consonantal pattern of proto-Indo-European, the semantic analysis of the reconstructed lexical system and affinities with proto-Semitic, South Caucasian and several ancient Near Eastern languages, they have concluded that the hypothetical Indo-European homeland existed in the 5th millennium BC in an area of eastern Anatolia, northern Mesopotamia and the southern Caucasus. We propose to accept the bulk of the arguments put forward by Gamkrelidze and Ivanov and to relate the 'homeland' to the establishment of the first settled agriculturalists in the Near East in the 8th and 7th millennia BC (cf. Renfrew 1987).

Proto-Indo-European probably originally belonged to a small agricultural tribe, but for unknown reasons was widely accepted as an intertribal *lingua franca* by early agricultural communities. Expanding with the spread of the farming economy, it became interlinked with the native languages, and underwent the divergence and devolution which finally resulted in the emergence of modern Indo-European languages. The key factor in the dispersal of these languages was the spread of the new subsistence, social and cultural patterns, and only to a very limited extent the migration of human groups.

Archaeological investigations indicate the trends in the economic and cultural development of the early farming communities of the Near and Middle East. In the course of the 6th millennium BC there occurred a general shift to the north. Large urban-like centres (e.g. Çatal Hüyük) evolved on the central Anatolian plateau, while in the Zagros foothills one may note the emergence of trends leading to the appearance of such large cultural units as the Hassunan and Samarran. This early cultural consolidation reached its peak in the Halaf horizon, characterized by the spread of the same pottery motifs and distinctive architectural styles over a vast area. The emergence of these cultural units was essentially a trans-ethnic phenomenon achieved by means of the extensive exchange of cultural information; its prerequisite was the existence of a common information medium, i.e. a common Indo-European language.

By the middle of the 6th millennium BC early agricultural settlements had evolved in the intermontane Transcaucasian (Kura and Araxes) depressions. They made up a distinct cultural unit, showing some links with the contemporary farming cultures of the Near East. This circumstance, as well as the absence of any relationships with the local substratum, enables it to be suggested that the Caucasian communities of this period were at least familiar with Indo-European dialects. At the same time, in western Georgia and along the Pontic coast, Neolithic groups whose material culture had affinities with the local Mesolithic and Epipalaeolithic continued to exist. One may suspect that these groups belonged to Caucasian-speaking communities.

The same period also sees the spread of the farming economy to the west, to the Balkan peninsula, and to the east, as far as the fringes of the Iranian plateau and the northern and southern piedmonts of the Kopet Dag mountains. All of the areas mentioned, as well as others situated further to the east, in the Indus river basin (Mehrgarh) show multifaceted relationships which may be regarded as indicating an early penetration of Indo-European dialects.

In the course of the 4th and 3rd millennia BC the climate of much of the Old World became cooler and drier, considerably diminishing agricultural potential in the areas of early farming. The adaptive mechanisms which were developed in response to this included an intensification of agriculture, involving the use of irrigation in a number of cases; the development of trans-humant herding; a rapid expansion of the metallurgy and mining industry; and an intensification of cultural and commercial links. One of the more remarkable manifestations of these phenomena was the Kuro-Araxian culture, which lasted from the end of the 4th to the end of the 3rd millennium BC. It was characterized by a uniformity in pottery and in other elements of material culture and spread over the whole of Transcaucasia and beyond, as far as northeastern Iran (Geoy Tepe and Yanik Tepe) and into Palestine (Khirbet Kerak; Mellaart 1960). It may be seen as a classic example of a trans-ethnic cultural phenomenon, including Caucasian, Semitic and other elements, apart from Indo-European ones. There is reason to believe that the earliest Caucasian and Semitic links of proto-Indo-European belong to this period.

The ecological crisis caused by the growing aridity became more acute in the second half of the 3rd millennium BC, resulting in a decline in agricultural productivity and increased competition. One of the important consequences of this situation was the breaking up of trans-ethnic entities and the emergence of more-ethnically related cultural units. It has been noted (Despres 1975, pp. 2–3) that the initiation and maintenance of ethnic boundaries are generally related to factors dependent on competition for economic resources.

Equally important was the accelerated social stratification – the elevation of the military élite and of local rulers as indicated by 'royal tombs' such as those at Majkop, Trialeti, Alaca Huyuk and Horoztepe. The Trialeti culture of the first half of the 2nd millennium BC in eastern Georgia features all of the elements of the developed chiefdom social pattern (Kuftin 1941, Japaridze 1973). It is important to stress that similar cultural elements were developing independently within such entities as this, without large-scale migration, although there were intensive cultural and trade contacts, particularly in the sphere of prestige items.

Political tension caused by the competition for scarce resources led to repeated military confrontations between ethnic groups, which are manifested in the levels of destruction often noticeable in archaeological records of this time (e.g. the burnt shrine of Beycesultan XVIIa, c. 2800 BC, or the destruction of Troy IIa, c. 2300 BC). The various economic, social and political manifestations apparent at this time, such as the emergence of the pastoral Pit Grave cultures in the North Pontic steppes, the appearance of ethnically based chiefdoms, and the repeated cross-cultural contacts and hostilities, should all be seen as interrelated phenomena, responses to an ecologically prompted socio-economic crisis. These processes occurred predominantly within the Indo-European speaking environment long ago established in the area.

The argument above seems to be contradicted by the comparatively late appearance of Indo-European names in written records, which are first mentioned in the documents of the Assyrian trade colony at Kanesh, c. 1940–1840 BC. The earliest written languages in use in the early oriental states were non-Indo-European: Sumerian, Elamite, Hattian, Hurrian-Urartian and Semitic (Akkadian). However, the explanation lies in the multi-ethnic character of early oriental state societies. It could well be the case that the ruling élite served by the written documents was ethnically alien to the bulk of the local population. The élite groups may well have originated from the substrate elements where Caucasian-affiliated languages were in use.

Conclusion

This chapter has sketched out some of the possibilities for the relationship between archaeological and linguistic entities in western Eurasia during a long span of prehistory. It has emphasized general long-term continuity in the linguistic provinces of the area, going back into the Palaeolithic in some cases. Such an emphasis is a natural corollary of the suggestion that the appearance and spread of proto-Indo-European languages is associated with the spread of agriculture, a view for which, as we have seen, there is now a considerable amount of evidence (cf. Renfrew 1987).

The social, economic, cultural, linguistic and ethnic processes prevalent over the long period discussed in this chapter were by no means constant in nature. It has been one of the main aims of this contribution to demonstrate that the traditional approach which links linguistic diffusion with the migration of ethnic groups is simplistic. Language can change without the movement of groups of people, whereas the nature of linguistic and ethnic processes varies a great deal according to the nature of the social and economic context. The interactions which characterized the multi-ethnic civilizations of the ancient Near East were very different from those of Palaeolithic hunter–gatherers, and were themselves not constant, but responded to the changing pattern of ecological pressures on the prevailing socio-economic system. Only an awareness of the range of possibilities and a sensitivity to the nature of the theoretical concepts and the limitations of the various disciplines which have an interest in past ethnic processes will lead to progress in this field.

References

Alexeyev, V. P. 1978. *Paleontropologiya zemnogo shara i formirovanie chelovecheskih ras*. Moscow: Nauka.
Alimen, M. H. 1982. Le Sahara: grande zone désertique nord-africaine. *Striae* **17**, 35–51.
Bouda, K. 1949. *Baskisch–kaukasische Etymologien*. Heidelberg.
Bromley, Y. 1984. *Theoretical ethnography*. Moscow: Nauka.
Clarke, D. L. 1968. *Analytical archaeology*. London: Methuen.
Despres, L. A. 1975. Introduction. In *Ethnicity and resource competition in plural societies*, L. A. Despres (ed.), 1–7. The Hague: Mouton.
Diakonoff, I. M. 1967. *Yazyki drevney peredney Azii*. Moscow: Nauka.
Dolukhanov, P. M. 1986. Natural environment and the Holocene settlement pattern in the north-western part of the USSR. *Fennoscandia archaeologica* **III**, 3–16.
Dolukhanov, P. M., J. K. Kozlowski & S. K. Kozlowski 1980. *Multivariate analysis of upper Palaeolithic and Mesolithic stone assemblages* (Prace Archeologiczne 30). Warsaw and Cracow: Panstwowe Wydawnictwo Naukowe.
Farrand, W. R. 1971. Late quaternary palaeoclimates of the Eastern Mediterranean area. In *The late Cenozoic glacial ages*, K. Turekian (ed.), 529–64. New Haven: Yale University Press.
Gamble, C. 1986. *The Palaeolithic settlement of Europe*. Cambridge: Cambridge University Press.
Gamkrelidze, T. V. & V. V. Ivanov 1984. *Indoevropeiskii yazyk i indoevropeicy*. Tbilisi: Izdatel'stvo Tbilisskego Universiteta.
Gimbutas, M. 1963. The Indo-Europeans: archaeological problems. *American Anthropologist* **65**, 815–36.
Gimbutas, M. 1965. The relative chronology of neolithic and chalcolithic cultures in Eastern Europe north of the Balkan peninsula and the Black Sea. In *Chronologies in Old World archaeology*, R. W. Ehrich (ed.), 459–75. Chicago: University of Chicago Press.
Hubschmid, J. 1966. *Mediterranische Substrate mit besonderer Berücksichtigung der baskischen und west-östlichen Sprachbeziehungen*. Bern.
Japaridze, O. M. 1973. The Trialeti culture in the light of the latest discoveries and

its relation to anterior Asia and the Aegean Sea. *Actes du VIIIe Congrès International des Sciences Pre- et Protohistoriques*, Vol. 3, 39–44. Belgrade.

Klimov, G. A. 1963. Ob etimologicheskoi metodike Karla Boudy. In *Etimologia* O. N. Trubachev (ed.), 268–74. Moscow: Nauka.

Kuftin, B. A. 1941. *Arheologicheskie raskopi v Trialeti*. Izdatel'stvo Akademiya Nauk, Grus. SSSR.

Laszlo, G. 1961. *Ostrotetetunk legkorabi szakaszai*. Budapest.

Leroi-Gourhan, A. 1981. Diagrammes polliniques des sites archéologiques au Moyen-Orient. In *Beiträge zur Umweltgeschichte des Vordernes Orients*, 121–33.

McCure, H. A. 1978. Ar Rub' Al Khali. In *Quaternary in Saudi Arabia*, J. G. Zoetl & S. S. Sayari (eds), 252–63. Wien: Springer.

Mellaart, J. 1960. *The Chalcolithic and Early Bronze Ages in the Near East and Anatolia*. Beirut: Khayats.

Meshveliani, T. 1986. O rannom etape vorhnego palaeolita Zapadnoi Gruzii. In *Arheologicheskie Inyskaniya*, 109–24. Tbilisi.

Renault-Miskovsky, J. 1986. Relations entre les spectres archéo-polliniques et les oscillations climatiques entre 12 500 et le maximum glaciaire. *Bulletin de l'Association Française des Etudes Quaternaires* **1/2**, 56–62.

Renfrew, C. 1973. Problems in the general correlation of archaeological and linguistic strata in prehistoric Greece. In *Bronze Age migrations in the Aegean*, R. A. Crossland & A. Birchall (eds), 263–75. London: Duckworth.

Renfrew, C. 1987. *Archaeology and language: the puzzle of Indo-European origins*. London: Jonathan Cape.

Renfrew, C., J. E. Dixon & J. R. Cann 1966. Obsidian and early cultural contact in the Near East. *Proceedings of the Prehistoric Society* **22**, 37–58.

Roberts, N., O. Erol & T. de Meester 1979. Radiocarbon chronology of Late Pleistocene Konya lake. *Nature* **281**, 662.

Ronen, A. 1975. The Palaeolithic archaeology and chronology of Israel. In *Problems in prehistory: North Africa and the Levant*, F. Wendorf & A. B. Marks (eds), 249–72. Dallas: Southern Methodist University Press.

Soffer, O. 1985. *The Upper Palaeolithic of the central Russian plain*. Orlando: Academic Press.

Spencer, P. 1979. Three types of ethnic interaction among Maasai-speaking people in East Africa. In *Space, hierarchy and society*, B. Burnham & J. Kingsbury (eds), 195–204. Oxford: British Archaeological Reports.

Thunell, R. C. 1979. The Eastern Mediterranean Sea during the last glacial maximum at 18 000 years BP. *Quaternary Research* **11**, 353–72.

Zytsar', Y. V. 1955. O rodstve baskskogo yazyka s kavkazskimi. *Voprosy yazykoznaniya* **5**, 52–64.

20 *Research with style: a case study from Australian rock art*

NATALIE R. FRANKLIN

The analysis of stylistic variation has been the concern of archaeologists for many years. The literature dealing with the term 'style' is extensive but often muddled, failing to draw distinctions between various coexistent models and definitions. Generally there has been a failure to distinguish between the broad quality 'style', and particular manifestations of that quality on prehistoric artefacts. This chapter is concerned with an investigation into a particular set of data – a sequence of styles in Australian prehistoric rock art. It therefore considers style as a particular manifestation of a 'highly specific and characteristic manner of doing something' (Sackett 1977, p. 370), or a particular effect produced on an artefact, which is peculiar to a specific time and place.

Style in these terms, along with *function*, has been used in two distinct models which explain artefactual variation. The models may be described as follows.

> *Model 1.* Style resides in particular sorts of artefacts which have a social rather than a practical function (for example, Beals *et al.* 1977). Part of this view is the widespread impression in ceramic studies that style is restricted to decoration, and does not reside in the shape of a pot, which is generally held to have only a practical function (for example, Childe cited in Trigger 1980).
>
> *Model 2.* Style resides in all sorts of artefacts, from ceramics to stone tools to prehistoric pictures, along with other qualities such as function. There may be more style and less function in some artefacts than others, and vice versa (for example, Dunnell 1978, Plog 1983, Sackett 1973, 1982).

Difficulties are frequently encountered in recognizing and differentiating these two aspects – style and function – from each other.

Style as a measure of social interaction and social boundaries

Whallon (1968, p. 126) has stated the two basic assumptions of the model which Plog (1983) labelled the 'social interaction' theory of stylistic variation:

1. . . . style has many aspects and levels of behaviour which may be analytically distinguished and measured. Many of these aspects of style are not intuitively obvious, and each aspect of stylistic behaviour may demand a separate and different method of analysis.

2. . . . the nature of the diffusion of stylistic ideas and practices both within and between communities will be determined by the nature of interaction among artisans. The aspect of style concerned, the rate of diffusion, and the directions and limits of diffusion, will be conditioned by the kind, frequency and channelling of interaction among the producers of the stylistic material.

Thus, in the social interaction model of style, two aspects have been stressed in attempts to infer the characteristics of prehistoric social organization.

(a)   The similarity between stylistic attributes in different areas of a site or at different sites within a region is measured, and is used in the second aspect.

(b)   The higher the stylistic similarity between sites and the lower the degree of stylistic homogeneity within sites are, the greater will be the interaction between social units (Plog 1980). This is actually a tenet which is used as a basis for the analysis of social interaction by measuring stylistic variation.

Use of these two aspects is apparent in many ceramic studies in the USA (Flannery 1976), and such an approach has been labelled 'ceramic sociology' (Sackett 1977). Within *pueblos*, residential wards where certain design elements clustered were believed to indicate the location of specific matri-lineages, since ceramic analyses were based on the assumption that women were the recent prehistoric potters, and that in matrilocal societies prefer-ences for particular designs would be passed on from grandmother to mother to daughter, and so on. One such study analysed stylistic behaviour in Arikara ceramics (Deetz 1965, cited in Whallon 1968).

Style has also been used to measure *social boundaries*, and as such has assumed two distinct forms. In the first style is a conscious statement of group solidarity or identity, expressed in items of material culture. It has a distinct referent, which is a particular social group. This form has been described by Wiessner (1983) as 'Emblemic style', represented by, for example, flags or emblems that transmit a message of group identity to a defined target population. Its function is to mark deliberately the boundaries and territories of a particular social group. As such it would form a clear-cut, discrete distribution.

At the unconscious level style relates to the individual's perception of the world from a culturally shaped perspective (Conkey 1978). I have labelled this form 'Stochastic style' (Franklin 1986), whereby each cultural trait may have its own pattern of diffusion and variation. Each trait has the potential to reveal style, and should be examined and analysed separately, which may or may not result in some traits revealing similar distribution patterns. However, we must start with the assumption that each attribute will reveal its own pattern of variation. An example is given below to support this contention, illustrating how different cultural features reveal different distributions within recent Australian prehistory. The notion that cultural traits may form their own patterns of distribution and variation parallels the theory of the polythetic distribution of cultural assemblages (Clarke 1978, fig. 67), where specific artefact-types reveal irregular distribution areas which overlap to varying degrees, with each artefact-type forming its own pattern of distribution. As occurs with polythetic cultural assemblages, Stochastic styles would only occasionally coincide with ethnographic boundaries of some sort.

Stochastic styles are randomly changing, since there are no influences which encourage change in one direction only, in the way that increasing efficiency in function lends direction to the evolution of functional artefact-types. However, the initial change from one style to another might not be random; as, for example, with the change from the Panaramitee style to the Simple Figurative styles in Australian rock art, which is discussed below. Stochastic styles can form several different types of distribution, ranging from clinal, with their frequency of occurrence declining gradually in any particular direction across space, to random, to even a discrete, distinct distribution like that which has been noted for Emblemic styles.

The notion that stochastic stylistic traits operate outside conscious formal boundaries is not new in archaeology. 'Cultural drift' (L. R. Binford 1963), for example, sees a stochastic process of incremental change in design habits over time and space, of which the artisans themselves are unconscious. In this context Sackett's (1982, 1986) 'isochrestic style' should also be considered. According to this concept, style is 'passive' in the sense that the properties which may serve as 'ethnic signalling' are not the result of self-conscious behaviour on the part of the artisans concerned, a view which has parallels with the Stochastic approach. In the 'isochrestic' approach, style exists wherever artisans make specific and consistent choices among the equally viable alternative means of achieving a given functional form, so style should reside in and be sought between artefacts of the same function. However, a translation of this idea to other fields of enquiry cannot be upheld. For example, in the analysis of rock art it would mean that style should be sought within depictions of the same function, i.e. within the same 'subjects' or 'motifs'. So, it is the way in which motifs are produced or depicted and not that they are depicted at all which is significant to the analysis of style. However, it will become apparent from the exploration of Australian rock art styles presented below that the motif itself, as well as the way in which it is depicted, may very well reflect a 'cultural choice' on the part of the producer, and therefore be significant in the analysis of style. Thus, the 'isochrestic' view finds a parallel with the 'stochastic' approach in that style is held to be the result of unconscious behaviour on the part of the artisan, but diverges in the idea that style should be sought between artefacts of the same function.

Given that two types of styles, Stochastic and Emblemic, have been identified, can both be recognized within archaeological data? It is probable that Emblemic styles occurred in the past, but their existence within the archaeological record cannot be positively ascertained, since the archaeologist cannot know whether a discrete distribution pattern indicates the existence and distribution of a particular social group or not, which is a necessary assumption behind Emblemic styles. However, use of Stochastic styles avoids this problem, since it recognizes that styles have their own patterns of variation and distribution, which do not necessarily coincide with a particular social group.

The work of Clarke (1978) and Hodder (1978) also indicates the greater archaeological usefulness of Stochastic styles. Clarke (1978) realized the problem of correlating the different hierarchical aspects of material culture with those of linguistics, social organization and genetics. He made the following important observations (Clarke 1978, p. 365):

> The complexities of the problem of equating archaeological entities with social, linguistic and racial groupings rapidly becomes apparent. There is no *a priori* reason why the different aspects should equate exactly one with another . . . simple and naive equation of these differently based entities is not possible and is demonstrably false, but lack of exact correlation between the entities does not mean that there is no correlation whatsoever – it simply emphasizes the complexity of the relationship.

The difficulty of isolating correlations is understandable in view of the fact that all of these entities are 'arbitrary horizons of unspecified definition' (Clarke 1978, pp. 366–7).

Ethnographic work undertaken by Hodder (1978) in the Baringo district of western Kenya found that the tribal groups studied were each characterized by distinctive styles of dress, especially ear decoration, and distributions of such items of material culture as basket drinking cups, wooden eating bowls and shields indicated clear breaks at the tribal boundaries. However, despite the fact that each group maintained distinct styles and customs, individuals were permitted to move across tribal borders and, on marriage into another tribe, usually changed their dress accordingly. So, although distinct styles can be discerned within the material culture of the Baringo district, distinct, sealed tribes cannot. It is clear from this analysis that even though material culture does not relate to social interaction, it very clearly relates to tribal boundaries as markers of self-conscious identity groups. The cultural items mentioned above would thus constitute examples of Emblemic styles. Although archaeologically each item may have been recognizable as such, since they would have formed discrete distributions, the movement of people and their adoption of another tribe's customs and styles would not have been. Thus, as Wiessner (1983) has observed, Emblemic styles convey information about the existence of groups or boundaries, not about the degree of interaction across or within them. However, in this instance there is also the possibility that the clear-cut distribution pattern revealed by the material culture might have been (wrongly) interpreted by the archaeologist as a manifestation of Stochastic styles.

The concept of Stochastic styles therefore appears to be of greater use in the analysis of archaeological remains, since it acknowledges the complexity of relationships between different classes of archaeological evidence. It does not assume what 'causes' the styles, i.e. Emblemic styles assume that particular 'tribes' or other social groups are responsible for the artefactual variation observed. Although it is true that the concept of Emblemic styles also points to archaeological investigation of whether a particular style is acting in an Emblemic fashion, i.e. revealing a discrete distribution and uniformity within the realm in which it functions, the 'cause' for the variation and distribution observed cannot be recognized archaeologically as a distinct social group.

Stochastic versus Emblemic: a case study

Maynard (1979, pp. 91–2) has presented a simple synthesis of prehistoric pictures in Australia:

> . . . there are within the whole corpus of Australian rock art, three major identifiable styles which can be placed in a relative sequence . . . . I have called the three major units, in the order in which I believe them to have been used in Australia, Panaramitee style, Simple Figurative styles, and Complex Figurative styles.

Maynard's styles are described as follows.

The Panaramitee style

This uses pecked engravings of macropod and bird tracks, human foot-prints, circles, dots, crescents, spirals, radiate designs and only a small proportion of figurative motifs other than tracks. The forms of the motifs consist of bands, thick outlines and solid figures. Such engravings reveal a pancontinental distribution, and are found over a large area of South and Central Australia, in western New South Wales, at Ingaladdi in the Northern Territory, in the Laura area of Cape York Peninsula, in the Mt Isa region of northwestern Queensland, in Tasmania, and at a site on the Scott River in the south-west of Western Australia (Fig. 20.1). The most significant feature of the sites in South and Central Australia and western New South Wales is the consistency of the relative proportions of motifs (Edwards 1966, 1971).

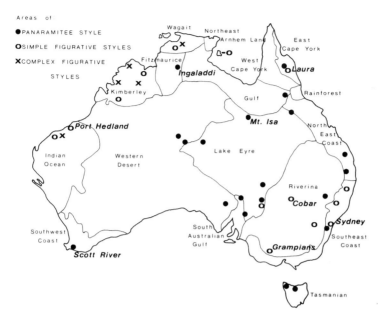

Figure 20.1   Map of Australia, showing the distribution of rock art styles (after Maynard 1979) compared with culture areas (after Peterson 1976), and the locations of sites mentioned in the text.

By contrast, engravings of this nature found in other regions of Australia do not reveal the same proportions of different motifs, but since they display identical techniques, forms and range of motifs, they too are included within the Panaramitee style (Maynard 1979).

Simple Figurative styles

These use figurative motifs, in engraved or painted, solid or outline form. Decorative details, although rare, consist of stripes, bars, dots, and the like, as infill, and different colours used for the outlining of painted solid figures. Motifs usually consist of simplified silhouettes of human and animal models. Maynard (1979, p. 99) claims:

> Most portrayals are strongly standardized. Human beings are depicted frontally, animals and birds in profile, snakes and lizards from above. Normally only the minimum visual requirements for recognition of the figure are fulfilled by the shape of the figure.

Animal tracks, although they occur in the Simple Figurative styles, are not as dominant as they are in the Panaramitee style. The Simple Figurative, like

Complex Figurative styles, is a large and generalized category consisting of a number of regional bodies of rock art which have the common stylistic characteristics described above. Simple Figurative styles occur around the northwestern, northern and eastern edges of Australia, as well as in western New South Wales, which constitute the furthest inland examples (Fig. 20.1).

Complex Figurative styles

These are extremely diverse, but 'their common characteristic, and that which distinguishes them from Simple Figurative styles, is that they are, in some respect, more sophisticated than crudely naturalistic' (Maynard 1979, p. 100). They are found exclusively in coastal regions of the northwestern corner of the continent, and examples are the Mimi and X-ray paintings of the Arnhem Land escarpment, the Bradshaw and Wandjina figures of the Kimberley region, and the engraved 'Kurangara' style found at certain sites in the Pilbara (Maynard 1979, Fig. 20.1).

Maynard proposed this sequence of rock art styles as an hypothesis to be tested and further discussed, not as 'a statement of proved fact . . . used to explain other facts' (Maynard 1979, p. 109). However, little work has yet been done within Australia to test the validity of this model.

To test Maynard's assumption that there are different styles within the entity 'Simple Figurative', several multivariate analyses were undertaken. One such example examined five regions of Simple Figurative art – the Sydney–Hawkesbury district (McMah 1965) and Port Hedland (McCarthy 1962) rock engravings; and the Laura (Trezise 1971), Cobar Pediplain (McCarthy 1976, Gunn 1983a) and Grampians (Gunn 1983b) rock paintings. The art from each region was described in terms of the classificatory scheme for Australian rock art proposed by Maynard (1977).

In this system each figure is described in terms of traits selected from five levels – Technique, Form, Motif, Size and Character. Following Maynard (1977), Form is defined as the visual organization of the marks making up a figure, whereas Character consists of those features which stand out in any way from 'photographic reality' (ibid., p. 398). This classificatory system relates to Maynard's definition of style, in that 'The style of a group of figures is the sum total of a small number of traits selected from each of the five descriptive levels' (ibid., p. 399).

In the multivariate analysis the data took the form of counts of traits selected from the first three descriptive levels – Technique, Form and Motif. Size was inconsistently recorded in the monographs used, whereas Character was considered to be more appropriate to the description of individual motifs than to the style of a whole assemblage.

The five regions under investigation were compared with each other through Correspondence Analysis (Bolviken et al. 1982). The results indicated that the Simple Figurative consists of a number of different styles, although there are some similarities between the regions in which the styles

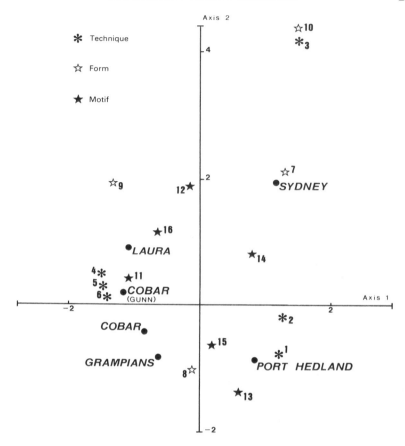

Figure 20.2 Correspondence analysis of five Simple Figurative assemblages from Australian rock art. The two axes account for 76% of the variation within the sample. Variables: 1, abraded; 2, pecked; 3, pecked-and-abraded; 4, stencilled; 5, imprinted; 6, painted; 7, outline, no infill; 8, solid; 9, outline, checkerboard infill; 10, continuous line, partially encloses space; 11, people; 12, macropods; 13, tracks; 14, fish, sea mammals, invertebrates, reptiles; 15, artefacts and objects; 16, others – birds, plants, indeterminates.

occur (Fig. 20.2). For example, Port Hedland and Sydney are similar in terms of technique (engraving) and motif (fish, sea mammals, invertebrates and reptiles), although they also differ in terms of other motifs, with Port Hedland having more tracks and artefacts and objects, and lacking macropods. These two sets of engravings are contrasted with the other three areas which have paintings. Differences also occur between these three painting regions, in that Laura has a predominance of macropods and birds, plants and indeterminates that have checkerboard infill, and the Grampians, where the motifs are solid, has none of these motifs and more tracks. Cobar reveals both similarities and differences to Laura and the Grampians. There were few variables common to all areas, which illustrates the broad nature of the similarities between the various styles of the Simple Figurative. These similarities are much less than those between the different regions of the Panaramitee style. Despite similarities, the differences between the five regions are marked and confirm Maynard's (1979) classification of them as distinct styles within the Simple Figurative.

If the concept of 'Emblemic styles' is employed, then one is *obliged* to conclude that the different styles are the result of individual 'tribes' or other rigidly defined social groups. However, in Australia it is clearly demonstrable that there is no one-to-one correlation between art styles and any other Aboriginal group as defined by the ethnography. White & O'Connell (1982) have noted that coherent recognizable clusters have not been derived from attempts to correlate such cultural features as art styles, languages, artefact forms, legends, or social and ritual practices. For example, in the highlands of southeastern Queensland, three culture areas, Northeast, Riverina and Lake Eyre, which are based on drainage basins (Peterson 1976), join, and yet, in terms of language, rock art style and communication networks as defined by the ethnography, the highlands form a distinct area in their own right (White & O'Connell 1982, Fig. 20.1). So, since different, distinct clusters cannot be recognized within different classes of material evidence for the recent past, we have little hope of recognizing such clusters in prehistory.

It is also apparent that certain kinds of 'stylistically and technologically similar archaeological data' (White & O'Connell 1982, p. 102) occur over larger areas than are occupied by any Aboriginal group. This phenomenon is exemplified in Australia by the Panaramitee style, which reveals a pancontinental distribution, and thus conforms to several of Peterson's (1976) culture areas (Fig. 20.1). Edwards (1971) has made some important observations regarding four 'constant features' of Panaramitee style engraving sites, such as their proximity to regular water supplies, their association with occupation sites, their advanced weathering and heavy patination, and consistent relative proportions of motifs. He states (*ibid.*, p. 363):

> It seems significant that this pattern cuts across the multiple divisions of customs, language, artefacts, and decorative and cave art recorded in these same areas.

So, in this case it is inappropriate to interpret the variation within Australian rock art in terms of the concept of Emblemic styles. Archaeologically, 'Emblemic style' is difficult to demonstrate. Use of the concept is only possible when the ethnographic context of the material under investigation is known.

However, if the concept of 'Stochastic styles' is employed, one is not forced to make conclusions that fit into predetermined 'pigeon-holes'.

Instead, one is able to delve more deeply into the archaeological meaning of the results obtained.

For example, one may ask: does such a change from homogeneity throughout Australia to diversity and regionalization, as documented by the change from the Panaramitee style to the Simple Figurative styles, imply social change? It would appear to do so, in that this explanation has been proposed to account for the supposed 'intensification' which occurred within Australia during the middle to late Holocene (Lourandos 1983, Morwood 1984). These changes include not only the introduction of the Simple Figurative styles (Morwood 1984, White 1984), but also: a major increase in site numbers and artefact densities (Hughes & Lampert 1982, Morwood 1984); movement of people into areas which hitherto had little or no occupation (Flood 1980, Ross 1981); the exploitation of new resources (Beaton 1982, Flood 1980, Lourandos 1983) and the introduction of the 'small tool tradition' (Morwood 1984, White & O'Connell 1982).

Social change has also been suggested to account for changes in European prehistory. S. R. Binford (1968) has noted a contrast between the absence of stylistic differences in the Acheulean and the presence of *style clines* in the Mousterian and *style zones* in the Upper Palaeolithic, and implies that some sort of social change has occurred to result in the increasing visibility of style zones in the archaeological record. She (*ibid.*, p. 275) states:

> The function of style is thought to be a means of either group or individual identification with a product or class of products.

Similarly, Gamble (1982, p. 105) observes:

> By concentrating upon a class of non-utilitarian display items, my intention has been to show that the significance of style lies in the possibilities that its investigation opens up for the study of palaeolithic social change.

He has noted that the homogeneity and pan-European distribution of the Upper Palaeolithic Venus figurines, his 'class of non-utilitarian display items', contrasts with the more localized occurrence of cave art.

It is probable that the change in Australia from the more homogeneous Panaramitee *style* to the heterogeneous Simple Figurative *styles* has implications in terms of social change, although what sort of change this entails is difficult to ascertain at present, and must await the results of future research.

It may also be profitable to view the change from the Panaramitee to Simple Figurative in terms of a decrease in the extent of social interaction and communication. As noted above, stylistic similarity between sites, as has been observed for the Panaramitee style, may imply a high degree of interaction, whereas differences in style between sites, as occurs in the Simple Figurative, may imply the opposite.

However, it should be stressed that the 'social interaction' theory of stylistic variation is just one way in which Australian rock art styles might be interpreted. There are examples in the literature which contradict the assertion that a high level of stylistic similarity implies interaction and a low level lack of interaction. As discussed above, in the Baringo district there are differences in the styles of the material culture items belonging to the different tribes, yet there is a high level of social interaction across the tribal boundaries (Hodder 1978).

References

Beals, R. L. H. Hoijer & A. R. Beals 1977. *An introduction to anthropology*. New York: Macmillan.

Beaton, J. M. 1982. Fire and water: aspects of Australian Aboriginal management of Cycads. *Archaeology in Oceania* **17**, 51–8.

Binford, L. R. 1963. 'Red Ochre' caches from the Michigan area: a possible case of cultural drift. *Southwestern Journal of Anthropology* **19**, 89–108.

Binford, S. R. 1968. Ethnographic data and understanding the Pleistocene. In *Man the hunter*, R. B. Lee & I. DeVore (eds), 274–5. Chicago: Aldine.

Bolviken, E., E. Helskog, K. Helskog, I. M. Holm-Olsen, L. Solheim & R. Bertelsen. 1982. Correspondence Analysis: an alternative to Principal Components. *World Archaeology* **14**, 41–60.

Clarke, D. L. 1978. *Analytical archaeology*. London: Methuen.

Conkey, M. W. 1978. Style and information in cultural evolution: toward a predictive model for the Palaeolithic. In *Social archaeology: beyond subsistence and dating*, C. L. Redman, M. J. Bergman, E. Curtin, W. Y. Langhorne Jr, N. M. Versaggi & J. C. Wanser (eds), 61–85. New York: Academic Press.

Dunnell, R. C. 1978. Style and function: a fundamental dichotomy. *American Antiquity* **43**, 192–202.

Edwards, R. 1966. Comparative study of rock engravings in South and Central Australia. *Transactions of the Royal Society of South Australia* **90**, 33–8.

Edwards, R. 1971. Art and Aboriginal prehistory. In *Aboriginal man and environment in Australia*, D. J. Mulvaney & J. Golson (eds), 356–67. Canberra: Australian National University Press.

Flannery, K. V. 1976. Introduction to Chapter 9: analysis of stylistic variation within and between communities. In *The early Mesoamerican village*, K. V. Flannery (ed.), 251–4. New York: Academic Press.

Flood, J. 1980. *The moth hunters: Aboriginal prehistory of the Australian Alps*. Canberra: Australian Institute of Aboriginal Studies.

Franklin, N. R. 1986. Stochastic versus Emblemic: an archaeologically useful method for the analysis of style in Australian rock art. *Rock Art Research* **3** (in press).

Gamble, C. 1982. Interaction and alliance in Palaeolithic Society. *Man (New Series)* **17**, 92–107.

Gunn, R. G. 1983a. *Preliminary investigations of Aboriginal rock art sites in the Cobar area of western New South Wales*. Unpublished report to the National Parks and Wildlife Service, New South Wales.

Gunn, R. G. 1983b. *Aboriginal rock art in the Grampians*. Records of the Victoria Archaeological Survey 16. Melbourne: Government Printer.

Hodder, I. 1978. The maintenance of group identities in the Baringo district, western Kenya. In *Social organisation and settlement: contributions from anthropology, archae-*

ology and geography, D. Green, C. Haselgrove & M. Spriggs (eds), 47–73. Oxford: British Archaeological Reports International Series (Supplementary) 47.

Hughes, P. J. & R. J. Lampert. 1982. Prehistoric population change in southern coastal New South Wales. In *Coastal archaeology in eastern Australia: proceedings of the 1980 Valla conference on Australian prehistory*. S. Bowdler (ed.), 16–28. Canberra: Australian National University Press.

Lourandos, H. 1983. Intensification: a late Pleistocene–Holocene archaeological sequence from southwestern Victoria. *Archaeology in Oceania* **18**, 81–94.

McCarthy, F. D. 1962. The rock engravings at Port Hedland, northwestern Australia. *Kroeber Anthropological Society Papers* **26**, 1–73.

McCarthy, F. D. 1976. *Rock art of the Cobar Pediplain in central western New South Wales*. Canberra: Australian Institute of Aboriginal Studies.

McMah, L. 1965. *A quantitative analysis of the Aboriginal rock carvings in the district of Sydney and the Hawkesbury River*. BA thesis, Department of Anthropology, University of Sydney, Sydney, New South Wales, Australia.

Maynard, L. 1977. Classification and terminology in Australian rock art. In *Form in indigenous art: schematisation in the art of Aboriginal Australia and prehistoric Europe*, P. J. Ucko (ed.), 387–402. Canberra: Australian Institute of Aboriginal Studies.

Maynard, L. 1979. The archaeology of Australian Aboriginal art. In *Exploring the visual art of Oceania*, S. M. Mead (ed.), 83–110. Honolulu: The University Press of Hawaii.

Morwood, M. J. 1984. The prehistory of the Central Queensland Highlands. In *Advances in world archaeology*, Vol. 3, F. Wendorf & A. E. Close (eds), 325–81. New York: Academic Press.

Peterson, N. 1976. The natural and cultural areas of Aboriginal Australia: a preliminary analysis of population groupings with adaptive significance. In *Tribes and boundaries in Australia*, N. Peterson (ed.), 50–71. Canberra: Australian Institute of Aboriginal Studies.

Plog, S. 1980. *Stylistic variation in prehistoric ceramics: design analysis in the American Southwest*. Cambridge: Cambridge University Press.

Plog, S. 1983. Analysis of style in artefacts. *Annual Review of Anthropology* **12**, 125–42.

Ross, A. 1981. Holocene environments and prehistoric site patterning in the Victorian Mallee. *Archaeology in Oceania* **16**, 145–55.

Sackett, J. R. 1973. Style, function and artefact variability in Palaeolithic assemblages. In *The explanation of culture change: models in prehistory*, C. Renfrew (ed.), 317–25. London: Duckworth.

Sackett, J. R. 1977. The meaning of style in archaeology: a general model. *American Antiquity* **42**, 369–80.

Sackett, J. R. 1982. Approaches to style in lithic archaeology. *Journal of Anthropological Archaeology* **1**, 59–112.

Sackett, J. R. 1986. Isochrestism and style: a clarification. *Journal of Anthropological Archaeology* **5**, 266–77.

Trezise, P. J. 1971. *Rock art of southeast Cape York*. Canberra: Australian Institute of Aboriginal Studies.

Trigger, B. G. 1980. *Gordon Childe: revolutions in archaeology*. London: Thames & Hudson.

Whallon, R. 1968. Investigations of late prehistoric social organization in New York state. In *New perspectives in archaeology*, S. R. Binford & L. R. Binford (eds), 223–44. Chicago: Aldine.

White, J. P. 1984. Australian prehistory: time for a reassessment? *The Quarterly Review of Archaeology* **5**(1), 11.

White, J. P. & J. F. O'Connell 1982. *A prehistory of Australia, New Guinea and Sahul.* Sydney: Academic Press.

Wiessner, P. 1983. Style and information in Kalahari San projectile points. *American Antiquity* **48**, 253–76.

21 Steppe traditions and cultural assimilation of a nomadic people: the Cumanians in Hungary in the 13th–14th century

ANDRAS PÁLÓCZI-HORVÁTH

The Carpathian Basin, the western end of the Eurasian steppe, was the last station in the wandering of nomadic peoples several times in history. Though the development and consolidation of the central and eastern European states put a stop to major popular movements from the 10th century, different nomadic peoples arrived from the East on the Pontus steppe one after the other: the Petchenegs, Uzes and Cumanians. The culture of all of these peoples was of central Asian origin.

In the 1060s a new archaeological culture appeared west of the Volga: new finds, burial customs, costume and new artistic remains, the funeral sculptures known as *kamennaya baba* (Rasovskiĭ 1937–1938, Pletneva 1958, Fedorov-Davydov 1966, Pletneva 1974). This ethnocultural unit – identical with the culture of the Cumanian-Kipchak tribes – disintegrated during the Mongol invasion, as a result of wars and migration in the whole area when the Cumanian tribes dispersed. Some of them lived on under Mongol rule within the Golden Horde, other groups fled southwards and westwards, to Bulgaria, to Moldavia, to the Latin Empire of Constantinople, and to Hungary (Rásonyi 1970, pp. 22–4).

In 1239, under the leadership of khan *Kuthen* ('Kötän'), the reigning prince of the disintegrated Cumanian confederacy of tribes, about 60–80 000 Cumanian people moved into Hungary. This ethnic group of steppe origin differed in every respect (ethnic, language, religion, customs, material culture, economy, etc.) from the population of feudal Hungary, who had followed a Western-type development since the turn of the 10th–11th century. When they moved into Hungary, their economy was based on extensive animal husbandry, they lived in nomadic quarters, in tents, in yurts. Though their social structure was rather stratified, it was more archaic than contemporary Hungarian society. After 300 years the Cumanians' assimilation into the Hungarian society was finished; they were completely integrated. Since the 16th–17th century they have formed one of the largest ethnic groups of the Hungarian people.

Before the Cumanians some of the neighbouring steppe peoples had already moved into Hungary. They were welcomed by the Hungarian kingdom because of their military importance, as the eastern peoples – fighting with nomadic tactics – could do the light cavalry's duties (advance guard and rearguard); the light cavalry was one of the traditional troops of the royal army. The Cumanian auxiliary troops played an important rôle in the 13th century, when the Hungarian kingdom led campaigns to obtain the leading position in Central Europe. Later their importance decreased, but until the middle of the 14th century they represented a considerable military power. The notabilities (*principales, domini*) and nobles (*nobiles*) of the Cumanians had to do military service for the king and they enjoyed equal rights with the Hungarian noblemen in every respect (Gyárfás 1873, pp. 439–41).

In Hungary the history of the Cumanian ethnic group can be regarded as a process of assimilation.

1. According to the sources, the first generation led its own life undisturbed in Hungary. In a similar fashion to other foreign peoples the Cumanians obtained territorial autonomy and collective privileges (1279: *Cumanian law I and II*, Gyárfás 1873, pp. 432–5, 438–43). When the relations between Hungarian society and the pagan Cumanians became strained it became necessary to arrange Cumanian affairs constitutionally. King Ladislaus IV (1272–90) depended on the Cumanians' military power against the barons to put an end to feudal anarchy, and it rather deepened the internal conflicts. From 1279 the Cumanians' violent conversion and rapid settling caused permanent problems which could not be solved. In 1280 the malcontent Cumanians rebelled and were defeated by the king at the battle at Hód-lake. After that they fled the country eastwards, decreasing in numbers by one-third (Györffy 1963, p. 56).

2. After the death of King Ladislaus IV (1290) the conflicts between Hungarian and Cumanian society were not so sharp: the Cumanians adapted themselves to the life of the country, they could keep their autonomy and adopted Christianity only formally. Little is known about their internal relations; they arranged their administrative and juridical affairs within the clans without charters, consequently the process of assimilation cannot be followed up year by year by means of written sources. In the first half of the 14th century the clan system began to disintegrate and differentiation inside Cumanian society accelerated. For a time the noble stratum was the primary preserver of the traditions, but later, in the middle of the 14th century, they wanted to resemble the Hungarian landed nobility. They expropriated the clan estates and wanted to create feudal private properties (Kring 1932, pp. 54–7, Pálóczi-Horváth 1975, pp. 322–5). At the same time the free common people were growing poor and some of them became servants (Györffy 1953, pp. 250–1).

3. In the 14th century the economy and society of the Cumanians

changed. The inner conditions for feudalization were good in the middle of the 14th century and the process of assimilation came to a turning-point. From this time more data can also be found in charters. In the second half of the 14th century nomadic winter shanties were replaced by permanent villages. The clan system changed into a territorial system: administrative–juridical seats (*sedes*) were established (Györffy 1953, pp. 248–50, 273–5). At the same time Christianity was really adopted and was an important stimulus to assimilation. For a while the Pope exempted the converted people from paying the tithe (Theiner 1859, p. 797, Mályusz 1971, p. 278). By the end of the 14th century the Cumanian light cavalry lost its military importance and noblemen's military duty changed into taxation (Györffy 1953, pp. 263, 266).

4. In the 15th–16th century the integration of the Cumanian ethnic group into Hungarian society was complete. The non-nobles were preserved in free peasant status by their collective privileges. The last stage of assimilation took place at the time of the Osmanli-Turk conquest, after 1541. When the population fled from the territories destroyed by the campaigns, the ethnical mingling intensified. By this time the Cumanian language had died out. Before it, for 200 years, there was bilingualism, the parallel use of the Cumanian and Hungarian language.

Several investigations have been carried out by different disciplines in order to reconstruct the process of Cumanian assimilation. Recent archaeological researches in particular have produced important results (Selmeczi 1971, Pálóczi-Horváth 1973, 1975). It has been possible to demonstrate the survival of the traditional steppe culture for 100–150 years and to distinguish the different stages of assimilation. The process of settling down and giving up the nomadic way of life is indicated by the new archaeological data. With the help of the complex analysis of different sources and interdisciplinary researches the cultural assimilation process can be examined in detail. The history of this ethnic group shows how a medieval nomadic people gave up its traditions, settled down and at the same time could preserve some elements of their original culture which distinguished them from the other groups of the Hungarian people.

Grave goods

In the Christian culture of medieval Hungary a rather small assemblage can be distinguished, associated with the Cumanians who insisted on their steppe traditions and followed a nomadic way of life. This assemblage comes from the tribal–clan–aristocracy's isolated graves following pagan ritual; the majority of the grave goods are characteristic of the steppe culture of the 13th century and are objects of Eastern origin. At the end of the 19th century it was suggested that the material of the auxiliary peoples who moved from the East should be traceable among the medieval Hungarian finds. It was hypothesized that the finds concerned were the weapons of Eastern origin of the 11th–14th centuries, together with horse equipment coming from burials of men with horses (Nagy 1893a, b). This assumption has been proved correct by the new finds which have come to light since then and by analyses of the steppe peoples. The characteristic grave goods of the Cumanian male graves are weapons and related objects (helmet, chain-mail, arrowheads, sabre, etc.), and the iron parts of the horse equipment (bit, sircingle buckle and stirrup). It can be observed that certain finds were the most modern types of the steppe culture, e.g. bits, stirrups and light-cavalry armour (Pálóczi-Horváth 1969, 1980, pp. 417–19).

Other sources, the wall-paintings and miniatures from the 13th and 14th centuries also indicate that the Cumanians brought into Hungary the newest forms of steppe costume, armament and horse equipment, innovations of Central-Asian origin, and that these types came into fashion in the Hungarian culture; for example, the saddle, reflex bow, felt-high-cap, etc. (László 1940, Kőhalmi 1974, pp. 642–4, Pálóczi-Horváth 1980, pp. 409–19). According to the written sources Cumanian costume greatly influenced Hungarian fashion at the end of the 13th and in the first half of the 14th century (Szentpétery 1937, p. 473, Pálóczi-Horváth 1980, p. 408). Although the pagan burials with rich grave goods ceased to exist at the beginning of the 14th century, the contemporary representations indicate that *the traditional Eastern costume survived until the beginning of the 15th century*; the Saint-Ladislaus legend with a representation of Cumanian warriors is a frequent subject of medieval Hungarian art. In the Middle Ages the costume is the expression of ethnic identity, one of the most traditional parts of Cumanian civilization.

There are finds of foreign origin in the Cumanian assemblage, which reached the steppe from the settled peoples by trade, tax or plunder, but these finds can be found among the first generation of Cumanians in Hungary as their own cultural elements and parts of their equipment: *Bánkút*, Chinese bronze mirror in a female grave (Banner 1931, pp. 195–8, Fodor 1972, pp. 225–33); *Kunszentmárton*, a double-edged sword with heraldic representation in a male grave (Selmeczi 1971, pp. 188–90).

The gold and silver gilt mount-decorated belts (*Kigyóspuszta, Csólyos* and *Felsőszentkirály*) are characteristic parts of the Cumanian assemblages, and played an important rôle in defining the find-group (Éri 1956). These belts are of Western type, and their analogies can be found in the 13th century in the costume of the knights; the motifs, representations and inscriptions of the mounts also refer to the culture of knighthood (Pálóczi-Horváth 1980, pp. 419–20). In Europe there are few similar and contemporary finds, consequently the definition of their origin is very difficult: there are South Italian products, French in style, among them, which reached Hungary by trade or through diplomatic relations in the second half of the 13th century. According to the royal account books, the Cumanian noblemen, especially the leaders of the royal light cavalry, often enjoyed grants and other presents; they may have got these belts as gifts from the prince (Pálóczi-Horváth 1982, pp. 95–101).

The silver jewellery from noble female graves is partly characteristic of the steppe costume (*Bánkút*, torques (Banner 1931, pp. 191–3); *Balotapuszta*, earring, head-dress of rings, torques (Pálóczi-Horváth 1980, pp. 422–4)), partly the products of a goldsmith's craft of Byzantine style (*Balotapuszta*, jewels with filigree decoration (Pálóczi-Horváth 1980, pp. 422); *Homok-Óvirághegy*, a thick necklace woven of silver (Selmeczi 1971, p. 189, Pálóczi-Horváth 1980, p. 421)). Possible sources of origin for these range from the Russian towns to Asia Minor and the Balkans, and they cannot be defined with absolute certainty; there are even analogies among the goldsmiths' works of the Hungarian Arpadian period (Kovács 1974, pp. 16–17). According to the historical data two hypotheses seem to be probable.

(a) The jewellery comes from a Balkan goldsmith's workshop. Very little is known about the Balkan centres, so they cannot be localized.

(b) There may have been a Cumanian goldsmith's workshop in the area of the Black Sea or on the Crimea, with Byzantine craftsmen working in it. Before the Mongol conquest such a workshop may have provided a large area with filigree silver objects, earrings, bracelets, and mounts which decorated the shirts, dress, high caps, etc. This latter hypothesis is supported by new research on the metalwork of the 13th–14th century in the Black Sea area and by a rich grave good belonging to a prince (*khan*) from the area of Zaporozh'e, from the first half of the 13th century (Kramarovskiĭ 1985, Magomedov & Orlov 1985).

Once they had moved into Hungary, the Cumanians lost their direct connections with the steppe culture after a while, but in the 14th century cemeteries some objects of eastern origin or superstitious customs connected with shamanistic belief can still be seen. The commoners' cemeteries of the 13th century were unknown for a long time, but research has recently revealed that the Cumanians were buried for centuries in the cemeteries of the villages which developed from the winter quarters, and that there is not a great difference between the burials of the pagans and those of later Christian Cumanian commoners with poor grave goods (Horváth 1978, pp. 123–4, Pálóczi-Horváth 1982, p. 103). There are only few authentic grave goods in the earliest layers of these cemeteries. Rich graves can be found again from the middle of the 14th century, indicating that the members of the noble stratum (*comes* and *capitaneus*) left their familiar burial places away from the settlements, gave up the important elements of the pagan rite (burial of horses, horse equipment and weapons) and were buried together with their people. By this time the metal parts of the jewellery, belts, dress were mostly Hungarian products showing that by the middle of the 14th century the Cumanians had already become connected with Hungarian internal trade (Pálóczi-Horváth 1982, p. 103). On the basis of the archaeological finds it can be seen that *in the 14th century the Cumanian culture became dual*. In Hungary the Anjou-age was the golden age of feudalism, and for the Cumanians it was the period of transformation when they had to give up the

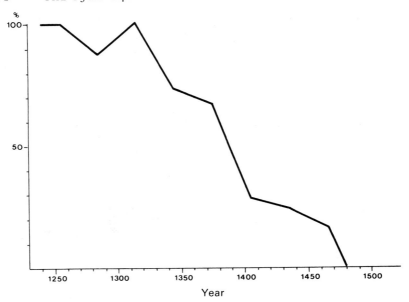

Figure 21.1   The change in Cumanian personal naming in the 13th–15th centuries.
The proportion of pagan personal names decreases gradually.

greater part of their traditions; for example, pagan and Christian elements
lived together in their *beliefs*.

These important cultural, linguistic and religious changes are indicated by
onomastic researches (Rásonyi 1967). From investigation of Cumanian personal names in charters it appears that the practice of giving first names
changed between 1360 and 1390: the pagan personal names, usually of
Turkish origin, disappeared from the sources and were replaced by Christian
first names (Fig. 21.1, Pálóczi-Horváth 1975, pp. 330–1). At the same time
personal names consisting of two parts also developed, when the former
Cumanian name as a distinction was used before the Christian name.

Settlements

When the programme of Cumanian archaeological research started at the
end of the 1960s it was obvious that *the plan had to be based on settlement
investigations*, as the traces of the noble stratum's graves could not be found.
These graves may have been low tumuli, and consequently they come to
light accidentally (Pálóczi-Horváth 1973, pp. 204–5). On the other hand, a
settlement reflects the everyday life and economic structure better than a
cemetery does.

King Béla IV (1235–1270) marked out the Cumanian settlement territory

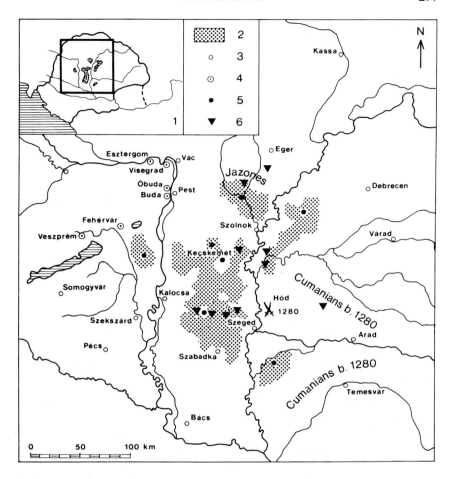

Figure 21.2 Cumanian settlement in Hungary in the 13th–14th century. 1, the Hungarian kingdom in the 13th–14th century; 2, the habitation area of the Cumanian clans and the Yass; 3, important Hungarian towns; 4, royal and queenly residences; 5, the centres of the Cumanian clans; 6, grave goods.

on the Great Hungarian Plain, on lands and royal estates which became depopulated during the Mongol invasion. The Cumanians divided their estates among clans. The habitation area of seven clans can be distinguished; it is about 8000 km² along the lowlands of the Danube and Tisza (Fig. 21.2, Pálóczi-Horváth 1975, pp. 319–27). In the Middle Ages Cumanian people lived in 100 villages and included the Iranian-speaking Yass (*Jazones*), who came from the Caucasus. In spite of the fact that most of the villages were destroyed during the Turkish wars at the end of the 16th century and during

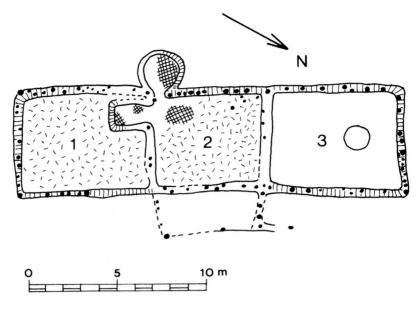

Figure 21.3   Ground plan of a house. Túrkeve-Móric, 15th century. 1, living
room; 2, kitchen; 3, pantry.

the 17th century, they can be localized and some of them were excavated.
According to the historical data, the place names and the archaeological
results *the Cumanian population may have lived in nomadic quarters for 100–120
years and began to settle down in the middle of the 14th century* (Pálóczi-Horváth
1975, pp. 329–33). The earliest layers of the open settlements can be dated to
the end of the 14th century. There is no archaeological evidence of the
nomadic winter quarters, but the cemeteries belonging to the villages existed
earlier than the permanent villages; consequently these cemeteries were
begun by the population of the winter quarters. The archaeological evidence
of the settlements of the 15th–16th centuries indicates a sedentary population
with a complex economy.

There are no important differences between the Cumanian and the
neighbouring contemporary Hungarian house-types, house-structures, personal belongings and implements. In the Cumanian settlements, as with
those on the Great Hungarian Plain, there were mud-walled houses with a
wooden structure and gabled roof; inside they had three rooms – a living
room, a kitchen and a pantry (Fig. 21.3). The fireplaces were modern, and
had two closed heating spaces: both – the outer clay oven and the stove in the
room – were heated from the kitchen, so the living room was free from
smoke and had a loft (Méri 1954, p. 146). This house-type is the antecedent
of the Middle-Hungarian house-type of modern times.

According to the archaeological results from some destroyed villages

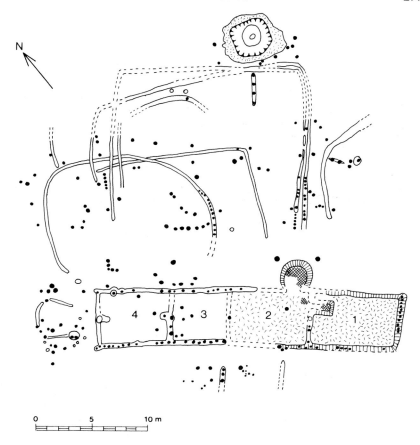

Figure 21.4   Ground plan of a toft. Lászlófalva-Szentkirály, 15th century. 1, living room; 2, kitchen; 3 and 4, pantry.

(*Túrkeve-Móric* – Méri 1954, *Karcag-Orgondaszentmiklós* – Selmeczi 1976, *Lászlófalva-Szentkirály* – excavation by the author) certain features of the 15th–16th century settlements are characteristic of the Cumanian ethnic group and can be traced back to the steppe traditions. For example, on the basis of the excavated animal bones, animal husbandry played a leading rôle in their economy (cattle, sheep, horse and pig), providing the basis of their subsistence, and it is reflected by the utensils and settlement structure. Usually the houses stand far from each other, the tofts are big, and there are buildings for animals near the houses. In medieval *Szentkirály* large open areas were enclosed behind the houses for the animals (Fig. 21.4). Such folds for extensive animal husbandry come to light only in Cumanian villages from this period; similar folds were used by Hungarian herdsmen in the

18th–19th century on the outer grazing lands. The archaeological work illustrates why the Cumanian settlements were called *szállás* (*descensus*) according to the medieval terminology, to distinguish them from the earlier Hungarian villages with other structures and a more intensive economy. It seems likely that further investigations will reveal other specific features of the Cumanian culture.

The medieval Christian state made every effort to convert and settle down the steppe peoples, but the process took more than a century. There were few changes in the first two phases of the assimilation process from the middle of the 13th century to the middle of the 14th century. In the third phase (in the second half of the 14th century) the process accelerated; over a period of 50 years important economic, social and cultural changes occurred and the Cumanian community became integrated into Hungarian society. Total ethnic and linguistic assimilation took a further 150–200 years. During this time their culture evolved a new structure as the evidence of a successful adaptation to Hungarian developments, but it was based on steppe traditions. The traces of these traditions are being investigated by archaeology.

References

Banner, J. 1931. A bánkúti lovassír. Das Reitergrab von Bánkút. *Dolgozatok* **7**, 187–204.

Éri, I. 1956. Adatok a kígyóspusztai csat értékeléséhez. Zur Frage der Schnalle von Kígyóspuszta. *Folia Archaeologica* **8**, 137–51.

Fedorov–Davydov, G. A. 1966. *Kochevniki Vostochnoĭ Evropy pod vlast'yu zolotoordynskikh khanov*. Moscow: Izdatel'stvo Moskovskogo Universiteta.

Fodor, I. 1972. Újabb adatok a bánkúti sír értékeléséhez. Further data to the evaluation of the Bánkút grave. *Folia Archaeologia* **23**, 223–42.

Gyárfás, I. 1873. *A jász-kúnok története (The history of the Cumanians and Yass*, Vol. 2: *Kr.u. 884–1301-ig. AD 884–1301)*. Kecskemét: Sziládi.

Györffy, G. 1953. A kunok feudalizálódása. (The feudalization of the Cumanians.) In *Tanulmányok a parasztság történetéhez Magyarországon a 14. században (Studies on the history of peasantry in Hungary in the 14th century)*, G. Székely (ed.), 248–75. Budapest: Akadémiai Kiadó.

Györffy, G. 1963. Magyarország népessége a honfoglalástól a XIV. század közepéig. (The population of Hungary from the conquest up to the middle of the XIVth century.) In *Magyarország történeti demográfiája (The historical demography of Hungary)*, J. Kovacsics (ed.), 45–53. Budapest: Közgazdasági Kiadó.

Horváth, F. 1978. Csengele középkori temploma. Die mittelalterliche Kirche in Csengele. *A Móra Ferenc Múzeum Évkönyve 1976–77*, **1**, 91–126.

Kovács, É. 1974. *Romanesque goldsmiths' art in Hungary*. Budapest: Corvina.

Kőhalmi, K. U. 1974. Die Bedeutung der Kulturgeschichte des Karpatenbeckens für die Erforschung der Kultur der zentralasiatischen Reiternomaden. In *Sprache, Geschichte und Kultur der altaischen Völker. Protokollband der XII. Tagung der Permanent International Altaistic Conference 1969 in Berlin*, G. Hazai & P. Zieme (eds). Akademie der Wissenschaften der DDR Zentralinstitut für Alte Geschichte und Archäologie: *Schriften zur Geschichte und Kultur des Alten Orients* **5**, 637–44.

Kramarovskiĭ, M. G. 1985. Serebro Levanta i khudozhestvennyi metall Severnogo Prichernomor'ya XIII–XV vekov (po materialam Kryma i Kavkaza). In *Khudozhestvennye pamyatniki i problemy kul'tury Vostoka*, V. G. Lukonin (ed.), 152–80. Leningrad: Iskusstvo.

Kring, M. 1932. Kun és jász társadalomelemek a középkorban. (The Cumanian and Yass social groups in the Middle Ages.) *Századok* **66**, 35–63, 169–88.

László, G. 1940. Adatok a kunok tegezéről. Beitrag zur Kenntnis des kumanischen Köchers. *Néprajzi Értesítő* **32**, 51–9.

Magomedov, B. V. & R. S. Orlov 1985. *Slavyane i Rus. Vystavka novykh arkheologicheskikh materialov k V Mezhdunarodnomu kongressu arkheologov-slavistov.* Prospekt, Akademiya Nauk Ukrainskoĭ SSR, Institut Arkheologii, Kiev: Naukova Dumka.

Mályusz, E. 1971. *Egyházi társadalom a középkori Magyarországon. (Ecclesiastical society in Medieval Hungary.)* Budapest: Akadémiai Kiadó.

Méri, I. 1954. Beszámoló a tiszalök-rázompusztai és túrkeve-mórici ásatások eredményéről. (Report on the results of the excavations at Tiszalök-Rázompuszta and Túrkeve-Móric.) *II. Archaeologiai Értesítő* **81**, 138–54.

Nagy, G. 1893a. A régi kunok temetkezése. (The burial customs of the Cumanians.) *Archaeologiai Értesítő* **13**, 105–17.

Nagy, G. 1893b. A magyarhoni lovassírok. (Horse-graves in Hungary.) *Archaeologiai Értesítő* **13**, 223–34.

Pálóczi-Horváth, A. 1969. A csólyosi kun sírlelet hadtörténeti vonatkozásai. Die kriegsgeschichtlichen Bezeihungen des kumanischen Grabfundes von Csólyos. *A Móra Ferenc Múzeum Évkönyve 1969*, **1**, 115–21.

Pálóczi-Horváth, A. 1973. Situation des recherches archéologiques sur les Comans en Hongrie. *Acta Orientalia Academiae Scientiarum Hungaricae* **27**, 201–9.

Pálóczi-Horváth, A. 1975. L'immigration et l'établissement des Comans en Hongrie. *Acta Orientalia Academiae Scientiarum Hungaricae* **29**, 313–33.

Pálóczi-Horváth, A. 1980. Le costume coman au moyen âge. *Acta Archaeologica Academiae Scientiarum Hungaricae* **32**, 403–27.

Pálóczi-Horváth, A. 1982. Régészeti adatok a kunok viseletéhez. Archäologische Angaben zur Tracht der Kumanen. *Archaeologiai Értesítő* **109**, 89–107.

Pletneva, S. A. 1958. Pechenegi, torki i polovcy v yuzhnorusskikh stepyakh. In *Trudy Volgo-Donskoi arkheologicheskoĭ ekspedicii, I. Materiali i issledovaniya po arkheologii SSSR* **62**, 151–226. Moscow and Leningrad: Nauka.

Pletneva, S. A. 1974. *Poloveckie kamennye izvayaniya.* Arkheologiya SSSR E4–2. Moscow: Nauka.

Rásonyi, L. 1967. Les anthroponymes comans de Hongrie. *Acta Orientalia Academiae Scientiarum Hungaricae* **20**, 135–49.

Rásonyi, L. 1970. Les Turcs non-islamisés en Occident (Pécénegues, Ouzes et Qiptchaks, et leurs rapports avec les Hongrois). *Philologiae Turcicae Fundamenta*, Vol. 3, First Part: *The Turks before Islamisation*. Wiesbaden: Steiner.

Rasovskiĭ, D. A. 1937–1938. Polovcy. III. Predely 'Polya polovetskago'. *Seminarium Kondakovianum* **9**, 71–85; **10**, 155–78.

Selmeczi, L. 1971. Angaben und Gesichtspunkte zur archäologischen Forschung nach den Kumanen im Komitat Szolnok. *A Móra Ferenc Múzeum Évkönyve 1971*, **2**, 187–97.

Selmeczi, L. 1976. The settlement structure of the Cumanian settlers in the Nagykunság. In *Hungaro-Turcica. Studies in honour of Julius Németh*, G. Káldy-Nagy (ed.), 255–62. Budapest: Akadémiai Kiadó.

Szentpétery, E. 1937. *Scriptores rerum Hungaricarum tempore ducum regumque stirpis Arpadianae Gestarum*, Vol. 1. Budapest.

Theiner, A. 1859. *Vetera monumenta historica Hungariam sacram illustrantia maximam partem nondum edita ex tabulariis Vaticanis deprompta, collecta ac serie chronologica disposita ab A. Theiner*, Vol. 1. Rome.

22 An ethnic change or a socio-economic one? The 5th and 6th centuries AD in the Polish lands

ZBIGNIEW KOBYLÍNSKI

Since at least the 19th century Polish historiography and archaeology have been engaged in a discussion concerning the original seat of the Slavs before the period of their great migrations in the 6th century AD and the emergence of their name in literary sources. From the very beginning of this discussion both autochthonic views (claiming that this seat was within the present Polish lands) and allochthonic ones (usually involving the identification of this seat east of present Polish territory) were voiced. Previous discussions of the linguistic evidence (summarized recently by Mańczak 1982) and historical sources (Łowmiański 1963, Machinski 1976, Kolendo 1981, Jażdżewski 1982, Hensel 1984) did not lead to a strong justification of any of the competing views. In this situation all the hopes have been laid on archaeology.

In the period immediately preceding the outbreak of World War II, when the discussion between Polish and German archaeologists acquired a political dimension, it seemed that the most important problem was the definition of the ethnicity of the Lusatian archaeological culture, which covered almost all of the Polish lands in the Bronze Age and the Early Iron Age. At present the centre of gravity of the discussion has moved to later times: to the explanation of sociocultural changes in the Polish lands at the decline of the Roman Empire and the beginning of the Early Medieval Period. This chapter presents the current state of the debate concerning these problems.

Two alternative views, both based on the same archaeological evidence, should be distinguished in this respect. According to the first view there was an absolute hiatus in the Polish lands in the second half of the 5th century and in the first half of the 6th century, i.e. there was social and cultural discontinuity, defined by the lack of archaeologically observable manifestations of human existence (Godłowski 1979, 1983, 1985). This discontinuity separated epochs which were totally different from each other in terms of the state of social development and in the field of culture. According to the other view, the 5th and 6th centuries were characterized by social and cultural continuity (Kostrzewski 1965, Hensel 1974, 1978, 1984, Jażdżewski 1959, 1982, Leciejewicz 1976) indicated by archaeologically observable manifestations of human existence, although relatively limited in quantity and quality.

These different interpretations of the meaning of the same facts indicate clearly the lack of uniform criteria for the interpretation of archaeological sources in terms of the continuity and discontinuity of the social systems that they reflect. Let me therefore briefly consider these problems.

In any given process, including a sociocultural process, continuity and discontinuity are inseparably interlinked, whereas the perception of them is related to the kind of changes of interest in the given case. Each process is characterized by the ever-present discontinuity of phenomena at the factual level accessible to direct observation, and the simultaneous relative continuity of the phenomena in terms of their essential characteristics. The continuity is 'relative', for, at a certain moment in the course of the process, the essence of the phenomenon observed can also change. A qualitatively new phenomenon can exhibit genetic continuity with respect to its predecessor, or no significant references, even when retaining functional continuity. The notions of identity and genetic continuity are subjective, because both the choice of characteristics observed and the evaluation of the degree of observed transformation at which the student still recognizes the relationship between phenomena as identity, are strongly influenced by the previously accepted theories on the nature of the phenomena in question.

In the case of complex systems, including interacting subsystems (as in a sociocultural system), the identification of continuity or discontinuity involves additional difficulties. A sociocultural system consists of subsystems operating at three ontological levels: (a) of the material base; (b) of biological human existence and social behaviour; and (c) of pure spiritual artefacts (Lipiec 1972, Chmielecki 1987). Obviously, all three levels are dynamically coupled with one another, so that, for example, almost every material artefact with a primarily utilitarian function also has a spiritual function. An obvious guarantee of the identity and preservation of the sociocultural system in the course of various processes occurring in it and around it would seem to be the biological continuity of the human population. Indeed, a break in this continuity causes the sociocultural system to become nonexistent. As the social sciences show, however, the continuity of the system is determined by the feeling of identity of the human population rather than its real identity (in an anthropological or linguistic sense). Social identity and continuity of a given group is conditioned by a phenomenon of ethnic consciousness (Zientara 1985) not necessarily related to common language or common history. Studies on the Germanic tribes of the late Roman period have shown that a tribe was a political organization involving elements of different origin and its ethnic distinctiveness was the result of a need to maintain unity (Wenskus 1961, Strzelczyk 1984).

This could mean that the question of the original seat of the Slavs is the result of a false assumption about the nature of ethnicity, influenced by modern notions of nationality. Arguably, the Slavs as a distinct ethos emerged just at that time when their name appeared in historical sources, because at that time their distinctiveness was noticed by outsiders. However, we should ask what was the process which led to the emergence of a uniform Slavic ethnicity at the beginning of the Early Medieval period in the Polish lands.

The most important problem in studying ethnicity in the light of archaeological evidence is the question of the existence of ethnospecific artefacts. It has been generally recognized that certain artefacts are some-times deliberately used as symbols of ethnic unity: these could be named ethnic idioms, or the artefacts of emblemic style (Wiessner 1983, Franklin, ch. 20, this volume). Others are only the results of some culturally deter-mined behaviour and can be named ethnic correlates. However, the identifi-cation of ethnic idioms and ethnic correlates in the archaeological evidence is subjective, and the territoriality of some artefacts and archaeologically visible forms of social behaviour is not necessarily related to the ethnic consciousness of the population studied. Most probably, those behavioural correlates which are not determined by a primarily techno–utilitarian func-tion should be considered as ethnospecific; however, even in this case we cannot be sure of their meaning because the identification of the primary function of a given artefact type is a projection of our image of past reality. Moreover, in the case of complex, polysemantic cultures (Lem 1968) some artefacts might be symbols of distinctiveness of smaller social units, rather than whole ethnic groups.

In beginning a more detailed analysis of the problem of possible ethnic continuity or change in the 5th and 6th centuries AD in the Polish lands we should therefore distinguish three aspects of continuity in a sociocultural system, and consider their archaeological visibility. They are settlement (population) continuity, cultural (stylistic) continuity and ethnic (conscious-ness) continuity. Since this ethnic factor is not observable archaeologically, it is possible to distinguish four situations theoretically occurring in the archaeological evidence (where S denotes settlement continuity, i.e. the determination of uninterrupted occupation of the same places, and C denotes continuity in cultural traits; later we will see how this continuity was understood in Polish archaeology):

	S	C
A	+	+
B	+	−
C	−	+
D	−	−

In each case ethnic continuity can either occur or be absent, whereas archaeologically it can be only inferred with some probability: high in cases A and C, lower in case B, and with hardly any or no probability in case D.

The notions of settlement and cultural continuity deserve some comment. Archaeological observation of any sociocultural process is discontinuous by definition. We can observe only a series of discrete states of the phenomenon being studied and compare the two which are closest together on the time axis. The course of the process between these points remains unknown. Thus, there is always the risk of observing at the later period a completely different community; for example, if there was a replacement of population at a given locality due to a migration. Such a community might well react against the preceding cultural tradition, contributing further to a discrepancy between these two sociocultural systems and their archaeologically tangible manifestations (cf. Wierzbicki 1976). This is why I consider case B as rather symptomatic of ethnic discontinuity. It therefore seems that the necessary requirement in the determination of settlement continuity is to identify 'mixed assemblages', combining the cultural features of both chronological states of the social system being studied. To the best of my knowledge (Kobyliński forthcoming) such assemblages have not been found so far in the Polish lands, although they are known from the Ukraine.

Next one should consider the archaeological indicators of the case denoted here as 'C'. Kostrzewski used to be one of the most devoted believers of continuity conceived in this way, whereas in recent times Jażdżewski and Leciejewicz have also supported the view. Jażdżewski (1982) for example, has written:

> the links are not limited to pottery (pots with egg-shaped and biconical bellies, bows, cups, vessels on partly hollow stems, roasters and small plate-like bowls), and to the way of making the pottery, but also include a large amount of basic metal (mainly iron) goods, (such as coulters, adzes, sickles, hammers, axes, cutting tools, scissors, spade fittings, knives, tweezers, keys, padlocks, spear and arrow heads), as well as rotating querns, building types and the characteristic burial ritual.

Apart from the fact that the similarities indicated by this eminent scholar apply in most categories to objects of a techno–utilitarian nature whose form was almost solely determined by their function and had no value for cultural differentiation, the assemblages of artefacts compared were chronologically distant from one another. Some arguments, as we will see later, were simply incorrect, but even if truly stated, such a cultural continuity would only be the continuity of some arbitrarily chosen cultural traits, not continuity of the whole cultural system.

Particular attention should be paid to possible continuity in those aspects of archaeologically visible cultural behaviour which are the potential correlates of ethnic consciousness. Arguably, the forms and decoration of clay vessels could be considered as examples of emblemic style, because pottery is both a field of production of fundamental importance for social existence, and is sufficiently flexible to provide a means of cultural manifestation.

All students agree that no later than the first half of the 5th century the large centres of pottery manufacture on the upper Vistula River and in Lower Silesia, which had made advanced 'grey' pottery, using the potter's wheel, stopped their production. However, a large number of archaeologists have attempted to demonstrate the existence of technological and stylistic links between the pottery of the late period of Roman influences and the pottery of the early stages of the early Middle Ages. These connections are supposed to be of two kinds. On the one hand, it has been repeatedly argued that Slavic pottery of the 6th century belonging to the so-called Prague type relates directly to the primitive 'kitchen'-ware of the late period of Roman influence (Jażdżewski 1958, Kostrzewski 1965, Hasegawa 1973, 1975). For Rusanova (1976) the identification of these links was of essential significance in her search for the origin of the early Slavic culture and the original seat of this people. However, as Godłowski (1979) has pointed out, even when it is assumed that these similarities are really significant, and are not accidental (which cannot be excluded in the case of simple plain pottery), such connections in terms of one element of archaeological culture cannot settle the question of cultural continuity. For Rusnova the vessel of the Prague type became a sort of symbol, the main and only indicator of the Slavic ethnos in material culture terms. This even led her to reject the Slavic nature of the Penkovka-type assemblages from the southern part of the Dnieper basin, when it is known from written sources that in the 6th century this region was inhabited by the Slavs.

Another aspect of the supposed connections between early medieval pottery and the pottery of the late period of Roman influence concerns the western part of Poland: Lower Silesia and the western part of Great Poland and southern Pomerania. Much has been said on the subject in Polish publications (for example, Kurnatowska 1981, Leciejewicz 1976). The latter stated:

> There is no doubt that in the 6th–7th centuries, at most sites in the Lowlands, pottery was produced by craftsmen using the potter's wheel. Some of the types, e.g. the bowls of Tornow-Klenica type, between the middle Elbe and the Warta River, or the early forms of the Feldberg type on both sides of the mouth of the Odra River, refer so distinctly to the late Roman period pottery in Silesia that it would be difficult not to discern a continuity of production skills.

Without rejecting the possibility of such references, it is necessary to point out that the groups of pottery vessels mentioned above do not represent the oldest medieval phase in the area in question. They were probably preceded by completely hand-made pottery of the Sukow-Dziedzice type in Pomerania, and the derivates of the Prague type in Lower Silesia. The chronology of these pottery groups is not stated precisely. According to some scholars, from the very beginning of the early Middle Ages wheel-made pottery was produced along with fully hand-made forms, and the opposite view is simply the result of an erroneous evolutionist approach, maintaining that a simpler form must always have preceded a more advanced one (recently: Żak 1985). At present it is impossible to solve this problem, and the discussion of it often acquires an emotional character. The acknowledgement or refutation of the existence of continuity in pottery forms and technology is a question of belief, rather than based on reliable scientific argument.

Unfortunately, the other evidence frequently cited to support the existence of cultural continuity is equally dubious. This is particularly the case with the alleged similarities in iron metallurgy (Leciejewicz 1976), which recent research (for example, Brzeziński 1983) indicates do not exist. In the late Roman period in the Polish lands there were large metallurgical centres and specialized production settlements, whereas at the beginning of the early Middle Ages iron was produced on a small domestic scale. The iron-firing furnace and chemical composition of the iron were also different.

Distinct differences can also be seen in the burial ritual of the two periods, although, in this respect, comparison is in vain, since the burial ritual of the older stage of the early Middle Ages is known only from a few cremation burials in urns. It can only be surmised that the basic type of burial ritual in the 6th century was connected to some rather indefinite form of cremation, involving the scattering of the burnt remains on the ground surface. It is often believed that the prototype of this form of burial ritual was the practice of burial with a cremation layer which was frequent in the late Roman period. In fact, as an argument against continuity it should be pointed out that all of the cemeteries of the late Roman period were abandoned about the middle of the 5th century. In contrast with the richly furnished graves of this period, the burials of the 6th century did not contain any furnishing at all (Zoll-Adamikowa 1975–1979).

The previous state of discussion, outlined above, on the problem of the cultural and ethnic continuity versus discontinuity in the Polish lands in the 5th and 6th centuries AD should be considered very unsatisfactory, because one of the alternative views is accepted simply on the basis of prior assumptions not based on any empirical data. A critical evaluation of this state of discussion led to the search for a category of archaeological sources which would be: (a) invariable with respect to depositional and post-depositional disturbances; (b) determined by factors of a cultural nature, i.e. ones which are indicators of cultural, or perhaps even ethnic, identity; (c) an important characteristic of the sociocultural system, and not merely one cultural trait. The use of space manifested in the spatial settlement structure, based on stable positions in sociocultural space, is arguably such a category. Multilevel settlement spatial structure seems to contain potentially both ethnic idioms and correlates, and at the same time is one of the most important characteristics of the whole system. Therefore, settlement structures were compared for two periods adjacent to each other on the time axis: the late Roman influenced period, between the 3rd century and the middle of the 5th century, and the older stage of the early Middle Ages, between the 6th century and the middle of the 8th century (Kobyliński, in press). Only the most important results of this analysis can be outlined here.

Most significantly, an essential difference was found between the two periods in terms of the model of settlement location in relation to the relief of the terrain and the soils accessible to the settlement inhabitants. The location of early medieval settlements appeared to be strongly determined by a tendency to ensure security to the inhabitants, whereas this factor was not significant in the preceding period. Another obvious difference was the emergence of strongholds in the late 6th century: fortified settlements, absent from the Polish lands in the period of Roman influences. Most probably, the emergence of fortified settlements, which were not inhabited permanently, was not the effect of social differentiation of previously uniform society. The hillforts of the 6th and 7th centuries seem to play an important rôle in social and religious ceremonies, being at the same time a visible symbol of group unity, maintaining the ethnic consciousness.

Distinct differences were also found in the settlement pattern at the semi-microlevel in the two periods. In several late Roman period settlements functionally differentiated features were found: the division of the settlement space into dwelling and service areas, and traces of buildings organized around a central empty space. None of these structural elements occurred in the model of spatial organization of the early Medieval settlement. Instead there were rather chaotic groupings of buildings, erected in rows rather than around a central place. Dwellings within the early Medieval settlement were less densely spaced than in the preceding period. Settlements were smaller, both in terms of space and number of dwellings, than the late Roman period settlements had been.

Essential differences were also found in the types of housing. None of the basic types of buildings from the late period of Roman influences was encountered within the early Medieval settlements. At the same time none of the basic types of dwellings in the older stages of the early Middle Ages had prototypes in the earlier period in this area. The most typical form of dwelling in the late Roman period was the overground rectangular post construction, whereas in the older stage of the early Medieval period two distinct types of buildings may be distinguished. In the southern and southeastern part of Poland we observe dwellings in the form of square subterranean huts with stone or clay ovens in one of the corners, usually the northeastern one. This type of dwelling is connected with assemblages of Prague-type pottery, and as a distinct cultural element occurs also in the Ukraine, Romania, Bulgaria, Yugoslavia, Czechoslovakia and the GDR (cf. Donat 1980). Godłowski (1979) showed that these two cultural traits (square huts and egg-shaped hand-made vessels), which cannot be dated earlier than the 6th century in the Polish lands, had analogies dated by metal artefacts at least a century earlier in the basins of the Boh, the Prut and Dniester River in the Ukraine (the 5th century or even the latter part of the 4th century). The identical nature of this form of dwelling over vast areas of central and southern Europe, and the clear chronological pattern of its occurrence, shows evidently that this building form was an ethnic idiom of the Slavs. However, the typical building form in the western, northern and central part of Poland in the 6th and 7th centuries is completely different from the square subterranean huts: it is an oval pit (about 2 × 3 m) slightly dug into the ground, most probably the subterranean part of an overground building of lightweight construction of unknown type. It is therefore evident that the groups connected with the square huts with stone ovens represent only part of the Slavic ethnos inhabiting Polish lands. Accordingly, a hypothesis was proposed that there were two crystallization centres of the early Medieval Slavic culture, one of which would have been in the Ukraine and the other in western Poland, where it would indicate the continuity of the late Roman period traditions (Zeman 1979, Kurnatowska 1981). Godłowski, who expressed the firm conviction that the Slavs came to the Polish lands only as a result of migration, no earlier than the second half of the 5th century, and probably even as late as the 6th century, discerned recently (Godłowski 1983) two directions of this migration: a southern one from the Ukraine, connected with the square huts, and a northern one, from Byelorussia. However, it is impossible to show a genetic link between the oval features in the Polish Lowlands and their alleged antecedents, either in the Polish lands or in Byelorussia.

The changes which occurred in the settlement structure between the late period of Roman influences and the early stage of the early Medieval period can be considered drastic. Should they be interpreted as ethnic changes, or, according to some scholars (for example, Żak 1985), as socio-economic changes caused by a breakdown in the previous system of productive relations and the formation of a new epoch based on a division of societies into classes? Personally, I would tend to support the first view, but at the same time I would argue that previous understandings of Slavic ethnic and cultural unity and the nature of its origin is misleading. In the light of the analysis of settlement structures at the beginning of the early Medieval period in the Polish lands, it seems that Slavic ethnic unity was formed relatively late, on the basis of several smaller groups, probably characterized by distinct ethnic consciousness. One of them, but not necessarily the most important one, came from the Ukraine; the origins and character of the others remain unknown.

References

Brzeziński, W. 1983. Zastosowanie urzadzeń ogniowych w gospodarce u schyłku starożytności i w poczatkach wczesnego średniowiecza na ziemiach Polski. PhD dissertation, Instytut Historii Kultury Materialnej PAN, Warsaw.

Chmielecki, A. 1987. Kultura duchowa: rozważania ontologiczne. In *Myśl przez pryzmat rzeczy*, Z. Kobyliński, B. Lichy & P. Urbańczyk (eds), in press.

Donat, P. 1980. *Haus, Hof und Dorf in Mitteleuropa vom 7.–12. Jahrhundert*. Berlin: Akademie Verlag.

Franklin, N. R. 1989. Research with style: a case study from Australian rock art. In *Archaeological approaches to cultural identity*, S. J. Shennan (ed.), ch. 20. London: Unwin Hyman.

Godłowski, K. 1979. *Z badań nad zagadnieniem rozprzestrzeniania se Słowian w V–VII w. n.e.* Kraków: UJ.

Godłowski, K. 1983. Zur Frage der Slawensitze vor der grossen Slawenwanderung im 6. Jahrhundert. *Settimane di studio del Centro italiano di studi sull'alto medioevo* **XXX**, Spoleto, 257–84.

Godłowski, K. 1985. *Przémiany kulturowe i osadnicze w południowej i środkowej Polsce w młodszym okresie przedrzymskim i w okresie rzymskim.* Wrocław: Ossolineum.

Hasegawa, J. 1973. *Z badań nad wczesnośredniowieczna ceramika zachodniosłowiańska.* Łódź: Ossolineum.

Hasegawa, J. 1975. Chronologia i rozprzestrzenienie ceramiki typu praskiego w Europie Srodkowej. *Prace i Materiały Muzeum Archeologicznego i Etnograficznego w Łodzi* **21**.

Hensel, W. 1974. *U źródeł Polski średniowiecznej.* Wrocław: Ossolineum.

Hensel, W. 1978. Zagadnienia etniczne. In *Prahistoria Ziem Polskich*, W. Hensel (ed.), Vol. 3, 197–204. Wrocław: Ossolineum.

Hensel, W. 1984. *Skad przyszli Słowianie.* Warsaw: SD.

Jażdżewski, K. 1958. Uwagi o chronologii zachodniosłowiańskiej ceramiki we wczesnym średniowieczu. *Przeglad Archeologiczny* **10**, 150–91.

Jażdżewski, K. 1959. Das gegenseitige Verhältnis slawischer und germanischer Elemente in Mitteleuropa seit dem Hunneneinfall bis zur awarischen Landnahme an der mittleren Donau. *Archaeologia Polona* **2**, 31–70.

Jażdżewski, K. 1982. Jak patrzeć na zasiedziałość i na rozprzestrzenienie Słowian w Europie Środkowej i Środkowo-Wschodniej w starożytności i w poczatkach wczesnego średniowiecza. *Prace i Materiały Muzeum Archeologicznego i Etnograficznego w Łodzi* **27**, 195–213.

Kobyliński, Z. forthcoming. *Struktury osadnicze na ziemiach polskich u schyłku starożytności i w poczatkach wczesnego średniowiecza.*

Kolendo, J. 1981. Zróda pisane w badaniach nad strefami kulturowymi i etnicznymi Europy środkowej w okresie rzymskim. In *Problemy kultury wielbarskiej*, T. Malinowski (ed.), 65–78. Słupsk: WSP.

Kostrzewski, J. 1965. *Zur Frage der Siedlungsstetigkeit in der Urgeschichte Polens von der Mitte des II. Jahrtausend v.u.Z. bis zum frühen Mittelalter.* Wrocław: Ossolineum.

Kurnatowska, Z. 1981. Główne kierunki rozwoju osadnictwa i kultury Słowian Połabskich. In *Słowiańszczyzna Połabska miedzy Niemcami a Polska*, J. Strzelczyk (ed.), 51–61. Poznań: UAM.

Leciejewicz, L. 1976. *Słowiańszczyzna zachodnia.* Wrocław: Ossolineum.

Lem, S. 1968. *Filozofia przypadku.* Kraków: Wydawnictwo Literackie.

Lipiec, J. 1972. *Podstawy ontologii społeczeństwa.* Warsaw: PWN.

Łowmiański, H. 1963. *Poczatki Polski*, Vol. 1. Warsaw: PWN.

Machinski, D. A. 1976. K voprosu o teritorii obitanya Slovyan v I–VI vekakh. *Arkheologicheski Sbornik* **17**, 82–100.

Mańczak, W. 1982. *Praojczyzna Słowian.* Wrocław: Ossolineum.

Rusanova, I. P. 1976. *Slovyanskie drevnosti VI–VII vv.* Moscow: Akademiya Nauk.

Strzelczyk, J. 1984. *Goci- legenda i rzeczywistość.* Warsaw: PIW.

Wenskus, R. 1961. *Stammesbildung und Verfassung.* Cologne & Graz: Böhlau.

Wierzbicki, Z. T. 1976. Metodologiczne rozważania o ponownych monografiach społeczności lokalnych. *Etnografia Polska* **20**, 35- 65.

Wiessner, P. 1983. Style and information in Kalahari San projectile points. *American Antiquity* **48**, 253–76.

Żak, J. 1985. O kontynuacji i dyskontynuacji społecznej i kulturowej na ziemiach nadodrzańskich i nadwiślańskich w V–V/VI w. n.e. *Folia Praehistorica Posnaniensia* **1**, 85–108.

Zeman, J. 1979. K problematice časne slovanske kultury ve stredni Evrope. *Pamatky Archeologicke* **70**, 113–30.

Zientara, B. 1985. *Świt narodów europejskich*. Warsaw: PIW.

Zoll-Adamikowa, 1975–1979. *Wczesnośredniowieczne cmentarzyska ciałopalne Słowian na obszarze Polski*, Vol. 1–2. Wrocław: Ossolineum.

Index

academic parochialism 72–3
accommodation and resistance, strategies of 86
acculturation 76, 85
actualistic research 98–102, 107–8
Agorsah, E. K. 138
adaptation systems 242–6, 247, 252, 254–6, 259, 260–4, 274
agriculture 197, 242, 248–51, 254, 255
  and ceremony 146–8
  spread of 268, 272–5
  swidden 125
Aguado, F. P. 143
alliance
  economic 79, 83, 86, 88, 229
  inter-ethnic 245
  marriage 151, 152, 237, 247, 281
  political 143, 144
anthropology 3, 35, 160, 171, 234
  cultural 49
  physical 8, 267, 268, see also inference
apartheid 68
archaeological cultures 17–18, 25, 43, 44, 59–60, 62–4, 186, 189–92, 196, 220–9, 271, 273, 291, 303
  concept of 13, 23, 45, 46
  as entities 5, 11, 157, 267–8
  and enthnicity 42, 47, 210
  political significance of 6–7, 62
archaeology and politics 50, 66–74, 138 see also nationalism
  appropriation of the past 78
archaeology in public education 50
Argentina 28, 242–56, 258–65
art-historical analysis 185
Atherton, J. H. 128, 136, 138
Australia 9, 29
  prehistory 280, 282–8
autonomy 127
Avars, the 186–93

Bakuba weavers, the 160–4, 170–1
Barnes, B. and D. Bloor 3
Baron Bolko von Richthofen 59
behaviour
  laws of 157

ritual see ritual
belief system 141, 144, 148, 151–2, 243 see also ideology
Bentley, G. C. 15–16, 19–20
Berry, B. 237
Bijelo Brdo culture, the 26
Binford, L. 4, 12, 20, 24, 94–108
Binford, S. R. 287
Bird, J. 263
Blume, E. 40
Boissevain, E. 89
boundaries
  ethnic 25, 26, 41, 47, 141, 153–4, 158, 229, 274, 279–82, 288
  political 27, 229
Bourdieu, P. 15
Boyd, R. and P. J. Richerson 22
Bray, W. 143
Britain, British 73, 79–80, 84
Bromley, Y. 269
Bulgaria, Bulgarian Turks 188, 190, 192
burial practices 27, 44, 77–9, 81–4, 86, 88–9, 106, 133, 188, 190, 192, 208, 212–17, 219–29, 291, 293–6, 308
Bushong, the 161, 170–1

Canada 9
capitalism 23, 66–9, 87
Carpathian Basin, the 186–93, 291
Cassius Dio 58, 60
centralisation, political 63, 137, 143
chiefdoms 128, 135, 219
Childe, V. G. 8, 13, 39, 44, 48
Clark, G. 48
Clarke, D. L. 13, 25, 143, 267, 281
class conflict 225
Colombia 141–54
colonisation 24, 25, 28, 141, 144, 154, 245, 264
  colonists 9, 79–81, 83–90, 243, 245, 251, 254
  indigenous response to 86, 234, 244–5
  in prehistory 258–60
computer systems 112–15, 120, 162, 167, 171

continuity
    and change 85
    of cultural practices 79, 83, 85, 89–90,
        306–8
    and discontinuity in social process 304,
        308
    ethnic 305–6, 308
    historical 24, 29, 45–6, 60, 275, 303–4
    in material culture 39, 46, 61, 127, 207–8,
        303–4, 306–8
    in use of style 170
cultural
    assimilation 29, 190, 191, 234, 292–300
    determinism 11–15
    differences 44, 153, 262–3, 309
    drift 263
    fragmentation 10
    past, accessibility of 96–107
    transmission 26, 174, 176–81, 240
    variation 5, 12, 28, 146
cultural identity 9–10, 35, 150, 153, 237–8
    and archaeological objectivity 37, 47–8
    in prehistory 27
    and variation in material culture 25
cultural-materialist approach 28, 244–56
culture 35
    change 262, 268
    concept of 9, 12, 46, 103, 105
    contact 76, 78–90, 234, 240
    deculturalisation 143
    as 'people' 1, 6, 41, 42
    provinces 39, 41, 125
    symbols 229
culture-historical paradigm 46, 48, 62, 157
Cumanians, the 291–300

David, N. and H. Hennig 136
Diaz-Polanco, H. 11
diffusion 13
dominance, domination 85, 89–90, 106, 143,
        229, 255

economy
    political 251–3, 255–6
    'subproduction' 250
ecosystem paradigm 24, 95–6, 101–2, 105–6
Edwards, R. 286
Eggert, M. K. H. 49
Eluyemi, O. 207
empiricism, in traditional research 95, 97
epistemology 68, 70, 76, 78
    limits in archaeological enquiry 94–8, 102,
        103, 107–8, 120, 121
    problems 118
Ertebolle culture, the 210
ethnic groups 6, 27, 29, 44, 89, 125–9, 135,

        137–9, 144, 151, 154, 181, 187, 199,
        200–5, 240, 269, 205, 240, 269, 275
    appearance of 15
    nature of 47
ethnic interpretation 39
    of archaeological data 36–7, 59, 186–91,
        210
    of early historical cultures 43, 185, 186–91
    the problem of 40, 47
    and the 'settlement archaeological method'
        9, 39–42
ethnic 'revival' 9
ethnicity, ethnic identity 6, 11–16, 22, 25,
        27, 28, 35–6, 64, 81, 125, 144, 147–8,
        151, 152, 153, 234–5, 267–8, 269, 279,
        303–5, 310
    and archaeology 14
    indicators of 133–5, 137–9, 158–9, 186–8,
        202–5, 207
    material expressions of 141, 211–17, 305
    nature of 12, 19
    origins of 14
ethnoarchaeology 20, 25, 26, 50, 101, 138,
        157–8
    importance of 24
ethnocentrism 49
ethnography 25, 49, 106, 125–8, 131–9, 143,
        174, 204–5, 281
    of archaeology 89
    condemnation of 103
    relationship with archaeology 118–19, 209
Europe, Palaeolithic of 269–72
exchange 147, 150, 151, 182, 197, 221, 248,
        251, 264

fascism 191
France 73
    Iron Age 27, 219–29
Fried, M. H. 11, 15
Friedman, J. 9
functionalism, 104, 105

Gamble, C. 270, 287
Gamkrelidze, T. V. and V. V. Ivanov 273
Geary, P. J. 11–12, 14, 15
Germany, Germans 7–8
    prehistory 30, 35–51
Gilbert, W. H. 237
Gimbutas, M. 273
Girtler, R. 7
Gibson, James 4
Gellner, E. 14–15
grave goods 82–3, 86–8, 192, 196, 208, 213,
        215–16, 219, 293–5

Harris, M. 244

Hawkes, C. 120
  'ladder of inference' 96
Harte, T. 237
Healey, P. 85
heritage 4, 28, 61
hierarchical model 267
hierarchy 252
  political 225, 275
historical materialism 62
history, the discipline of 117
Hitler, Adolf 61 *see also* nazis
Hodder, I. 94, 106, 157, 229, 281
Hodson, F. R. 43
Hollis, M. and S. Lukes 1, 2
Horton, R. 3–4
Hubschmid, J. 272
human perception 4, 88, 159
  emic 28, 151
  etic 28, 151, 244
Hungary, Hungarians 26, 29, 186–93,
  291–300
Huns, the 186, 188
hunter-gatherers 242, 254, 255, 263, 268, 276
hunters 135

identity
  aspects of 20
  cultural *see* culture
  ethnic *see* ethnicity
  national 305
  personal 16, 157
  physical 233, 236
  social 125, 138, 157–8, 181, 304
  tribal 84, 87, 89
ideology 50, 69, 84–5, 118
  identity 239
  in ideological aspects of human behaviour
    77
  influence on interpretation 23, 66, 72–3,
    76, 94
  personal 115
imperialism 23, 70, 71
inference
  anthropological 119
  natural 118
  rules of 113–16, 120
interaction 252, 255, 281
  cultural 85, 89, 229
  'distance' 176–9
  economic 79, 83, 86, 88, 197, 242, 244–5,
    251
invented tradition 90
Irish Celts, the 229

Jacob-Friesen, K. H. 41
Jahn, M. 40, 41

kinship 26, 243, 251–2
  models of 174–5, 179, 181
Klejn, L. S. 43
Kossinna, G. 7–9, 23, 27, 36–43, 46, 48–50,
  59, 61
Kostrzewski, Josef 40, 60–1, 306
knowledge, exchange of 144
Kubaruwa, the 146–53
Kuhn, T., Kuhnian arguments 68, 97–100,
  102–3
Kup, A. P. 129
Kuranko, the 125–39

land ownership 143, 175
language 29, 126, 144, 268, 272–6, 286, 293
  chant 144–5, 146–7, 150, 153
  nature of 269
  religious 143–6
Laotitian refugees 160–71
legitimacy 84, 88
  historical 7, 9, 10, 23–4, 62
  marxist perceptions of 11
  political 90, 107
Limba, the 125–39
local semantics 110, 113–14
Locher, P. J. and C. F. Nodine 159
logicist analysis 112–15
Lüning, J. 44–6, 49
Lüning paradigm, the 45–6

McGuire, R. H. 36
McLoughlin, W. G. 85
Mann, M. 11
Marnian Variant, the 219–29
Marx, K. 66
marxism 118, 185
  neo-marxist theories of science 98
material culture 47, 125
  distributions 4, 8, 25, 26, 45, 87, 210,
    281–2, 287
  as indicator of ethnic identity 131–9, 157,
    186–9
  variation in 18, 148–51, 211–12, 234
Maynard, L. 283–4, 286
Menghin, O. 41
middle range theory 98, 101–2, 108
migration 13, 23, 127, 186–8, 189–90, 250,
  255, 258, 261, 273, 291
  seasonal 254
  theories 11, 59–64, 258–9, 268, 276
Miller, D. and C. Tilley 71
missionaries, Christian 127, 144, 145, 171,
  254, 255
Moberg, Carl Axel 60
Montelius 39
multiculturalism 119, 141–54

Murra, V. J. 146
mythology 86, 141–5, 148, 149, 150, 153

Narr, K. j. 47
Nassaney, M. S. 106–7
national socialism 38, 61
nationalism 37, 40, 50, 303
    changing patterns of 26, 191, 192
    romantic 7, 9
nation-building 9
Native Americans 12, 23–4, 28, 76–90,
        233–40
    Cajuns, the 237
    mestizo groups 235–8
    Narranganseti, the 23–4, 76, 79–90, 106–7,
        237
    relations with Europeans 76, 78–90
Nazis, the 23, 38, 48, 50
Needham, R. 141–3
New Archaeology 17, 35, 48, 76, 94–8, 102
    and the problem of epistemic limits see
        epistemology
normativist theory 104–6
North America 9, 12, 76, 79–90, 160–1, 167,
        233–40, 279
Nunamiut, the 101

objectivism 3, 24, 71, 76, 101
    anti- 106
    v. contextualism 94, 97, 98, 103, 106–8
objectivity 2, 12, 50
    in interpretation 22, 24, 29–30, 77, 89–90,
        94, 105–6, 112, 115, 209
    v. subjectivity 119
Olmstead, G. S. 229
oral tradition 141–5, 146–7, 150, 153, 207–9
    oral history 128, 133, 135

paradigm relativity 103–5
Peacock, D. P. S. 174
Piggott, S. 101, 120
    'ladder of inference' 96
Pliny 58–9
Plog, S. 278
Poland 23, 29, 58–60, 303–10
    Iron age 60
polythetic classification 141–3, 267, 280
positivism
    in archaeology 98
    in scientific theory 95
pottery 149, 274, 279
    and cultural transmission 174–82
    ethnographic studies of 136–7
    as expression of cultural entities 44–5, 59
    as indicator of ethnic identity 136–7,
        306–7

power
    economic 10, 67, 79, 89, 90
    political 10, 87, 89, 90, 242
    relationships 143
    religious 242
    in society 11, 66, 69
prehistory, evolutionary approaches to 40,
        42
pressure, economic 225
primary theory 4
problems in interpretation 1–30, 47, 48,
        89–90, 94–108, 119, 209, 217, 219, 281,
        303–5, 308–10
production
    artefacts of 83
    of commodities 83–4, 244
    domestic mode of 249, 253, 255
    economic relations of 87
    of knowledge 78
    techniques of 210
Przeworsk culture, the 59–60, 62–4

racist ideology 8, 23, 38, 40
rationality 86
    and relativism 1–5
relativism in interpretation 115 see also
        rationality
religion 58, 126, 143–4, 197, 253, 256
    Christianity 127, 293 see also missionaries
    external, affect on ritual practice 127
    Islam 127
    religious language see language
Renfrew, C. 29
ritual 143, 153
    behaviour, material aspects of 133–5, 138,
        264
    practices 125, 126–7, 133–5, 137, 286
    space 77, 88, 133–5
Robinson, P. 82
Rochereau, H. J. 145
rock art 29, 278, 282–8
rock shelters 128
Roman Empire, the 58, 63, 303
Rozoy, J. G. 224

Sackett, J. R. 18
Sangmeister, E. 46
Scandinavia 59, 61
    mesolithic 27, 210–17
Schortman, E. M. 20
Schuchardt, Carl 40
Service, E. R. 128
Shanks, M. and C. Tilley 3
Shi Ji, historical records 195, 199, 204
Sierra Leone 125–38
    Iron Age 127
    Neolithic 127

Simmons, W. S. 84
slavery 80, 89, 137, 199, 200, 236–7
Slavs, the 29, 60–1, 187, 188–9, 303–10
Smith, A. D. 7, 9, 10, 14
Smith, M. G. 27, 28
Smolla, G. 51
social
    change 67, 68, 70, 76, 88, 90, 216, 272,
        296, 303
    integration 67
    organisation 63, 67, 137, 141, 197–9, 215,
        234, 242, 281
    structure 126, 182, 199, 216, 291, 295
spatial order, conceptions of 88
spatial variation 14, 19
    in material culture 5, 6, 12, 17, 219
    and political entities 27, 225–9
'state' 128
Stonehenge 66
Stopp, G. H. 237
style
    assertive 18–22, 157
    Darwinian models for 21–2
    emblemic 18–22, 29, 157, 279–86, 305,
        306
    ethnic 158–71
    and identity 18, 20–1
    as a measure of socal interaction 279,
        281–2
    nature of 17, 278
    in society 174, 181
    stochastic 29, 279–86
stylistic variation 13, 18, 21–2, 151, 157–9,
        278, 286
    isochrestic variation 18–22, 29, 280
    'social interaction' theory of 278–9, 287–8
subjectivity 3, 12, 36, 47, 115, 304, 305
submission, tactics of 87

Sutherland, R. D. 150

Tacitus 58
Ticul, Maxico 174–81
Toba, the 28, 242–56
tribes, tribal 157, 161, 199, 210, 219, 221,
        234, 242, 273, 281, 286, 304 see also
        identity
typology 39, 44, 62, 185

universal laws 24
universal semantics 110–11, 113
universalism 4
U'wa, the 25, 142–54

Vandals, the 23, 57–64
Venezuela 141–54

Wahle, E. 38, 41, 47
Wenskus, R. 43
Whallon, R. 278
White, J. P. and J. F. O'Connell 286
Wiessner, P. 18–20, 22, 157, 279, 282
Williams, Roger 79, 81, 87
Wobst, M. 18
Woods, F. J. 237
World Archaeological Congress Second
        Announcement 115
'world systems perspectives' 20
world view 154
Wylie, A. 120

Yalunka, the 125–39
Yoruba, the 27, 207–9
Yunnan area, China 26, 195–205
    Bronze Age 196, 205

Zaire 160–1